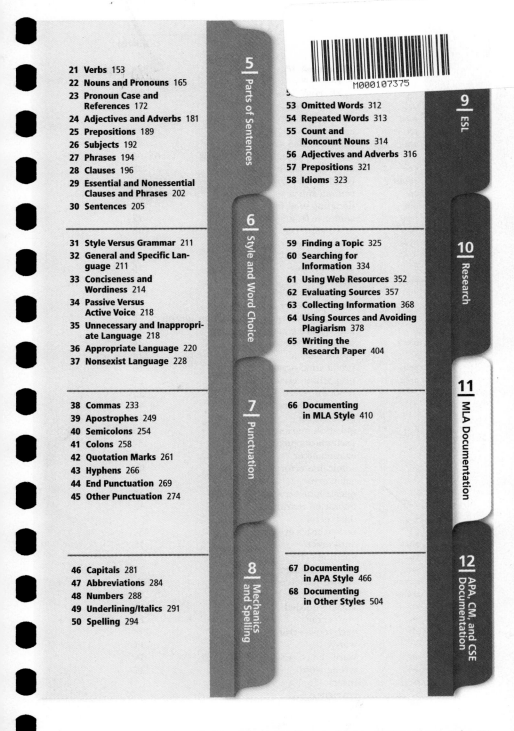

RESPONSE SYMBOLS

Symbol	Explanation	Chapter(s)
ab	abbreviation error	47
adj	adjective error	24
adv	adverb error	24
agr	agreement error	11
art	article error	24b
awk	awkward construction	15–18
ca	case error	23
cap	capitalization error	46
cit	citation missing/error in format	66–68
coh	coherence needed	3b
coord	coordination error	17a
cs	comma splice	10a
dm	dangling modifier	13a
frag	sentence fragment	12
fs	fused sentence	10b
hyph	hyphenation error	43
ital	italic/underlining error	49
lc	use lowercase	46
log	logic	4d
mm	misplaced modifier	13b
num	number use error	48
¶/no ¶	paragraph/do not begin new paragraph	3
//	parallelism error	14
pass	unneeded passive	34
pl	plural needed	22a
pred	predication error	16
prep	preposition error	25
ref	pronoun reference	23b
p	punctuation error	38–45
.	period error	44a
?	question mark error	44b
!	exclamation point error	44c
︿	comma error	38
;	semicolon error	40
:	colon error	41
˅	apostrophe error	39
" "	quotation marks error	42
—	dash error	45a
( )	parentheses error	45c
shft	shift error	15
sp	spelling error	50
sxt	sexist language	37
subord	subordination error	17b
trans	transition needed	19
var	variety needed	20
v	verb error	21
vt	verb tense error	21c
w	wordy	33
wc	word choice error	36
ww	wrong word	36
^	insert	
⌐/tr	transpose	
℘	delete	

PRENTICE HALL REFERENCE GUIDE

Muriel Harris,
with contributions from Jennifer L. Kunka

Custom Seventh Edition

Taken from:

Prentice Hall Reference Guide, Seventh Edition
by Muriel Harris

Custom Publishing

New York   Boston   San Francisco
London   Toronto   Sydney   Tokyo   Singapore   Madrid
Mexico City   Munich   Paris   Cape Town   Hong Kong   Montreal

2009240116

KW

**Pearson
Custom Publishing**
is a division of

www.pearsonhighered.com

ISBN 10: 0-558-20971-8
ISBN 13: 978-0-558-20971-1

Preface

TO THE STUDENT

The *Prentice Hall Reference Guide* may look like others you've used or seen, but there are some important differences that will make it easier—and more helpful—for you to use:

- **This handbook assumes that you are like all other writers and that you are unlike all other writers.** The *Prentice Hall Reference Guide* offers numerous strategies for writing correctly and effectively. Some will be helpful for you; others won't work as well for you—but that's OK. Try them out, and use what works.

- **This handbook is designed for easy use.** This book is arranged so that you can look up answers to your questions without knowing all grammatical terms.

  - If you have a specific question, turn to the "Question and Correct" list. If you don't know what to ask but you know your sentence or paragraph just doesn't seem right, turn to "Compare and Correct." (There is, of course, also an index if you know the point of grammar you want to check.)

  - "Try This" boxes offer practical and concise strategies for overcoming common writing problems, like finding a topic to write about. "Checklist" boxes offer "to-do" lists to keep your writing processes on track and to help you evaluate your work. "Hint" boxes offer tips for avoiding errors and writing efficiently.

  - Each tabbed page lists the contents within that tab and questions you might ask to find the information you need in that section of the book.

- **This handbook concentrates only on the most essential points of grammar and the most frequently made errors.** You won't find an exhaustive list of grammatical terms or seldom-used rules in this book. We've worked to keep the guide complete enough to answer all your questions without becoming thick enough to be a doorstop.

- **This handbook doesn't talk down to you.** I've tried to write this handbook in a comfortably informal style. I don't like being lectured at, and I assume that you don't either.

- **This handbook offers exercises in a useful format.** To practice your understanding of various topics, try the exercises in some chapters. You'll notice that most exercises are paragraphs, rather than separate sentences. The subjects of these paragraphs may even add to your storehouse of minor facts with which to amaze your friends.

I've tutored students in a writing center, elbow to elbow, for many years, and seeing them gain confidence in their writing has been incredibly rewarding. They, in turn, have helped me greatly with my writing. This handbook is my attempt to work with you, too, so that you become the confident, competent writer I know you can be.

TO THE INSTRUCTOR

This book is the result of many years of field testing. Throughout all the editions of this reference guide, I've kept in mind the countless students whom I've worked with as a writing tutor and also the stacks of papers I've read as a teacher. I have included all the advice that I've passed along, emphasized topics I know are major sources of confusion, and included strategies I know students find useful. I have also included hints, strategies, and feedback my students have shared with me.

Ease of Use: *Prentice Hall Reference Guide's* Hallmark Feature

This book reflects my efforts to produce a reference guide that all writers can use, even when they don't know much grammatical terminology. I've answered hundreds of grammar questions and sat with hundreds more students who know what problem they need to solve but don't know how to find the handbook page that will help them. The following features were designed with them in mind:

- **"Question and Correct"** and **"Compare and Correct."** In the "Question and Correct" list, students can find many of their questions with accompanying references to the pages in the book they need. But it is sometimes difficult to phrase a question, so I have also included "Compare and Correct," where students will find examples of typical troublesome constructions that may be similar to theirs. Again, references will guide them to appropriate places in the book.

- **"Try This," "Hint,"** and **"Checklist" boxes.** Because students are busy, the boxes in this guide are designed to stand out from the main text for quick, easy reference.

- **Organization.** This book introduces students to the "big picture" processes and genres of writing first and then covers sentence-level concerns before moving on to the complexities of doing research and documenting sources. Tabs divide the major sections for easy reference:
    - **Writing Processes** reviews the concerns of all writers as they move through various stages of writing and includes discussion of argument, visual argument, and document design.

- **Common Categories of Writing** covers writing about literature; public writing such as business letters, memos, e-mail, Web pages, and résumés; and portfolios.

- **Revising Sentences** provides rules and suggestions for constructions beyond the word level. Students should fully understand the important concepts of whole sentences and how the parts fit together before tackling the parts of speech that compose a sentence.

- **Parts of Sentences** explains parts of speech, grammatical terms having to do with single words, and concepts about phrases, clauses, and sentence types.

- **Style and Word Choice** offers suggestions for avoiding sexist language, wordiness, and clichés, along with guidelines for tone and word choice.

- **Punctuation** covers guidelines for the most frequently used forms in these areas.

- **Mechanics and Spelling** covers mechanics, such as capitals and abbreviations, as well as proofreading, the use of spell-checkers, and useful spelling rules.

- **ESL and Multilingual Writers** includes explanations of American writing style and those aspects of English grammar most needed by students learning English as another language.

- **Research** moves through the processes of finding a topic, searching for information, taking notes, avoiding plagiarism, and evaluating and using sources. It also includes information on conducting research online, using Web resources, and evaluating and citing Internet resources.

- **Two Documentation** sections cover documenting in MLA, APA, CM, and CSE styles.

- A **Glossary of Usage** and a **Glossary of Grammatical Terms** provide a quick reference for students who know the terms they're having trouble with.

■ **Multi-purpose exercises.** In the exercises that follow key sections, students will learn interesting bits of information about lighter topics (such as the origin of the phrase "it's a doozy" and the increasing popularity of pigs) and about relevant, current topics (such as the problems of waste disposal). The exercises are set up so that students can practice several types of skills simultaneously such as proofreading, sentence combining, and writing their own sentences while applying various rules.

Features New to the Seventh Edition

Preparing the seventh edition provided an opportunity to add important new material, to clarify some explanations, and to clean up minor infelicities. The major additions reflect new directions writing programs have taken, and needs today's students urgently express. With these additions, I'm confident that this book is more inclusive in terms of both its audience and the types of writing assignments for which it offers help:

- New "Try This" boxes for quick, easy reference
- More extensive coverage of writing processes, including discussion of the rhetorical triangle
- More material on writing arguments and composing visual arguments
- New material on the medium of a writing project and on multimedia presentations
- Help with compiling portfolios, including e-portfolios
- New student paper on a work of literature
- Extensive updates to coverage of document design
- New material and updates on research writing, with greater emphasis on doing research using online resources
- Visual guides to documentation
- Dozens more examples of MLA and APA citation format
- New student paper in MLA style
- Updates from 2007 *APA Style Guide to Electronic References*
- Revised examples, models, and explanations throughout the book
- Removable Quick Reference Card for documentation format

Available Supplements

The following supplements accompany the seventh edition of the *Prentice Hall Reference Guide*:

For the Instructor

Strategies and Resources for Teaching Writing *with the* Prentice Hall Reference Guide, *Seventh Edition,* ISBN 0-13-237955-4

Offering advice from instructors on planning and teaching composition, this instructor's manual includes sections covering: Strategies for Teaching Writing, Collaborative Writing, The ESL Writer in the Composition Class, Workplace and Public Writing, Integrating Computers into the Writing Classroom, The Role of Visual Rhetoric in Writing, and more. In addition, the manual provides instructors with a guide to the special features of the handbook and offers strategies for encouraging students to use them.

Online Answer Key

The textbook answer key for the *Prentice Hall Reference Guide,* Seventh Edition, is available for download by instructors from the Instructor Resource Center at www.prenhall.com/harris. The answer key provides suggested answers for all exercises included in the handbook.

Prentice Hall Resources for Writing

This set of supplements for the instructor is designed to support a variety of popular composition topics, including:

- *Teaching Writing Across the Curriculum* by Art Young, ISBN 0-13-193664-6, is written for college teachers in all disciplines and provides useful advice on teaching writing across the curriculum.

- *Teaching Civic Literacy* by Cheryl Duffy, ISBN 0-13-168060-9, offers advice on how to integrate civic literacy into the composition classroom.

- *Teaching Visual Rhetoric* by Susan Loudermilk Garza, ISBN 0-13-168058-7, provides an illustrated look at visual rhetoric and offers guidance on how to incorporate this topic into the classroom.

- *Teaching Writing for ESL Students* by Ruth Spack, ISBN 0-13-168059-5, addresses various strategies that can be employed to teach writing to nonnative speakers.

For the Student

Practicing Grammar and Usage, ISBN 0-13-237954-6

This student workbook provides additional exercises addressing important topics from each section of the text. The workbook also contains suggested answers for each exercise to guide students and reinforce learning.

www.prenhall.com/harris

This useful Web site includes self-graded exercises, relevant Web links, and a wealth of additional online resources for the composition student.

For the Instructor and Student

MyCompLab® Online writing support created by composition instructors for composition instructors and their students.

MyCompLab (www.mycomplab.com), including an electronic and interactive version of *Prentice Hall Reference Guide,* Seventh Edition, offers comprehensive online resources in grammar, writing, and research in one dynamic, accessible place:

- Grammar Resources include *ExerciseZone*, with more than three thousand self-grading practice questions on sentences and paragraphs; and *ESL ExerciseZone*, with more than seven hundred self-grading questions.

- Writing Resources include a hundred writing activities involving videos, images, and Web sites; guided assistance through the writing process, with worksheets and exercises; and an extensive collection of sample papers from across the disciplines.

- Research Resources include *ResearchNavigator™*, which provides help with the research process, the *AutoCite™* bibliography maker, and access to *ContentSelect™* by EBSCOhost and the subject-search archive of the *New York Times*; and *Avoiding Plagiarism*, which offers tutorials in recognizing plagiarism, paraphrasing, documenting sources in MLA or APA style, and other topics.

MyCompLab includes an intelligent system called *Grade Tracker* so students can track their work, communicate with instructors, and monitor their improvement.

And more . . . *MyCompLab* includes even more resources to help students use this book and improve their writing. They can use the site on their own, or their instructor may direct them to portions of it as part of their course assignments.

- Downloadable checklists and other materials from the book

- More than a thousand electronic exercises

- Video tutorials that supplement the book's explanations

- Hundreds of links to other Web sites providing additional help with the book's topics

- Sample research papers from various academic disciplines

- Usage flashcards on tricky words and phrases

Pearson Tutor Services, Powered by SMARTHINKING

Submit your papers, essays, or other written work to Pearson Tutor Services for personalized and detailed feedback on how to improve your paper. Highly qualified writing tutors review your writing and return it to you with their feedback for improvement. Please visit www.mycomplab.com for more detailed information.

Acknowledgments

This book first took shape in the mind of Phil Miller, former president of Humanities and Social Science at Prentice Hall, as he patiently listened to my griping about grammar handbooks. His quiet wisdom and calm persistence brought this book into existence. This latest version benefited from the wisdom and guidance of the Prentice Hall editorial and production teams. I've profited also from the extremely helpful comments, corrections, and suggestions of the many reviewers and users—including writing center tutors—who have added their voices and insights to each edition of this book. For their advice on the seventh edition, I would like to thank the following instructors: Jeanette Adkins, Tarrant County College; Matthew Allen, College of DuPage; Robert Arnold, University of North Carolina Charlotte; Martha Bachman, Camden County College; Lee Barnes, College of Southern Nevada; Greg Barnhisel, Duquesne University; Keri Bjorklund, Sheridan College; Emily Bobo, University of Kansas; Donna Bontatibus, Middlesex Community College; Dawn Brickey, Charleston Southern University; Elaine Burklow, Vincennes University; Stephania Byrd, Lakeland Community College; Shelley Caraway, Panola College; Patricia Cearley, South Plains College; John Chapin, University of Maryland University College; Gregory Clark, Brigham Young University; Mark Coley, Tarrant County College; Tammy Conard-Salvo, Purdue University; Susan Jaye Dauer, Valencia Community College; Anne Dennis, Mohave Community College; Ralph Dirksen, Western Illinois University; Doug Downs, Utah Valley State College; Ann Dee Ellis, Brigham Young University; Hank Galmish, Green River Community College; Larry Garcia, St. Philip's College; Catherine Golden, Skidmore College; Carey Goyette, Clinton Community College; Annie Gray, Pellissippi State Technical Community College; Andrew Green, University of Miami; Maggie Griffin Taylor, New Mexico Tech; Karen Harrel, Tarrant County College; Judy Hatcher, University of Houston Clear Lake; Loraine Hourani-Stout, West Virginia University at Parkersburg; Schahara Hudelson, South Plains College; Clair Juenell Owens, Vincennes University; Paul Kellermann, Penn State University; Patricia Kramer, Rock Valley College; Anne Kuhta, Northern Virginia Community College; Richard Lee, SUNY College at Oneonta; Nancy Long, Bethune Cookman University; William Joseph Marinelli, Hofstra University; Susan Medina, Grantham University; Linda Mitchell, San Jose State University; D'Juana Montgomery, Southwestern Assemblies of God University; Sherry Moseley, Lanier Technical College; Richard Nanian, George Mason University; Julie Nash, University of Massachusetts; Beverly Neiderman, Kent State University; Allen Nelson Swords, Clemson University; Sara Newman, University of North Carolina Charlotte; Ellen Nichols, Middlesex Community College; Patricia Nolan, Clark College; Troy Nordman, Butler Community College; Megan O'Neill, Stetson University; Laura Osborne, Stephen F. Austin State University; Juenell Owens, Vincennes University; Dianne Parker, Lanier Technical College; Frank Perez, Tarrant County College; Maureen Phillips, Liberty University; Nancy Raferty, Camden County College; Sherry Rankins-Robertson, Arizona State University; Robin Redmon Wright, University of Texas at San Antonio; Sharon Reedy, Pellissippi State; Althea Rhodes, University of Arkansas at Ford Smith; Doug Rigby, Lehigh Carbon Community College; Denise Rogers, University of Louisiana at Lafayette; Art Scheck, Tri-County Technical College; Kelly Shea, Seton Hall University; Linda Simon, Skidmore College; Jeffrey Steichmann, Michigan State University; Karen Stewart, Norwich University; Norma Sullivan, College of DuPage; Carol Teaff, West Virginia Northern Community College; Alice

Templeton, The Art Institute of California-San Francisco; Richard Turner, Ozarks Technical Community College; Michael Van Meter, Central Oregon Community College; Trish Verrone, Caldwell College; Martha Vertreace-Doody, Kennedy-King College; Carol Westcamp, University of Arkansas at Ford Smith; Clarissa West-White, Florida A&M University; Brian Whaley, Utah Valley State College; Lowell Mick White, Texas A&M University; Grace Wilson, College of the Albemarle; Rita Wisdom, Tarrant County College; and Guangping Zeng, Pensacola Junior College.

Special thanks to all who contributed or assisted with the writing samples included in this edition, including Joseph M. Liethen, Amy McAllister, Liza Bryant, Ronald D. Carter, Suzanna Jackson, R. Taylor Bunn, Lynn Hanson, and Brookgreen Gardens. Thanks also to those who provided information and support during the writing of this text, including Christopher Johnson, John Sutton, Heather E. Epes, Rachel Corbett, Lauren Tomlinson, Sarah Carpenter, Francis Marion University, and especially Andrew J. Kunka.

I owe a huge debt of gratitude to Jennifer Kunka who has joined me in working on this edition. Her depth of knowledge and experience, as well as her commitment to working closely with students, enriches this edition far beyond what I have added. And many, many thanks to Barbara Schneider, who lent her skills and expertise to the larger structure of this edition and added needed material to the text, and to Susan Hoehing, who helped to revise the ESL material. My belief that collaboration results in a product far stronger than merely combining the individual efforts of people working separately is strengthened by seeing how Jennifer, Barbara, and Susan enhanced and improved this edition. I also owe a great debt of gratitude to student writers, who over the years have patiently listened to my attempts to help them and who revised into coherent papers the endless questions, doodles, diagrams, handouts, and bits of advice I kept giving them. As for my husband, Samuel, and our children—Rebecca, her husband Daniel, and their children, Hannah and Eitan, and our son, David, and his wife, Megan—I prefer to think that my appreciation for them and for what they mean to me is always evident in our lives, not on pages of books.

—*Muriel Harris*

COMPARE AND CORRECT

Examples of Sentence Problems	Refer to Page(s)	Symbol*
1. The students supported a change in the campus policy, the administration denied their request. **_Revised:_** The students supported a change in the campus policy, _but_ the administration denied their request.	1. Comma splice. See **pp. 108–109**	**cs**
2. Dr. Hwong recommended a low-sugar diet she also referred her patient to a specialist for additional medical tests. **_Revised:_** Dr. Hwong recommended a low-sugar diet; she also referred her patient to a specialist for additional medical tests.	2. Fused or run-on sentence. See **pp. 109–110**	**fs**
3. The professor _come_ to class at noon. **_Revised:_** The professor _comes_ to class at noon.	3. Incorrect subject-verb agreement. See **p. 111**	**agr**
4. Either the accountant or his lawyers _is_ going to speak to the media. **_Revised:_** Either the accountant or his lawyers _are_ going to speak to the media.	4. Incorrect subject-verb agreement. See **p. 112**	**agr**
5. Each of the candidates _have_ a different opinion about the tax bill. **_Revised:_** Each of the candidates _has_ a different opinion about the tax bill.	5. Incorrect subject-verb agreement. See **p. 113**	**agr**

*You can find a complete list of Response Symbols on the page facing the title page.

Examples of Sentence Problems	Refer to Page(s)	Symbol*
6. These people *is* expected to donate more money to charity this year. **Revised:** These people *are* expected to donate more money to charity this year.	6. Incorrect subject-verb agreement. See **pp. 113–114**	**agr**
7. There *is* several questions that need to be answered. **Revised:** There *are* several questions that need to be answered.	7. Incorrect subject-verb agreement. See **p. 115**	**agr**
8. He is one of those film actors who *performs* well in both dramas and comedies. **Revised:** He is one of those film actors who *perform* well in both dramas and comedies.	8. Incorrect subject-verb agreement. See **pp. 115–117**	**agr**
9. Thousands of people die each year from malaria. *Which is commonly spread by mosquitoes.* **Revised:** Thousands of people die each year from malaria, *which is commonly spread by mosquitoes.*	9. Sentence fragment. See **pp. 117–121**	**frag**
10. *When starting the project, it was* difficult to decide on a topic. **Revised:** *When starting the project, I found it* difficult to decide on a topic.	10. Dangling modifier. See **pp. 121–124**	**dm**
11. Sara read a book about the ebola virus *at the coffeehouse.* **Revised:** *At the coffeehouse,* Sara read a book about the ebola virus.	11. Misplaced modifier. See **pp. 124–125**	**mm**

Examples of Sentence Problems	Refer to Page(s)	Symbol*
12. The student finished her writing project *by checking for misspelled words and corrected the comma errors.* ***Revised:*** The student finished her writing project *by checking for misspelled words and <u>correcting</u> the comma errors.*	12. Faulty parallelism. See **pp. 127–128**	**//**
13. When a person exercises in hot weather, *you* should drink plenty of water. ***Revised:*** When a person exercises in hot weather, *<u>he or she</u>* should drink plenty of water.	13. Shift in person. See **pp. 128–129**	**shft**
14. *A firefighter faces* many dangerous situations. *They* always have to be prepared to risk *their* lives to save others. ***Revised:*** *<u>Firefighters face</u>* many dangerous situations. *They* always have to be prepared to risk *their* lives to save others.	14. Shift in number. See **pp. 128–129**	**shft**
15. When the movie *ended,* the lights *come* on. ***Revised:*** When the movie *ended,* the lights *<u>came</u>* on.	15. Shift in verb tense. See **p. 130**	**vt**
16. As the soccer player *ran off the field,* the crowd *cheers.* ***Revised:*** As the soccer player *ran off the field,* the crowd *<u>cheered</u>.*	16. Shift in verb tense. See **p. 130**	**vt**

Examples of Sentence Problems	Refer to Page(s)	Symbol*
17. After analyzing the sales figures and compiling the financial data, the stockbroker *screwed up* and forgot to send the report to his supervisor. ***Revised:*** After analyzing the sales figures and compiling the financial data, the stockbroker <u>*made an error*</u> and forgot to <u>send</u> the report to his supervisor.	17. Shift in tone. See **p. 130**	**shft**
18. The legislator stated that the law needs to be changed, but *his reasons were not explained for this*. ***Revised:*** The legislator stated that the law needs to be changed, but <u>*he did not explain his reasons for this*</u>.	18. Shift in voice. See **pp. 130–132**	**shft**
19. The teacher told the students *that the weather would be cold* and *bring your coats*. ***Revised:*** The teacher told the students <u>*that the weather would be cold*</u> and <u>*they should bring their coats*</u>.	19. Shift in discourse. See **p. 132**	**shft**
20. *The cause* of our city's high unemployment rate *is the result of* corporations transferring jobs to other countries. ***Revised:*** Our city's high unemployment rate <u>*is caused by*</u> corporations transferring jobs to other countries.	20. Faulty predication. See **pp. 133–134**	**pred**

Examples of Sentence Problems	Refer to Page(s)	Symbol*
21. The river crested above flood stage, and their homes were destroyed. ***Revised:*** *Because* the river crested above flood stage, their homes were destroyed.	21. Inappropriate coordination. See **pp. 134–136**	**coord**
22. Najee is a civil engineer, *and* he is a computer genius, *so* he designed the bridge near the Wabash River, *but* the bridge is still under construction. ***Revised:*** *Najee,* a civil engineer and a computer genius, *designed* the bridge under construction near the Wabash River.	22. Excessive coordination. See **pp. 134–136**	**coord**
23. *When I enrolled* in a neonatal nursing program, *it was last year*. ***Revised:*** *I enrolled last year* in a neonatal nursing program.	23. Inappropriate subordination. See **pp. 136–138**	**subord**
24. *Shady conditions are best* for growing hostas *because* they thrive in moist soil *and* adapt well to covered areas, *which* can be found next to buildings *and* under tree limbs. ***Revised:*** *Hostas thrive* in shady conditions with moist soil *and adapt* well to covered areas next to buildings or under tree limbs.	24. Excessive subordination. See **pp. 136–138**	**subord**

Examples of Sentence Problems	Refer to Page(s)	Symbol*
25. I bought an *MP3 player* after my *CD player* broke. My *MP3 player* can hold 1,500 songs. My *CD player* broke when I dropped it. **Revised:** *After I dropped and broke my CD player*, I bought an *MP3 player* that holds 1,500 songs.	25. Sentences move from unknown to known. See **p. 139**	**awk**
26. The corporation will *never* make a profit if it *fails* to satisfy customers. **Revised:** The corporation *will make a profit by satisfying customers*.	26. Negative language. See **p. 139**	**log**
27. The Web site did *not* have *no* information about the author's credentials. **Revised:** The Web site did *not* have *any* information about the author's credentials.	27. Double negative. See **p. 140**	**log**
28. *The decision* of the president will be made this afternoon. **Revised:** The president will *decide* this afternoon.	28. Uses a noun instead of a verb. See **pp. 140–141**	**w**
29. *It* was the dream of Tamika to visit Paris. **Revised:** *Tamika* dreamed of visiting Paris.	29. Sentence subject not the intended subject. See **p. 141**	**w**
30. A change *was* made in my class schedule *by my advisor*. **Revised:** *My advisor made a change* in my class schedule.	30. Uses passive instead of active. See **pp. 141–142**	**pass**

Examples of Sentence Problems	Refer to Page(s)	Symbol*
31. This city shows signs of urban sprawl. Many businesses have closed in the downtown area. New chain stores have opened near the city limits. The downtown area can be revived. ***Revised:*** This city shows signs of urban sprawl. *For example*, many businesses have closed in the downtown area. *Also*, new chain stores have opened near the city limits. *However*, the downtown area can be revived.	31. Needs transitions. See **pp. 142–148**	**trans**
32. High school students need to study more science. They also need to study more math. This is true for American students. This is important to succeed. This is needed in technology fields. ***Revised:*** *American* high school students need to study *more science and math to succeed* in technology fields.	32. Monotonous sentence rhythm. See **pp. 148–152**	**var**
33. He has *wrote* his paper and has *began* his next project. ***Revised:*** He has *written* his paper and has *begun* his next project.	33. Incorrect verb tense. See **pp. 157–162**	**vt**
34. If the conference room *was* available, we would schedule the meeting for 2:00 p.m. ***Revised:*** If the conference room *were* available, we would schedule the meeting for 2:00 p.m.	34. Incorrect verb mood. See **pp. 163–165**	**v**

Examples of Sentence Problems	Refer to Page(s)	Symbol*
35. College students take classes to pursue their *interest* and *career goal*. ***Revised:*** College students take classes to pursue their *interests* and *career goals*.	35. Incorrect use of plurals. See **pp. 165–168**	**pl**
36. The manager sent a memo to Mr. Andrews and *I*. ***Revised:*** The manager sent a memo to Mr. Andrews and *me*.	36. Incorrect pronoun case. See **pp. 172–177**	**ca**
37. In comic books, *they* often have secret identities. ***Revised:*** In comic books, *superheroes and villains* often have secret identities.	37. Vague pronoun reference. See **pp. 177–181**	**ref**
38. When seals and penguins meet on the Antarctic ice shelf, *they* will attack. ***Revised:*** When seals and penguins meet on the Antarctic ice shelf, *the seals* will attack.	38. Unclear pronoun reference. See **pp. 177–181**	**ref**
39. He recited the poem very *good*. ***Revised:*** He recited the poem very *well*.	39. Incorrect use of adjective. See **pp. 181–184**	**adj**
40. The Web site is updated on *a* hourly basis. ***Revised:*** The Web site is updated on *an* hourly basis.	40. Incorrect use of *a*. See **pp. 184–185**	**art**
41. Canada is one of the *most largest* countries in the world. ***Revised:*** Canada is one of the *largest* countries in the world.	41. Incorrect comparison. See **pp. 186–189**	**adj**

Examples of Sentence Problems	Refer to Page(s)	Symbol*
42. The executive board had to decide *among* Chicago and Milwaukee for the location of their new manufacturing plant. ***Revised:*** The executive board had to decide <u>*between*</u> Chicago and Milwaukee for the location of their new manufacturing plant.	42. Incorrect preposition. See **pp. 189–192**	**prep**

Examples of Style Problems	Refer to Page(s)	Symbol*
43. *At the present time*, I plan to arrive at 9:00 p.m. *in the evening*. ***Revised:*** I plan to arrive at 9:00 p.m.	43. Wordiness. See **pp. 214–217**	**w**
44. It is *better to be safe than sorry*, so Congress should stop *beating around the bush* and pass the proposed budget. ***Revised:*** Congress should <u>*take preventative measures*</u> and <u>*quickly*</u> pass the proposed budget.	44. Clichés. See **pp. 218–219**	**wc**
45. The lawyer was *straight* until he *dissed* the judge. ***Revised:*** The lawyer was <u>*doing well*</u> until he <u>*insulted*</u> the judge.	45. Slang. See **pp. 225–227**	**wc**
46. When the phone rang, Brooke *mashed* a button and *cut it off right quick*. ***Revised:*** When the phone rang, Brooke <u>*pressed*</u> a button and <u>*shut it off quickly*</u>.	46. Regionalism. See **pp. 225–227**	**wc**

Examples of Style Problems	Refer to Page(s)	Symbol*
47. *You are requested* to re-*mainder* your *exterior attire* in the *appointed repository*. **Revised:** *Please leave your coats in this closet*.	47. Inflated expression. See **pp. 227–228**	**w**
48. The next mayor must consult with *his* advisors more frequently. **Revised:** The next mayor must consult with *his or her* advisors more frequently.	48. Sexist language. See **pp. 228–229**	**sxt**
49. *Each voter* will need to cast *his or her ballot* at *his or her designated polling station*. **Revised:** *All voters* will need to cast *their ballots* at *their designated polling stations*.	49. Needs alternatives to male or female pronoun. See **pp. 229–231**	**w**

Examples of Punctuation Problems	Refer to Page(s)	Symbol*
50. Congress should work to balance the federal budget and the president should encourage these efforts. **Revised:** Congress should work to balance the federal budget, and the president should encourage these efforts.	50. Comma needed in compound sentence. See **pp. 234–236**	**,**
51. When the polar ice caps melt the ocean level will rise. **Revised:** When the polar ice caps melt, the ocean level will rise.	51. Comma needed after introductory clause. See **pp. 236–238**	**,**
52. George Clooney who starred in the film *Syriana* won an Academy Award for his performance. **Revised:** George Clooney, who starred in the film *Syriana*, won an Academy Award for his performance.	52. Comma needed to set off nonessential clause. See **pp. 239–241**	**,**

Examples of Punctuation Problems	Refer to Page(s)	Symbol*
53. One of Charles *Dickens* greatest novels is *Bleak House*, an expansive story that captured the Victorian *publics* imagination. ***Revised:*** One of Charles *Dickens'* greatest novels is *Bleak House*, an expansive story that captured the Victorian *public's* imagination.	53. Incorrect uses of the apostrophe. See **pp. 249–251, 252–254**	'
54. The city council announced *its'* plans to change the policy. ***Revised:*** The city council announced *its* plans to change the policy.	54. Apostrophe incorrectly used with possessive pronoun *its*. See **pp. 252–254**	'
55. The public is concerned about rising energy costs, therefore, automobile makers would be wise to focus on building environmentally friendly vehicles. ***Revised:*** The public is concerned about rising energy costs; therefore, automobile makers would be wise to focus on building environmentally friendly vehicles.	55. Semicolon needed between independent clauses. See **pp. 254–256**	;
56. Women can take steps to prevent osteoporosis, such as: exercising daily, consuming calcium-rich foods, and taking vitamins. ***Revised:*** Women can take steps to prevent osteoporosis, such as exercising daily, consuming calcium-rich foods, and taking vitamins.	56. Unnecessary colon. See **pp. 260–261**	:

Examples of Punctuation Problems	Refer to Page(s)	Symbol*
57. The corporate spokesman stated that "he would provide details about the merger at Monday's press conference." *Revised:* The corporate spokesman stated that he would provide details about the merger at Monday's press conference.	57. Incorrect use of quotation marks with an indirect quotation. See **pp. 261–263**	" "

58. The judge asked, "How do you plead?" The defendant responded, "I plead guilty, your honor."
 	
Revised:
    The judge asked, "How do you plead?"
    The defendant responded, "I plead guilty, your honor."
	58. Incorrect presentation of dialogue.
	See **pp. 261–263**
		" "

59. William Butler Yeats' poem, Leda and the Swan, is a sonnet. *Revised:* William Butler Yeats' poem, "Leda and the Swan," is a sonnet.	59. Quotation marks needed. See **p. 263**	" "
60. Did the mayor say, "The city will lower taxes next year?" *Revised:* Did the mayor say, "The city will lower taxes next year"?	60. Incorrect use of the question mark with quotation. See **p. 264**	?
61. Their son started reading when he was only *two-years-old*. *Revised:* Their son started reading when he was only *two years old*.	61. Incorrect use of hyphens. See **p. 267**	p

Examples of Punctuation Problems	Refer to Page(s)	Symbol*
62. *Twenty five* men and *thirty two* women auditioned for the play. **Revised:** *Twenty-five* men and *thirty-two* women auditioned for the play.	62. Needs hyphenation of two-word units. See **p. 267**	**p**

Examples of Problems with Mechanics and Spelling	Refer to Page(s)	Symbol*
63. Both the *republicans* and *democrats* in *congress* should work together to meet the challenges of the *Twenty-First Century*. **Revised:** Both the *Republicans* and *Democrats* in *Congress* should work together to meet the challenges of the *twenty-first century*.	63. Incorrect capitalization. See **pp. 281–284**	**cap**
64. *15* football players were suspended after the brawl. **Revised:** *Fifteen* football players were suspended after the brawl.	64. Incorrectly written number. See **pp. 288–291**	**num**
65. "Lost" is one of the best television shows of the decade. **Revised:** *Lost* is one of the best television shows of the decade.	65. Needs italics. See **pp. 291–292**	**ital**
66. Maple trees *loose there* leaves in cold weather. **Revised:** Maple trees *lose their* leaves in cold weather.	66. Needs proofreading. See **pp. 294–295**	**sp**
67. The *theif decieved* the police *cheif*. **Revised:** The *thief decieved* the police *chief*.	67. Spelling error (*ie/ei*). See **pp. 296–300**	**sp**

Examples of Problems with Mechanics and Spelling	Refer to Page(s)	Symbol*
68. She *mispelled* some words and had to *re-do* her paper. ***Revised:*** She *misspelled* some words and had to *redo* her paper.	68. Incorrect prefixes. See **pp. 296–300**	**sp**
69. Drug *trafficing* is a *real* big problem in this city. ***Revised:*** Drug *trafficking* is a *really* big problem in this city.	69. Incorrect suffixes. See **pp. 296–300**	**sp**
70. When he completes his master's *theses*, he will graduate and become an *alumni* of the university. ***Revised:*** When he completes his master's *thesis*, he will graduate and become an *alumnus* of the university.	70. Spelling error (plurals). See **pp. 300–301**	**pl**
71. Overexposure *too* sun can *effect* one's vision in the *dessert*. ***Revised:*** Overexposure *to* sun can *affect* one's vision in the *desert*.	71. Incorrect soundalike words. See **pp. 302–303**	**sp**

Examples of Concerns of ESL Students	Refer to Page(s)	Symbol
72. Hsuan has *planning* his trip to Los Angeles. ***Revised:*** Hsuan has *planned* his trip to Los Angeles.	72. Verb forms with helping verbs. See **pp. 306–308**	**v**
73. If Jill had more information, she *may* change her mind. ***Revised:*** If Jill had more information, she *would* change her mind.	73. Verbs with conditionals. See **pp. 306–308**	**v**
74. I need to *hand* my paper at 8:00 a.m. ***Revised:*** I need to *hand in* my paper at 8:00 a.m.	74. Phrasal verbs. See **pp. 309–310**	**v**

Examples of Concerns of ESL Students	Refer to Page(s)	Symbol*
75. Zahara promises *playing* her song another time. ***Revised:*** Zahara promises *to play* her song another time.	75. Verbs with *-ing* and *to* + verb. See **pp. 310–312**	**v**
76. Svetlana *asking* her professor about *assignment*. ***Revised:*** Svetlana *is* asking her professor about *the* assignment.	76. Omitted words. See **p. 312**	^
77. The food at the restaurant *it* was delicious. ***Revised:*** The food at the restaurant was delicious.	77. Repeated words. See **p. 313**	⸮
78. You should watch the *weathers* during hurricane season. ***Revised:*** You should watch the *weather* during hurricane season.	78. Count and noncount nouns. See **pp. 314–316**	**pl**
79. Dirk drives a *blue small* car. ***Revised:*** Dirk drives a *small blue* car.	79. Adjective order. See **pp. 317–318**	**adj**
80. Whenever I watch *new movie*, I always want to know *titles* of other movies by *same director*. ***Revised:*** Whenever I watch *a* new movie, I always want to know *the* titles of other movies by *the* same director.	80. Articles (*a/an/the*). See **pp. 318–321**	**art**
81. Elena had to work *less* days after school started. ***Revised:*** Elena had to work *fewer* days after school started.	81. Incorrect choice of *less/fewer*. See **p. 321**	**wc**

Examples of Concerns of ESL Students	Refer to Page(s)	Symbol*
82. Joo-Won left his coat *on* the classroom *at* Friday. ***Revised:*** Joo-Won left his coat *in* the classroom *on* Friday.	82. Incorrect prepositions. See **pp. 321–323**	**prep**

TRY THIS

Below you'll find a complete list, with page numbers, of the TRY THIS boxes in the text. This section reprints some key TRY THIS strategies from Tab 2, Writing Processes, as these are some of the challenges students encounter most often.

TRY THIS: To Find a Topic

■ What is a problem you'd like to solve?

_____ is a problem, and I think we should _____.

■ What is something that pleases, puzzles, irritates, or bothers you?

What annoys (or pleases) me is _____.

■ What is something you'd like to convince others of?

What I want others to agree on is _____.

■ What is something that seems to contradict what you read or see around you?

Why does _____?" (or) "I've noticed that _____, but _____.

■ What is something you'd like to learn more about?

I wonder how _____.

■ What is something you know about that others around you may not know?

I'd like to tell you about _____.

TRY THIS: To Get Beyond Writer's Block

TRY THIS: To Revise Your Draft

TRY THIS: To Edit and Proofread for Later-Order Concerns (LOCs)

TRY THIS: To Write an Effective Introduction

■ Cite an interesting statistic:

Nearly 25 percent of colleges and universities now require first-year students to have their own laptops.

■ Suggest the long-term effects of your topic:

Notebooks, pens, and textbooks will, in the near future, no longer be taken to classes. Instead, students will appear with their laptops, ready to take notes and refer to their online textbooks.

■ Offer an analogy:

Like freshman beanies worn years ago, a new laptop is now a sign of a first-year college student.

■ Pose a question:

Why are so many colleges and universities requiring students to buy laptops before starting college?

- Relate an anecdote:

  When I was accepted at State University, I thought my big expense for classes would be textbooks. To my surprise, I found the most costly item on my shopping list was a new computer.

- Make a surprising statement:

  The laptop computer was developed primarily for use by people in the business world; designers had no idea they'd become standard equipment for college students.

- Introduce a quotation.

  "The standard laptop computer now weighs less than most textbooks students used to drag to class, thus relieving them of backaches from those overstuffed backpacks," said Michael Modin, a spokesperson for Macintosh computers.

- Acknowledge an opinion or approach that differs from yours.

  Some college faculty have expressed concern as more and more students carry laptop computers to classes. According to these instructors, students no longer look up at the board, spend time in class checking their e-mail, and too often lose their notes when their hard drives crash.

- Offer a definition. (Note: This approach should be used only when you need to help your readers understand a concept or when you want to clarify or limit how you are using a particular term.)

  When college admissions offices instruct first-year students to bring their own laptops to campus, they do not mean the Blackberry or any similar all-in-one device. They are referring to the familiar folding portable computer.

TRY THIS: To Write an Effective Conclusion p. 24

Conclusions can look either backward or forward.

If the paper has a complex discussion, *look backward* by doing any of the following:

- Summarize the main points to remind the reader of what was discussed.
- Emphasize important points you don't want the reader to forget.
- Refer to something in the introduction, thus coming full circle.

If the paper is short or doesn't need a summary, *look forward* by doing any of the following:

- Pose a question for the reader to consider.
- Offer advice.

- Call for action the reader can take.
- Consider future implications of your topic.

TRY THIS: To Establish Common Ground p. 34

Try out some of the patterns below in order to establish common ground with your reader(s):

- I hold the view that _____, but you hold the view that _____.
- Your objections to my view are _____.
- But what you and I share about this subject is _____.
- My view builds on this shared view because _____.

TRY THIS: To Explore Topics for Argument p. 37

Another good strategy is to start with something very ordinary and then keep asking "SO WHAT?" or "WHY?" (or both) to everything you write.

Example: I need a new backpack.

SO WHAT?   **WHY?**

?   Because my books are so heavy they're wearing out my current backpack.

SO WHAT?   **WHY?**

Students are asked to bring too many   ?
texts to class. Texts should be available
electronically.

This writer might want to argue that publishers should provide, and teachers should use, electronic versions of textbooks. (Note that the writer has a possible topic for her argument, but she still needs to work on her thesis.)

TRY THIS: To Organize Your Argument pp. 42–43

- Start with the common ground you share with the audience.
  You and I both agree that _____.
- Bring up points that favor your opponents' side of the argument early in the paper.
  You claim that _____, because _____, and this is important to remember _____.
- Start with the claim and follow with a discussion of the reasons.
  I claim that _____ because _____ and because _____.

- Try a problem-and-solution pattern if that seems more appropriate.

  The problem is _____, and the way to solve it is _____.

- Try a cause and effect pattern.

  The problem is _____ and is caused by _____. The effects of this problem are _____.

- Establish the criteria or standards by which to judge a claim, and then show how your claim meets these criteria.

  I claim that _____ and my standards (or "criteria" or "basis for judgment") are _____, and my claim meets these standards because _____.

- Move through your points and then announce your thesis or claim. This can be particularly effective when your conclusion is one that an audience is not likely to be receptive to at first.

  One fact (or example or outcome) is _____. Another is _____, and another is _____. Therefore, I claim that _____.

1

THINKING ABOUT WRITING

1a THE RHETORICAL TRIANGLE

Every time we write, we write about something (a topic) to someone (an audience). The interaction among writer, topic, and audience is often portrayed as a "rhetorical triangle":

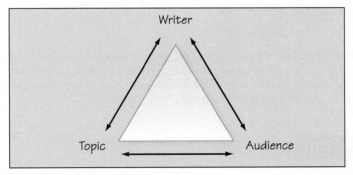

Figure 1.1 The Rhetorical Triangle

Every act of writing also takes place in a specific context, which, together with writer, audience, and topic, makes up the "rhetorical situation" of writing. Successful writers keep the rhetorical situation in mind as they produce their drafts.

Consider the situation of Alissa, a college student writing a paper about electronic voting for her political science class. Alissa, like all writers, will produce writing that reflects who she is, including her skill level, personal interests, and degree of motivation. She will need to consider her topic carefully: will it hold her interest through the writing process? Is the topic appropriate for the assignment? At the same time, she'll need to consider her audience. Will her topic interest her intended reader(s)? How much does this audience already know about her topic, and how much information will she need to provide to explain her point clearly and effectively?

Writer, topic, and audience are the basic elements of the triangle, but there are other important factors to consider. To write effectively, Alissa will also need to determine her purpose for writing. What would she like her reader(s) to think (or do) after reading the paper? She will also need to determine her thesis—what it is she wants to say about her topic. In most cases, she will need to work within the context of an assignment and its time limits. All of these aspects of writing are explained more fully in the sections that follow.

1b **TOPIC**

The topic of a piece of writing may be something the writer chooses, or it may be assigned. If you choose your own topic, remember that topics that are tired or overdone can result in tired, flat papers. The following is a short list of topics that have been overused:

- capital punishment
- gun control
- legalizing marijuana
- lowering the drinking age
- the pro's and con's of abortion
- drug addiction
- parental control of Internet chat rooms
- campus parking problems

Many instructors have become reluctant to read more papers on these topics, so it's better to avoid them. If you are asked to choose your own topic and nothing comes to mind, try one or more of the strategies suggested in the following Try This box.

Try This

TO FIND A TOPIC

- **What is a problem you'd like to solve?**
  _____ is a problem, and I think we should _____.
- **What is something that pleases, puzzles, irritates, or bothers you?**
  What annoys (or pleases) me is _____.
- **What is something you'd like to convince others of?**
  What I want others to agree on is _____.
- **What is something that seems to contradict what you read or see around you?**
  Why does _____? (or) I've noticed that _____, but _____.
- **What is something you'd like to learn more about?**
  I wonder how _____.
- **What is something you know about that others around you may not know?**
  I'd like to tell you about _____.

If you're writing an argument or a persuasive paper, see 4c for more advice on finding a topic.

1c AUDIENCE

As you define your purpose and topic, decide who your intended audience is. The information and details you include in your writing, the tone you take, and the assumptions you make about your readers' level of interest in a subject are important considerations that shape your writing. For example, if you are writing a newspaper article about a new medication, you can assume that in this situation, or context, your readers are likely to be most interested in the health benefits, possible dangers, and cost of taking the medication. But if you were writing the article for the drug company's newsletter (a different situation or context), you might choose instead to emphasize how the medication will fare against its competition.

Checklist

DEFINING AUDIENCE

When you start to write, define your audience by asking yourself the following questions:

- **Who is my audience?** (peers? a potential boss? a teacher? readers of a particular publication?)
- **What information should be included?** What do your readers already know about the subject? What will they need to know to understand what you are writing about? What do you want them to learn?
- **What is the audience's attitude?** Are readers likely to be interested in the subject, or will you need to create some interest? Are they sympathetic, neutral, or hostile to your views?
- **What is the audience's background?** How would you characterize your readers in terms of education, specialized knowledge, religion, race, cultural heritage, political views, occupation, and age? Will this background determine in part what and how you write? (For example, if you are writing about how the holiday of Cinco de Mayo was celebrated as you grew up, would a non-Hispanic audience be likely to know the reasons for celebrating this holiday?)

1d PURPOSE

Writing is a powerful multipurpose tool. We write to convey information, to persuade others to believe or act in certain ways, to help ourselves and others remember, and to create works of literary merit. Writing also allows us to explore more fully what we are thinking so that we learn while expressing ourselves.

Through writing, then, we can achieve a variety of purposes:

- *Summarizing.* Stating concisely the main points of a piece of writing
- *Defining.* Explaining the meaning of a word or concept
- *Analyzing.* Breaking the topic into parts and examining how these parts work or interact
- *Persuading.* Offering convincing support for a point of view
- *Reporting.* Examining all of the evidence and data on a subject and presenting an objective overview
- *Evaluating.* Setting up and explaining criteria for evaluation and then judging the quality or importance of the object being evaluated
- *Discussing or examining.* Considering the main points, implications, and relationships to other topics
- *Interpreting.* Explaining the meaning or implications of a topic
- *Exploring.* Exploring either our thoughts or a topic by putting mental notions into written form

1e MEDIUM

As we develop ideas for writing projects, we also need to consider the medium in which the writing will appear. Formal papers, multimedia presentations, Web pages, and e-mail all have their advantages—depending on the topic, audience, and purpose. Choosing the correct medium and adapting our language to suit it will ensure that we communicate effectively and appropriately. For example, the abbreviated language used in instant-messaging programs would generally be considered far too informal for academic research papers or serious professional writing situations. Similarly, the style of a professional letter is too formal for a personal e-mail.

Checklist

CHOOSING THE RIGHT MEDIUM FOR YOUR MESSAGE

In academic writing situations, your instructor may indicate the medium for your assignment. If you can choose the medium, consider the following questions:

- Am I writing for an academic, professional, or personal audience?
- Is my writing situation considered formal, semiformal, or informal?
- Which technology is available to me?
- Will my message need to be delivered orally? In person? Online? On paper?

- Would a beginning-to-end or hypertext organization be most effective for communicating my message?
- Could my audience conveniently access hyperlinks if they were provided?
- Would images, sound, animation, or video enhance or distract from my message?

1f THESIS

After you consider the elements of the rhetorical situation, you can decide on a comment you'll make about your topic. Then you will have a thesis, or main point, to express in your writing. Sometimes the comment part of a thesis is developed in a writer's mind early in the writing process, and sometimes it becomes clear as the writer works through various writing processes.

Topic	Comment
Television commercials	should not insult competing brands or companies.
Effective document design	helps technical writers present complex material more clearly.

Narrowing the topic is an important stage of writing because no one can write an effective paper that is vague or promises to cover more than is possible in the space allotted. Answering the questions about audience in the Checklist on page 3 will help you narrow your subject. Being specific about topic, audience, or both, is a good way to limit the scope of a paper. As an example, if you determine that your audience is not all college students but specifically students who depend on financial aid from the government, you will need to supply less background information. Instead of writing a short paper about how the Internet can be useful in college classes, for example, you could write about a more specific topic, such as how online tools can allow students to "virtually" dissect animals in college biology classes.

Some examples of thesis statements that have been effectively narrowed follow.

Too General	Narrowed
Lost is one of the best series on television.	*Lost* remains a popular television series because it combines action-packed plots with fascinating characters and innovative storytelling strategies.

Too General	Narrowed
Education needs to improve.	To keep the United States competitive in the global marketplace, American high school students need more exposure and hands-on training in technology, science, and engineering.
Global warming is a problem we should deal with.	Global warming can be slowed by developing environmentally safe and renewable fuel sources such as sunlight, wind energy, and hydrogen-fueled engines.

If you're writing an argument or persuasive paper, see 4d for more advice on developing an appropriate argument.

2

WRITING PROCESSES AND STRATEGIES

As we write, we plan, draft, organize, revise, edit, perhaps go back to plan some more, revise, maybe reread what we've written, reorganize, put the draft aside for a while, write, and so on. All of these writing processes are part of the larger act of producing a piece of writing, and there is great variety in how writers move back and forth through these processes. Because moving through all of these processes takes time, most writers (especially good ones) realize that they have to start early and that they'll be engaged in some hard work.

2a   PLANNING

During the planning process, you track down the material you want to include in your writing. The following useful strategies can help you find material.

Brainstorming

Once you have a general topic in mind, one way to start planning is to turn off the editor in your brain (that voice that rejects ideas before you've had a chance to consider or develop them) and let thoughts tumble out either in conversation or on paper. Ideas tend to generate other ideas, and a variety of thoughts will surface.

During a brainstorming session with a writing center tutor, one writer took the following notes as she considered whether she would support term limits for the members of the United States Congress:

For term limits
- Prevents one person from gaining too much power and representing only one faction of the public.
- Keeps bringing newcomers into office so they represent different parts of the public in their district.
  - New political views
  - That means that the groups who give political donations will change.
- In the last term, that person can put his or her energies into working on laws, not just on getting reelected.
- Stay in office too long, maybe not doing important work?

Against term limits
- People really get to know their job and have seniority.
- Leaders (speaker of the House . . . who else? majority leader? powerful committee heads?) have to have a lot of experience to do a good job.

Some facts to find out
- How many congressional representatives stay in office a long time?
- What happens to them after long terms in office?
- Do leaders really have to have a lot of experience? (Check on role of advisers and staff.)

Freewriting

Some writers find that they produce useful material when they start writing and keep writing without stopping. The writing is "free" in that it can go in any direction that occurs to the writer as he or she writes. The important part of freewriting is to keep going. You can also use freewriting as a "mind dump," recording everything you know about the subject you're going to write about. One student writer, analyzing a stereotype he had encountered, began his freewriting for his assignment as follows:

My dream even from when I was a child was always to be a farm manager. Back in seventh grade, I remember my social studies class was having a discussion of vocations in life. Never once did anyone talk about a profession in the line of agriculture, so when I asked, "What about farm management?" I was blasted with laughter and crude comments. The comments they made were false stereotypes that people have. People think all ag students are "countrified" or are just "farm boys." Just "hicks." Another stereotypical view is that farmers are lazy, just plant and sit around at the local coffeeshop and gossip. My father's farm is very diversified. We grow mint, onions, and corn. The mint and onions keep us busy all year. Many farmers get a job in town to supplement their farm income. Farmers need to keep complicated records and take hard ag courses in college. I use a hand-held computer to collect data for crop and field planning. The right software programs can make a great difference in successful farming.

Outlining

Outlines are plans. As a first stage in planning, many writers begin to find ideas by outlining (or listing) what they know about a subject. This also helps clarify what information they will need before they start to write, but writers may or may not follow that first outline because it can change as the paper develops. In that case, a later outline, developed after an early draft, helps writers to see how the paper will be structured. But if a paper can't be outlined, the writing could lack a reasonable structure or perhaps supporting detail. If some idea or subtopic doesn't seem to fit within the outline, it could be because it doesn't belong in the document. All main topics should support or explain the thesis.

Outlines can take many shapes and serve a variety of purposes. You might need them for taking notes on assigned reading or material you read for research papers, for an essay you're writing, for a speech or PowerPoint, or for other documents, and your instructor may ask you to include an outline with your finished draft. Depending on the writing to be done, you'll find that outlines serve useful purposes:

Uses

- *Listing* what you know and what you want to write about.

- *Organizing* your material. (You can order material chronologically, perhaps for presenting historical development; cause-and-effect order can help you organize the relationship of one thing to another; and compare-and-contrast organization can help you structure items you are discussing. Outlining can also be useful later in the writing process because it helps to group related ideas together and to reorder material into the best logical structure. Outlines also can clarify which ideas are related and more important than other ideas.)

- *Visualizing* the design or structure of the document and whether or not it seems balanced. (That is, you can then see what the main ideas and subsections of main ideas are and whether one main idea is dominating the whole paper while other main ideas are not discussed adequately.)

Types of outlines

- *Informal.* Informal outlines are often lists or notes briefly jotted down as they occur to you and then perhaps re-ordered, if needed.

Some people call this a "working outline," and it's easy to revise as you work more on the paper. You may use words or phrases, and an ordering system of numbers or letters may not be needed. When Adit was preparing to write her personal essay to apply to a school of veterinary medicine, she jotted down the following:

What experiences have I had with animals?
  — Summer assistant in local vet's office
    — Cleaned equipment
  — Helped with animals during treatment
  — Got to know how much work is involved
    — My own pets
    — Learned to care for a variety of animals
Should I list my course work? high school clubs?
  — Helped a cousin show her sheep
  — Had to groom two sheep

■ *Formal.* For formal outlines, consistently use sentences, words, or phrases in a system that clearly indicates relationships and indicates levels of coordination. You can show how various headings and subheadings relate by using Roman numerals for main headings (usually capitalizing all major words), capitals letters (and capitals for the first word of each top sublevel), and lowercase for minor subheads (with first word capitalized or all lowercase for the subhead content), or decimals (especially for technical writing). Logically, if you have a I, you will need a II, and if you have an A, you will need a B.

A. Main Idea
  1. Subheading
    a. Less important support-
      ing idea
    b. Less important support-
      ing idea
  2. Subheading
B. Main Idea
C. Main Idea

I. Main Idea
  A. Subheading
    1. Less important idea
    2. Less important idea
  B. Subheading
II. Main Idea
III. Main Idea

For decimals, you can use the following structure:

1.0
  1.1 (or) 1.a (or) 1a
  1.2 (or) 1.b (or) 1b
2.0
  2.1 (or) 2.a (or) 2a
  2.2 (or) 2b (or) 2b

A sample formal outline (this one is for a problem/solution paper) follows:

I. Show Need for Food for Local Homeless
   A. Current level of homeless in the community
      1. Homeless shelters overcrowded
      2. Food banks empty by end of the month
   B. Donations not keeping up with demand
   C. Major local donor (restaurant) out of business
   D. Projections for future unemployment when auto parts plant closes
II. Offer Solutions
   A. Local media (newspapers, TV) used to present problem
   B. Requests for donations sent to local churches and synagogues
   C. New commercial sources sought
      1. Local supermarkets
      2. College residence hall cafeterias
      3. Restaurants
   D. Volunteer food collectors and distributors sought

Most word processing programs have software that will help you create outlines. Headings have to be consistent (all headings at the same level are words, all are phrases, or all are sentences) and should be in parallel form (see 14a for help with parallel structure).

Clustering and Branching

Clustering establishes the relationships between words and phrases. Begin by writing a topic in the middle of a sheet of paper and circling it. Then as related ideas come to mind, draw lines to connect these ideas to other ideas. The other ideas will become the center of their own clusters of ideas as the topic branches out. When you keep an open mind, ideas spill out onto the page. You can rework them in a more orderly way by putting the main idea at the top of the page and reordering the branches. The writer who created the cluster on page 11 was exploring the topic of divorce and its effect on children.

Conversation or Collaboration

Some writers prefer to plan by themselves; others benefit from talking with a peer response group, a writing center tutor, or a friend. Talk produces more talk, and if the listener asks questions, even more ideas can develop in the writer's mind. If you find talk useful and you are in a situation where you can't engage in conversation, try picturing yourself addressing an imaginary audience.

Writer's Notebook or Journal

Ideas tend to float to the surface of our minds when we're engaged in other activities, such as walking to class, cooking, or taking a shower. You can capture those thoughts by recording them in a notebook or personal digital assistant (PDA). Some writers regularly keep journals, writing brief

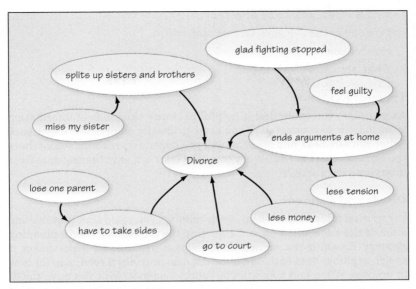

Figure 2.1   Clustering Example

entries at least once a day. You can refer to your journal, PDA, or notebook for ideas when you write.

Reading

An important source of material for your writing is the reading you do. You can search relevant information in libraries or on the Internet. You can also find connections to your topic when you read the newspaper, magazines, or readings for other classes. Your writer's notebook is a useful place to record these connections.

Who? What? When? Where? How? Why?

Journalists often use these question words as they gather information for news articles. Such words can be useful in helping them think more fully about a topic. *Who* or *what* might be involved or affected? *Why?* Is the location (*where?*) important? *How? What* connects the people or things involved? Try using these question words in a variety of combinations, and jot down your answers. For example, for a paper about the effect of too much exposure to sun on human skin, you might ask these questions while gathering information:

What damage can the sun cause to human skin? Why?

What illnesses result?

How serious are these?

Who is most likely to be affected?

How can these illnesses be treated?

How widespread is the problem?

What are the warning signs?

Types of Evidence

As you plan, you could find it helpful to clarify the kinds of information to include in your paper. Will you draw primarily on personal experience (what you see, hear, and read), or will you depend on reading, researching the work of others in the library or on the Internet, or gathering data from interviews or research?

Divide and Conquer

For writing projects that seem overwhelming, you could find that making a list of the steps involved in completing the project is a useful planning strategy. Breaking the writing into groups of manageable tasks makes it easier to plunge into each one. Your list also provides a road map for how to proceed. When and how will you collect evidence? Will you go to the library tomorrow afternoon? What will you need to read before you start writing? What questions do you want to discuss with a writing center tutor?

Try This

TO GET BEYOND WRITER'S BLOCK

Like other writers, sometimes you could find it difficult to get started. When that happens, consider the following strategies.

■ **Bounce ideas off a friend or classmate by e-mail or in person.** Encourage the person to ask questions that help you clarify your thoughts. (Offer to return the favor the next time your friend faces an assignment.)

■ **Start writing.** Write anything to get some words out. That's often the hardest part of writing.

■ **Turn off your mental editor.** This keeps telling you what you have written or thought isn't perfect. Selecting what you want to keep will come later.

■ **Choose a time and place where your mind can roam freely.** For some people, that happens in the shower. For others, sitting outside helps.

■ **Make a list of the "have to's" that keep you from writing.** For example, the list could include "I have to write a perfect first sentence

▶

before I can write more" or "I have to worry about the grammar of my sentences the first time I write them" or "I have to have my thesis sentence in mind when I start." If these "have to's" keep you from starting to write, hit the delete key in your mind so that they disappear.

■ **Start well in advance of your deadline.** Watching the clock to hurry yourself along isn't an effective technique. Try to remember you will need time to put an early draft away and come back to it later to revise and improve it.

2b DRAFTING

Some writers prefer to do most of their planning in their heads, and as a result, they have the general shape of a paper in mind when they start writing. Others have to write and rewrite early drafts before a working draft begins to take shape. In general, early drafts are very rough as writers add, change, and rework. Some writers are ready to share their early drafts with others, to get advice, to hear how the draft sounds when read aloud (by a writing center tutor, a peer response group, or themselves), and to get more ideas for revision. Other writers aren't ready to share their early drafts, and they prefer to delay reader input until a later draft. Because many good writers work collaboratively, they seek readers of their drafts before they are finished.

Writers who have time to put a draft aside for a while often find that something they hear or read triggers suggestions for new material. This is yet another reason for starting early—to allow for that "percolating" time. In the same way, when you have a short period away from a draft, you gain distance so that you can be more objective about what revisions are needed. When you reread a freshly written draft, it is hard to separate what is still in your head from what is on the page, and it is even harder to see what is missing or needs reworking.

2c ORGANIZING

As your draft takes shape, compare it to the outline you created (see pages 8–10). If you're a writer who outlines after drafting rather than before, try outlining your draft now. Checking your draft against an outline helps you see whether the organizational structure is sound and whether any sections need more material. If you're working on the computer, experiment with cutting and pasting parts of the outline in different places until you see a logical flow that makes sense to you.

2d   COLLABORATING

1. Responding to Writing

Most writers benefit from reader comments while drafting a paper. Readers' feedback can give you a fresh perspective—a view from the outside—on how the paper is progressing. Those reader comments are only suggestions, though. The final decisions as to how to revise in light of those comments are matters for you to decide.

Following are some ways you can get feedback from readers.

Meet with a Writing Center Tutor

If you have access to a writing center, ask a tutor to respond to the draft. The tutor is likely to ask what your concerns are, so come prepared with questions you had about that draft as you wrote it (for example, "Does the conclusion seem sort of weak?" "Does my thesis seem clear?" "Are my examples OK?" "Does this fit the assignment?"). Some writing centers also work with students online, so check to see whether this service is available on your campus.

Meet with a Small Group of Students in Your Class

If your class has peer response groups or workshop days, you can exchange papers and offer reader feedback for each other, in person or online. When you act as a reader, you not only are helping other writers but also are sharpening your own critical skills. That practice in critically reading someone else's writing improves your ability to read your own papers critically. You'll begin to notice that you will more easily think of suggestions for revising your own papers. To make the responses within your small group more useful, consider the following suggestions.

When You Meet in Person

- *Spend a few minutes comparing how you feel about hearing responses to your writing.* Some writers welcome comments from readers, but others are fearful or hesitant. Some readers also are hesitant to suggest changes, either because they aren't sure how valid their own comments are or because they don't want to offend fellow students. A few minutes spent discussing how to overcome these barriers can make the rest of the session more useful.

- *Come prepared with copies of your paper and some questions.* Since most readers can follow along more easily if they are reading your draft as they hear it, come prepared with enough copies to distribute to everyone. And think of some useful questions you have about your draft that you want your readers to answer.

- *Decide on ground rules for how your group will proceed.* Does your group want to have the writer or someone else read the paper aloud?

(Most writers benefit from this stage of response because they can catch mistakes as they read or listen and hear how the writing flows.) How long will the group spend on each paper? Will all the responses be oral, or do you want group members to write down any comments? Does your group want to draw up a uniform response sheet with itemized questions?

■ *Decide what questions readers will respond to.* Before starting to read, your group should spend a few minutes working up a list of questions to guide the responses. Possible questions include the following:

1. Since the first comments from readers should be positive ones, you can start by asking what the readers like about this draft. What worked well? (Writers need to know what's working well in addition to what might be revised.) What are some strong points of this draft? (interesting topic? effective introduction? strong feelings expressed? good examples? good use of humor? effective word choice?)

2. What do you think is the main point of this paper?

3. Are there any sections that are unclear and need more explanation?

4. Does the paper fit the assignment?

5. Who is the appropriate reader or audience for this paper?

6. Are there any sections that seem out of order?

7. Are there any parts of the paper where the writing seems to stray from the topic?

8. Does the paper flow? (That is, does the paper seem to progress smoothly, or are there abrupt shifts or missing connections?)

9. What else do you want to know about the paper's topic?

10. If you had to prioritize, what is the most important revision you would suggest to the writer?

When You Meet Online

■ *Follow the guidelines for meeting in person.*

■ *Decide on a procedure for how your group is going to interact.* If you're "meeting" via e-mail only, decide the following: Will everyone write specific comments in the text of the file? If so, use "track changes" or a different font or color to distinguish your comments from the writer's words. Will everyone read everyone else's comments? If so, the file has to be forwarded from person to person and eventually back to the author. If you're using a peer review or text-sharing program that allows the papers and comments to be posted online, be sure that all group members have access to and understand how the system works.

■ *Before sending or posting your comments or responses, reread what you have written.* Your tone of voice, body language, and facial expression are missing, so your reader could misinterpret what you are writing.

■ *Decide in advance what each person has to do, and set deadlines for each group member's work to be finished.*

Form a Writing Group on Your Own

If you want reader feedback but have no writing center or classroom opportunities to get that feedback, you may want to form a writing group. A writing group is a small group of people willing to come together, either in person or online, on a regular basis to read each other's writing. A writing group may take on a personality of its own as members learn from each other and learn how to critique writing. Some groups that work well stay together for years.

2. Writing Together

Some writers are asked to write as a group (a common practice in the business world, where team reports are assigned). If you find yourself writing in such a group project, your group will need to set ground rules. The first task will be to decide whether all members will work on the whole paper or everyone will be responsible for a part.

If each part is assigned to a different writer, your group should decide the following in advance:

1. How will your group break the project into parts? A brainstorming session can be helpful at this stage; if you're successful, the final product of this session (or additional sessions) will be an outline.

2. Will your group meet in person, online, or both?

3. Who will do each part of the outline?

4. Who will be assigned to put all of the parts together and produce the final product?

5. What are the deadlines for drafts of each part? When the group meets to read drafts, you can use the suggestions listed on pages 14–15 to guide your discussion.

6. When you meet to read a draft of the whole paper, how will the group decide on revisions? Should revisions be agreed to by a majority vote, or should there be a project leader who oversees the drafting of the final product?

7. When there is a draft with all parts revised, will all members of the group see the final document and suggest any last-minute changes?

If the whole paper is to be co-authored, your group needs to decide how to proceed. Some steps to consider include the following:

1. Spend time discussing your topic, refining it, and deciding on the major areas of content. This will take several meetings, and since ideas will evolve as you talk, someone needs to take notes. If this discussion proceeds online, be sure there is a record of what has been discussed.
2. Try writing separate drafts. When the group comes together, you may find that you can cut and paste from different writers' drafts to form a whole.
3. Have each writer rewrite the whole that has been created. Then meet to see how the drafts have been refined. More cutting and pasting may be needed here.
4. If you're meeting in person, have a final meeting at which the last draft is read aloud, and ask all members to suggest final revisions. If you're working online, post the last draft and invite revisions.

2e REVISING

A particularly important part of writing is revising, which means re-seeing the whole and then reworking it. Because this can be difficult to do, some writers make the mistake of handing in a paper that is really an early draft that hasn't been adequately revised. The low grades they get are not indications of inadequate writing but a result of handing in a paper too early in the writing process. (Think, for example, of similar problems caused when software is released too early, before the bugs are worked out.)

One effective way to revise is to read the paper as if you were someone else, not the writer. It's difficult but important to get some mental distance from your own writing. Another effective way to re-see your paper is to put it aside for a few days (that's the advantage of getting early drafts done days before the due date). When you come back to the paper, you will be able to read it with more objectivity.

Try This

TO REVISE YOUR DRAFT

Start at the beginning of the draft. Whenever you return to your paper, read from the beginning of the draft to the section where you will be working. This helps you get back into the flow of thought, and it permits you to revise what you've written so far.

▶

Use "track changes" or create multiple drafts. If your software has a "track changes" feature, turn it on; this will allow you to see everything you change and allow you to undo it if you have second thoughts. If you don't have this feature or don't use it, save each of your drafts with a new file name. If you decide to delete something, you'll still have the deleted material in an earlier file in case you want to put it back in.

Print out hard copies. As you're working on a computer, it may help to look at a printed copy of your draft to get a sense of the whole paper.

Change the view to check paragraphs. Switch to "print preview" so that you can see each whole page on the screen. Is one paragraph noticeably shorter than the others? If so, it might need more development. Is there a paragraph that seems to be too long and to need condensing or breaking into two paragraphs?

Highlight sentence length. If you're working on your computer, hit the return key after every sentence so that each one looks like a separate paragraph. Are all of your sentences about the same length? If so, you might need some variety. Do all of the sentences start the same way? If so, you might need to use some different sentence patterns. (See Chapter 20 on sentence variety.)

During the revision process, many writers are helped considerably by collaborative feedback from others. Writers who publish their work often get feedback and helpful advice from their editors, and scholars who submit articles and books to scholarly publications ask colleagues to read their manuscripts. Reader response can be very useful when you are revising your paper. It's important, though, to remember that you are the writer, and you must decide which advice to listen to. (See 2d for help with collaborating with your readers.)

To revise effectively, use the following checklist to review your draft for all major qualities of good writing, those aspects referred to as the higher-order concerns (HOCs) by Thomas J. Reigstad and Donald McAndrew in their book *Tutoring Writing: A Practical Guide for Conferences* (Portsmouth, NH: Boynton/Cook, 2001). (The later-order concerns, or LOCs, are discussed on page 19.)

Checklist

REVISING FOR HIGHER-ORDER CONCERNS (HOCs)

Purpose. What is the purpose of this paper? Have you achieved the purpose? If not, what's needed?

Thesis. Is the thesis clearly stated? Has it been narrowed sufficiently? Is it appropriate for the assignment? Can you summarize your thesis if

▶

asked? If you think of the thesis as a promise that you will discuss this statement, have you kept all parts of that promise?

Audience. Who is the audience for this paper? What assumptions have you made about the members of your audience? Did you tell them what they already know? Is that appropriate? If you are writing for your teacher or some expert in the field, does he or she expect you to include background material? Did you leave out anything your audience needs to know?

Organization. What is the central idea of each paragraph? Does that idea contribute to the thesis? Do the paragraphs progress in an organized, logical way? Are there any gaps from one part to another? Is the reader likely to get lost in any part? Do your transitions indicate when the writing moves to a new aspect of the topic?

Development. Are there places where more details, examples, or specifics would help? Are there details that are not relevant and should be omitted?

2f EDITING AND PROOFREADING

Editing is the fine-tuning process of writing. When you edit, you attend to what are called the later-order concerns (LOCs)—details of grammar, usage, punctuation, spelling, and other mechanics. Errors in grammar and usage send the wrong message to your readers about your general level of competence in using language, and such errors will cause you to get lower grades. For a list of strategies for correcting these errors, see the Try This box below.

Try This

TO EDIT AND PROOFREAD FOR LATER-ORDER CONCERNS (LOCs)

- **Use online tools.** Online spell-checkers cannot flag problems with wrong forms of words such as *it's/its* or *advice/advise*. Grammar-checkers catch some but not all grammar problems and can only offer suggestions. For example, the program may highlight constructions such as *there is* or *there are,* but it cannot tell you whether your choice is appropriate.

- **Edit on a hard copy.** It may be easier to print a draft and mark that for editing changes.

- **Put the paper aside for a bit.** It's easier to see problems when the paper is not as fresh in your mind.

- **Slide a card down each line as you reread.** This will help your eye slow down.

▶

■ **Point to each word as you read if you tend to leave out words.** Be sure that you see a written version of every word you say.

■ **Keep in mind a list of the particular problems you tend to have when writing.** Which grammatical problems have teachers frequently marked? Which do you frequently have to check in a handbook? Here are some of the most common problems to look for in your papers:

fragments	omitted commas
subject-verb agreement	verb tenses
comma splices	spelling errors
misplaced apostrophes	run-on sentences
pronoun reference	unnecessary commas
omitted words	missing transition words

■ **Keep this book close by as you edit and proofread.** If you have a question and don't know which section to check, see the **Question and Correct** section in the front of this book. If you have a written example, check the **Compare and Correct** section in the front of this book to find a similar example.

The most effective time to edit is when you've finished revising so that you've shaped the paper and won't be making any more large-scale changes. It is more efficient to fine-tune sentences you know will be in the final version than to spend time on work that might be deleted in a later draft. Another reason for not editing until the paper is close to completion is that you may be reluctant to delete sentences or words you have already corrected. Even if a sentence needs to be rewritten or doesn't belong in the paper, there's a natural tendency to want to leave it in because it is grammatically correct. Don't let yourself fall into that trap.

Proofreading is the final editing process of writing, the last check for missing words, misspellings, format requirements, and so on. If you have a list of references you consulted while writing your paper, this is the time to do a final check on the information and the format of the entries. To check your spelling, try the proofreading suggestions listed in 50a.

3

PARAGRAPHS

Each paragraph in a paper is a group of sentences that work together to develop one idea or topic within the larger piece of writing. Effective paragraphs are unified, coherent, and developed.

3a UNITY

A unified paragraph focuses on one topic and does not include unnecessary or irrelevant material. To check the unity of each of your paragraphs, ask yourself what the paragraph is about. You should be able to answer in a sentence that either is implied or appears in the paragraph as the topic sentence. Any sentence not related to this topic sentence is probably a digression that doesn't belong in the paragraph.

3b COHERENCE

Every paragraph should be written so that each sentence flows smoothly into the next. If your ideas, sentences, and details fit together clearly, your readers can follow along easily without getting lost. To help your reader, use the suggestions in Chapter 19 for repeating key terms and phrases and using synonyms, pronouns, and transitional devices between sentences and paragraphs. Equally important, try to check for missing information that causes a break in the chain of ideas, explanation, or argument.

Hint

MAKING YOUR WRITING "FLOW" BY ADDING MISSING LINKS

Sometimes writers skip a step or two in their writing, introducing what is sometimes referred to as "lack of coherence" or breaking the "flow" of the paper. This can happen when the writer forgets to put some information in the paper that is in her mind or when a writer thinks the instructor knows some information that doesn't have to be repeated. Such connections between sentences and paragraphs are often necessary for clear communication.

Example: It has recently been shown that some bacteria can shine in the dark. This important source of bioluminescence is being studied closely, especially by a group at Princeton where members are finding many species like this.

[Ask yourself: What's missing between the first and second sentence? Does the intended audience know what "bioluminescence" is? Why is it being studied? Why is it important? There is some missing information here that needs to be added.]

3c DEVELOPMENT

A paragraph is well developed when it covers the paragraph topic fully, using details, examples, evidence, and other specifics the reader needs as well as generalizations to bind these specifics together. You can check the development of each of your paragraphs by asking yourself what else your reader might need or want to know about that topic. Some specifics help explain or support the more general statements, and other specifics help make bland generalizations come alive.

3d INTRODUCTIONS AND CONCLUSIONS

Some writers need to write their introduction before the body of the paper, and others find it easier to write their introduction after revising the body. Some writers even write the introduction last. As you draft your introduction and conclusion, consider the following points.

Introduction

The purpose of the introduction is to bring the reader into the writer's world, to build interest in the subject (why should someone read this?), and to announce the topic. The introduction also gives the reader a chance to mentally create a sense of who the author is and what attitude the reader should assume while reading, much as we formulate a mental sense of others when we are introduced to them. By the end of an effective introduction, readers also have a clear sense of what the topic is and how the paper will be organized. This will help readers follow the progression of the paper more easily as they read and not get lost in details or complex arguments. Think of the introduction as a plan or map for your readers. See the Try This box below for some specific strategies for writing an introduction.

Try This

TO WRITE AN EFFECTIVE INTRODUCTION

■ Cite an interesting statistic.

Nearly 25 percent of colleges and universities now require first-year students to have their own laptops.

■ Suggest the long-term effects of your topic.

Notebooks, pens, and textbooks will, in the near future, no longer be taken to classes. Instead, students will appear with their laptops, ready to take notes and refer to their online textbooks.

■ Offer an analogy.

Like freshman beanies worn years ago, a new laptop is now a sign of a first-year college student.

■ Pose a question.

Why are so many colleges and universities requiring students to buy laptops before starting college?

▶

■ **Relate an anecdote.**

When I was accepted at State University, I thought my big expense for classes would be textbooks. To my surprise, I found the most costly item on my shopping list was a new computer.

■ **Make a surprising statement.**

The laptop computer was developed primarily for use by people in the business world; designers had no idea they'd become standard equipment for college students.

■ **Introduce a quotation.**

"The standard laptop computer now weighs less than most textbooks students used to drag to class, thus relieving them of backaches from those overstuffed backpacks," said Michael Modin, a spokesperson for Macintosh computers.

■ **Acknowledge an opinion or approach that differs from yours.**

Some college faculty have expressed concern as more and more students carry laptop computers to classes. According to these instructors, students no longer look up at the board, spend time in class checking their e-mail, and too often lose their notes when their hard drives crash.

■ **Offer a definition. (NOTE: Use this approach only when you need to help your readers understand a concept or when you want to clarify or limit how you are using a particular term.)**

When college admissions offices instruct first-year students to bring their own laptops to campus, they do not mean the Blackberry or any similar all-in-one device. They are referring to the familiar folding portable computer.

Conclusion

Conclusions are important parts of papers and are needed for several reasons:

■ Readers are likely to remember conclusions more than the body of a paper.

■ The conclusion is your opportunity to summarize your major points.

■ You can introduce a new idea that the paper has been building to and that your reader will now agree with, having read your paper.

■ The conclusion is a clear signal to the reader that the paper is ending, much as a piece of music needs a conclusion and a conversation on the phone needs a signal that you're about to hang up.

See the Try This box on page 24 for some specific strategies for writing a conclusion.

Try This

TO WRITE AN EFFECTIVE CONCLUSION

Conclusions can look either backward or forward.

- **Look backward.** If the paper has a complex discussion, try any of the following:
    - *Summarize the main points* to remind the reader of what was discussed.
    - *Emphasize important points* you don't want the reader to forget.
    - *Refer to something in the introduction,* thus coming full circle.
- **Look forward.** If the paper is short or doesn't need a summary, try the following:
    - *Pose a question* for the reader to consider.
    - *Offer advice.*
    - *Call for action* the reader can take.
    - *Consider future implications* of your topic.

3e PATTERNS OF ORGANIZATION

Paragraphs can be organized in a great variety of ways, starting with a statement that is the main point of the paragraph and then including reasons, data, evidence, or other support for the main idea; following chronological order; moving from general to specific information or from specific to general; or following some spatial order, such as top to bottom, side to side, or front to back.

The patterns used in the following paragraphs illustrate ways of thinking about and organizing ideas. You can also use these patterns during planning as you think about your topic. The information about the current job market and future employment trends contained in these sample paragraphs was found during a brief search of resources on the Internet. (See Chapter 60 for a discussion of search methods.)

Narration

Narratives tell stories (or parts of stories), with the events usually arranged in chronological order to make a point that relates to the whole paper.

> With the rapid growth in opportunities for physical therapists, a recent graduate in this field found that her job search was a particularly pleasant experience. Offered dozens of jobs around the country, she began by deciding where she wanted to travel as well as where she might want to live. On her interview trips, she explained, "I was treated royally. Recruiters in three different cities—Atlanta,

Seattle, and Tucson—paid all my expenses for on-site interviews."
When she opted to stay in Seattle for some sightseeing, her hotel and
food expenses were paid for two additional days. After her Seattle
trip, she went to Atlanta, where recruiters offered her a particularly
generous relocation package and sign-on bonus. Her experience is one
more example of the fact that while job searching in many fields today
is disheartening, the need for physical therapists is causing employers
to compete for applicants.

Description

Description includes details about people, places, things, or scenes drawn
from the senses: sight, sound, smell, touch, and taste.

In the offices and laboratories of many companies, people work in
groups, sitting around a table, talking and trading ideas. Interacting
with colleagues can be enjoyable when the group keeps its sense of
humor and maintains an informal atmosphere. Bottles of flavored
spring water are passed out, doughnut crumbs are scattered over
reports and charts, and aging pizza boxes are stacked up along the
conference room wall. But that does not mean real work isn't getting
done. There is an art to group effort because everyone has to learn how
to work smoothly with a diversity of personalities. One member of the
group may want to dominate the conversation or try to assert his
ideas, his loud voice like a refrain above all the other noise as he insists
that everyone listen to him. Another person may find that, in order to
be heard, she has to lean forward, elbows on the table, to insert her
voice in the conversation. Early in the morning, some members of
the group are trying to wake up by slurping coffee, and late in the
afternoon, others want to give up and take the work home. However,
even with the continuous need to be effective in blending different
people into the group, employers are finding that the results are
usually better than if each employee were left alone to do his or her
part of the project.

Cause and Effect

Cause-and-effect paragraphs trace causes or discuss effects. The paragraph may start with effects and move backward to analyze causes or
start with causes and then look at the effects. The following paragraph
starts with a cause, the age of the U.S. population, and then looks at the
effects of demographics on the job market.

The growth and direction of the job market in the future is greatly
affected by population trends, so government agencies such as the
Bureau of Labor Statistics study population changes in order to
determine where the growth in jobs will be in the next decades. A major
factor that influences jobs is the age of the population. Because the

number of Americans over age eighty-five will increase about four times as fast as the total population, there will be a major increase in the demand for health services. With the shift to relatively fewer children and teenagers, there will also be greater demand for products and services for older people. For example, older people with stable incomes will travel more and have more money for consumer goods, so some jobs will focus more on tending to their needs. The job market, present and future, is shaped by the age of America's population, present and future.

Analogy

Use analogies to compare things that may initially seem to have little in common but that can offer fresh insights when compared.

It's a mistake to think that the best way to look for a job is to apply for available openings. Over 75 percent of the jobs being filled every year are not on those lists. A better way of looking for a job is very much like inventing a successful item to sell in the marketplace. The "hot" sellers are not merely better versions of existing ones; they are totally new, previously unthought-of consumer goods or services. In the same way, the majority of the jobs being filled are not ones that existed before, and like a successful new children's toy or some new piece of electronic equipment, they did not exist because no one realized the work needed to be done. Good executives, managers, and business owners often have ideas for additional positions, but they haven't yet developed those ideas into full-blown job descriptions. Like the inventor who comes up with the concept for a new consumer product, a job seeker can land a position by asking potential employers about changing needs in their corporation and suggesting that he or she can take on those responsibilities. Finding a new need is definitely a strategy that works as well for job seekers as it does for inventors.

Example and Illustration

Frequently, writers discuss an idea by offering examples to support the topic sentence, or the writer may use an illustration, which is an extended example.

Examples

According to the Bureau of Labor Statistics, America's workers are an increasingly diverse group. Whereas white non-Hispanic men have historically made up the largest segment of the labor force—about 78 percent—that is no longer true. By 2005, Hispanics had added about 6.5 million workers, an increase of 64 percent over 1995 levels. African

Americans, Hispanic Americans, and Asian Americans now account for roughly 35 percent of all labor force entrants. Another factor that is increasing the diversity of the workplace is the growing number of women. Although the number of women under the age of forty entering the working world is increasing more slowly than in the past, women fill about 48 percent of all jobs. All these groups contribute to the diversity of America's labor pool.

Illustration

The Bureau of Labor Statistics' study of employment trends for the future reports that the fastest-growing areas for jobs are in occupations that require higher levels of education. Office and factory automation and offshore production greatly reduced the number of people needed in jobs that could be filled by high school graduates. Now the need is for more executives, administrators, managers, and people with professional specialties—occupations that require people with higher education. Moreover, in a complex world dominated by high-tech electronics and international markets, a high school education is no longer adequate. High school graduates increasingly find themselves limited to the service sector, working in areas such as fast-food service, where the pay is low and there is little potential for advancement. The trend toward the need for people with higher education is expected to continue for the foreseeable future.

Classification and Division

Classification involves grouping or sorting items into a group or category based on unifying principles. Division starts with one item and divides it into parts.

Classification

As America moves from being a nation that produces goods to one that produces services, the major growth in employment will be in the service-producing industries. Included in this group, according to the Bureau of Labor Statistics, are five major categories of service employment. First, there are the service industries, which include the health services needed by a growing and aging population; all the business service industries that supply personnel for offices and for computer and data processing; the education field, which will need more teachers for more students as the population continues to grow; and the social services areas, such as child care and family services. The second major category of service-producing jobs includes those in the wholesale and retail trade, spurred in part by rising incomes and a greater demand for clothing, appliances, and automobiles. Finance, insurance, and real estate make up the third major category, and government is a fourth area of service in which the number of jobs will increase. Finally, the category of transportation, communications, and public utilities will be a major area for expansion of jobs, with truck transportation accounting for 50 percent of the new jobs in this area. Jobs in communications, however, will decline about 12 percent.

Division

As we look more closely at marketing and sales occupations, which the Bureau of Labor Statistics defines as a growing service area, we can see that it includes a wide variety of jobs. People who work in this area sell goods and services in stores, on the phone, and through catalogs and mail order. They also purchase commodities and properties for resale, act as wholesalers for others, and scout out new stores and franchises to open. Travel agents and financial counselors both aim to increase consumer interest in their services. Others study the market for growth trends and consumer needs or analyze sales in the United States and abroad. Marketing and sales occupations indeed span a broad spectrum of interests, though they all have the consumer in mind.

Process Analysis

A process paragraph analyzes or describes the way something is done or the way something works. Such paragraphs can also explain how to complete some process and are ordered chronologically.

When you scout the job market, here are some steps to follow to improve your opportunities for finding the job you want. First, do not limit yourself to the jobs listed by various companies. Those lists represent only a small percentage of the jobs available, and they will draw dozens—maybe even hundreds—of applicants. Instead, draw up a list of companies you'd like to work for by browsing through their annual reports and other materials available in a job counselor's office. Don't forget the Yellow Pages, particularly if you know the city where you want to work. Then call the company and ask for the name of someone who is likely to have hiring authority. If possible, get a name other than that of the personnel manager—that person's job is often to screen out unqualified candidates. Next, send a clear, well-focused résumé directly to that person, and don't be bashful about listing your accomplishments in terms of that company's needs. In the cover letter, state why you are the ideal person for that organization. Make your reader see why the company will be better off with you, not anyone else. Be sure to conclude the cover letter with a request for an interview and explain that you will be following up with a phone call within the next few days. At the interview, explore all of the options you can, helping the other person see how you might fit in, even if there is no vacancy at the present time. You might help the person create a new position for which you'd be the best applicant. Finally, be sure to write a short letter thanking the interviewer for meeting with you.

Comparison and Contrast

One way to discuss two subjects is to compare them by looking at their similarities or contrast them by looking at their differences. There are two options for organizing such a paragraph: present first one subject and then the other, or discuss both subjects at the same time, point by point.

Two Subjects, One at a Time

A government study of occupations in forestry and logging indicates that people employed in these two fields represent two rather different areas in terms of the kinds of work they do. Forestry technicians compile data on the characteristics of forests, such as size, content, and condition. Generally, they are the decision makers, traveling through sections of forest to gather basic information about species of trees in the forest, disease and insect damage, seedling mortality, and conditions that may cause forest fires. One of their main responsibilities is to determine when a tract of forest is ready to be harvested. Less skilled than forest technicians are forest workers, whose job includes more physical labor. They plant new tree seedlings to reforest timberland, remove diseased or undesirable trees, spray herbicides where needed, and clear away brush and debris from camp trails, roadsides, and camping areas. Like forest technicians, though, forest workers spend long hours outdoors in all kinds of weather.

Two Subjects, Point by Point

Many students who graduate with economics majors take one of two very different types of jobs, either as government economists or as market research analysts for large companies. Those who go to work for the government assess economic conditions in the United States and abroad and estimate the economic effects of specific changes in legislation or public policy. Market research analysts, by contrast, are concerned with the design, promotion, price, and distribution of a product or service. Another area of difference is that government economists analyze data provided by government studies, whereas market research analysts often design their own surveys and questionnaires or conduct interviews. Whether they work as economists for the government or as analysts for private companies, however, most people in this field find that they often work under pressure of deadlines and tight schedules. In spite of the pressure, some economists and analysts combine full-time jobs with part-time or consulting work in academia or other settings.

Definition

A definition of a term or a concept places it in a general class and then differentiates it from others in that class, often through the use of examples and comparisons.

> Skill in problem solving is a crucial mental ability that job interviewers look for when they meet applicants, but it is not clear what this mental process is. Problem solving is an ability that assists a person in defining what the problem is and how to formulate steps to solve it. Included in this complex cognitive act are a number of characteristic mental abilities. Being flexible—remaining open to new possibilities— is a great asset in solving a problem, though a good problem solver also draws on strategies that may have worked in other settings. In addition, problem solving involves keeping the goal clearly in mind so that a person doesn't get sidetracked into exploring related problems that don't achieve the desired goal. Employers want problem solvers because having such a skill is far more valuable than having specific knowledge. Problem-solving abilities cannot be taught on the job, whereas specific knowledge often can be, and specific knowledge can become outdated, unlike the ability to solve problems.

4

ARGUMENT

Reading and writing persuasive arguments are parts of your everyday life. You've seen plenty of advertisements that attempt to persuade you to buy certain products, and you may have received letters from charitable organizations or political candidates persuading you to donate time or money to their causes. You may also have written a business proposal to persuade your boss to implement a plan or an application to persuade an organization to grant you admission to a program or give you funding. The use of reasons as well as emotional appeals to persuade an audience is part of normal interaction with the world. People actively persuade you to believe, act on, or accept their claims, just as you want others to accept or act on your claims. If you think of this in terms of the rhetorical triangle (see page 1), your topic is the action that you (the writer) want to convince your reader to take.

However, persuasion is not the only purpose for writing an effective argument. You might argue to justify to yourself and others what you believe and why you hold those positions. You might also create arguments to solve problems, or you might argue about how to evaluate something. Most of your college writing will involve some form of argument. Position papers, reviews of films and books, and literary analyses are all forms of argument. Outside the classroom, your resume and cover letter will be an argument to hire you, and in the workplace, you will often be engaged in argument to make decisions and solve problems.

The ability to argue effectively is a skill everyone needs. Argumentation involves researching to find support for your claims as well as reasoning to explain and defend actions, beliefs, and ideas. Therefore, you need to think about finding information and to consider how you present yourself as a credible writer to your audience, how your audience will respond to you, how you select topics to write about, and how you develop and organize your material into persuasive papers. These topics are discussed in this chapter.

4a WRITING AND READING ARGUMENTS

As a writer, you have to get your readers to listen to you and let you make your case. To gain your reader's trust and respect, your writing should indicate that you know what you are talking about, that you are truthful, and that you are reasonable enough to consider other sides of the argument. As the reader of an argument, you need to consider the writer's credibility. For example, if you were to read an article that claims cigarette smoking is not harmful to our health and then discover that the writer works in the tobacco industry, you would question the writer's credibility. Similarly, you need to establish your own credibility with your audience.

Checklist

ESTABLISHING CREDIBILITY

The following suggestions will help you establish your credibility with your audience:

Show that your motives are reasonable and worthwhile. Give your audience some reasonable assurance that you are arguing for a claim that is recognized as being for the general good or that shares the audience's motives. For example, are you writing an argument to a group of fellow students for more on-campus parking because you personally are having a parking problem or because you recognize that this is a problem many students are having? If you want action to solve your personal problem, you are not likely to get an attentive hearing. Why should others care?

Avoid vague and ambiguous terms and exaggerated claims. Words such as *always, never, best,* or *worst* usually invite someone in your audience to find an exception. Vague arguments such as "everyone says" (who is "everyone"?) or "it's a huge problem" (how big is "huge"?) raise doubts about the writer's knowledge and ability to write authoritatively. Exaggerations such as "commercialism has destroyed the

▶

meaning of Christmas" or "no one cares about the farmer's problems anymore" are inflated opinions that weaken the writer's credibility.

Acknowledge that you have thought about opposing arguments by including them. Readers who don't agree with you want to know that you aren't ignoring their views.

Cite knowledgeable, credible people as sources for your evidence. If your audience is not likely to know your sources by name, be sure to indicate who they are and why they should be trusted. Institutional affiliations, publications, and awards and other forms of recognition are usually effective as grounds for credibility.

4b CONSIDERING THE AUDIENCE

1. Types of Appeals

As you form the topic for your argument, think about your audience. If the people you are writing to are likely to disagree with your position, think about how to acknowledge and address their reasons for disagreeing, and think about what types of appeals would be most effective in conveying your argument.

Logical Appeals

Logical reasoning is grounded in sound principles of inductive and deductive reasoning. Writers of strong arguments avoid logical fallacies and base proofs on factual evidence gathered from data and events, as well as on deduction, definitions, and analogies. Logical proof appeals to people's reason, understanding, and common sense. (See pages 39–40 for more on logical reasoning.)

For example, for a paper attempting to persuade readers that a particular state's job training program has worked and should therefore continue to be funded, logical arguments could include data showing the number of people in the program and the success rate of their employment after being in the program. The paper could then compare those figures to data for a similar group of people who did not take part in the program.

Showing readers the evidence you have gathered is always more persuasive than telling them what to think. A very persuasive way to present logical appeals is through the use of data in charts, graphs, comparison tables, and other images. The arrangement of those pieces of evidence can be used to show the relationships among them or between two opposing results. (See pages 43–51 for more on visual argument and pages 51–70 for document design.)

Emotional Appeals

Emotional appeals arouse the audience's emotions—sympathy, patriotism, pride, anger, and other feelings based on values, beliefs, and motives. Appeals to emotions may include examples, descriptions, and narratives.

For example, for the paper on job training programs, an effective example might be the story of a woman who was previously unemployed for a long period of time despite intensive job seeking but who found a good job after acquiring new skills in the program. Her testimony would appeal to the audience's sympathy and to the belief that most people want to work and would be able to do so if they could just get some help in upgrading their skills.

Ethical Appeals

Ethical appeals act on the audience's impressions, opinions, and judgments about the person making the argument. In other words, these appeals establish the writer's credibility. As a writer, you need to give your audience proof that you are knowledgeable, do not distort evidence, and have some expertise on the subject. You should also show that you are fair and trustworthy, especially when addressing your opponents. To establish credibility, you can draw on personal experience, explain your credentials or those of your sources, and offer appropriate logical proof. For example, the author of the job training paper might draw on her own experience working for the program or explain that the data she is presenting come from a highly credible source, such as county or state records. The writer also might appeal to the values she shares with her readers. For example, she might show how cutting the funding to the state's job training program will increase unemployment rates, and more unemployment will increase the financial burden on all taxpayers. Because the writer assumes that her readers are also taxpayers, she shows how they share values on this issue.

In constructing your argument, always consider what your audience is likely to value most as evidence. Do your readers value education or experience more? Are they respectful or suspicious of authority? Will they focus only on your logic no matter what experience or credentials you might offer?

2. Common Ground

An important step in gaining a hearing from your audience is to identify the common ground—the values, beliefs, interests, motives, or goals—you share. Think, for example, of some strong conviction you hold. If someone with an equally strong stand on the opposite side started arguing for that opposing position without appealing to common ground, would you be likely to listen attentively, or would you instead start marshaling arguments for your side? A writer who firmly believes in everyone's right to own a gun would probably have more success appealing to equally firm advocates of gun control by establishing a shared concern about safety and street crime at the beginning. Without starting on neutral territory, neither side would be likely to listen to the other. (On the other hand, if you and your audience are in total agreement, there is no need to offer an argument. An appropriate topic for a persuasive paper will fall between extremes, with both opposing views to consider and common ground to find.)

Because the search for common ground is so important, let's examine how it might be discovered. Suppose a legislator wants to introduce a bill requiring motorcyclists to wear helmets, but the legislator knows he will be voted down because many other legislators oppose laws they believe restrict people's freedom to decide. One place to find some common ground would be to establish that everyone has a concern for the safety of bikers. It's also likely that everyone in the legislature will agree that bikers have a right to be on the road and that motorists often aren't sufficiently careful about avoiding them. When the legislator makes his listeners aware that they share this much common ground, he is likely to get a hearing.

Let's consider one more example. Suppose you are writing a proposal to the city council to spend funds beautifying a public playground. If you believe the council is likely to turn down your proposal, you need to think about the council members' possible reasons for rejecting it. Is the city budget so tight that the council is reluctant to spend money on any projects that aren't absolutely necessary? If so, what appeals could you make in your proposal? Your opening argument could be a logical appeal, including some facts about the low cost of the beautification project. Perhaps you could begin with an emotional appeal about the children who use the playground. What common ground do you share with the council? You and they want a well-run city that doesn't go into debt. If you acknowledge that you share those concerns and that, like the council, you don't want to put the city budget in the red, you will be more likely to get the council to listen to your proposal.

Try This

TO ESTABLISH COMMON GROUND

Try some of these patterns to establish common ground with your reader(s):

- I hold the view that _____, but you hold the view that
  _____.
- Your objections to my view are _____.
- What you and I share about this subject is _____.
- My view builds on this shared view because _____.

Getting ready to write a persuasive paper requires thinking about yourself as the writer and about the audience who will read your arguments. You also have other considerations as you move through this writing process. How do you find a topic? How do you find the material you want to use in the development of your arguments? How do you build sound arguments? How do you organize all of this information into a paper? The rest of this chapter offers help with these important parts of the process.

4c FINDING A TOPIC

1. Arguable Topics

Topics for persuasion are always topics that can be argued, that have some cause for debate between two or more sides. Arguable topics are different from statements of fact, which are generally considered to be true or can be easily verified. For example, no one can deny that the total number of reported rapes has increased nationally over the past fifty years, so a claim that reported rapes have gone up would not be a topic for a persuasive paper—it is simply a fact that can be checked in lists of national crime statistics. But there are multiple sides to other issues about rape. Are those numbers higher because the population has grown, because of more accurate reporting, because more rapes are being committed, or because women are more inclined to report such attacks? A persuasive paper might therefore take a stand about the causes of the increase in reported rapes.

2. Interesting Topics

When preparing to write a persuasive paper on a topic of your choice, think about the wide range of matters that interest you or that are part of your life. What do you and your friends talk about? What have you been reading lately in the newspaper, in magazines, or on the Internet? What topics have you learned about on television? What are some ongoing situations around you, events that are happening or about to happen? What unresolved public or family issues concern you? What topics have you been discussing or reading about in your classes? What matters concerning yourself are unresolved and need further consideration? What event happened to you that made you stop and think? get mad? cheer?

Checklist

EXPLORING TOPICS FOR ARGUMENT

If you can't think of opinions or topics to argue, try some of these patterns:

■ I believe that _____ because _____.

Example: I believe that there should not be a military draft because _____.

▶

- Presently, we do/don't do this _____, but we ought to _____ because that is better _____.

  Example: Presently, we don't have funds but need to repair our national highways. To raise money we ought to raise the price of drivers' licenses because that's better than _____.

- The problem is _____, and the way to solve it is _____.

  Example: The problem is that the amount of air pollution continues to rise, and the solution is _____.

- _____ is/is not _____ because _____.

  Example: Whistleblowing is not an act of company disloyalty because _____.

3. Local and General Topics

In the "so what" strategy in the Try This box on page 37, the writer started to develop a topic by thinking it through on a local or personal level and then enlarging it. You can start the same way with some new rule, guideline, or restriction on your campus, such as a new electronic device that searched you as you left the library to see if you had a book you hadn't checked out. Is that something that bothers you? Do you see it as an invasion of privacy, a waste of the school's money, or a way to stop all library theft you know is going on in your school? These are local views of the matter, and any one might be a springboard for a paper in which you argue that the antitheft system is or is not a beneficial addition to the library. Another option is to move to a larger view beyond your own library or campus or city. Is this instance part of a larger issue of new technology that implies everyone should be checked for dishonest behavior? Should we accept that new library device or airport scanners as a means to safeguard our security and well-being? Why? These are powerful questions that will help us think more deeply.

4d   DEVELOPING YOUR ARGUMENTS

1. Claims, Support, and Warrants

To develop your arguments, start by clarifying what your main point or claim is, what support you are going to offer for that claim, and what warrants or unspoken assumptions are present in the argument. This system for arguments was developed by Stephen Toulmin, a modern philosopher.

Claim

A *claim* is the proposition, the assertion, or the thesis that is to be proved. There are three types of claims: of fact, of value, and of policy. We can find these types of claims by asking questions that identify what an argument is trying to prove:

■ Is there a *fact* the argument is trying to establish?

Does global warming contribute to the intensity of hurricanes?
Is the amount of television advertising increasing in relation to the amount of programming?
Do infants benefit from being read to by their parents?
Does hosting the Olympic Games help the host country's economy?

■ Is there an issue of *values* in the argument?

Should schools provide sex education for children?
Should scientists be permitted to do stem-cell research?
Should same-sex marriage be a matter for each state to decide?
Should the beliefs of major religions be taught in public schools?

■ Is there an issue of *policy* in the argument?

Should legislators be allowed to hold office for an unlimited number of terms?
Should your college provide free parking for students?
Should people who buy things on the Internet pay sales tax?
Should airports continue conducting random searches of passengers for security reasons?
Should police be allowed to use racial profiling to detain people?

Try This

TO EXPLORE TOPICS FOR ARGUMENT

Another good strategy is to start with something very ordinary and then keep asking "**SO WHAT?**" or "**WHY?**" (or both) to everything you write.

Example: I need a new backpack.

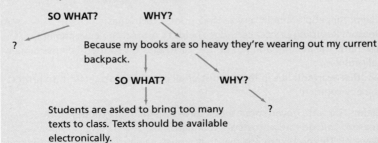

This writer might want to argue that publishers should provide and teachers should use electronic versions of textbooks. (Note that the writer has a possible topic for her argument, but she still needs to work on her thesis.)

Support

The *support* for an argument provides the reasons or evidence used to convince the audience. Such support or proof may include facts, data, examples, statistics, and the testimony of experts. Support may also include appeals to our emotions. If a claim is made that baseball is no longer the nation's favorite summer sport, facts or statistics are needed to show that it once was the nation's favorite summer sport and that it has declined in popularity. If a claim is made that the U.S. Postal Service should issue commemorative stamps honoring famous American heroes of World War II, the argument might use an emotional appeal to our patriotism, asking us to remember these great people who served our country so bravely.

Warrant

The *warrant* is an underlying assumption, belief, or principle in an argument that logically connects the claim with the reasons or evidence used to back that claim. Some warrants are clearly stated, while others are left unstated. Whether or not your audience shares your assumption determines if your audience will accept or reject your argument. If you hear someone say that she didn't learn a thing in her history class because her teacher was dull, an unstated warrant is that the teacher is solely responsible for what students learn or that dull teachers can't help students gain knowledge. In such an argument, it may be easy to spot the warrant, but other arguments have warrants that are not as obvious.

Warrants are important because an argument can fail if the underlying warrant isn't necessarily true.

> **Claim:** More police are needed to patrol the streets of inner-city neighborhoods.
> **Reason:** An increase in patrol cars will reduce illegal drug trafficking in these neighborhoods.
> **Warrant:** This claim assumes that patrolling police are able to find and arrest drug dealers.

> **Claim:** All people should recycle their printer cartridges.
> **Reason:** Recycling printer cartridges helps to protect the environment.
> **Warrant:** The accumulation of printer cartridges is a substantial environmental problem.
> **Another warrant:** It is in the interest of all people to take actions to protect the environment.

> **Claim:** The state government should give colleges more money.
> **Reason:** College tuition costs are too high.
> **Warrant:** This argument assumes that money given to colleges from the state government will be used to lower tuition costs, not for some other purpose.

As writers develop their arguments, they have to be aware both of what warrants exist in their arguments and of what warrants exist in the audience members' minds. If an audience shares the writer's warrants, the argument is likely to be more effective and convincing. If the audience does not share the writer's warrants, the audience will be hard to persuade. When you see a commercial that shows a well-known athlete endorsing some new pizza chain, several warrants or unspoken assumptions are operating behind the claim that this company has good pizza and the support that the pizza is good because the athlete says so. One warrant is that this athlete is not just making a statement because he has been paid to do so. Another is that this athlete really knows what good pizza is or that his standards and tastes in pizza are the same as yours. If you accept such warrants, you are likely to be convinced that the pizza is good because the support was adequate for the argument. If you don't, then the athlete's statement was not adequate support, and you are not likely to be enticed to try the pizza.

Similarly, for the argument you build, you should also examine the warrants in the opposing arguments. What assumptions are left unsaid in the case made by the opposing side? Does the opposing argument rest on underlying assumptions or accepted beliefs that your readers ought to know about? For example, let's say you're arguing against physician-assisted suicide for the terminally ill. The opposing side may not have presented any evidence that shows that doctors always know when a patient is terminally ill; this might be a warrant in their case. Would your audience accept that warrant? If not, then you make your argument stronger by calling attention to it.

2. Logical Arguments

Another consideration as you build your argument is the logical development of the argument. For the claim you make, is it appropriate to move from a statement of a general principle to a conclusion? If so, you will develop your argument deductively. Is it instead more appropriate to construct your case from particular instances or examples that build to a conclusion? If so, your argument is an inductive one.

Deductive Reasoning

When you reason deductively, you start with a generalization or major premise and reason logically to a conclusion. The conclusion is *true* when the premises are true and is *valid* when the conclusion follows necessarily from the premises. This involves stating that all items you name (A) are in some category (B). Then name some specific member (C) of the (A) group. You can then conclude that the specific member (C) is a part of the category (B).

Example:
All dogs (A) are mammals (B).
A Dalmatian (C) is a type of dog (A).
Therefore, Dalmatians (C) are mammals (B).

Inductive Reasoning

When you reason inductively, you come to conclusions on the basis of evidence, and arrive at a statement of what is generally true of something or of a whole group of things. For example, if you try a certain medication a few times and find that each time you take it, it upsets your stomach, you conclude that this medication bothers you. Inductive conclusions are, however, only probable at best. New evidence might prove the conclusion false. The amount and quality of evidence are also key. Suppose you want to find the most popular major on your campus, and you decide to stand outside the engineering building. You ask each student entering and leaving the building what his or her major is, and the vast majority of the students say that they are majoring in engineering. The conclusion that engineering is the most popular major on campus is not reliable because the sample does not represent the whole campus. If you moved to the agriculture building and stood there and asked the same question, it's likely you would inductively conclude agriculture to be the most popular major.

4e RECOGNIZING AND AVOIDING FALLACIES

Letters to the editor, advertisements, political campaign speeches, and courtroom battles sometimes offer proofs that have not been carefully thought through. As you develop your own arguments and read the arguments of others, check for mistakes in their reasoning. It is unfortunately easy to fall into a number of traps in thinking.

- *Hasty Generalization.* A conclusion reached with too few examples or with examples that are not representative.

   Example: Your friend complains that the phone company is run by a bunch of bumblers because they never send a bill that is correct.

   Hint: Many hasty generalizations contain words such as *all, never,* and *every.* You can correct them by substituting words such as *some* and *sometimes.*

- *Begging the Question (Circular Reasoning).* An argument that goes around in circles, assuming that what has to be proved has already been proved.

   Example: When a salesperson points out that the product she is selling is "environmentally friendly," you ask why. Her reply is that it doesn't pollute the atmosphere. Why doesn't it pollute the atmosphere? Because, she explains, it's environmentally friendly.

   Hint: Check to see whether there is no new information in the development of the argument. If the argument goes around in circles, look for some outside proof or reasoning.

- *Doubtful Cause (Post Hoc, Ergo Propter Hoc).* A mistake in reasoning occurs when one event happens and then another event happens, and people mistakenly reason that the first event caused the second when in fact no such relationship exists. (The Latin phrase *post hoc, ergo propter hoc* means "after this, therefore because of this.")

  Example: If a school institutes a dress code and vandalism decreases the next week, it is tempting to reason that the dress code caused a decrease in vandalism, but this sequence does not prove a cause-and-effect relationship. Other factors may be at work, or incidents of vandalism might increase next week. More conclusive evidence is needed.

  Hint: Do not automatically assume that because one event follows another, the first event caused the second event. Check for a real cause-and-effect relationship that can be repeated many times with the same results.

- *Irrelevant Proof (Non Sequitur).* A line of reasoning in which the conclusion is not a logical result of the premise. (The Latin phrase *non sequitur* means "it does not follow.")

  Example: That movie was superb because it cost so much to produce.

  Hint: The proof of a statement must be a logical step in reasoning with logical connections. In the example given here, the amount of money spent on filming a movie is not necessarily related to its quality and is therefore an irrelevant proof.

- *False Analogy.* The assumption without proof that, if objects or processes are similar in some ways, they are similar in other ways.

  Example: If engineers can design those black boxes that survive plane crashes, they should be able to build the whole plane from that same material.

  Hint: Check whether other major aspects of the objects or processes being compared are not similar. In the example, the construction materials used in a huge and complex plane cannot be the same as those for the little black boxes.

- *Personal Attack (Ad Hominem).* Focusing on aspects of the person who is advancing an argument in an attempt to undermine or dismiss the argument. (The Latin phrase *ad hominem* means "against the man.")

  Example: If an economist proposes a plan for helping impoverished people, her opponent might dismiss her plan by pointing out that she's never been poor.

  Hint: Avoid reasoning that diverts attention from the quality of the argument to the person offering it.

■ *Either . . . Or.* Establishing a false either/or situation that does not allow for other possibilities or choices that may exist.

Example: Either the government balances the budget, or the country will slide into another Great Depression.

Hint: When offered only two alternatives, look for others that might be equally or even more valid.

■ *Bandwagon:* An argument that claims to be sound because a large number of people approve of it.

Example: In a political campaign, we might hear that we should vote for someone because many other people have decided this person is the best candidate.

Hint: Do not accept an argument just because some or even many other people support it.

4f ORGANIZING YOUR ARGUMENT

The organization of an argument depends in part on how you analyze your audience. See the Try This box below for some ways to organize an argumentative paper to best suit your audience.

Try This

TO ORGANIZE YOUR ARGUMENT

■ *Start with the common ground* you share with the audience.
You and I both agree that _____.

■ *Bring up points that favor your opponents' side of the argument* early in the paper.
You claim that _____ because _____, and this is important to remember because _____.

■ *Start with the claim* and follow with a discussion of the reasons.
I claim that _____ because _____ and because _____.

■ *Try a problem-and-solution pattern* if that seems more appropriate.
The problem is _____, and the way to solve it is _____.

■ *Try a cause-and-effect pattern.*
The problem is _____ and is caused by _____. The effects of this problem are _____.

■ *Establish the criteria or standards* by which to judge a claim, and then show how your claim meets these criteria.
I claim that _____ and my standards (or "criteria" or "basis for judgment") are _____, and my claim meets these standards because _____.

▶

■ *Move through your points and then announce your thesis or claim.* This can be particularly effective when your conclusion is one that an audience is not likely to be receptive to at first.

One fact (or example or outcome) is _____. Another is _____, and another is _____. Therefore, I claim that _____.

5

VISUAL ARGUMENT

We see visual arguments all around us. Logos, commercials, print ads, Web sites, blogs, photographs, charts, graphs, and cartoons are used for a variety of purposes—to inform, to educate, and to entertain, but also to persuade us to buy merchandise or adopt certain beliefs. As readers, we need to understand the strategies used in visual arguments to determine whether those arguments are credible and if we should act on them. As writers, we can use visual arguments to reinforce our written arguments and to appeal to our readers logically, emotionally, and ethically. Developing strategies for using visual arguments can help us communicate more effectively and persuasively with our audiences.

5a SIMILARITIES AND DIFFERENCES BETWEEN WRITTEN AND VISUAL ARGUMENTS

Both written and visual arguments depend on the connections between claims and evidence. In visual arguments, **claims** can be in the wording accompanying an image, such as a title provided for a graph or chart. More often, however, claims in visual arguments are implied rather than stated openly. For example, advertisements for products don't usually state "you need these products." Rather, that claim is implied through the presentation of images in the ad.

Evidence in visual arguments is presented through the content, positioning of items in an image, and accompanying wording. For example, evidence in print ads includes pictures of the products and people who interact with the products, corporate logos, slogans, and other descriptive text. Graphs and charts show visual representations of data with labels and titles. Photographers rely on the content and layout of their photos to communicate with viewers.

Creators of visual arguments rely heavily on an assumption of **common ground** with viewers, especially when the purpose of the argument is to persuade. The claims and evidence of visual arguments are often based on social, cultural, or factual knowledge they assume the

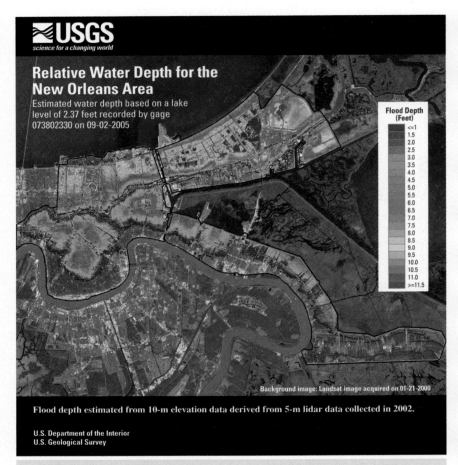

Flood depth estimated from 10-m elevation data derived from 5-m lidar data collected in 2002.

U.S. Department of the Interior
U.S. Geological Survey

▲ **Figure 5.1   Reading Visuals**   This topographical map from the U.S. Geological Survey illustrates data about the depth of flooding in New Orleans' neighborhoods on September 2, 2005, four days after the landfall of Hurricane Katrina. Providing this information in visual form—as opposed to a table or textual explanation—quickly helps readers to locate the most severely flooded areas of the city.

◄ **Figure 5.2**
Logical Argument
This image of New Orleans was taken on Aug. 30, 2005—one day after the landfall of Hurricane Katrina—and shows the failure of the city's levy system to withstand a major hurricane. © *Smiley N. Pool/Dallas Morning News/CORBIS. All Rights Reserved.*

Figure 5.3 ►
Emotional Argument
This image was taken at the New Orleans Convention Center on Sept. 3, 2005. Americans felt sympathy for those left homeless by Hurricane Katrina, as well as outrage that dead bodies remained on street sidewalks five days after the hurricane's landfall. *Shannon Stapleton/Corbis/Reuters America LLC.*

◄ **Figure 5.4   Ethical Argument**
This photo, taken on Sept. 5, 2005, shows evacuees resting in a makeshift camp in the Houston Astrodome. The American flag, facing backward, is posed prominently over the field. The layout of this photo raises ethical concerns, inviting readers to question whether the American government provided the best assistance it could for its citizens in a time of need. © *Ken Cedeno/CORBIS. All Rights Reserved.*

reader will already have. Creators of visual arguments, therefore, must know their audiences well to communicate effectively.

Checklist

READING VISUAL ARGUMENTS

As you interpret a visual argument, ask yourself these questions:

- ■ **What is the purpose of the visual?** (To inform? To persuade? To educate? To entertain? For another purpose?)
- ■ **Who is the target audience for the visual argument?** For a print ad, think about the publication in which you saw it. Who are the target readers of that publication?
- ■ **What is the claim of the visual argument?** Remember that it may be implied rather than stated.
- ■ **What kinds of evidence are provided in the visual argument?** Think about the content of the image and how those content items are arranged. Also examine any wording that appears in the image.
- ■ **In what ways does the visual argument rely on common ground?** This may include cultural, social, historical, political, or other knowledge.
- ■ **What kinds of assumptions are made in the visual argument?**

The visuals included on pages 44 and 45 illustrate ways to effectively present information.

5b APPEALS IN VISUAL ARGUMENT

We see a variety of **argumentative appeals** when we read visual arguments.

Logical Appeals

Visual arguments sometimes use images and text to prove a claim based on logic and facts. Visual arguments can be used to draw a comparison between items, which can be effective in convincing a reader to accept those differences. Graphs, charts, and maps, which depend on data, can be particularly effective in showing a logical appeal. Photographs also can be used to provide evidence. When news photographers take pictures of a scene, for example, they document the facts of the event, and the pictures can help to inform readers and prove a claim about that event.

Emotional Appeals

Visual arguments can be particularly effective in appealing to readers' emotions. Well-composed photographs can evoke feelings of happiness,

CAN A BALL GAME LEAVE A CHILD
WITH PERMANENT SIDE EFFECTS?

React to sports with rage and kids learn aggressive behavior. Keep your cool
and kids learn to do the same. To learn more about preventing aggressive or violent behavior,
call 877-ACT-WISE for a free brochure. Or visit ACTAgainstViolence.org.

   You're always teaching. *Teach carefully.*

MetLife Foundation

ACT Against Violence is a joint project of the American Psychological Association
& the National Association for the Education of Young Children.

▲ **Figure 5.5   Visual Argument 1**   This ad for the Act Against Violence
campaign poses a logical argument by making a comparison: when parents
display violent or aggressive behavior at their children's sporting events,
they hurt their children, leaving emotional wounds that are as significant
as physical injuries. This ad also makes an emotional appeal, connecting to
parents' needs to protect their children and keep them safe. The boy's facial
expression helps parents to see how they can inadvertently hurt their own
children through violent behavior. *The Adults and Children Together Against
Violence (ACT) campaign is a joint project of the American Psychological Association
and the Advertising Council. Reprinted by permission.*

A Mind is a Terrible Thing to Waste

▲ **Figure 5.6 Visual Argument 2** This ad invites readers to donate to the United Negro College Fund. Claiming that "A Mind is a Terrible Thing to Waste," the UNCF makes a visual argument by showing that children have amazing, inventive ideas literally bursting out of their heads. Support for educational causes like the UNCF can "launch" these children to reach their full potential. *Reprinted by permission of the United Negro College Fund and the Advertising Council.*

pride, affection, sympathy, or anger. We can relate to the feelings displayed by people in photographs. Similarly, images of animals, natural scenes, and symbols can stir our emotions.

Advertisers use visual arguments to show how their products will help to fulfill readers' needs. For example, an ad for antibacterial soap featuring an image of a sick child can remind us of our desire to keep ourselves and our families healthy and safe. Similarly, a men's cologne ad that features a couple kissing can trigger readers' needs for love and sexual fulfillment. Critical readers of visual arguments will question whether those products actually lead to fulfilling the need.

Ethical Appeals

Visual arguments can establish the credibility of the creator or sponsor of an image. They can also invite us to confirm or to question the trustworthiness of the individuals or organizations featured in the image.

Such ethical appeals can be created by using visual perspective. Imagine a photograph of a man standing in front of his desk at work; the camera has been positioned three feet from the ground and pointed up toward his head. This camera angle emphasizes the man's authority because the photograph suggests he is superior to the viewer. Now imagine the camera positioned three feet above the man's head with the camera angled down. In this position, the viewer is placed in a position of judgment and invited to question his credibility.

Ethical appeals can also be created by the use of contrast. For example, imagine a photograph of a homeless veteran sleeping on a park bench with the dome of the United States Capitol building in the background. The placement of the homeless veteran in contrast to an important symbol of the U.S. government may invite questions about the justice of this situation.

Corporations and organizations carefully design their logos, slogans, and images to build and reinforce their audience's positive feelings about their products and services. This is known as establishing a company's **brand identity**. Think about the images and feelings that come to mind when you see the Nike swoosh, the golden arches of McDonald's, or Microsoft's multicolored windows. Companies and organizations hope that when we repeatedly see their logos and associate them with positive images, we will trust them and buy their products or services.

5c LOGICAL FALLACIES IN VISUAL ARGUMENT

As with all arguments, readers must consider whether the visual arguments they see are valid and trustworthy. For example, when advertisers display photographs showing the effects of using a specific product, they want these images to be considered as evidence of that product's effectiveness. Because photographs can be so easily altered, however, the truthfulness of such photos is open to question.

Readers should also be aware of **logical fallacies** in visual arguments. For example, stereotypes are easy to portray in visual arguments. An advertisement that contrasts an image of an attractive young man using a brand-name product with a picture of a "nerd" using a competing product may show the fallacy of hasty generalization—encouraging readers to draw conclusions based on limited or misrepresentative information. Similarly, a dramatic image might evoke a very strong emotional reaction from readers; however, the emotional impact of that image may overshadow flaws in the logical argument.

Advertisements often commit the fallacy of appealing to a false authority. Imagine a television commercial in which a celebrity endorses a brand of vitamins. Is the celebrity a physician or an expert in nutrition? If not, why should we accept him or her as an authority on the quality of the vitamins?

Irrelevant proof, false analogies, personal attacks, bandwagon appeals, and either/or situations are often the subjects of logical fallacies in visual arguments.

5d   WRITING VISUAL ARGUMENTS

A visual argument can be an effective method of proving your claim and achieving your purpose. To create effective and reliable visual arguments, consider the following.

Readability

Your visual should be easy to read and understand. Visuals are most effective when they communicate ideas more efficiently than could be described in a written format. If the information you want to display is too complex to be portrayed clearly in a visual, then a written argument might be a more useful choice.

Titles, Labels, and Captions

Sometimes, images require labels or titles to clarify the meaning of the visual. When creating graphs or charts, label your data accurately and clearly. Photos and images often make more sense to readers when they are paired with a caption or title. Contrasts and connections between images and text can enhance the logical, emotional, or ethical appeals of visual arguments.

Credibility

Readers will consider visual arguments to be credible when they include strong images that clearly and responsibly convey meaning. Data should be accurately represented in graphs and charts. Overemphasizing some figures or ignoring other important data could make readers question the results.

Credible creators of visual arguments also use good judgment when evoking readers' emotions. Readers may feel unfairly influenced by a visual argument that has an overwhelming emotional appeal without strong logical connections.

CREATING EFFECTIVE VISUAL ARGUMENTS

When developing visual arguments, ask yourself these questions:

- **Will using a visual argument improve my ability to communicate with my reader?** If so, which types of visuals would be the most effective for my rhetorical situation?

- **What is my purpose in communicating with my audience?** Would logical, emotional, or ethical appeals (or some combination of these) be most useful in achieving my purpose?

- **Who is my audience, and how can I show its members that we share common ground?**

- **What should be the tone of my image?** Serious? Funny? Inspiring?

6
DOCUMENT DESIGN

The words and images we use to express ourselves to an audience are obviously important, but the appearance and format of our documents are also important. Good document design does the following:

- *It makes your documents easier to read and understand.* Appropriate spacing, alignment, tabs, headers, bullets, and text formatted with bold or italics should draw your readers' attention to important information. Overcrowded pages, too little white space, and lengthy sections of text without paragraph or section breaks will make readers more likely to miss key points or decide not to read the document.

- *It projects a positive image of the writer.* Our society is visually oriented, so it judges documents in part on the way they look. Your well-designed document can help present you as positive and professional and convince your readers of your credibility and authority. By contrast, a poorly designed document may cause readers to view a writer as unorganized and lacking attention to detail.

- *It attracts readers and draws them into your writing.* When appropriate, images such as graphs, tables, and photographs can also help grab your readers' attention.

- *It appeals to visually oriented readers.* Thanks to the hours people spend viewing Web sites, television, films, and other media, many readers find it easier to understand information in a document that skillfully blends visuals with text. Digital cameras, scanners, and software programs have made it easier than ever to add visuals to your writing to strengthen the content and attractiveness of your documents.

6a   PRINCIPLES OF DOCUMENT DESIGN

Listed here are some principles for creating well-designed, readable pages.

Apply Design Elements Consistently

The design elements (such as bullets, white space, spacing, font types, and so on) you apply at the beginning of your document should be used consistently throughout. Shifts in design can make your writing look unorganized and confuse your reader.

Include White Space

Well-used white space makes documents more readable by offering some visual relief from heavy-looking blocks of text. White space in the margins helps to frame the text, leaves room for a reader to make notes, and can indicate section breaks. For documents such as research papers, reports, and business letters, allow space between headings and paragraphs, indent lists, and consistently place visuals such as graphs and tables in the center or to the left or right. For brochures and newsletters, use white space to frame text headings and visuals.

Avoid Clutter

When experimenting with design, writers sometimes overdo it, adding so many design and visual elements that they distract readers. With document design, less is more. A few well-placed design elements will strengthen the meaning of the document more than several poorly integrated visual features. Try to keep your pages clean and uncluttered with no more than two or three different fonts. Use standard fonts such as Times New Roman, Arial, Georgia, Tahoma, and Verdana. Fonts that look like scripted handwriting can be difficult to read in text-heavy documents.

Use Contrasting Design Elements for Emphasis

Variations in font size and type and the insertion of indentations, graphics, and background shading can help to highlight selected elements of your text. For example, bold or italic fonts can add emphasis by making words stand out from regular text. As with any design element, however, don't overuse such fonts because they can distract your reader.

Insert Headings and Subheadings

Use words and phrases to announce new topics or subsections of a document. Bold, italics, larger font sizes, or a combination of these will make your headings and subheadings more noticeable.

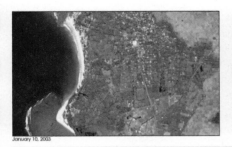 

January 10, 2003   December 29, 2004

▲ **Figure 6.1   Comparing Images**   These satellite photographs by NASA show the devastation of the Indonesian city of Lhoknga by the tsunami that struck on December 26, 2004. Placed next to each other, these before-and-after photos demonstrate the force of the tidal waves.

6b   INCORPORATING VISUALS

Visuals such as images, graphs, charts, and tables can help you communicate clearly, concisely, and effectively. They can also make your documents more informative and interesting.

Images

Images such as photographs, diagrams, maps, and illustrations add color, variety, and meaning to your documents. They can help your readers see a subject in a new perspective, follow steps in a process, or pinpoint a location. Images can also provide a logical, emotional, or ethical appeal in an argument, as well as set a tone or produce a stylistic effect. Multiple images placed next to each other can be used to show contrast or changes over a period of time (see above).

Photographs can be edited using image-production software such as Macromedia Fireworks and Adobe Photoshop. These programs enable users to crop photos to desired heights and widths, as well as sharpen, blur, brighten, color, rotate, or magnify images. As with all evidence you present, however, be sure that your editing of an image does not distort its meaning.

Hint

REDUCE FILE SIZE

Before pasting an image into your work, you may want to reduce its file size (or number of bytes) to help it load more quickly in a word-processed document, multimedia program, or Web page. By "exporting" in Macromedia Fireworks or "optimizing" in Adobe Photoshop, you can convert your image to a smaller .jpeg or .gif file while retaining the physical size and original formatting.

Graphs and Charts

Graphs and charts are used to illustrate data in visual form and explain relationships between items. They can be produced easily in a spreadsheet program such as Microsoft Excel. (See pages 55–56.)

Tables

Tables, which show relationships between items, can be created in Microsoft Word or other word-processing software. (See page 56.)

Checklist

ADDING VISUALS TO A TEXT

Visuals can add a great deal to a written text but not without the proper context. Be sure to observe the following when you include visuals:

- **Include a title:** Graphs, charts, and images are labeled as *figures*, and tables are labeled as *tables*. Add a title to each figure and table that explains its content, such as "Figure 1: Increases in Voter Registration" or "Table 5: Number of Registered Voters in Each Wisconsin County." Figures and tables should have separate numbering systems in your document.

- **Add labels:** In graphs and charts, provide a label on the X (horizontal) axis and Y (vertical) axis to specify values indicated in each area of the visual. Column headings in a table also need to be labeled clearly.

- **Place visuals in their appropriate location in the text:** In professional writing documents and MLA-formatted papers, visuals can be placed in the body of a text. In such cases, introduce visuals directly before they are inserted in the text.

  Example: The number of people registering to vote has changed dramatically over the last decade (see Figure 1).

  After each visual, briefly explain the importance of the information:

  Example: Voter registration reached all-time highs immediately prior to the most recent elections, suggesting the success of voter registration drives during this time period.

  In APA-formatted papers, visuals appear on separate pages at the end of the paper, with tables first, then figure captions, and then figures. The text should include a reference to each table or figure.

- **Cite your sources:** To show that information has been gathered from outside sources, use the format appropriate for the documentation style you are using. See, for example, MLA-style source references for the thematic map, Figure 6.5, and the table, Figure 6.7, on page 56.

Figure 6.2 Pie Chart

Pie graphs are used to show parts of a whole. They can be formatted to show numerical data, percentages, or both.

(**HINT:** Use contrasting colors or shading to distinguish between different slices of the pie.)

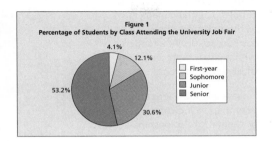

Figure 1
Percentage of Students by Class Attending the University Job Fair
4.1%
12.1%
53.2%
30.6%
First-year
Sophomore
Junior
Senior

Figure 6.3 Bar Graph

Bar graphs are primarily used to show relationships among items. They also may be used to illustrate increases or decreases over time.

The *X*- and *Y*-axes (horizontal and vertical axes) must be labeled to indicate the meaning of the data.

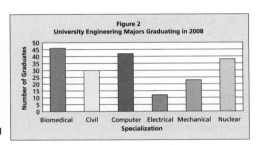

Figure 2
University Engineering Majors Graduating in 2008
Number of Graduates
50
45
40
35
30
25
20
15
10
5
0
Biomedical
Civil
Computer
Electrical
Mechanical
Nuclear
Specialization

Figure 6.4 Line Graph

Line graphs are used to show change over a period of time. The *X*- and *Y*-axes must be labeled to show data types.

(**HINT:** If the graph has multiple lines, use different colors or line types, such as dotted or dashed, to distinguish each from the others.)

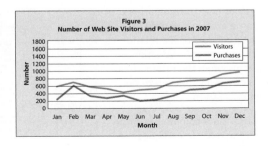

Figure 3
Number of Web Site Visitors and Purchases in 2007
Number
1800
1600
1400
1200
1000
800
600
400
200
0
Visitors
Purchases
Jan
Feb
Mar
Apr
May
Jun
Jul
Aug
Sep
Oct
Nov
Dec
Month

Figure 6.5 Map

Maps are used to identify locations. Thematic maps, such as this one from the U.S. Census Bureau, provide readers with a visual representation of demographic data.

Always include a legend with your map to indicate spatial or thematic relationships.

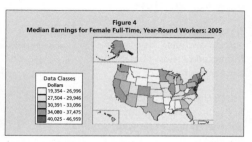

Figure 4
Median Earnings for Female Full-Time, Year-Round Workers: 2005

Data Classes
Dollars
19,354 - 26,996
27,504 - 29,946
30,391 - 33,096
34,080 - 37,475
40,025 - 46,959

Source: United States, Census Bureau, "M1902. Median Earnings for Female Full-Time, Year-Round Workers (in 2005 Inflation-Adjusted Dollars): 2005," U.S. Census Bureau Factfinder, 2005, 26 Oct. 2006 <http://factfinder.census.gov/>, path: Search; M1902 2005.

Figure 6.6 Flowchart

Flowcharts help readers follow a process or show options in making decisions.

(**HINT:** Use colors and shapes to differentiate between levels of decision making.)

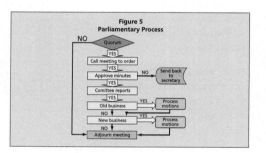

Figure 5
Parliamentary Process

NO — Quorum
YES
Call meeting to order
YES
Approve minutes — NO — Send back to secretary
YES
Committee reports
YES
Old business — YES — Process motions
NO
New business — YES — Process motions
NO
Adjourn meeting

Figure 6.7 Table

Tables help to summarize large amounts of data and help readers to see relationships between and among items when the information is not easily reduced to numerical form.

Offer clear column headings in the table to categorize information.

Table 1
Growing Conditions for Rose Varieties

Name	Height	Light Conditions	Soil Conditions	Growing Climate
English Roses	3–6'	Full sun to partial shade	Moist	Moderately cool to moderately warm
Musk Roses	4–6'	Full sun to partial shade	Moist	Warm
Rambler Roses	20–50'	Full sun	Moist	Moderately cool to warm
Tea Roses	4–7'	Full sun	Moist	Warm

Source: Susan A. Roth, Better Homes and Gardens Complete Guide to Flower Gardening (Des Moines, IA: Meredith Books, 1995) 364–74.

6c PAPER PREPARATION

1. Page Preparation

Paper

Print on 8½-by-11-inch white paper, preferably the usual 20-lb. weight paper, and use only one side of each sheet.

Line Spacing

Double-space throughout, including every line in the title, the text of the paper, headings, footnotes, quotations, figure captions, all parts of tables, and the bibliography section.

Margins

Leave margins of one inch at the top and bottom and at both sides of the page, but put page numbers one-half inch from the top at the right side of the page. Justify margins at the left, but do not justify at the right margin unless that is the style your instructor requests or is the style used for publications at your place of work.

Order of Pages

ORDER OF PAGES	
MLA Style	**APA Style**
1. First page, with appropriate information followed by text of paper (see 66d) **2.** Notes (optional section, starting on a separate page) **3.** Works Cited (starting on a separate page)	**1.** Title page (see 67d) **2.** Abstract **3.** Text of paper **4.** References (start on a separate page) **5.** Appendixes (optional, start each on a separate page) **6.** Footnotes (list together, starting on a separate page) **7.** Tables (optional, start each on a separate page) **8.** Figure captions (use only if figures are included and list together, starting on a separate page) **9.** Figures (optional, place each on a separate page)

Titles and Title Pages

In MLA format, research papers and reports do not need a title page. (If your instructor asks for one, follow his or her instructions on formatting.) On the first page of your paper, leave a one-inch margin at the top and then put your name, your instructor's name, the course number, and the date submitted at the left-hand margin. Double-space this information. Then double-space and type the title, centered on the page. If you need more than one line for the title, double-space between these lines. Then double-space between the title and the first line of the text.

In APA style, include a title page (all double-spaced) with the title centered between left and right margins and positioned in the upper half of the page. Depending on your instructor's preference, either include just your name and college (as per APA guidelines and the sample page in 67d) or include your name, instructor's name, course, and date, with each line double-spaced and centered below the title.

Page Numbers and Identification

In MLA style, number pages at the upper right of each page, one-half inch from the top and flush with the right margin. Include your last name before the page number (to prevent confusion if pages are misplaced), and don't use *page* or *p.* before the number (see the sample essay in 66d). In APA style, place the number one-half inch from the top and flush with the right margin. Include an abbreviated form of the paper's title (known as a "running head") five spaces before the page number, with no comma between the title and page number (see the sample essay in 67d).

Do not use any punctuation in page numbering. In word processing, the numbering and name or title identification is done automatically after you set up the header appropriately.

Fonts

Use 10- to 12-point type and a standard font that is easy to read, such as Times New Roman, Arial, or Palatino. Do not use fonts that resemble handwriting, appear unusually shaped, or are difficult to read.

Indentations

Indent the first line of every paragraph one-half inch or five spaces from the left-hand margin. For long quotations (block quotations) within paragraphs, indent one inch or ten spaces from the left-hand margin in MLA style; indent one-half inch or five spaces in APA style. (See 42a for more information about quotations.)

Lists

In long research papers and professional writing documents, lists can present information clearly and efficiently. Lists include phrases or sentences containing key points and supporting details, often organized with bullets, dashes, or numbers.

Example: Physical fitness levels were measured in the following groups of athletes:

1. Track and field team members
   - Long-distance runners
   - Sprint runners
   - Pole vaulters
2. Football players

Introduce your list with an independent clause (see 28a) to explain what is going to be listed, and end the clause with a colon. If each item in the list is a complete sentence, use a period at the end of each entry.

Appendixes

Appendixes are located at the end of a document and contain details that are not essential in the body of a paper. The use of appendixes avoids interrupting the flow of the main document, and readers who do not need the details can skip them. Details to include in appendixes may be questionnaires, lists, forms, and other information. If you have just one appendix, label it "Appendix." If you have more than one, use a label such as "Appendix A," "Appendix B," and so on, and title each one. In your document, refer to each appendix by its label.

Example: Citizens overwhelmingly approve of the proposed changes to the state law (see Appendix A for survey information and Appendix B for the state law).

2. Titles

An essay's title serves several purposes. It indicates to readers what they can expect as to the topic and the author's perspective in the essay. Some titles state in a straightforward manner what the essay will be about; for example, the title "The Physical Benefits of Yoga" is a clear indication of the content and the author's plan to address it directly, in a formal manner. Other titles, particularly of personal essays, may offer the reader only a hint about the topic—a hint that becomes clearer as you read the essay. "A Tale of a Tail" might be the title for an essay describing a frightening experience with a rat or a humorous experience with a kite.

Choosing a Title

A title helps the writer organize a topic and select the emphasis for a particular essay. Writers who select the title before or during the early stages of writing may need to check at a later stage to see that the title still relates to the essay as it evolves and develops.

Good titles are brief and usually consist of no more than six or seven words. Good titles are also clear and specific. An example of an overly general title for an essay would be "Depression" because it does not indicate what aspect of depression will be discussed. Even a title such as "Issues in Educational Reform" is too general for a short essay because so much material could be discussed under this heading.

A title should stand alone. The title should not be part of the first sentence, and it should not be referred to by a pronoun in the first sentence. For example, in a research paper titled "Influences of Fast-Food Advertising on Children," the first sentence should not read as follows:

Incorrect Opening Sentence: This is a topic of great concern both to parents and physicians who think fast-food advertising negatively affects children.

Revised: While the toys and cartoon characters that appear in ads for fast-food restaurants appeal to children, parents and physicians are alarmed that such advertising tactics may contribute to increasing childhood obesity rates.

Capitalizing a Title

Capitalize the first and last words of a title, plus all other words except articles (*a, an, the*), short prepositions (*by, for, in, to, on,* etc.), and short joining words (*but, and, or,* etc.). Capitalize both words of a hyphenated word and the first short word of a subtitle that appears after a colon. (For more on capitalization, see Chapter 46.)

Pursuing a Career in Chemical
  Engineering
A History of the Corset
Going Green: Building
  a Solar-Powered Business

The World Through My Veil
Daytime Dramas: The Rise
  of Telenovelas
The Final Bell

Punctuating a Title

For your own essays, do not put the title in quotation marks, and do not use a period after the title. (For more information on using quotation marks and underlining, see Chapters 42 and 49.)

3. Headings and Subheadings

Headings are the short titles that define sections and subsections in long reports and papers. Headings provide visual emphasis by breaking the paper into manageable portions that are easily seen and identified. Headings with numbers also indicate relationships because the numbers tell the reader which parts are segments of a larger part, which are equal, and which are of less importance. Subheadings are the headings of less importance within a series of headings. Headings and subheadings do not substitute for the transitions you provide for your readers, but they do help your readers see the organization of the paper and locate material more easily. Use the headings and subheadings consistently so that your reader follows your organizational pattern for what is more important (in the headings) and what is less important (in the subheadings).

Use top- or first-level headings in boldface for main points, and center them on the page. Second- and third-level headings can be used for subsections, with the second level in boldface at the left margin. A third-level heading also starts at the left margin and can be underlined. MLA format does not use periods with headings. Keep your headings and subheadings short and specific.

MLA Example

Technological Advances in Spying

New Types of Surveillance Equipment

Listening devices

In APA format, only one level of heading is recommended for short papers, centered on the page, with each word (except short prepositions and articles) capitalized. If two levels are needed, use levels 1 and 3, and if three levels are needed, use levels 1, 3, and 4. Level 2 is centered, in italics, with the beginning of each word capitalized following APA title capitalization style. Level 3 starts flush left, italicized, with capitals for the first letter of each word. Level 4 is indented and italicized, with only the first word capitalized and ending with a period.

APA Example

Level 1:   Purpose of Experiment

Level 2:   *Two Groups of Participants*

Level 3: *Control Group*

Level 4:   *Methods used.* After the group was introduced . . .

For outlines or reports or other documents with a table of contents, number each item, usually with Arabic numerals, although the decimal system is often used in technical and professional fields. Both systems can be combined with letters. Always have at least two entries at each level.

Decimal Numbers	**Arabic Numerals**
1.0	1.
1.1 (or) 1.a. (or) 1a	A.
1.2 (or) 1.b. (or) 1b	B.
2.0	1)
2.1 (or) 2.a. (or) 2a	a.
2.2 (or) 2.b. (or) 2b	b.

For all headings and subheadings, use the same grammatical form to start each phrase. (See Chapter 14 on parallelism.)

Not Parallel	**Revised into Verb Phrases**	**Revised into Noun Phrases**
A. For Preliminary Planning	A. Planning the Paper	A. The Preliminary Draft
B. The Rough Draft	B. Writing the Rough Draft	B. The Rough Draft
C. Polishing the Draft	C. Polishing the Draft	C. The Polished Draft

4. Spacing for Punctuation

Punctuation	Spacing	Example
End punctuation	Leave no space before end punctuation. Leave one space before the next sentence.	. . . next year. After the term of . . .
Periods after abbreviations	Leave no space before the period and one space after. When a sentence ends with an abbreviation, use only one period.	Dr. Patel and Mrs. Paz discussed . . . . . . at 8 A.M. The next day . . .
Commas, semicolons, colons	Leave no space before the mark and one space after.	skilled, dedicated musician Paulo, an architect; Mariana, a graphic designer; and . . .
Apostrophes	Leave no space within a word. At the end of a word, leave no space before the apostrophe, one space after.	shouldn't customer's request swans' necks
Quotation marks	Leave no space between the quotation marks and what they enclose, no space between double and single quotation marks, and one space afterward in the middle of a sentence.	"For real?" was his favorite expression. "'The Flower Duet' is one of my favorite classical music pieces," she explained.
Hyphen	Leave no space before or after. If the hyphen shows the connection of two prefixes to one root word, put one space after the hyphen after the first prefix. (Hyphens should not be used with most prefixes and suffixes.) Do not use hyphens at the end of lines to divide words. Instead, begin the word on the next line. If your word processing program has a hyphenation function, turn it off.	a four-story building pre- and post-Victorian literature

Punctuation	Spacing	Example
Dash	Type two hyphens, with no space before or after, to form a dash, or insert a dash.	All of my cats-- Dodger, Dora, and Gilbert--loved their new catnip toys.
		All of my cats— Dodger, Dora, and Gilbert—loved their new catnip toys.
Slash	Leave no space before or after except for marking lines of poetry, when one space is left before and after.	and/or
		a writer/director
		He commented on these two powerful lines from Robert Browning's poem: "This grew; I gave commands; / Then all smiles stopped together."
Brackets, parentheses	Leave no space before or after the material being enclosed.	"When [the fund-raising group] pre-sented its report (not previously published), the press covered the event."
Ellipsis	An ellipsis consists of three periods. Leave one space before and after each pe-riod. If what precedes the ellipsis ends a sentence, first insert a period to end the sentence, with no space after the last word, and then add the three el-lipsis points, spaced evenly.	The senator com-mented upon . . . the debate. "The workers dis-agreed with the new policies. . . . On the following day, they held a public protest."
Underlining or italics	Ask your instructor whether italics or underlining is preferred.	Pride and Prejudice *Pride and Prejudice*

Figure 6.8 Sample Slides

▲ **Title slide.** All of the slides in this presentation use consistent design elements. The dark green background is professional and complements the "green" message of the presentation.

▲ **Introductory slide.** With this introductory slide, the speaker can ask a question, pause, and invite responses from audience members, thereby investing them in the argument. The digital image provides evidence for the author's argument.

6d   MULTIMEDIA PRESENTATIONS

Multimedia software programs such as Microsoft PowerPoint have changed the ways writers deliver oral presentations. Strategic use of multimedia can enhance presentations. Be aware, however, that PowerPoint can limit the power of your message by oversimplifying complex ideas or reducing powerful prose to bulleted items. For an example that reduces a famous speech to six overly simple slides, see Lincoln's Gettysburg Address in PowerPoint at http://norvig.com/Gettysburg/.

1. Organizing Your Presentation

A clear organizational structure can make the information you provide easier for your audience to follow.

1. *Title slide:* Provide the title of your presentation, your name, and your organization (if appropriate). An image can be added to increase your audience's interest in your topic.

2. *Introductory slide(s):* Grab the attention of your audience with questions, striking images, or an interesting quotation to lead into your main point.

3. *Thesis slide:* Use this slide to present your main point—or thesis statement—to your audience. On your thesis slide, map out your supporting claims or topics for discussion in short, bulleted statements.

4. *Body slides:* Prepare several slides to support claims listed on your thesis slide.

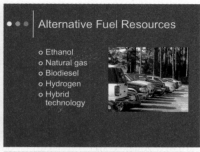

▲ **Thesis slide.** The thesis slide previews the supporting claims covered in the rest of the presentation. Note the parallel structure of the verb phrases in the bulleted items.

▲ **Body slide.** This body slide covers the first point listed in the thesis slide. Note how the digital photograph complements the topic of the slide.

5. *Conclusion slide(s):* Complete your presentation by recapping your main points. Conclude with a strong written and visual statement that will make a lasting impression on your audience.

6. *Reference slide(s):* List all sources used in the presentation in the appropriate documentation style format.

2. Designing Multimedia Slides

It's easy to get caught up in the sparkle of multimedia presentations. Too many graphic elements, however, can clutter your slides and interfere with your ability to communicate clearly. Remember, *less is more* when designing multimedia slides.

Background

Programs such as PowerPoint contain many preprogrammed background selections. Choose backgrounds that complement the tone and content of your presentation. As a general rule, the simplest ones are the best.

Color

Use light-colored text on a dark background or dark-colored text on a light background to create contrast and make your presentation easy to read. Try to avoid background colors that are too bright; they can be distracting. Blue backgrounds promote trust with your readers, and dark colors convey a professional tone.

Fonts

Use fonts such as Times New Roman, Arial, Georgia, Tahoma, and Verdana that can be found on most computers. The fonts in your presentation rely on the font files stored on the computer where the slides were designed, so make sure your presentation computer has the fonts you used to create the presentation.

Vary your font sizes. Titles should be somewhat larger (32–42-point font) than text on the body of the slide (20–32-point font). Words in fonts smaller than 20 point may be too difficult for your audience to read.

Graphics

Graphics can improve the impact of your presentation by explaining a fact, illustrating a point, and educating your audience. Digital photographs can look professional, engage interest, and reinforce your points. Clip art, on the other hand, can be boring and look childish, so use it sparingly. If you use any visuals, be sure to cite your sources properly in your presentation. See Chapter 60 for more information about copyright guidelines.

Animations

PowerPoint offers many choices for adding movement to the text and graphics in your presentation. As usual, less is more. Using just one or two animation elements per presentation will help to emphasize your key points and to build interactions with your audience. For example, you can ask a question that you animate with a mouse click. You can then pause and give your audience time to respond to your question, and then click your mouse again to reveal your answer.

Layout

Balance your use of text and images on each slide to emphasize main points. Words, descriptive phrases, or short sentences—known as **talking points**—should be set off in bullets so your audience members can easily follow your arguments, and each slide should have no more than 30–35 words. Place images to the left or right of your text (rather than above or below it) to achieve a proportioned look.

Consistency is critical for developing a strong multimedia presentation. Don't switch background colors, font styles, or animation styles midway through your presentation. Set a tone with your opening slides and stick with it throughout your presentation.

3. Presenting with Multimedia

You are the main point of interest, and your PowerPoint slides are merely a supplement. Instead of including your whole speech on your slides and reading it word-for-word, list key talking points on the slides and follow them as you talk, using notes if necessary.

Before your presentation, check the location and computer on which your multimedia presentation will be displayed. Make sure you have saved your presentation on a storage device (flash drive, disk, or CD-ROM) compatible with the computer to be used for the presentation. It is a good idea to come prepared with back-up transparencies or handouts of your presentation in case you are interrupted by a technical failure.

Checklist

FINE-TUNING YOUR PRESENTATION

- *Beforehand,* **practice your presentation several times.** Coordinating your speech with the speed of the mouse clicks ahead of time will help you to be more confident during your presentation.

- *When you present,* **try not to click too rapidly through your slides.** Give your audience time to absorb your visuals along with your oral presentation. Also speak loudly enough to get everyone's attention. This is particularly necessary when computers and digital projectors are humming in the background.

- *As you conclude your presentation,* **pass out handouts to leave with your audience.** Providing handouts at the beginning of your presentation (except in case of a technical failure) can distract audience members from paying attention. Instead, leave a lasting impression with your audience by distributing handouts at the end.

6e   WEB PAGE DESIGN

A well-designed Web site weaves together color, sound, graphic elements, hyperlinks, and clear, informative, concise text. Web pages can be made by using word-processing programs such as Microsoft Word. They can also be written in HTML (hypertext markup language) or created with WYSIWYG ("what you see is what you get") programs such as Macromedia Dreamweaver.

Developing a clear navigational plan will help you organize your pages and lead readers through your site. Start with the home page, and then lay out all of the pages to be included in your site and the hyperlinks that will connect them together. Provide page titles and determine the content of each page to avoid repetition. Check to see that every page has a link back to the home page. (See page 69 for an example of a student's plan for her Web site.)

When you begin designing your site, think about how you will define your online style. To develop ideas, it can be helpful to look at other Web sites and note the visual elements you find appealing. To give your site a consistent design, consider creating a template so that visual elements are repeated.

Place your title near the top of your home page. Then add images or other graphics that provide an appealing focal point to it. Navigational aids, such as buttons, can be placed together at the top, side, or bottom of the page.

When you develop additional pages for your site, try to limit each page to two or, at most, three screen lengths of textual material. Rather than double-spacing text like a traditional print paper, use single-spacing on Web pages to fit more text on a screen. Skipping a line between blocks of text will help your readers process information more efficiently as they scroll down the page. Also clearly identify your links with underlines or different colored lettering so readers will find them.

Fonts

Easily readable fonts help readers understand your text on your Web pages. Use widely available fonts such as Times New Roman, Arial, Georgia, Tahoma, and Verdana so they will work for most readers. If special fonts are important, use an image-production program such as Adobe Photoshop or Macromedia Fireworks to create image files with words typed in those fonts, and then insert those files into your Web page.

Color

Use color to draw attention to specific items on your Web page. Background colors that contrast with text colors make text easy to read. Avoid overly bright backgrounds and combinations of red and blue, which are difficult for readers to view online.

Images

Include images that improve your site content instead of being simply page decorations. Digital photographs can add a sense of style and sophistication to your Web site. Well-placed animated images can be effective, but use them sparingly because they can distract the reader from your content. Also be sure to give credit to all sources you use. See Chapter 60 for information about copyrighted images.

Once your site is posted, be sure to update it regularly. If you include an e-mail link (mailto:youraddress@yourprovider.com), readers can contact you to ask questions or share their views, but companies that collect addresses for spamming will also find you. Try searching for a program that will hide your address or that will open a window for the message and mail it to you.

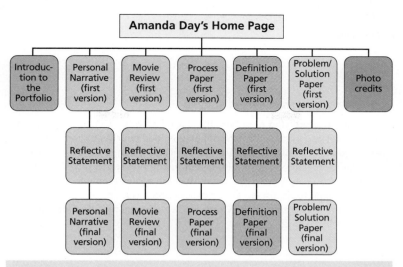

▲ **Figure 6.9   Flowchart for Planning a Web Site**   Amanda Day is creating an e-portfolio, an online version of her process portfolio, for her composition course. This flowchart illustrates the layout of her Web site. Amanda's home page will provide hyperlinks to each of her papers, her introduction, and her photo credits. She will also insert links between the first version, reflective statement, and final version of each paper.

▲ **Figure 6.10   Designing a Home Page**   For her writing class, Amanda has focused on topics that revolve around the theme of "space." The design elements of this page reinforce this theme. This page has a clearly stated title, and the image of Saturn provides a distinctive focal point. The light-colored fonts contrast against the black background, making the words easy to read. The images next to the text guide readers through the e-portfolio's organizational structure.

Hint

LOAD IMAGE FILES ON YOUR SERVER

Unlike word-processing files, Web files (.html or .htm files) will not save the images that you paste into them. When you load your Web files onto your server, you also need to load each image file (.gif, .jpg, .png, and others) onto your server. If you do not load your image files separately, they will not appear on your Web pages when they are accessed online.

For unusual fonts, use an image-production program such as Adobe Photoshop or Macromedia Fireworks to create image files that include text incorporating such fonts.

www. **Web Design Resources**

www.webstyleguide.com/index.html

Web Style Guide, 2nd ed., by Patrick Lynch and Sarah Horton, which includes extensive online information on site and page design, graphics, and multimedia

www.webdesignfromscratch.com/basics.cfm

Ben Hunt's user-friendly guide to page layout and graphic design

www.w3schools.com/default.asp

Refsnes Data's comprehensive step-by-step tutorials on HTML, XHTML, JavaScript, CSS, and more

www.adobe.com/devnet/dreamweaver/getting_started.html

Information about designing Web sites using Macromedia Dreamweaver

wdvl.internet.com/WebRef/Help/Begin.html

The Web Developer's Virtual Library guide for beginners designing their first Web page

www.lib.virginia.edu/science/guides/html/html.htm

The University of Virginia Library's introduction to HTML

NOTES

NOTES

7

WRITING ABOUT LITERATURE

Why write about literature? When we read various types of literature, such as stories, poems, and plays, we do so to enjoy the work and to learn more about the world as seen through the eyes of the writer whose work we're reading. One way to understand the work more deeply is to write about it. As we do so, we learn how to interpret literature more skillfully.

7a WAYS TO WRITE ABOUT LITERATURE

Before you can write about a creative work, you should have something to say about it. This involves analyzing, so begin by reading a work closely and considering its meaning. How can the work be interpreted? Think about its language in terms of such things as images, rhythms, use of dialogue, or symbolism. Consider analyzing the piece in one of the following ways:

- *Analyze a theme or how the plot displays the theme.* For example, what are some of the conflicts? How do events connect to each other? Do some events foreshadow others? Does the writer offer a lesson to be learned or a way of looking at life or the world? Is the author responding to some event he or she experienced or recalling some past moment?

- *Analyze characters.* Consider their behavior, how they are described, what they say, and how all this fits into the plot or theme of the work or its setting. Does your interpretation tell you anything more about the characters or the theme or the culture or time period in which the work is set? Do the characters change or stay the same? Is there a minor character worth analyzing in terms of the theme or plot or effect on a major character?

- *Analyze the structure of the work.* Is it chronological? Does it skip around? Are you given clues by the writer as to what will happen?

- *Analyze the narrator.* Who is telling the story, someone outside the events or one of the characters? Does the narrator tell the reader the characters' thoughts? Does the author write in the first person, using *I*? What is the narrator's tone or attitude?

- *Look at type or genre of the work.* Is it a tragedy, comedy, sonnet, mystery, or science fiction? How does it compare to others of its type? Does it blend several types of literature? Does it use elements common to this type of work? Is it an effective example of this type of work? Why?

■ *Analyze the historical or cultural background.* How does the work reflect values and beliefs of the time and place in which it is set or in which it was written? For example, if the work is set in Boston in the late nineteenth century, what were the attitudes toward immigrants then? How does the work reveal those attitudes? What are some of the social or political forces that were at work at the time or that affected the author? Would contemporary readers interpret it differently than readers at the time it was written?

■ *Analyze the work in terms of gender.* How does the work portray women or men? How does it define their roles in the family? in society? in the workplace?

■ *Focus on the reactions of the audience to the work.* Why do readers respond as they do to this work? If the meaning of the text is constructed by readers, what is a reader response to this work?

■ *Research the life of the author.* What about the author's life is reflected in this particular work? For example, if you are reading *The Diary of Anne Frank,* what were the events at the time (World War II and the Holocaust) that are the background against which she wrote?

■ *Resist the obvious meaning of the work.* Read skeptically, look for internal inconsistencies, and focus on ambiguities in the work. How would you interpret the work?

7b WRITING THE ASSIGNMENT

Be sure to read the assignment carefully, checking the key terms that define your task. Are you asked to remain objective and inform the reader, persuade the reader, respond personally to the work, or offer an evaluation? Who is the audience for your paper? In addition to the instructor, you may be asked to write for a particular audience, and that will help you decide how much background information the reader will need.

Here are the steps you should take when writing about a literary work.

1. Read the work all the way through.

2. Ask yourself some questions: What aspect of the work interests, surprises, pleases, or upsets you? What questions does the work raise in your mind? What characters or literary devices (such as setting, images, or language) stand out in your mind? What new insights did you gain from your reading?

3. Put the answer to your question into an assertion or thesis. Does that assertion seem so obvious that it's not fresh or interesting to write about? Try delving more deeply to see the complexity behind the obvious, or choose another question to answer.

> ### Hint
>
> **AVOIDING PITFALLS IN WRITING ABOUT LITERATURE**
>
> Students often make two kinds of errors in writing about literature.
>
> ■ **Writing a plot summary instead of writing an analysis or doing re-search.** Unless you are specifically asked to write a plot summary, summarize only when you need to in order to support a point.
>
> ■ **Leaving out needed information.** Some writers make the mistake of thinking that if the instructor knows a lot about the work, they don't have to include such information in their paper. They forget that part of the purpose of the paper is to show the instructor that they have read and understood the work and that they have learned what has been taught in the course.

4. If possible, read the whole work again, or skim it to look for evidence of what you want to write about. A second reading can help you find support for your thesis that may not have been apparent as you read the work the first time. Are there examples of dialogue that help support your point? Can you find something a character did or said, an incident in the story, a recurring image, or a surprise twist that supports your point? If the work is printed in a book you own, use your highlighter or take notes in the margins. If the book is not yours, write your notes on the computer. In either case, keep a list of the page numbers you will want to refer to when you write your paper.

5. Support your main point with reasoned arguments and evidence from the work itself. You can also use secondary sources to offer additional evidence to support your ideas. (On the difference between primary and secondary sources, see 60a.)

As you write your first draft, be prepared to discover new insights or connections you hadn't originally thought of. Writing is often an act of discovering what we think, so your paper may change shape or go off in a slightly different direction. Then you'll need to go back and revise the thesis and perhaps the introductory section as well.

www. **Web Sites for Primary Texts and Secondary Sources**

vos.ucsb.edu
   Voice of the Shuttle

www.bartleby.com
   Bartleby.com ▶

7c CONVENTIONS IN WRITING ABOUT LITERATURE

Verb Tense

Use present tense as you write about a fictional work.

> Because Gambel **uses** her characters to speak for her, we know that when Melissa **says** she **is angered** by society's attitudes toward children of mixed-race parents, Gambel **is expressing** her own viewpoint.

Use past tense, however, when you write about historical background for a work or make reference to the past as context for the work.

> Mark Twain **was** also an author of travel books and **worked** as a reporter.

Documentation Style

For most classroom assignments involving literature, use MLA or CM style for citations and for the list of works cited at the end of the paper (see Chapter 66 and 68a).

Poems and Plays

Cite short poems by line number, and cite plays by act and scene. If needed, add line numbers in plays. Use either arabic numbers (1, 2, 3, and so on) or Roman numerals (I, II, III, and so on). For example, for Shakespeare's *Macbeth,* both of the following are acceptable:

> *Mac.* 2.4.123–34   (*or*)   *Mac.* II.iv.123–34

> In Sidney Lanier's poem "The Symphony," he explores the power of music to deepen our understanding of religion's message to love one another: "Music is Love in search of a word" (line 368).

> In his play *A Doll's House,* Henrik Ibsen has Nora's husband, Torvald, use such affectionate terms as "my little lark" and "my little squirrel" to address Nora (1.1).

Quotations

When you introduce quotations from the work or from secondary sources, prepare your reader by explaining the point or relevance of the quotation first. That helps integrate the quotation smoothly into your writing and prepares your reader to understand the quotation. (For more on quoting, see 42a and 64e.)

> When Sarah realizes she must give up her right to see her own daughter, she wants Maria to remember that she is Maria's biological mother, and so she tells Maria, "You must always remember that it was me who held you in my womb and who brought you into the world, nursed you, and rocked you at night when you couldn't sleep" (252).

If you omit some of the quotation, use an ellipsis (see 45e) to indicate where words are omitted from the text. Use brackets (see 45d) around any words of your own that you added to the quote.

Author's Name

Use the author's full name when first mentioned in your paper, and then use only the last name. Use only last names in parenthetical citations.

Italics and Quotation Marks

Italicize (or underline) titles of books, journals, plays, and other works published as a complete entity and not part of a larger work. Use quotation marks to enclose titles of short stories, essays, songs, short poems, and portions of larger works (see 42b and 49a).

7d SAMPLE LITERATURE PAPER

A sample paper, beginning on page 76, provides a detailed analysis of a character in Graham Greene's *The End of the Affair*.

1 INCH

1/2 INCH

Amy McAllister

Dr. W. Ramsey

English 415

29 April 2007

DOUBLE SPACE

Saint Sarah: Tracing the Impact of Sarah's Sainthood

in The End of the Affair

Graham Greene's The End of the Affair is a largely religious novel despite the main character's disbelief in God. The story is narrated from the first-person point-of-view of Maurice Bendrix, a writer who expresses his disbelief in God throughout the narrative. Though the novel begins and ends with Bendrix, the transformational story of The End of the Affair really belongs to Sarah, who is often seen only as a supporting character in Bendrix's larger narrative. However, it is Sarah's path to sainthood that shapes key events throughout the novel—even after her death.

1 INCH

1 INCH

Greene initially presents Sarah as an unreligious but passionate person stuck in the rut of a dull marriage to an even duller man. Unexpectedly, she finds love with Maurice Bendrix, and they begin an adulterous affair. Though religious readers might be appalled by the immorality of this relationship, even in the midst of her affair Sarah expresses a certain amount of saintliness. Critic Deryl Davis believes that in many of Greene's characters, "corruption is a path to salvation, or at least to recovery of the soul." Throughout the novel, Sarah's sinful path leads her toward a religious reconciliation.

In his critique of the writings of Graham Greene, critic A. A. DeVitis argues that even though Sarah seems to love Bendrix more than she has ever loved any man before, "At this period of her life, there is nothing of the saint in Sarah; there is no thought of God in her promiscuous life" (109). DeVitis's claim that Sarah doesn't think of God at this time is supported by the text of the novel; however, the claim that there is no presence of sainthood in her at the time of the affair is not justified. Greene foreshadows the God-like love

1 INCH

McAllister 2

within Sarah while describing Bendrix's jealousy. Bendrix constantly accuses Sarah of committing infidelities during their relationship. He does not understand how Sarah can be in love with him and not be jealous, and her lack of distrust and suspicion angers him. Sarah tries to make him understand that she is not jealous because she loves him, and she says, "'I'm only saying I want you to be happy. I hate your being unhappy. I don't mind anything you do that makes you happy'" (Greene 55). Though she loves Bendrix, she would rather he would be with someone else if it would make him happy. Her love for him is purely unconditional and selfless. She places no stipulations on it and lets him know that she loves him completely.

Sarah reveals this saintliness again when she makes the vow that forever alters their relationship. The house in which Bendrix and Sarah meet for their adulterous liaisons is bombed during the Blitz. After Sarah sees Bendrix and concludes that he is dead, Sarah reveals her complete selflessness. Instead of beginning to mourn her loss or simply walking away, Sarah prays to a God in whom she has never believed. She pleads with God to make Bendrix come back to life, ultimately making her vow: "'I love him and I'll do anything if you'll make him alive. . . . I'll give him up forever, only let him be alive . . .'" (Greene 95). Even though giving up Bendrix is the last thing Sarah wants to do, she is willing to sacrifice her desires in order for him to live. This self-sacrificial love is pivotal in Sarah's saintly development. As critic Georg Gaston acknowledges, Sarah's love is divine, and indeed, "[her love] imitates the passion of Christ" (Gaston 47). Her vow is symbolic of Christ's death as atonement for the transgressions of mankind as she willingly allows a part of her emotional self to die so that Bendrix might live.

Sarah shows the depth of her love by keeping her promise even when she wants nothing more than to be with Bendrix. This faithfulness to God revealed through Sarah's keeping of the vow is

McAllister 3

just another reflection of her goodness as she feels that she must stay true to it for Bendrix's sake. However, she begins to wonder about the existence of God like she never has, and before she realizes it, she finds herself in a relationship based on a more spiritual kind of love.

DeVitis argues that Sarah must have this love relationship with God because, as he says, "Having experienced perfect human love with Bendrix, Sarah renounced him for God, and nothing short of divine love will satisfy her" (109). DeVitis's point is further validated when Bendrix calls Sarah to let her know he is coming to visit. Sarah rushes out into the rain to avoid Bendrix, and she immediately heads to a church. Bendrix assumes that he will win the battle between God and himself for Sarah's love because he can physically touch her. However, at the end of the scene, Sarah does not tell him that she loves him; instead, she dismisses him with "'God bless you'" (Greene 131). With this, Bendrix realizes that the battle is lost, and though Sarah still loves him as she always has, she loves something else more.

Even after Sarah's death, her saintly characteristics still affect Bendrix. After Sarah's death, Bendrix begins to associate some "miracles" with her. Though each miracle could be explained by some other natural occurrence, the reader agonizes along with Bendrix over the idea that Sarah might really have a hand in the events that happen. At Sarah's funeral, Bendrix arrives with a young lady he does not know well, and upon realizing that he does not want her there, he begs Sarah, "Get me out of it. I don't want to begin it all again and injure her. I'm incapable of love. Except of you, except of you . . . " (Greene 159). He says this, Sarah's mother approaches him, and the young lady disappears. Later, as he recounts this experience in his head, he begins to wonder if Sarah might have done this for him, and he attempts to convince himself that thinking Sarah might possess some saintly power is a foolish notion. Though Bendrix wants to dismiss this circumstance as mere coincidence, other aspects of the story leave him unable to do so. As critic Michael Gorra argues, the events in Book Five of <u>The End of the Affair</u> seem to work "as if through the intercession of a saint." In Book Five, the reader sees other "miracles" occur. As much as Bendrix would like to reject the notion that God exists and enables Sarah to play a role in these events, he cannot.

However, her saintliness is not tied solely to the miracles for which she is given credit. Throughout the entire novel, Sarah loves without reservation. For Sarah, love is largely about devotion, and just as she is devoted to Bendrix during their affair, she pledges that same devotion to God as she acknowledges Him. This idea of complete devotion and all-encompassing love is a saintly trait, and in fact, Greene scholar R. H. Miller says that Sarah's character is inspired by the story of Saint Catherine, a saint who devoted her life to others in need. As Miller sees it, "Sarah is a modern type of St. Catherine, moving in her own way through London, searching for God, performing tender acts of love, and touching in her special way the lives of those around her" (Miller 85). If it was Greene's intention that Sarah possess some saintly qualities, it is impossible to ignore her arrival at a state of sainthood at the novel's end. In fact, it is truly Sarah's love for God that creates the rivalry Bendrix perceives between himself and God. It is that very rivalry that helps Bendrix to begin to ascertain his belief in God by the novel's conclusion.

By the end of the novel, it seems as though Bendrix is aware that something about Sarah was different all along. Near the beginning of their affair, Bendrix said, "She had so much more capacity for love than I had" (Greene 51), and this shows that he saw her as having a gift for love. Bendrix expresses a similar idea in his final encounter with Sarah in the church. As he begins to leave, he looks back, and while watching Sarah, he thinks, "[All] I know is that in spite of her mistakes and her unreliability, she was better than most. It's just as well that one of us should believe in

McAllister 5

her: she never did in herself" (Greene 131). She moved through life affecting each person with whom she came into contact. Her path to sainthood made an impression on every person she encountered. Sarah's life is not some mere tale of a serendipitous tawdry romance, but instead reveals the story of a simple woman who became a saint.

1 INCH   1/2 INCH
McAllister 6

Works Cited

Davis, Deryl. "Instruments of Grace: For Novelist Graham Greene and His Characters, Corruption Could Be a Path to Salvation." Sojourners 34 (2005): 38–41. InfoTrac OneFile. Thomson Gale. Francis Marion U, Rogers Lib., Florence, SC. 16 Apr. 2007 <http://web7.infotrac.galegroup.com>.

DeVitis, A. A. Graham Greene. New York: Twayne, 1964.

Gaston, Georg M. A. The Pursuit of Salvation: A Critical Guide to the Novels of Graham Greene. New York: Whitston, 1984.

Gorra, Michael. "On The End of the Affair." Southwest Review 89 (2004): 109–25. InfoTrac OneFile. Thomson Gale. Francis Marion U, Rogers Lib., Florence, SC. 16 Apr. 2007 <http://web7.infotrac.galegroup.com>.

Greene, Graham. The End of the Affair. 1951. New York: Penguin, 2004.

Miller, R. H. Understanding Graham Greene. Columbia, SC: U of South Carolina P, 1990.

1 INCH   1 INCH

1 INCH

(Follow MLA guidelines by starting your Works Cited list on a separate page. Space limitations of this book do not permit the Works Cited list above to be on its own page.)

8

PROFESSIONAL WRITING

8a MEMOS

Memos are brief communications to others in an organization and are written for a number of purposes. They inform readers about new information, answer questions, make recommendations, offer progress reports, summarize, make requests, and so on. They are usually brief, no more than a page or two dealing with a single topic, and are written in a semiformal tone. Even with brief memos and memos sent by e-mail, headings and bulleted lists help highlight and convey information quickly and concisely. When the memo is sent by e-mail, the subject line should be short and state the subject clearly.

Memos generally begin with the reasons for writing or the most important points first and then move to supporting details. This is particularly useful when informing others. If the purpose of the memo is to persuade, however, a more effective organization is to begin with an appeal or offer reasons or evidence before stating the course of action you are recommending.

Memos, like business letters, are single-spaced, with double spacing between paragraphs. Handwrite your initials after your name in the heading (see Figure 8.1). Unless an organization has its own internal conventions or format, use the following guidelines for page arrangement.

- *Heading.*

To:	(recipient's name and job title)
cc:	(anyone other than the recipient listed in the "To" line who will receive a copy)
From:	(your name and job title)
Date:	(complete date)
Subject:	(concise statement of what the memo is about, with the first word capitalized)

- *Summary.* If the memo is longer than a page, you can include a summary to provide a brief statement of the key points. A heading indicating the specific content of the summary will help your reader. You may want to wait until you write the complete memo before coming back to write the summary.

- *Body or discussion section.* This is the information you wish to convey by writing the memo.

- *Closing.* Include a closing paragraph with a courteous ending that states the action you want your reader to take. Your memo will be more effective if you explain how the reader will benefit from the action and how you are making the action easier for the reader. For

---

To: New student tour guides
From: Cheryl Houston, Admissions Counselor   CH
Date: April 5, 2007
Subject: Training sessions for campus tours

Please plan to attend one of the following training sessions for campus tours. Remember that summer tour guides must attend one of the April sessions. All others may attend in April or August. Sessions are held in Jewell Hall, Room 120.

Monday, April 9	6:00-8:30 p.m.
Thursday, April 12	7:00-9:30 p.m.
Saturday, April 14	9:00-11:30 a.m.
Monday, August 13	5:00-7:30 p.m.
Tuesday, August 14	6:00-8:30 p.m.
Saturday, August 18	9:00-11:30 a.m.

Please call me at extension 7556 to let me know which session you plan to attend. Thank you for your cooperation.

Figure 8.1 A Sample Memo

example, you might close with a sentence such as "Your approval of this plan will allow my committee to move forward on this vital project, and I will be glad to stop by your office on Tuesday to answer any questions you may have as you make your decision."

■ *Attachments.* If you need to attach documentation, lists, graphs, or any other material to your memo, mention the attached information in the memo and list those documents here.

Attached: Diagram of the Planned Expansion
            Dilman Construction Company's Estimate of Costs

8b E-MAIL COMMUNICATIONS

E-mail is a widely used means of communication and has very different patterns of organization, levels of formality, and purposes. Some e-mails are quick, personal notes to friends while others are really electronic memos or business letters.

Remember that business e-mail is *public:* anyone in the company or group—and perhaps even outside of it—can read it. Here are some guidelines to keep in mind when writing business e-mail messages:

■ Keep the subject line short and appropriate.

■ Begin an e-mail with a standard salutation followed by a colon:

Dear Dr. Jones:

- Keep your message brief. Many people find it difficult to read long screenfuls of text, so keep your paragraphs short and your entire message limited to one screen, if possible. Your reader will appreciate not having to scroll down to read the whole message.

- Although e-mail is less formal than printed documents and usually uses contractions and *I* and *you,* proofread your messages to correct any grammatical errors, misspellings, and typos.

- Reread your message to be sure that it is not possible for the recipient to misinterpret the tone. Some e-mail can sound inadvertently curt, rude, or confusing because the message was written too quickly or the writer failed to reread and revise.

- Close the message with your name and title, if applicable. Most e-mail programs display your e-mail address, so you don't need to include it. However, if you are e-mailing to a listserv or group, your address may not be displayed, so you may wish to add it to your signature.

- If you have an "auto-signature"—text with your name, title, and other identifying information—that automatically appears at the end of your messages, be sure it looks professional (without unnecessary quotations, designs, or comments) and includes your e-mail address.

Checklist

DRAFTING AND SENDING EFFECTIVE E-MAILS

- Consider the purpose and audience of your message when you choose an appropriate tone and writing style.

- Avoid using all capital letters, which are the electronic equivalent of shouting at your reader.

- Don't quote from or forward someone else's e-mail without that person's permission.

- Double-check the address line before hitting the send key. If you are replying to a message that was sent to many people, make sure that only those you want to receive your message are included in the address line.

- Remember that people other than the recipient may read your message. Never write anything that might embarrass you or anyone else.

- If your message is emotional or very important, save it in your draft file before sending it. Do something else for a while, and then reread it to make sure that it communicates in a way that is respectful of your audience and represents you well.

8c   BUSINESS LETTERS

When you are writing documents for an audience that includes busy people who want to know quickly why you are writing and what information you have for them, keep the following guidelines in mind.

- State your purpose at the beginning of your letter.

- Use a clear topic sentence to start each paragraph. Topic sentences can help you to unify your ideas and guide your reader through your letter.

- Remember that you are often writing for multiple audiences who are reading the document for different purposes and may skim rather than read. These different audiences may need different types of information. So before writing the letter, think about all of the audiences who might read your letter and what they will need to know. How and where in your document will you include all of this information? If some of your readers may want specific data or other information, can you put that in an attachment?

- Provide the background your readers may need. For example, if you are writing a letter in response to a customer's order, remind the customer of the specific order you are writing about. If you are requesting some information, the reader will most likely need some context as to what you are seeking and for what purpose. Make sure you provide all of the information needed for your reader to act on your request. For information on cover letters when you send your résumé, see 8d.

- Make your letter clear, concise, professional, objective, courteous, and friendly.

- Proofread all documents you send out to be sure they are grammatically correct, are spelled correctly, and have no typographical errors.

- If your business letter is sent as an e-mail attachment (as many letters are), it is especially important to keep it short and to use word processing software that is generally available so that the attachment can be opened and read.

Parts of Letters

Business letters are single-spaced, with double spacing between paragraphs, on one side of a sheet of paper. The parts of the letter are as follows (see the example in Figure 8.2).

- *Return address (information about you).* Place this at least one inch from the top of the page, at the left margin. If the letter is short, start this farther down the page. Don't include your name. Include, as the top line, your street address, then city, state, and ZIP code in the next line, and then the date in the line below. You can also create a template with your own letterhead to use. If you are using stationery with a printed letterhead or your own template that includes the address, add only the date.

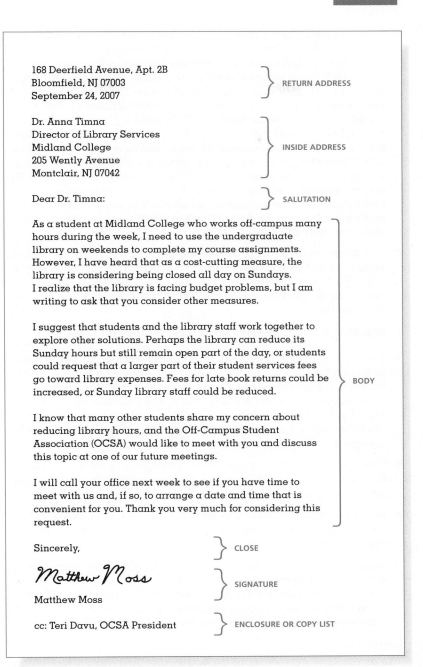

168 Deerfield Avenue, Apt. 2B
Bloomfield, NJ 07003   } RETURN ADDRESS
September 24, 2007

Dr. Anna Timna
Director of Library Services
Midland College   } INSIDE ADDRESS
205 Wently Avenue
Montclair, NJ 07042

Dear Dr. Timna: } SALUTATION

As a student at Midland College who works off-campus many
hours during the week, I need to use the undergraduate
library on weekends to complete my course assignments.
However, I have heard that as a cost-cutting measure, the
library is considering being closed all day on Sundays.
I realize that the library is facing budget problems, but I am
writing to ask that you consider other measures.

I suggest that students and the library staff work together to
explore other solutions. Perhaps the library can reduce its
Sunday hours but still remain open part of the day, or students
could request that a larger part of their student services fees
go toward library expenses. Fees for late book returns could be   } BODY
increased, or Sunday library staff could be reduced.

I know that many other students share my concern about
reducing library hours, and the Off-Campus Student
Association (OCSA) would like to meet with you and discuss
this topic at one of our future meetings.

I will call your office next week to see if you have time to
meet with us and, if so, to arrange a date and time that is
convenient for you. Thank you very much for considering this
request.

Sincerely,   } CLOSE

Matthew Moss   } SIGNATURE

Matthew Moss

cc: Teri Davu, OCSA President } ENCLOSURE OR COPY LIST

Figure 8.2 Sample Business Letter

■ *Inside address (information about the person to whom the letter is being sent).* At the left margin, include the person's name (starting with any title that person has) and the complete address (including, on separate lines, company name; street address; and then the city, state, and ZIP code on the last line). If you are responding to a letter you received or a job advertisement with this information stated in the ad, you will have the necessary information. Otherwise, be sure to double-check that you have addressed the letter to the right person, spelled the person's name correctly, and used the person's proper title. These things are important because the person you are writing to may no longer be there or the position title may have changed. Incorrect spelling or wrong names or titles can make the writer look uninformed, so it's wise to check by phone. You don't want to rely on getting the information from an online directory or company document that may be out-of-date.

■ *Salutation (the greeting to the person receiving the letter).* At the left margin, start the salutation with "Dear," then a name, followed by a colon. Write to a specific person. If you don't know the recipient's name, use the job title, and if you don't know the person's gender, use the whole name.

    Dear Mr. Patel: **Dear Personnel Director:**   **Dear Jan Spivak:**

■ *Body (the content of the letter).* Begin at the left margin, with no indentation for each paragraph, and double-space between paragraphs. Keep the paragraphs short. Do not start the letter with your name (for example, "My name is Mark Smith, and I am seeking information about …") because your name will be in the signature section of the letter. End with a courteous close, thanking the person if that is appropriate.

■ *Close (the closing greeting).* At the left margin, capitalize only the first word, and end with a comma. A typical close is "Sincerely," "Sincerely yours," or "Yours truly."

■ *Signature (your signature and name).* Type your name two double spaces below the close, and sign your name in the space between the close and your typed name.

■ *Enclosure or copy list.* At the left margin, note with the word "Enclosure" any enclosures that will be included with the letter. This helps match up the enclosure if it gets separated from your letter. If you are sending copies to anyone else, type "cc:". List the other recipients' names alphabetically, with an explanatory title, if needed.

Letter Style

The placement of the parts of the letter noted here and illustrated in Figure 8.2, with all elements beginning at the left margin, is referred to as "full block" style (no paragraph indentations and all parts starting at the left margin). This is considered the most formal arrangement of a letter and also more current usage than "modified block" style in which the return address, close, and signature appear on the right half of the page.

www. Web Resources for Business Letters

writing.colostate.edu/guides/documents/bletter

The Writing Center at Colorado State University's Writing Guides on Business Letters

owl.english.purdue.edu/handouts/pw/index.html

The Purdue University Online Writing Lab (OWL), which documents business letters and résumés

8d COVER LETTERS

When you are applying for a job and submitting a résumé, you should always have a cover letter that introduces you, states the job you are applying for, and adds depth and explanation to the qualifications on your résumé. Consider this letter as presenting an argument—that is, showing your reader why you are an outstanding candidate for the position. The goal of the letter is to get an interview.

Even if you are generally modest, sell yourself to the reader. Show why that company would benefit from hiring you, and demonstrate that you have all the qualifications, skills, and requirements for the job. Don't overlook any of the qualifications mentioned in the job listing. They are the keys to what the employer is looking for.

It is critically important to proofread your letter carefully. Candidates who submit letters and résumés with grammatical and mechanical mistakes in them are the first to be weeded out.

Opening Section of the Letter

If you have had personal contact with someone in the company or if you have been invited to apply, mention that in the opening sentence or two.

Indicate the title of the specific job you are applying for and the source of your information. Did you see the job listed on your campus recruitment board, on the company's Web site, in the newspaper, or at Monster.com or another job search site?

Identify yourself in terms of your qualifications by summarizing what you can offer this company.

Middle Section of the Letter

Make strong connections between your qualifications and those listed in the job description.

Refer the reader to your enclosed résumé. Then expand on your experience, education, and qualifications, and add background that enhances your appeal as an employee but that isn't evident in the résumé. For example, if leadership or supervision skills are important and you indicate that you held an elected office in the student government, you might note that you won by a wide majority in a large field of candidates. This fact shows that you're liked by people, you're seen as a leader, and you stand out in a crowd.

Closing Section of the Letter

Conclude with an action step. What do you want your reader to do? Contact you? If so, how can you be contacted? Are you available to come for an interview? When?

Thank the reader for considering your résumé. Indicate below your signature that the résumé is enclosed. At the left border, under your name, note an enclosure:

Enclosure: Résumé

A sample cover letter is presented in Figure 8.3.

Additional Letters

If you haven't heard from the employer in a week or two, you can write a follow-up letter to see whether your letter was received. If you have an interview, write a letter of thanks afterward, again reminding the interviewer of your qualifications and your interest in working for that company. The final step after you have decided to accept or reject the job offer is to write a letter indicating your decision. Acceptance letters can repeat the conditions of employment to be sure that you and your future employer agree on matters such as salary, starting date, title, and responsibilities. If you reject the offer, you can politely note that although you are unable to accept the job, you were pleased to be offered the position by a company you admire.

8e   RÉSUMÉS

An effective résumé focuses on the organization to which you are applying, so select the details that display your particular skills and achievements for that job. When you are applying for positions in different companies or for different jobs, you will need to tailor your résumé to fit each one. Because readers are likely to take only a short time to look at your résumé, they need to see the information easily and quickly. They won't search for your strong points.

Résumés for entry-level positions are usually one page in length, but two pages may be used for people with significant job experience. When designing your résumé, try to fill your page and avoid too much blank space. Show a prospective employer that you have much to offer through the layout of your page.

As you create your résumé, keep the following guidelines in mind:

- Create a visually appealing, uncluttered format.

- Avoid overloading the résumé with too much information.

25 Oregon Way
Austin, TX 78221
April 18, 2007

Ms. Margaret Whitmore
Bankers Trust
John Hancock Building, Suite 45B
138 Trujillo Way
Darleton, TX 75219

Dear Ms. Whitmore:

At the suggestion of Jim Mendez, one of your colleagues in the
Human Resources Department, I am applying for the position
of bank teller listed in the *Darleton Times* last week. My skills
in accounting, my summer experience working as a customer service
assistant in the bank in my hometown of Monroe, Mississippi, and
my college courses in financial computing will allow me to be a
productive employee at Bankers Trust.

As you will see from the enclosed résumé, I am about to graduate
from the University of Texas at Austin with a B.A. in Finance. My
courses in financial computing have been particularly useful in
learning how bank records are kept and how software is utilized. In
addition to pursuing extracurricular campus activities, which
allowed me to further develop my communication skills, I served as
the treasurer for my fraternity, keeping accurate records of our
$150,000 annual budget.

I am available for an interview anytime after May 15, and I can meet
with you in your office in Darleton. I will telephone in about ten days
to arrange a convenient time and to learn whether you need any
additional information. If you prefer, you can call me at (466) 555-1212
or e-mail a message to blalock@tu.edu to schedule a meeting.

Thank you for considering my résumé. I am looking forward to
meeting with you in person.

Sincerely,

William Blalock

William Blalock

Enclosure: Résumé

Figure 8.3 A Sample Cover Letter

- Use headings and bullets for emphasis and clarity.
- Use white space strategically to divide sections of your résumé.
- Organize to emphasize your strongest skills.
- Use action verbs (see the accompanying Hint box), and keep lists in parallel structure (see Chapter 14).
- Check very carefully for misspellings or typos.

For information on scannable résumés, see 8e3.

Hint

USING ACTION VERBS IN YOUR RÉSUMÉ

To help the prospective employer see you as an active worker, use action verbs such as the following:

act	generate	persuade
adapt	get	plan
administer	govern	prepare
advise	guide	present
analyze	handle	process
assess	head	produce
build	hire	program
calculate	implement	promote
catalog	improve	provide
compile	increase	raise
complete	initiate	recommend
conduct	install	recruit
coordinate	integrate	reorganize
create	maintain	represent
decide	manage	revise
define	market	schedule
demonstrate	modify	select
design	monitor	sell
develop	motivate	send
direct	negotiate	speak
distribute	obtain	supervise
edit	operate	survey
establish	order	train
evaluate	organize	transmit
examine	oversee	update
forecast	perform	write

1. Sections of the Résumé

The order of the sections will depend on what is appropriate to the job you are seeking. The name of the section might vary according to the content. For example, if you haven't had much work experience but have other experience you want to highlight, such as being treasurer of a campus organization or doing publicity work for a local group, use "Experience" rather than "Work Experience." If you submit a résumé online, section names may be set by the company or job listing service.

Name

Generally, you should use your full name, not initials or a nickname.

Address

Include your college and permanent addresses if they are different so that your prospective employer can contact you at either place. Include phone numbers, dates that you will be at both addresses, and other contact information such as a fax number, cell phone number, e-mail address, or Web page address. Make sure your e-mail address is appropriate for professional situations; if it is too informal, you might want to set up a new e-mail account with a more appropriate address. Also, include your Web page only if it is professional in appearance and does not include personal pictures or other features that you don't want a prospective employer to view.

Mark Daniel Kane

College Address	**Permanent Address**
521 Cary Quadrangle	1523 Elmwood Drive
West Lafayette, IN 47906	Nobleton, IN 46623
(765) 555-0224	(765) 555-8789; fax (765) 555-4527
cell: (765) 427-1111	cell: (765) 427-1111
markkane@purdue.edu	mkane@aol.com
(Until May 15, 2007)	(After May 15, 2007)

Career Objective

Not all résumés include a career objective, but if you do have one, it can be labeled "Career Objective," "Objective," "Professional Objective," or the like. It is placed immediately below your name and address and contains one to three lines of text describing the position you are applying for and summarizing your main qualifications. Some writers choose sentence format; others use descriptive phrases with minimal punctuation. Follow these guidelines.

- Relate this section directly to the job you want, and tie in the skills you have acquired, your education, and your activities.

- Include the job title you seek and the skills you can offer. The rest of your résumé proves that you have the necessary skills, education, and experience.

- Don't emphasize what you want from the job ("to learn" or "to gain experience"). Instead emphasize what you can do for the company.

- Be specific. The most common problem is being too vague or too general.

   Too General: A position utilizing my skills and experience

   More Specific: A position allowing me to use my professional writing skills and management experience to write technical documentation for software products

Profile Statement

Instead of an objective statement, you might use a profile statement instead. This section is usually labeled "Profile," "Profile Statement," or "Summary of Qualifications." It is usually written as a descriptive phrase outlining your key qualifications or skills followed by three to five bulleted statements that highlight additional information about your work experience, education, and professional skills. Like the objective statement, the profile statement is placed immediately below your name and address. This strategy is a particularly good choice for people who want to emphasize skills that they have developed in school or volunteer situations rather than on the job. Follow these tips:

- Emphasize in your descriptive phrase the most important traits that are likely to appeal to a prospective employer.

- Start your bulleted statements with active verbs to describe your skills and experiences.

- Use a parallel sentence structure for each of your bulleted statements.

   Profile

   A graduating professional writing major with strong leadership experience and excellent skills in marketing and public relations
   • Excels in leading major group projects through to completion
   • Communicates effectively with supervisors, co-workers, and customers
   • Creates effective business and marketing documents, including letters, memos, brochures, and newsletters

Education

This is a major section for most students. Include the following:

- Names of colleges attended (with the most current listed first)

- Degrees and graduation dates (month and year)

- Major, minor, or specialization

- Grade point average (optional). Include your GPA first, then a slash, and then the highest possible GPA at the school. You can also indicate your major GPA, calculated by averaging your grades in courses in your major.

GPA: 3.7/4.0

Arrange the information in the order according to the aspect you want to emphasize, the college or the degree.

Purdue University
Bachelor of Science, May 2007
Major: Chemical Engineering; GPA: 3.7/4.0
(*or*)
Bachelor of Science in Chemical Engineering, May 2007, Purdue University
GPA: 3.7/4.0

You may want to list some upper-level courses you've taken that are particularly significant to the job you are applying for, or you might list special courses that are different from those everyone in your major must take. Use a specific heading such as "Public Relations Courses" rather than a vague "Significant Courses." If appropriate, indicate programming languages you know and software you can use.

Under the heading "Special Projects," you can highlight unique features of your education that make you stand out from other applicants. Describe special projects you have completed, reports you have written, or conferences you have attended. Briefly give the most important details.

Work Experience or Experience

Before deciding how to arrange and present this information, make a list of the following items:

- Job titles, places worked, locations, and dates. Include part-time, temporary, and volunteer work as well as cooperative programs and internships.

- Duties you performed and skills you acquired.

You can organize this information as a functional or chronological résumé. Use action verbs in this section.

Research Analyst

Kellogg Co., Montack, Michigan, Summer 2007

- Supervised nine assistants gathering information on cows' eating habits.
- Researched most recent information on cows' nutritional needs.
- Analyzed data to determine how to reduce number of feeding hours while maintaining nutritional quality.

Skills

Not all résumés include a skills section, but this is a useful way to emphasize skills you acquired from various jobs and activities. List the following:

■ Jobs, club activities, projects, special offices, or responsibilities.

■ Skills you have developed from these experiences. For example, as president of a club, you led meetings, delegated responsibilities, and coordinated activities.

Group your skills under three to five categories that relate to the job you are seeking, as described in your objective or profile statement, and use those categories as your headings.

Management
- Chaired a committee to prepare and institute new election procedures for the Student Union Board.
- Evaluated employees' work progress for monthly reports.

Communication
- Wrote weekly advertisements for student government entertainment activities.
- Represented my sorority in negotiations with university administrators.
- Spoke to potential funding groups for student-organized charity events.

Programming
- Analyzed and designed a program to record and average student grades for a faculty member.
- Designed a program to record and update items of the sorority's $90,000 annual budget.

Activities or College Activities

This section demonstrates your leadership and involvement and can include college activities, honors, and official positions or responsibilities you have had. You may need to explain in a phrase or two what the various organizations are because prospective employers will probably not be familiar with the fact that the Tomahawk Club is an honorary service organization on your campus or that Alpha Gamma Alpha is a first-year honors council at your school.

References

It is advisable to be selective about who gets a copy of your list of references. Therefore, you should write "References available on request" on your résumé. List the names of your references on a separate sheet, with addresses (including e-mail) and phone numbers. You can mail or fax the list if the potential employer asks for it. Be sure that you have first asked each person you wish to list whether he or she will serve as a reference.

2. Résumé Styles

There are two basic approaches for organizing a résumé: by date and by skills.

Reverse Chronological Résumé

This résumé presents your educational background, starting with the most recent degree, followed by work experience, beginning with the most recent job. List address (city and state) of the employer and dates of employment, and include a description of your duties, responsibilities, and acquired skills. This type of résumé highlights your current job and employer. (See Figure 8.4 for an example.)

Skills Résumé

This résumé emphasizes your skills and abilities gained through jobs, experiences, and activities and allows you to relate them to the job you want. Arrange the skills from the most to the least relevant. If appropriate, include the name and location of companies and dates of employment. This approach is particularly useful when the skills you've acquired are more impressive than the jobs you've had or when you want to highlight a significant skill acquired from different experiences and jobs.

Checklist

WRITING AN EFFECTIVE RÉSUMÉ

- **Organization.** Put the most important sections first. For example, is your work experience more important than your education? Are your college activities more important than your past jobs?
- **Visual appeal.** Use white space and lists to make your résumé visually appealing and easy to read. Highlight your headings with different kinds of type, underlining, boldface, capital letters, and indenting to show your organizing abilities. But don't clutter by using too many different fonts or types of headings.
- **Parallel headings.** Be sure your headings and lists are in parallel form.
- **Length.** Many companies prefer one-page résumés, but length may vary according to your field and career objective.
- **Uniqueness.** Your goal is not to make your résumé like all the others in the pile; instead, highlight your unique capabilities.

Many applicants combine both types of résumés by beginning with skills and then listing employment and educational history.

Joseph M. Packer, C.P.A.
5 Bay Ave. • Milwaukee, WI 53021 • (414) 555-1892 • jmp@webmail.com

---

OBJECTIVE

To utilize my education and experience in accounting, auditing, and loan processing to facilitate financial services at a banking institution

EDUCATION

• B.B.A. in Accounting, University of Wisconsin   August 2003–May 2007
  • GPA: 3.68/4.00, graduated *cum laude*

SKILLS SUMMARY

• Project Management   • Professional Presentations
• Data Analysis   • Financial Budgeting
• Computer Proficiency   • Accounting/Booking
• Flowcharting   • Mortgage Loan Servicing

PROFESSIONAL EXPERIENCE

Internal Auditor II, Wislake Bank, Milwaukee, WI   June 2005–Present
• Lead various operation and financial audit projects working with both external auditors and federal examiners
• Coordinate a compliance revision of 3000 loan files involving five department heads and twenty staff members
• Train team members on Microsoft Excel applications

Financial Analyst Intern, Riversgate Home   August 2004–June 2005
Mortgage, West Bend, WI
• Selected portfolio loans to be sold to outside service agencies
• Maintained data for mortgage servicing rights, including reconciliation of receivable and payable accounts
• Analyzed mortgage market trends and fluctuating growth rates

ACTIVITIES

• Treasurer, Wislake Bank Political   August 2006–Present
  Awareness Forum
• Co-Chair, United Performing Arts Fund   July 2006–Present
  for Wislake Bank

HONORS

• Member, Beta Gamma Sigma Honor Society,   August 2006–May 2007
  University of Wisconsin
• Member, Phi Eta Sigma Honor Society,   May 2005–May 2007
  University of Wisconsin

References available on request

Figure 8.4 A Reverse Chronological Résumé

3. Electronic Job Search

If you are job hunting on the Internet, there are a number of sites you can access to check on jobs or to post your résumé. If your local newspaper or newspapers from locations where you want to look for a job have Web sites, you can check the classified advertisements online. You can also check sites listing online newspapers, and you can post your résumé in online databases. Your college may also maintain a Web site where students can post résumés.

Online Sites for Job Seekers

- Major newspapers with classified ads online

New York Times	jobmarket.nytimes.com/pages/jobs
Wall Street Journal Careers	www.careerjournal.com
Washington Post	www.washingtonpost.com/wl/jobs/

- Sites listing jobs

America's Job Bank	www.ajb.org
Career Builder	www.careerbuilder.com
Career Magazine	www.careermag.com
Federal Jobs Digest	www.jobsfed.com
HigherEdJobs.com	www.higheredjobs.com
Monster.com	www.monster.com
NationJob Network	www.nationjob.com
True Careers	www.truecareers.com
USAJOBS	www.usajobs.gov
Yahoo Classified	hotjobs.yahoo.com/jobs

Scannable or Searchable Résumés

You can submit your résumé online, have it posted on the Web, send paper copies, or give paper copies to recruiters at job fairs. In most large companies, paper copies will be scanned so that they can be entered into the company's résumé database that can search résumés by keywords. (If you send an electronic copy, send along a laser-printed original on white 8½-by-11-inch paper if possible, with print that is not faint or light.) These résumés will contain the same information as the résumé described in 8e1, but the formatting and design must be kept very simple so that it can be scanned or searched accurately.

It is very important to use concise, specific language. When scannable résumés are searched by keyword, the computer is often looking for nouns, not verb forms. So instead of verbs, use nouns as your strong words: instead of *supervised, managed,* or *taught,* use *supervisor, manager,* or *instructor.* It is also helpful to include a keyword list at the beginning of the résumé just below your name and address.

To make the résumé readable by a scanner and interpreted correctly in a database search, follow these design principles:

- Avoid images.

- Use a standard font such as Times New Roman, Palatino, or Arial, in 10- or 12-point size.

- Avoid punctuation as much as possible. No punctuation mark should touch a word.

- Separate each part of a phone number with a space, as in this example: 765 123 4567

- Use no more than one color in the document.

- Avoid horizontal or vertical lines.

- Do not use highlighting techniques such as italics, underlines, or bullets.

- Start every line at the left margin.

- Do not use columns.

- If you have more than one address, one should be placed below the other.

Checklist

PREPARING FOR YOUR JOB SEARCH

- Ask at least three people who know you in a professional or academic capacity to serve as your references. Get their permission before sending out your résumé.

- Review your online presence to see whether you project a professional image of yourself on the Web. Type your name into Google and see what comes up. Would you be comfortable with a potential employer checking your Web site, blog, MySpace page, or Facebook page? If not, make adjustments to ensure you project a professional image online before sending out your résumé.

- Consider your e-mail address. Does it sound professional? If not, you might want to set up a new e-mail account to use exclusively for your job search.

- Think about the message that potential employers will hear if they call and reach your answering machine or voice mail. Does your phone message sound professional? If not, offer a more professional greeting.

- Consider posting an online portfolio (also known as an *e-portfolio*) that provides potential employers with your résumé and samples of your best professional work (see Chapter 9 for information about creating and posting a presentation e-portfolio).

- Check with the career services office at your college or university for information about open positions with local employers.

8f NEWSLETTERS AND BROCHURES

Like other effective documents, newsletters and brochures are produced by first determining their purpose and their intended readers. The purpose might be to inform, to entertain, to gain readers' attention, to make sales, or to promote a cause.

Newsletters

Newsletters are published periodically and are often sent as attachments to an e-mail. They have many purposes, such as establishing and maintaining a network or updating and informing readers. Newsletters can contain any combination of the following:

- Short news articles
- Columns or essays contributed on an ongoing basis
- Legislative or policy updates
- Contributions from readers
- Notices of upcoming events
- Analyses of issues relevant to the group
- Book reviews
- How-to information
- News about members of the group
- Advertisements

Planning for a newsletter also involves making decisions about length, format, tone (formal or informal), graphics, cost, frequency and manner of publication, and means of distribution. When you put the newsletter together, you will need to know how to use desktop publishing software to create the master copy or have that stage of producing each issue done commercially.

The design or layout of a newsletter is based on several principles.

- *Alignment.* Everything on every page should align with something else on the page. A grid is an especially effective tool to ensure that the text and images align. The alignment, which holds the whole design of the page together, should be broken only sparingly if needed for emphasis.
- *Margins.* Margins for newsletters should not be the same on all sides. The inside margins where two pages meet should be smaller than the outside margins of those pages. Bottom margins are usually the largest margins and top margins the next largest.
- *Front page identification.* The front page should contain a banner across the top with the name of the newsletter, the date, and identification of the group that produces the newsletter and possibly the

audience for whom it is intended. (A sample front page of a newsletter is presented in Figure 8.5.)

- *Size.* For 8½-by-11-inch pages, consider visually dividing the pages into halves or thirds. Place elements on the page within these halves or thirds for a more interesting and visually appealing layout. Use larger graphics and font sizes to call attention to the most important information.

- *Contrast.* Pages that have no contrasting elements can be dull. Use boxes, borders, or frames as design elements to break up the page and to organize, emphasize, or group related information.

- *Consistency.* Keep the look of each page the same even when the content changes from page to page. One way to achieve consistency is to use a template for the entire publication.

Brochures

Although they follow many of the same principles as newsletters, brochures are normally distributed to readers on a one-time basis, not periodically. The cover of a brochure also has to draw in its readers quickly and entice them to pick it up and read it. Because the purpose of a brochure is often to announce something, the front page should be very clear about its topic or purpose. (Figure 8.6 shows a sample front page and two inner pages from a brochure.)

Brochures are normally folded, with each "page" of the brochure containing small chunks of text. This usually means short paragraphs and no more than two or three sentences to each paragraph. It is important to keep clear margins between those pages, to leave enough white space so that the page looks easy to read, and not to overdo the use of graphics and design elements.

CAM AT THE NIH

FOCUS ON COMPLEMENTARY AND ALTERNATIVE MEDICINE

VOLUME XIV, NUMBER 1   WINTER 2007

Survey: Older Americans' Discussion of CAM With Doctors

© Jupiterimages

Do Americans age 50 or older discuss complementary and alternative medicine (CAM) with their physicians? More than two-thirds do not, according to a new survey.

The telephone survey of more than 1,500 participants, which AARP conducted in collaboration with NCCAM, provides a look at the participants' discussion of CAM use with their physicians. It also yields information about their use of CAM and over-the-counter and prescription drugs.

Previous surveys have looked at CAM use by American adults of all ages or at CAM use for specific diseases and conditions. However, this survey focused on Americans age 50 or older and their dialogue with their physicians about CAM use.

According to Margaret A. Chesney, Ph.D., Deputy Director of NCCAM, "These results confirm previous research that people 50 or older are frequent users of CAM. However, most people in our survey were not talking to their doctors about their CAM use." She noted, "Each of us, no matter what our age,

(continued on pg. 2)

N𝒞𝒜M

NATIONAL CENTER FOR COMPLEMENTARY
AND ALTERNATIVE MEDICINE

**NATIONAL INSTITUTES
OF HEALTH**

**U.S. DEPARTMENT OF
HEALTH AND HUMAN
SERVICES**

Thinking About CAM Therapies for Young People

© Jupiterimages

- "It worked when I had the flu, so why shouldn't it work for my daughter's flu? I'll just give her a smaller amount."
- "This supplement claims to prevent colds in kids. Does it work?"
- "My grandson has migraines. I read on the Internet about a hands-on therapy that's supposed to be good for migraine."
- "The pediatrician recommended vitamin D for my breastfed baby. I wonder if she should be on fish oil supplements, too. My grandmother always made her children take cod liver oil."

Can complementary and alternative medicine (CAM) be helpful to children? Are CAM therapies safe? This article presents some general points to consider in addressing these questions.*

* Many people also use other terms in addition to or instead of "CAM," such as "integrative medicine," "holistic medicine," and "non-allopathic medicine."

(continued on pg. 4)

Figure 8.5 Sample First Page of a Newsletter

Source: United States, National Institutes of Health, National Center for Complementary and Alternative Medicine, <u>CAM at the NIH</u> *14.1 (2007),* <u>National Institutes of Health</u>, *28 March 2007 <http://nccam.nih.gov/news/newsletter/pdf/2007winter.pdf>.*

Brookgreen Gardens
Sculpture Workshops and Master Classes

Fighting Stallions by Anna Hyatt Huntington

P. O. Box 3368
Pawleys Island, SC 29585-3368

http://www.brookgreen.org

Grandmother (Rita) by Richard Blake

The Fountain of the Muses by Carl Milles

Brookgreen Gardens

In 1931, Archer and Anna Hyatt Huntington founded Brookgreen Gardens, a non-profit organization to preserve the native flora and fauna and display objects of art.

Today, Brookgreen Gardens is a National Historic Landmark with one of the most significant collections of figurative sculpture by American artists in the world. It has the only zoo accredited by the American Zoo and Aquarium Association on the coast of the Carolinas. Within its more than 9,000 acres are the Lowcountry History and Wildlife Preserve, the Huntington Sculpture Garden, and the Center for American Sculpture.

The Center for American Sculpture was created at Brookgreen Gardens in 2001 to consolidate the Kenan Master Sculptor program, Master Sculptor Classes, workshops, and lectures. In 2003, the Carroll A. Campbell, Jr. Center for American Sculpture opened, providing a venue for these activities, including a spacious studio, library and archives, and staff offices.

Call of the Sea by Harriet Frishmuth

Sculpture Workshops

Two Kids by Oronzio Maldarelli

Modeling the Cat with Carter Jones: Students will learn cat anatomy and bone to muscle kinetics in order to create feline sculptures. March 17–19, $450 plus supplies; beginners to intermediates.

Moldmaking with Fred Brownstein: This course is designed to teach students how to transfer their clay models to more permanent materials. March 27–31, $650 plus supplies; beginners.

Sculpture, Composition, and Relief with Stanley Bleifeld: Students will learn how to use the elements of design. April 24–28, $650 plus supplies and model fee; beginners to intermediates.

Human Anatomy for Sculptors and Painters with David Klass: Students will learn to construct anatomical figures. Klass's three dimensional approach is an effective method for understanding and learning anatomy. May 15–20, $700 plus supplies and model fee; beginners.

Sculpting the Portrait Bust with Anthony Antonios: A model will be used in the workshop. August 21–25, $650 plus supplies and model fee; beginners to intermediates.

Figure Sculpture in Wax for Bronze with Jack Kreutzer: Small reliefs will be created in wax. For an additional fee, the instructor can take the sculptures to Colorado to be cast and shipped back to students. September 25–29, $650 plus supplies and model fee; beginners to intermediates.

Head Portraiture with Leonda Finke: Students will learn to make head portraitures. October 23–27, $650 plus supplies and model fee; intermediates.

Figure 8.6 Sample Cover and Two Inner Pages from a Brochure

Brochure created by Ronald D. Carter, Suzanna Jackson, and R. Taylor Bunn, Francis Marion University. Reprinted by permission of the authors, Brookgreen Gardens, Lynn Hanson, Louise Peterson, and Richard Blake.

9

WRITING PORTFOLIOS

A portfolio is a collection of a writer's work. There are two key types of portfolios:

- *Process portfolio.* This portfolio type includes a series of rough drafts and final papers that are arranged chronologically to illustrate the growth of a writer's skills.

- *Presentation portfolio.* Presentation portfolios showcase a writer's best work. Writers may be asked to submit these portfolios for course or program evaluation. Sometimes job applicants also compile presentation portfolios that include an introductory statement, a résumé, and samples of their best work. Presentation portfolios are particularly helpful for graduating students who hope to impress prospective employers with their writing and design skills.

Portfolios are either done in print or electronically (as *e-portfolios*). Whether print or electronic, portfolios often contain images, color, and special fonts that illustrate the personality of a writer (see Chapter 6).

Review and Revision

In putting together your portfolio, you have the chance to revise your work. Consider the following questions as you review each paper:

- Does the overall message of your paper need to be expanded or narrowed?

- How can your thesis statement be stated more clearly and specifically?

- How can you make your introductory paragraph(s) more appealing?

- How can you improve on the logical connections in your argument?

- Would additional research help you support your claims? If so, what kinds of evidence would help you to back your thesis more effectively?

- Would reorganization make your argument more persuasive?

- Can you adjust your tone to appeal to your audience more effectively?

- Which word choices might communicate your message better?

Follow your revision process by editing and proofreading your work.

Reflection

Both types of portfolios typically include *reflective statements* or a *reflective essay* that explains choices made in the drafting and revision process as well as the significance of each work. For a *process portfolio,* consider the following questions as you reflect on your papers:

- Why did you choose to write on the selected topic(s)?

- How did you define your audience?

- Why did you take the position(s) you chose in your paper(s)?

- Which areas of writing did you struggle with? What steps did you take to tackle your difficulties?

- How do you think the selected papers demonstrate the growth and improvement of your writing skills? (This is especially important.)

Also explain the choices you made in the revision process between your first and final draft(s):

- Include details about why you changed your thesis statement, content, paragraph order, or other features of your paper(s). How do those changes help communicate your ideas more effectively?

- Discuss any additions or omissions. How do these changes improve your paper(s)?

- Reflect on strategies for improving your introduction, topic sentences, conclusion, tone, and/or word choices. Why do you believe these changes make your paper(s) stronger?

- Explain any changes in researched material. How does the addition of new material help you prove your argument(s) more effectively?

If you are constructing a *presentation portfolio,* consider the following questions as you write your reflective essay:

- Why did you choose to include these particular documents?

- What writing or other skills do they demonstrate?

- What growth or change in your abilities do they reveal?

- What do they show about how well you have achieved the goals of the course or goals you set for your professional development?

Arrangement

The arrangement of your portfolio should reinforce your purpose. In assembling a process portfolio, arrange documents chronologically. In assembling a presentation portfolio, you can decide on the best organizational strategy. A *thematic arrangement* can help you to show connections among topics. Arranging texts by type or *genre* can help you to show your range of skills. A *chronological arrangement* highlights the progression of a project or course of study. The title you create for your portfolio helps your reader see thematic connections between works, and showcases who you are as a writer.

Design and Construction

Print version   When you assemble a print portfolio, create a cover page that has the title of the portfolio, your name, and other information your instructor asks for. On the cover page, you can also include color, decorative fonts, photographs, and other images that relate to the theme and tone of your work in the portfolio. But try not to include so many of these choices that the page looks cluttered. White space is also part of your design and gives the page a clean, contemporary look. Also include a matching table of contents page that lists all the works in the portfolio and the page numbers where they are. (See a sample table of contents page in Figure 9.1.)

Your readers will appreciate your writing more when the design and format choices are appealing and effective. You'll also want design elements to be appropriate for the topics and themes of the documents in the portfolio. You may want photographs and other images to add more interest to your writing. And readable fonts help your readers follow along with ease. You can also add splashes of color to highlight paper titles or key points that make you stand out as a writer.

E-portfolio   E-portfolios require special attention to planning, design, and presentation. They can be created simply, using word-processing software, or they can be developed using more sophisticated Web-authoring software. (Your school might use portfolio software that helps you arrange and display your work.)

The Internet has made us all aware of how important visual presentation is and how fluid it can be. So it's important for anyone creating an electronic portfolio to think about the visual aspects of the pages, and that includes the design elements that are chosen. Consider all the factors for which you have to make choices: format, design, color, fonts, and joining images with text. As you choose each of these, think about how they relate to each other and how they work together to enhance the themes of your portfolio. And most important, think about how all these choices will help your reader to create an impression of you, the writer.

To construct an e-portfolio, collect the electronic files for all of your work, as well as any other material you wish to include, such as digital photographs and other images, background textures, sound clips, and video. It is a good idea to back up these files on a storage device, such as a USB key or CD-ROM, to ensure the protection of your data as you work.

Designing a map of your navigational plan (see 6c) helps you consider how your e-portfolio pages could be most effectively connected together

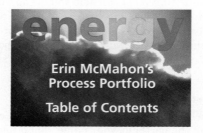

Erin McMahon's
Process Portfolio

Table of Contents

Figure 9.1 Table of Contents Page for a Print Portfolio
www.photos.com/Jupiter Images

so that the ordering is clear to your readers. Your map can also help you see where you need to insert hyperlinks to pages within your e-portfolio as well as add links to outside Web sites. It can also help you plan where to insert images files, sound files, or other media.

Creating your portfolio's home page is both fun and an important part of developing an e-portfolio. Think of your home page as the handshake with which you greet your readers and set the tone for their interaction with you. What type of design best reflects your personality and your purpose?

10

COMMA SPLICES
AND FUSED SENTENCES

A **comma splice** and a **fused sentence** (also called a **run-on sentence**) are punctuation problems in compound sentences. (See 30b2 on compound sentences.) There are three patterns for commas and semicolons in compound sentences:

1. Independent clause,   and   independent clause.
                        but
                        for
                        nor
                        or
                        so
                        yet

No one has registered for that class yet, **but** the deadline is approaching.

2. Independent clause;   independent clause.

Jamielle majored in American history; **he** is now a high school history teacher.

3. Independent clause;   however,   independent clause.
                        therefore,
                        moreover,
                        consequently,
                        (etc.)

Rami did agree to lend his computer to his roommate Matt; **however,** he clearly asked Matt to return it in an hour or two.

Commas in Compound Sentences

Use a comma when you join two independent clauses (clauses that would be sentences by themselves) with any of the following seven joining words:

and   but   for   nor   or   so   yet

The game was over, **but** the crowd refused to leave.

Some variations:

- If both independent clauses are very short, you may omit the comma.

  Lucinda may come or she may stay home.

■ Some people prefer to use a semicolon when one of the independent clauses already has a comma.

> Every Friday, depending on the weather, Sam plays tennis; but sometimes he can't find a partner.

Try This

TO REMEMBER THE SEVEN CONNECTORS THAT TAKE COMMAS

Think of FAN BOYS:

F: for **B:** but
A: and **O:** or
N: nor **Y:** yet
S: so

Hint

USING COMMAS WITH *AND*

Don't put commas before every *and* in your sentences. *And* is frequently used in ways that do not require commas.

Semicolons in Compound Sentences

If you use connecting words other than *and, but, for, nor, or, so,* or *yet,* or if you don't use any connecting words, you'll need a semicolon.

> The game was over; **however,** the crowd refused to leave.

> The game was over; the crowd refused to leave.

10a COMMA SPLICES

The **comma splice** is a punctuation error that can occur in one of two ways:

■ When independent clauses are joined only by a comma and no coordinating conjunction.

■ When a comma is used instead of a semicolon between two independent clauses.

> **Comma Splice:** In Econ 150, students meet in small groups for an extra hour
>
>   *and*
> each week, this helps them learn from each other.

Comma Splice: The doctor prescribed a different medication⸱/ however, it's

not helping.

10b FUSED OR RUN-ON SENTENCES

The **fused** or **run-on sentence** is a punctuation error that occurs when there is no punctuation between independent clauses. This causes the two clauses to be "fused" or "run on" into each other.

, and (or) ;

Fused or Run-On Sentence: I didn't know which job I wanted I

couldn't decide.

Try This

TO FIX COMMA SPLICES, FUSED SENTENCES, AND RUN-ONS

■ Add one of the seven joining words (*and, but, for, nor, or, so, yet*) preceded by a comma.

■ Separate the independent clauses into two sentences.

■ Change the comma to a semicolon. (See 10a.)

■ Make one clause dependent on the other clause. (See 17b and 20c.)

Exercise 10.1 Proofreading Practice

Some sentences in the following paragraph contain comma splices. Highlight or underline the sentences that contain this error, and place either a semicolon or the correct coordinating conjunction in the appropriate sentence.

(1) Office gossip no longer takes place at the water cooler. (2) Companies that are online have a better way to relay gossip, e-mail is the medium. (3) Some court cases have made corporate executives rethink policies on transmitting e-mail and destroying old messages. (4) Seemingly harmless conversations between colleagues have been retrieved, this information has been used in sexual harassment cases and other lawsuits. (5) A single employee can store thousands of pages of e-mail messages, however, the mail is not censored or monitored. (6) Consequently, companies are eager for systems that review and spot-check e-mail. (7) Company executives are employing programs that censor e-mail and block messages containing inappropriate material, this monitoring prevents embarrassing situations. (8) CEOs understand that Big Brother has a better view since employees began hitting the Send button.

Exercise 10.2 Pattern Practice

Combine some of the short sentences listed (and change a few words if you need to) so that you have five compound sentences that follow the pattern shown here. Be sure to punctuate correctly with a comma.

Independent clause, | and | independent clause.
but
for
nor
or
so
yet

There are many varieties of chocolate.

All varieties come from the same bean.

All varieties are the product of fermentation.

Once fermented, beans must be dried before being packed for shipping.

Chocolate pods cannot be gathered when they are underripe or overripe.

Chocolate pods are usually harvested very carefully by hand.

In the processing different varieties of chocolate are produced.

Dutch chocolate has the cocoa butter pressed out and alkali added.

Swiss chocolate has milk added.

Conching is the process of rolling chocolate over and over against itself.

Conching influences the flavor of chocolate.

Chocolate is loved by millions of people all over the world.

Some people are allergic to chocolate.

11

SUBJECT-VERB AGREEMENT

Subject-verb agreement occurs when the subject and verb (or helping verb) endings agree in number and person.

11a SINGULAR AND PLURAL SUBJECTS

The subject of every sentence is either singular or plural, and that determines the ending of the verb (or helping verb).

1. Singular

Singular nouns, pronouns, and nouns that cannot be counted, such as *news, time,* and *happiness* (see Chapter 55), take verbs with singular endings.

I chew.   Water drips.   Time flies.   You laugh.   The news is dull.

2. Plural

Plural nouns and pronouns take verbs with plural endings.

We know.   The cups are clean.   They stretch.   The stamps stick.

11b BURIED SUBJECTS

It is sometimes difficult to find the subject word when it is buried among many other words. In that case, disregard prepositional phrases; modifiers; *who, which,* and *that* clauses; and other surrounding words.

Almost **all** of Metha's many friends who are invited to her party **are bringing**
   (SUBJECT)   (VERB)
gifts.

[In this sentence, *Almost* is a modifier, *of Metha's many friends* is a prepositional phrase, and *who are invited to her party* is a *who* clause that describes *friends.*]

Try This

TO FIND THE SUBJECT AND VERB

1. It's easier to find the verb first because the verb is the word or words that change when you change the time of the sentence, from present to past or past to present.

Jaime **walks** to class.
(VERB—PRESENT TENSE)

Yesterday, Jaime **walked** to class.
            (VERB—PAST TENSE)

Tomorrow, Jaime **will walk** to class.
            (VERB—FUTURE TENSE)

▶

2. Eliminate phrases starting with the following words because they are normally not part of the subject:

including	along with	together with
accompanied by	in addition to	as well as
except	with	no less than

Everyone in our family, including my sister, **has taken** piano lessons.
(SUBJECT)   (VERB)

11c COMPOUND SUBJECTS

Subjects joined by *and* take a plural verb (X *and* Y = more than one, plural).

The (dog) and the (squirrel) are running around the tree.

The (company) and its (subsidiary) manufacture auto parts.

Sometimes, though, the words joined by *and* act together as a unit and are thought of as one thing. If so, use a singular verb.

(Peanut butter and jelly) is a popular filling for sandwiches.

11d OR AND EITHER/OR IN SUBJECTS

When the subject words are joined by *or, either . . . or, neither . . . nor,* or *not only . . . but also,* the verb agrees with the subject word closer to it.

Gang **colors** or dyed (hair) is not allowed in that school.

Either **Aleeza** or her (children) are going to bed early.

Neither the **actors** nor the (director) is ready for the performance.

Not only the **clouds** but also the (snow) was gray that day.

11e CLAUSES AND PHRASES AS SUBJECTS

When a whole clause or phrase is the subject, use a singular verb.

(What I want to know) is why I can't try the test again.

(Saving money) is difficult to do.

(To live happily) seems like a worthwhile goal.

However, if the verb is a form of *be* and the noun afterward (the complement) is plural, the verb has to be plural.

What we saw <u>were</u> pictures of the experiment.   [What we saw = pictures]

11f INDEFINITES AS SUBJECTS

Indefinite words with singular meanings, such as *each, every,* and *any,* take a singular verb when they are the subject word or when they precede the subject word.

Each <u>has</u> her own preference.

Each book <u>is checked in</u> by the librarian.

However, when indefinite words such as *none, some, most,* or *all* are the subject, the number of the verb depends on the meaning of the subject.

Some of the book <u>is</u> difficult to follow.
[The subject of the sentence is a portion of the book and is therefore thought of as a single unit and has a singular verb.]

Some of us <u>are leaving</u> now.
[The subject of this sentence is several people and is therefore thought of as a plural subject with a plural verb.]

All she wants <u>is</u> to be left alone.

All my sweaters <u>are</u> in that drawer.

11g COLLECTIVE NOUNS AND AMOUNTS AS SUBJECTS

Collective nouns are nouns that refer to a group or a collection (such as *team, family, committee,* and *group*). When a collective noun is the subject and refers to the group acting as a whole or as a single unit, the verb is singular.

Our **family** <u>has</u> a new car.

In most cases, a collective noun refers to the group acting together as a unit, but occasionally the collective noun refers to members acting individually. In that case, the verb is plural.

The **committee** <u>are</u> unhappy with each other's decisions.
[The subject here is thought of as different people, not a single unit.]

When the subject names an amount, the verb is singular.

Twenty-five **cents** is cheap.   Four **bushels** is enough.
More than 125 **miles** is too far.   Six **dollars** is the price.

11h PLURAL WORDS AS SUBJECTS

Some words that have an -s plural ending, such as *civics, mathematics, measles, news,* and *economics,* are thought of as a single unit and take a singular verb.

Physics is fascinating.   The **news** is disheartening.

Measles is unpleasant.   Modern **economics** shows contradictions.

Some words, such as those in the following list, are treated as plural and take a plural verb, even though they refer to one thing. (In many cases, there are two parts to these things.)

Designer **jeans** are fashionable.   **Eyeglasses** are inexpensive.

Pants cover his tan.   **Shears** cut cloth.

Scissors cut paper.   **Thanks** are not necessary.

Clippers trim hedges.   **Riches** are his dream.

11i TITLES, COMPANY NAMES, WORDS, AND QUOTATIONS AS SUBJECTS

For titles of written works, names of companies, words used as terms, and quotations, use singular verbs.

All the King's Men is the book assigned for this week.

General Foods is hiring people for its new plant.

Thanks is not in his vocabulary.

"Cookies for everyone!" is what she said.

11j LINKING VERBS

Linking verbs agree with the subject rather than the word that follows (the complement).

Her **problem** is frequent injuries.

Short **stories** are my favorite reading matter.

11k   *THERE (IS/ARE), HERE (IS/ARE),* AND *IT*

When a sentence begins with *there* or *here,* the verb depends on the complement that follows the verb.

There is an excellent old movie on TV tonight.

There are too many old movies on TV.

Here is the sun.

Here are my friends.

However, *it* as the subject always takes the singular verb, regardless of what follows.

It was bears in the park that knocked over the garbage cans.

11l   *WHO, WHICH, THAT,* AND *ONE OF* AS SUBJECTS

When *who, which,* and *that* are used as subjects, the verb agrees with the previous word it refers to (the antecedent).

They are the students **who** study hard.

He is the student **who** studies the hardest.

In the phrase *one of those who* (or *which* or *that*), it is necessary to decide whether the *who, which,* or *that* refers only to the one or to the whole group. Only then can you decide whether the verb is singular or plural.

Renata is **one of** those shoppers **who** buy only things that are on sale.

[In this case, Renata is part of a large group, shoppers who buy only things that are on sale, and acts like others in that group. Therefore, *who* takes a plural verb because it refers to *shoppers.*]

The *American Dictionary* is **one of** the dictionaries on the shelf **that** includes Latin words.

[In this case, the *American Dictionary,* while part of the group of dictionaries on the shelf, is specifically one that includes Latin words. The other dictionaries may or may not. Therefore, *that* refers to that *one* dictionary and takes a singular verb.]

Exercise 11.1 Proofreading Practice

In the following paragraph, choose the verb that agrees with the subject.

How children's drawings develop (1. is, are) a fascinating subject. For example, a two-year-old and sometimes even a three-year-old (2. does not, do not) create any recognizable forms when scribbling, and most of the children recently studied by a child psychologist (3. seem, seems) not to be aware of the notion that a line stands for the edge of an object. Typically, by the age of three, children's spontaneous scribbles along with their attempts at drawing a picture (4. become, becomes) more obviously pictorial. When a child has drawn a recognizable shape, either the child or some nearby adult (5. attempt, attempts) to label the shape with a name. By the age of three or four, there (6. is, are) attempts to draw images of a human, images that look like a tadpole and consist of a circle and two lines for legs. Psychologists, especially those who (7. study, studies) the development of people's concepts of reality, (8. conclude, concludes) that young children's tadpolelike drawings (9. is, are) a result of inadequate recall of what people look like. However, Layton Peale is one of a number of psychologists who (10. insist, insists) that young children do have adequate recall but (11. isn't, aren't) interested in realism because they prefer simplicity. Once the desire for realism (12. begin, begins), it leads to the more complex drawings done by older children.

Exercise 11.2 Pattern Practice

Write two sentences of your own modeled after each of the following patterns of correct subject-verb agreement.

Pattern A: Compound subject joined by *and* with a plural verb

The whole flower exhibit and each display in it were carefully planned for months.

Pattern B: An amount as a subject with a singular verb

Ten dollars is a small price to pay for that.

Pattern C: A title, company name, word, or quotation with a singular verb

The Mysteries of the Universe was an educational TV series.

Pattern D: An item that is a single unit but is thought of as plural (such as pants, scissors, and jeans) with a plural verb

The scissors need sharpening.

Pattern E: Plural words (such as *physics, economics,* and *measles*) with a singular verb

The news of the election results is being broadcast live from the election board office.

Pattern F: *Or, either . . . or, neither . . . nor,* or *not only . . . but also*
with a verb that agrees with the nearest subject

Either Avi or his friends are capable of handling that job.

Pattern G: A whole clause as the subject with a singular verb

Whatever the finance committee decides to do about the subject is acceptable to the rest of us.

Pattern H: A *who, what,* or *that* clause with a verb that agrees with the correct antecedent

Psycho is one of those movies that shock us no matter how many times we see them.

12
SENTENCE FRAGMENTS

A **sentence fragment** is an incomplete sentence.

To recognize a fragment, consider the basic requirements of a sentence:

- A sentence is a group of words with at least one independent clause (see 28a).

After buying some useful software for her computer, Nurit splurged on
several computer games to play   (INDEPENDENT CLAUSE).

- A clause has at least one subject and a complete verb, plus an object or complement if needed. (See 11j and Chapter 22.)

During the evening, the mosquitoes avoided the campfire.
                         (SUBJECT)   (VERB)   (OBJECT)

12a   UNINTENTIONAL FRAGMENTS

Fragment Without a Subject or Verb

One type of fragment lacks a subject or a verb.

Fragment: The week spent on the beach just relaxing and soaking up the sun.

[*Week* is probably the intended subject here, but it has no verb.]

Revised: The week spent on the beach just relaxing and soaking up the sun
        (SUBJECT)

was the best vacation I had in years.
(VERB)

Fragment: She selected a current news item as the topic of her essay. Then wondered if her choice was wise.

[The second of these two word groups is a fragment because it has no subject for the verb *wondered*.]

Revised: She selected a current news item as the topic of her essay. Then <u>she</u> <u>wondered</u> whether her choice was wise.
(SUBJECT)   (VERB)

Try This

TO FIND FRAGMENTS

1. Be sure that each word group has both a subject and a complete verb. Remember that -*ing* words are not complete verbs because they need a helping verb. (See 21b.)

2. Make up a *who* or *what* question about the sentence. The predicate is all the words from the sentence used in the *who* or *what* question, and the subject is the rest.

   My grandmother lived in a house built by her father.

   [Who lived in a house built by her father?]

   Predicate: lived in a house built by her father

   Subject: My grandmother

3. Try thinking of a sentence as a group of words that you could say to someone and then walk away, knowing you've made a statement that is complete. For example, you could say, "The manual's instructions were not clear." Your listeners would hear a statement. But if you said, "Because the manual's instructions were not clear," your listener would be waiting for the rest of the idea. So? What happened because the manual's instructions were unclear?

4. Consider whether or not you've written a dependent clause (see 28b) and put a period at the end of the clause even though it is a fragment. Think of a dependent clause as one part of a two-part pattern. That pattern can start with a marker word for adverbial dependent clauses (see 28b) or can be in reverse order: If A, → B, or in reverse order, B → if A.

   <u>Because the instructions were not clear, I couldn't install the wiring.</u>
         (BECAUSE A,)   →   (B)

5. Read the sentence out loud. If it goes on for so long that you lose the thread, you might have a fragment.

▶

Fragment: The planning team, which met to see whether or not there
(SUBJECT)
would be enough funds to carry out a five-year project aimed at cleaning up the polluted waterway overloaded with fertilizer runoff caused by the heavy rains that resulted in floods every spring.

[There is no complete verb for the subject planning team. What did the planning team do?]

Fragment Caused by a Misplaced Period

Most fragments are caused by detaching a phrase or dependent clause from the sentence to which it belongs. A period has been put in the wrong place, often because the writer thinks a sentence has gotten too long and needs a period. Such fragments can be corrected by removing the period between the independent clause and the fragment.

Ever since fifth grade, I have participated in one or more team sports./

beginning
~~Beginning~~ with the typical grammar school sports of basketball and volleyball.

[The second word group is a detached phrase that belongs to the sentence preceding it.]

Travelers to Europe should consider visiting in the spring or fall./

because
~~Because~~ airfares and hotels are often cheaper then.

[The second word group is a dependent clause that was detached from the sentence before it.]

Hint

FINDING FRAGMENTS

1. Read your paper backward, from the last sentence to the first. You will be able to notice a fragment more easily when you hear it without the sentence to which it belongs.

2. To find dependent clauses separated from the main clause, look for the marker word. (See 28b.) If the clause is standing alone, attach it to the independent clause that completes the meaning.

Fragment: Denise had breakfast at the doughnut shop near Hafter

after
Hall./ ~~After~~ she went to her 8 a.m. biology class.

▶

3. To identify a dependent clause incorrectly punctuated as a sentence, ask yourself whether it answers a yes/no question. If it doesn't, it's likely a fragment.

They often spend Sunday afternoons watching football games on TV.

[Do they often spend Sunday afternoons watching football games on TV? This question yields a yes/no answer, so the statement is an independent clause.]
Because they often spend Sunday afternoons watching football games on TV.

[Do because they often spend Sunday afternoons watching football games on TV? This is not a reasonable question, so the statement is not an independent clause and cannot stand as a sentence.]

12b INTENTIONAL FRAGMENTS

Writers occasionally write an intentional fragment for its effect on the reader. Intended fragments should be used only when the rest of the writing clearly indicates that the writer could have written a whole sentence but preferred a fragment. In the following three sentences, the second word group is an intended fragment. Do you like the effect it produces?

Fragment: Dilek walked quietly into the room, unnoticed by the rest of the group. *Not that she wanted it that way.* She simply didn't know how to make an effective entrance.

Exercise 12.1 Proofreading Practice

These paragraphs contain both complete sentences and fragments. Read through the passage, and highlight or underline the fragments.

(1) If you've ever doubted your child's identity, advanced technology makes it easy and affordable to set your mind at ease. (2) DNA testing, a procedure that determines genetic relationships, is now available to the average person. (3) For a fee of around $500. (4) Previously, DNA testing was used in criminal cases and in custody disputes involving celebrities. (5) When large sums of money were at stake. (6) Now the average person can find out if a child is in fact his or her biological offspring.

(7) The procedure is fast and easy. (8) The parent and child need to provide a sample from the inside of the cheek. (9) With a cotton swab collecting the tissue that is needed. (10) The sample is then sent to the lab, and an answer can be obtained within ten days. (11) In some areas, the sample can be sent through the mail. (12) Instead of being given at the lab.

(13) Advanced technology requires responsibility and caution. (14) Especially when a family's happiness is at stake. (15) Many people feel that

DNA testing has caused the breakdown of otherwise happy families. (16) Ethical issues involved in the testing. (17) Doctors have been urging labs that offer the testing to encourage counseling for the people involved. (18) Discovering that your child is not your own is a very complex issue. (19) And not a matter to be taken lightly.

Exercise 12.2 Pattern Practice

Read the following paragraph, and note the pattern of dependent and independent clauses (see Chapter 28) in each sentence. Practice by following those patterns to write your own sentences, and check to see that you haven't written any fragments. As a guide to help you, one sentence has been done. For your own sentences, you may wish to write about another modern convenience.

Pattern: Independent clause + dependent clause.

Sample Sentence: Those hot air dryers in public restrooms are a nuisance because it's impossible to dry your face without messing up your hair.

(1) The communications industry has made billions of dollars because Americans love instant gratification. (2) The average American can be heard talking on a cellular phone in the oddest of places, including the stall of a public restroom. (3) A high school student carries a cellular phone, and her most noticeable fashion accessory is a headset. (4) When a friend calls another friend, she may be subjected to "call waiting" and put on hold. (5) The telephone company offers instant-gratification services such as call forwarding, conference calling, and voice mail. (6) Because many people have become distracted while talking and driving, law enforcement agents have given more tickets related to cell phone use in the past year than in the previous three years combined.

13

DANGLING AND MISPLACED MODIFIERS

13a DANGLING MODIFIERS

A **dangling modifier** is a word or word group that refers to (or modifies) a word or phrase that has not been clearly stated in the sentence. When an introductory phrase does not name the doer of the action, the phrase then refers to (or modifies) the subject of the independent clause that follows.

Having finished the assignment, Jillian turned on the TV.

[*Jillian,* the subject of the independent clause, is the doer of the action in the introductory phrase.]

However, when the intended subject (or doer of the action) of the introductory phrase is not stated, the result is a dangling modifier.

Having finished the assignment, the TV was turned on.

[This sentence says that the TV finished the homework. Since it is unlikely that TV sets can get our work done, the introductory phrase has no logical or appropriate word to refer to. Sentences with dangling modifiers say one thing while the writer means another.]

Characteristics of Dangling Modifiers

■ They most frequently occur at the beginning of sentences but can also appear at the end.

■ They often have an *-ing* verb or a *to* + verb phrase near the start of the whole phrase.

Dangling Modifier: After getting a degree in education, more experience in

the classroom is needed to be a good teacher.

Revised: After getting a degree in education, Lu needed more experience in

the classroom to be a good teacher.

Dangling Modifier: To work as a lifeguard, practice in CPR is required.

Revised: To work as a lifeguard, you are required to have practice in CPR.

Try This

TO REVISE DANGLING MODIFIERS

1. Name the doer of the action in the dangling phrase.

▶

Dangling Modifier: Without <u>knowing</u> the guest's name, it was difficult for Marina to introduce him to her husband.

Revised: Because Marina did not <u>know</u> the guest's name, it was difficult to introduce him to her husband.

2. Name the appropriate or logical doer of the action as the subject of the independent clause.

Dangling Modifier: <u>Having arrived</u> late for practice, a written excuse was needed.

Revised: <u>Having arrived</u> late for practice, the team member needed a written excuse.

Exercise 13.1 Proofreading Practice

The following paragraph contains several dangling modifiers. Identify them by highlighting or underlining them.

(1) According to some anthropologists, the fastball may be millions of years older than the beginning of baseball. (2) To prove this point, prehistoric tool-making sites, such as Olduvai Gorge in Tanzania, are offered as evidence. (3) These sites are littered with smooth, roundish stones not suitable for flaking into tools. (4) Suspecting that the stones might have been used as weapons, anthropologists have speculated that these stones were thrown at enemies and animals being hunted. (5) Searching for other evidence, historical accounts of primitive peoples have been combed for stories of rock throwing. (6) Here early adventurers are described as being caught by rocks thrown hard and fast. (7) Used in combat, museums have collections of these "handstones." (8) So stone throwing may have been a major form of defense and a tool for hunting. (9) Being an impulse that still has to be curbed, parents still find themselves teaching their children not to throw stones.

Exercise 13.2 Pattern Practice

Using the patterns of the sample sentences given here in which the modifiers do not dangle, write your own sentences. One sentence is given as an example.

Pattern: After realizing there were no familiar faces at the party, Josh returned home to watch television.

Sample Sentence: While cleaning the house, Kristina looked for her lost ring.

1. To finish the New York City Marathon, runners must train on a daily basis.
2. Unlike high school, college offers independence and freedom.
3. Rather than fail the test, Carla decided to stay home and study.
4. They had a great party, having plenty of food and good music.

13b MISPLACED MODIFIERS

A **misplaced modifier** is a word or word group placed so far away from what it refers to (or modifies) that readers may be confused. Modifiers should be placed as closely as possible to the words they modify in order to keep the meaning clear.

Misplaced Modifiers: The assembly line workers were told that they had been fired by the personnel director.

[Were the workers told by the personnel director that they had been fired, or were they told by someone else that the personnel director had fired them?]

Revised: The assembly line workers were told by the personnel director that they had been fired.

Misplaced modifiers are often the source of comedians' humor, as in this classic used by Groucho Marx:

The other day I shot an elephant in my pajamas. How he got in my pajamas I'll never know.

Single-word modifiers should be placed immediately before the words they modify. Note the difference in meaning in these two sentences:

I earned nearly $30.

[The amount was almost $30 but not quite.]

I nearly earned $30.

[I almost had the opportunity to earn $30, but it didn't work out.]

Try This

TO AVOID MISPLACED MODIFIERS

When you proofread, check these words to be sure they are as close as possible to the words they refer to.

almost	hardly	merely	only
even	just	nearly	simply

Exercise 13.3 Proofreading Practice

Some of these sentences contain misplaced modifiers and unclear modifiers. Underline each misplaced modifier and draw an arrow to the more appropriate location.

After finishing a huge dinner, he only ate a few cherries for dessert.

(1) The man who was carrying the sack of groceries with an umbrella walked carefully to his car. (2) He only bought a small amount of food for his lunch because he was going to leave town that afternoon. (3) He whistled to his huge black dog opening the car door and set the groceries in the trunk. (4) The dog jumped into the trunk happily with the groceries.

Exercise 13.4 Pattern Practice

Choose one of the one-word modifiers listed in the preceding "Try This" box, and use the word in several places in a series of sentences to create different meanings. Write out the meaning of each sentence.

Here is an example using the word *almost:*

Almost everyone in the office earned a $500 bonus last year.
[Most of the people earned a $500 bonus, but a few people did not.]

Everyone in the office **almost** earned a $500 bonus last year.
[There was a chance to earn a bonus, but it didn't work out. Therefore, no one earned a bonus.]

Everyone in the office earned **almost** a $500 bonus last year.
[Everyone earned a bonus, but it was less than $500.]

14

PARALLEL CONSTRUCTIONS

14a PARALLEL STRUCTURE

Parallel structure involves using the same grammatical form or structure for equal ideas in a list or comparison. The balance of equal elements in a sentence helps show the relationship between ideas. Often the equal elements repeat words or sounds.

Parallel: The instructor carefully explained how to start the engine and

(1)

how to shift gears.

(2)

[1 and 2 are parallel phrases in that both start with *how to:* how to start the engine; how to shift gears.]

Parallel: <u>Getting the model airplane off the ground</u> was even harder than
(1)

<u>building it from a kit</u>.
(2)

[1 and 2 are parallel phrases that begin with -*ing* verb forms: <u>Getting
the model airplane off the ground</u>; <u>building</u> it from a kit.]

Parallel: She often went to the aquarium <u>to watch the fish</u>, <u>to enjoy the</u>
(1)

<u>solitude</u>, and <u>to escape from her roommate</u>.
(2)   (3)

[1, 2, and 3 are parallel phrases that begin with *to* + verb.]

Parallelism is needed in the following constructions:

■ Items in a series or list

Parallel: Items often overlooked when camping include

    1. All <u>medications</u> normally taken on a daily basis

    2. <u>Books</u> to read during leisure time

    3. <u>Quinine</u> tablets to purify water

[parallelism with a series of nouns in a list]

Parallel: The three most important skills for that job are

    1. <u>Being</u> able to adapt to new requirements

    2. <u>Knowing</u> appropriate computer languages

    3. <u>Keeping</u> lines of communication open

[parallelism with -*ing* verbs]

■ *Both . . . and, either . . . or, whether . . . or, neither . . . nor, not . . . but,
not only . . . but also* (correlative conjunctions)

Parallel: Both <u>by the way</u> he dressed **and** <u>by his attempts</u> at humor, it was
clear that he wanted to make a good impression.

[parallelism with *by the . . .* phrases]

■ *And, but, or, nor, yet, for, so* (coordinating conjunctions)

Parallel: Job opportunities are <u>increasing</u> in the health fields **but** <u>decreasing</u>
in many areas of engineering.

[parallelism using -*ing* verbs]

■ Comparisons using *than* or *as*

Parallel: The mayor noted that it was easier <u>to agree</u> to the new budget **than**
<u>to attempt</u> to veto it.

[parallelism in a comparison with *to* + verb]

14b FAULTY PARALLELISM

Nonparallel structure (or **faulty parallelism**) occurs when like items are not in the same grammatical form or structure.

Many companies are <u>reducing</u> their labor force as well as ~~eliminate~~ *eliminating* some
          (1)   (2)
employee benefits.

When the investigator took over, he started his inquiry by <u>calling</u> the
                                                        (1)
witnesses back and ~~requested~~ *requesting* that they repeat their stories.
                              (2)

The article looked at <u>future uses of computers</u> and <u>~~what~~ their role ~~will be~~</u>
                                   (1)   (2)
in the next decade.

Try This

TO PROOFREAD FOR PARALLEL STRUCTURE

1. As you proofread, **listen** to the sound when you are linking or comparing similar elements. Do they balance by sounding alike? Parallelism often adds emphasis by the repetition of similar sounds.
2. As you proofread, **visualize** similar elements in a list. Check to see that the elements begin in the same way.

Not Parallel: Isaiah wondered <u>whether to tell</u> his girlfriend that he forgot or <u>if he should make up</u> some excuse.

Revised: Isaiah wondered whether <u>to tell</u> his girlfriend that he forgot or <u>to make up</u> some excuse.

Revised: Isaiah wondered <u>if he should tell</u> his girlfriend that he forgot or <u>if he should make up</u> some excuse.

Exercise 14.1 Proofreading Practice

Highlight or underline the parallel elements in each sentence in this paragraph.

One of the great American cars was the J-series Duesenberg. The car was created by Fred and August Duesenberg, two brothers from Iowa who began by making bicycles and who then gained fame by building racing cars. Determined to build an American car that would earn respect for its excellent quality and its high performance, the Duesenbergs completed the first Model J in 1928. The car was an awesome machine described as having a 265-horsepower engine and a top speed of 120 mph. Special features of the car were its four-wheel hydraulic brakes and extensive numbers of lightweight aluminum castings. The masterpiece was the Duesenberg SJ, reputed to have a 320-horsepower engine and to accelerate from zero to 100 mph in 17 seconds.

Exercise 14.2 Pattern Practice

Write your own sentences using the same patterns for parallel structures as those in the examples below. You may want to write about some favorite vehicle of your own, such as a car or bike.

1. A common practice among early Duesenberg owners was to buy a bare chassis and to ship it to a coach builder, who would turn the chassis into a dazzling roadster, cabriolet, or dual-cowl phaeton.
2. Duesenbergs that were originally purchased for $6,000 or so and are now being auctioned off for more than $1 million are still considered superb examples of engineering brilliance.
3. After the Duesenberg first appeared on the market and people realized its excellence, the phrase "It's a doozy" became part of American slang.

15
CONSISTENCY (AVOIDING SHIFTS)

Consistency in writing involves using the same (1) pronoun person and number, (2) verb tense, (3) tone, (4) voice, and (5) indirect or direct form of discourse.

15a SHIFTS IN PERSON OR NUMBER

Avoid shifts between first, second, and third person pronouns and between singular and plural. The following table shows the three persons in English pronouns:

PRONOUN PERSON		
	Singular	**Plural**
First person		
(the person or persons speaking)	I, me	we, us
Second person		
(the person or persons spoken to)	you	you
Third person		
(the person or persons spoken about)	he, she, it, him, her, it	they, them

Some readers consider first or second person writing as too personal or informal and suggest that writers use third person for formal or academic writing. Second person, however, is appropriate for giving instructions or helping readers follow a process.

First, (you) open the hood of the car and check the water level in the battery.

[The pronoun *you* can be used or omitted.]

First person is appropriate for a narrative about your own actions and for essays that explore your personal feelings and emotions. Some teachers encourage writers to use first person to develop a sense of their own voice in writing.

1. Unnecessary Shift in Person

Once you have chosen to use first, second, or third person, shift only with a good reason.

In a person's life, the most important thing ~~you do~~ *he or she does* is to decide on
(THIRD) (SECOND)

a type of job.

[This is an unnecessary shift from third to second person.]

2. Unnecessary Shift in Number

To avoid pronoun inconsistency, don't shift unnecessarily in number from singular to plural (or from plural to singular).

Women can face
~~A woman faces~~ challenges to career advancement. When they take
(SING.) (PLUR.)

maternity leave, they should be sure that opportunities for promotion
(PLUR.)

are still available when they return to work.

[The writer uses the singular noun *woman* in the first sentence but then shifts to the plural pronoun *they* in the second sentence.]

15b SHIFTS IN VERB TENSE

Because verb tenses indicate time, keep writing in the same time (past, present, or future) unless the logic of what you are writing about requires a switch.

Narrative writing can be in the past or present, with time switching if needed. Explanatory writing (exposition) that expresses general truth is usually kept in present time, although history is written in past time.

Necessary Shift: Many people today <u>remember</u> very little about the Vietnam War except the filmed scenes of fighting they <u>watched</u> on television news at the time.

[The verb *remember* reports a general truth in the present, and the verb *watched* reports past events.]

Unnecessary Shift: While we <u>were watching</u> the last game of the World Series, the picture suddenly <u>breaks up</u>.

[The verb phrase *were watching* reports a past event, and there is no reason to shift to the present tense verb *breaks up*.]

Revised: While we <u>were watching</u> the last game of the World Series, the picture suddenly <u>broke up</u>.

15c SHIFTS IN TONE

Once you choose a formal or informal tone for a paper, keep that tone consistent in your word choices. A sudden intrusion of a very formal word or phrase in an informal narrative or the use of slang or informal words in a formal report or essay indicates the writer's loss of control over tone.

The job of the welfare worker is to assist in a family's struggle to obtain

children's
funds for the ~~kids'~~ food and clothing.
          ^

[The use of the informal word *kids'* is a shift in tone in this formal sentence.]

15d SHIFTS IN VOICE (ACTIVE/PASSIVE)

Don't shift unnecessarily between active and passive voice in a sentence. (See 21d for an explanation of active and passive verbs. For more on passive voice, see Chapter 34.)

Active: He <u>insisted</u> that he was able to perform the magic trick.

Passive: The magic trick <u>was not considered</u> difficult by him.

He <u>insisted</u> that he was able to perform the magic trick, which ~~was not~~ *he did not*

consider
~~considered~~ difficult ~~by him~~.

When choosing between passive and active, remember that many readers prefer active voice verbs because they are clearer, more direct, and more dramatic or lively. Also, the passive voice usually requires more words and can therefore drag out the writing unnecessarily. Compare the pairs of sentences here. In each pair which do you prefer? Why?

Passive: A resolution shall be made by us that a new birth of freedom shall be had by this nation, under God.

Active: [W]e here highly resolve that . . . this nation, under God, shall have a new birth of freedom.

[excerpt from Abraham Lincoln's *Gettysburg Address*]

Passive: How is it known by you when invisible ink has been used up by you?

Active: How do you know when you're out of invisible ink?

[quotation from Steven Wright]

The active voice also forces us to think about the doer of the action. For example, in the following sentence, the writer uses the passive voice rather than state who the doer is:

Many arguments are offered against building a fence along the Mexican/U.S. borders.

[By whom?]

However, there are occasions to use the passive:

■ When the doer of the action is not important or is not known

The pep rally <u>was held</u> before the game.

For the tournament game, more than five thousand tickets <u>were sold</u>.

■ When you want to focus on the action or the receiver of the action, not the doer

The records <u>were destroyed</u>.

Luisa <u>was chosen</u> to get the first prize.

■ When you want to avoid blaming, giving credit, or taking responsibility

The candidate conceded that the election <u>was lost</u>.

- When you want a tone of objectivity or wish to exclude yourself

The experiment was performed successfully.

It was noted that the results confirmed our hypothesis.

15e SHIFTS IN DISCOURSE

When you repeat someone's exact words, you are using **direct discourse,** and when you change a few of the words in order to report them indirectly, you are using **indirect discourse**.

Mixing direct and indirect discourse within sentences results in unnecessary shifting, a problem that causes lack of parallel structure as well.

Direct Discourse: The instructor said, "Your reports are due at the beginning of next week. Be sure to include your bibliography."

Indirect Discourse: The instructor said that our reports are due at the beginning of next week and that we should be sure to include our bibliographies.

Unnecessary Shift: The instructor said that our reports are due at the beginning of next week and be sure to include your bibliography.

[This sentence also mixes a statement and a command, two different moods. For more on mood, see 21e.]

Exercise 15.1 Proofreading Practice

As you read the following paragraph, proofread for consistency, and correct any unnecessary shifts. You may want to omit some words or phrases.

Many people think that recycling material is a recent trend. However, during World War II, more than 43 percent of America's newsprint was recycled, and the average person saved bacon grease and other meat fat, which they returned to local collection centers. What you would do is pour leftover fat and other greasy gunk from frying pans and pots into tin cans. Today, despite the fact that many people are recycling, less than half of Americans' waste is actually recycled. The problem is not to get us to save bottles and cans but to convince industry to use more recycled materials. There is a concern expressed by manufacturers that they would be using materials of uneven quality and will face undependable delivery. If the manufacturer would wake up and smell the coffee, they would see the advantages for the country and bigger profits could be made by them.

16

FAULTY PREDICATION

Faulty predication occurs when the subject and the rest of the clause (the *predicate*) don't make sense together.

> **Faulty Predicate:** The <u>reason</u> for her sudden success <u>proved</u> that she was talented.

[In this sentence, the subject, *reason,* cannot logically prove "that she was talented."]

> **Revised:** Her sudden success proved that she was talented.

Faulty predication often occurs with forms of the verb *be* because this verb sets up an equation in which the terms on either side of the verb should be equivalent.

Subject		Predicate
2 × 2	=	4
2 × 2	is	4
Dr. Streeter	is	our family doctor.

> **Faulty Predication:** Success is when you have your own swimming pool.

[The concept of success involves much more than having a swimming pool. Having a pool can be one example or a result of success, but it is not the equivalent of success.]

> **Revised:** One sign of success is having your own swimming pool.

Hint

AVOIDING FAULTY PREDICATION

Faulty predication often occurs in sentences that contain the following constructions:
  is when . . .   is why . . .   is where . . .   is because . . .
It is best to avoid these constructions in academic writing.

The reason I didn't show up is ~~because~~ *that* I overslept.

Exercise 16.1 Proofreading Practice

Rewrite the following examples of faulty predication so that they are correct sentences.

1. Relaxation is when you grab a bowl of popcorn, put your feet up, and watch football on television for two hours.

2. Computer science is where you learn how to program computers.

3. One of the most common ways to improve your math is when you get a tutor.

4. The next agenda item we want to look at is to find the cost of purchasing decorations.

5. His job consisted mainly of repetitious assembly line tasks.

Exercise 16.2 Pattern Practice

The patterns of the following five sentences avoid faulty predication. Practice these patterns by completing the second sentence in each set. Be sure to use the same pattern even though your subject matter will be different.

1. A good science fiction movie is one that has an exciting plot and amazing special effects.

   A good _____ is _____.

2. His job as a receptionist is to direct people to the right office.

   His job as a _____ is _____.

3. One sign of her excellent memory is her ability to remember the punch lines of all the jokes she hears.

   One sign of her _____ is _____.

4. The reason I didn't buy those boots is that they are overpriced.

   The reason _____ is that _____.

5. Stage fright is a kind of apprehension accompanied by a dry mouth, sweaty hands, and a fluttery stomach.

   _____ is _____.

17

COORDINATION AND SUBORDINATION

17a COORDINATION

When an independent clause is added to another independent clause to form a sentence, both clauses are described as **coordinate** because they are equally important and have the same emphasis.

1. Appropriate Coordination

Independent clauses are joined by coordinating words and appropriate punctuation (see Chapter 10, 28a, and 38a). Two types of words join co-ordinate clauses.

■ **Coordinating conjunctions** (the seven coordinating words used after a comma) are the following words:

and   but   for   nor   or   so   yet

■ **Conjunctive adverbs** (coordinating words used after a semicolon in a compound sentence) include the following words:

consequently	however	otherwise	thus
furthermore	moreover	therefore	nevertheless

The following sentences illustrate appropriate coordination because they join two clauses of equal importance and emphasis.

Ingeborg is doing well as a real estate broker, **and** she hopes to become wealthy before she is thirty-five.

Some people take vitamin C tablets for colds; **however,** other people prefer aspirin.

Hint

USING COMMAS WITH COORDINATING WORDS

The *coordinating conjunctions* listed above need commas before them when they join two independent clauses (see 28a and 38a). Some writers make the mistake of putting commas before these joining words whenever they appear in a sentence even if they don't join two independent clauses.

Unnecessary Comma: Economists debate the need for studying rising costs for entertainment/ and the growing practice of watching movies at home on DVDs.

Similarly, *conjunctive adverbs* take semicolons before them when they join independent clauses. They can also be used as adverbs, and they can be moved around in the sentence and don't need semicolons. If they are used as nonessential words (see 29b), they will need commas before and after them.

Necessary Commas: Waiting more than a week for merchandise to be de-livered, however, will cause some customers to cancel their orders.

2. Inappropriate Coordination

Inappropriate coordination occurs when two clauses that either are unequal in importance or have little or no connection with each other are joined together as independent clauses.

Inappropriate coordination can be corrected by making one clause depend on the other. However, if there is little connection between the clauses, they may not belong in the same sentence or paragraph.

Inappropriate Coordination: Winter in Texas can be very mild, and snow often falls in New England during the autumn.

[The connection between these two clauses is very weak; they don't belong together unless the writer can show more connection.]

Inappropriate Coordination: Brian was ill, and he went to the doctor.

Revised: Because Brian was ill, he went to the doctor.

[In this case, the first clause can be shown to depend on the second clause.]

3. Excessive Coordination

Excessive coordination occurs when too many equal clauses are strung together with coordinators. As a result, the sentence can ramble on and become tiresome or monotonous.

Excessive coordination can be corrected by breaking the sentence into smaller ones or by making the appropriate clauses into dependent ones.

Excessive Coordination: Kirsten is an exchange student from Sweden, and she is visiting the United States for the first time, so she decided to drive through the Southwest during her vacation.

Revised: Kirsten, an exchange student from Sweden visiting the United States for the first time, decided to drive through the Southwest during her vacation.

17b SUBORDINATION

When one clause has less emphasis or is less important in a sentence, it is **subordinate** to or dependent on the other clause.

1. Appropriate Subordination

Marker words that begin subordinate clauses show the relationship of the dependent or subordinate clause to the main clause. (See Chapters 17 and 28.) The following are some common marker words (called **subordinating conjunctions**):

after	before	though	whether
although	if	unless	which
as	once	until	while
as though	since	when	who
because	that	whereas	whose

Although I like snow, I enjoy Florida vacations in winter.

Mr. Papandrous, **who** never missed a football game, was one of the team's greatest supporters.

The house **that** she grew up in was torn down.

2. Inappropriate Subordination

Inappropriate subordination occurs when the more important clause is placed in the subordinate or dependent position and has less emphasis.

> **Inappropriate Subordination:** A career that combines a lot of interaction with people and opportunities to use my creative talents is my goal.

> **Revised:** My career goal is to combine a lot of interaction with people and opportunities to use my creative talents.

3. Excessive Subordination

Excessive subordination occurs when a sentence has a string of clauses subordinate to each other. As a result, readers have difficulty following the confusing chain of ideas that are dependent on each other.

To eliminate excessive subordination, place the string of dependent clauses in separate sentences with independent clauses.

> **Excessive Subordination:** These computer software companies should inform their employees about advancements and promotions with the company because they will lose them if they don't compete for their services since the employees can easily find jobs elsewhere.

> **Revised:** These computer software companies should inform their employees about advancements and promotions with the company. If these companies don't compete for the services of their employees, the companies will lose them because the employees can easily find jobs elsewhere.

Exercise 17.1 Proofreading Practice

Correct the sentences in the following paragraph that have inappropriate coordination and subordination.

(1) Most people think of pigs as providers of ham, bacon, and pork chops, and they think of pigs as dirty, smelly, lazy, stupid, mean, and stubborn, but there's more to pigs than this bad press they've had, so we should stop and reevaluate what we think of pigs. (2) President Harry Truman once said that no man should be allowed to be president who does not understand hogs because this lack of understanding indicates inadequate appreciation of a useful farm animal. (3) Some people are discovering that pigs make excellent pets. (4) In fact, pigs have been favorite characters in children's fiction, and many people fondly remember the cartoon character Porky Pig; Miss Piggy, the Muppet creation; and the heroic pig named

Wilbur in E. B. White's *Charlotte's Web.* (5) Now there are clubs for people who keep pigs as pets, and they are not just on farms where they have long been favorites as pets for farm children, who are likely to be fond of animals. (6) People with pigs as pets report that their pigs are curious, friendly little animals that are quite clean despite the "dirty as a pig" saying though they are not very athletic and have a sweet tooth. (7) Pigs can be interesting pets and are useful farm animals to raise.

Exercise 17.2 Pattern Practice

To practice using subordination and coordination appropriately, combine the following clauses using coordinating and subordinating words listed in this chapter.

Plastic used to be considered a cheap, shoddy material.

Plastic took the place of many materials.

Cars are made of plastic.

Boats, airplanes, cameras, fishing rods, watches, suitcases, toothpaste tubes, and plates are made of plastic.

Plastic replaced the glass in eyeglasses.

Plastic replaced the wood in tennis rackets.

Plastic replaced cotton and wool in our clothing.

Plastic seems new.

Plastic has been with us for a long time.

Celluloid is a nearly natural plastic.

Celluloid was developed in 1868 as a substitute for ivory in billiard balls.

Celluloid proved to be too flammable.

New types of plastic, such as glow-in-the-dark plastic, are mushrooming.

The use of plastics steadily increases.

By the mid-1970s, plastic had become the nation's most widely used material.

18

SENTENCE CLARITY

The suggestions offered in this chapter will improve the clarity of your sentences. These suggestions are based on what is known about how to help readers follow along more easily and understand sentence content more fully.

18a ## MOVING FROM KNOWN (OLD) TO UNKNOWN (NEW) INFORMATION

To help readers understand your writing, begin your sentences with something that is generally known or familiar before you introduce new or unfamiliar material later in the sentence. Then, when that new material is known, it becomes familiar, or "old," and you can introduce more new material. Note how these sentences move from familiar (or old) information to new:

Familiar Before Unfamiliar:

Every semester, after final exams are over, I'm faced with the problem of

what to do with lecture notes. They might be useful someday, but they just
     (OLD) ⟶ (OLD) ⟶ (OLD) ⟶

keep cluttering my computer's hard drive. Someday, the computer will crash
                    (NEW) ⟶   (NEW)

with all the information I might never need.

The next example is not as clear.

Unfamiliar Before Familiar:

Second-rate entertainment is my categorization of most movies I've seen
     (NEW)   (OLD)

lately, but occasionally, there are some with worthwhile themes. In the
                                              (NEW)

Southwest, the mysterious disappearance of an Indian culture is the topic of
                          (NEW)   (OLD)

a recent movie I saw that I would say has a worthwhile theme.
                                          (OLD)

You probably found these sentences hard to read because the familiar information comes after the new information.

18b ## USING POSITIVE INSTEAD OF NEGATIVE STATEMENTS

Use the positive (or affirmative) instead of the negative because negative statements are harder for people to understand.

> **Unclear Negative:** Less attention is paid to commercials that lack human interest stories.

> **Revised:** People pay more attention to commercials that tell human interest stories.

18c **AVOIDING DOUBLE NEGATIVES**

Use only one negative at a time in your sentences. Using more than one negative word creates a double negative, which is grammatically incorrect and leaves the reader with the impression that the writer isn't very literate. Some double negatives are also hard to understand.

Double Negative: He did <u>not</u> have <u>no</u> money.

Revised: He had no money. (*or*) He did not have any money.

Double Negative: I <u>don't</u> think he <u>didn't</u> have money left after he paid for his dinner.

[This sentence is particularly hard to understand because it uses both a double negative and negatives instead of positives.]

Revised: I think he had some money left after he paid for his dinner.

Try This

TO AVOID DOUBLE NEGATIVES

1. Watch out for contractions with negatives in them. If you use the following contractions, don't use any other negatives in your sentence.

aren't	doesn't	hasn't	weren't
couldn't	don't	isn't	won't
didn't	hadn't	wasn't	wouldn't

She doesn't want ~~no~~ *any* more riders in the car.

2. Watch out for other negative words:

| hardly | no one | nobody | nothing | scarcely |
| neither | no place | none | nowhere | |

They hardly had ~~no~~ *any* popcorn left.

18d **USING VERBS INSTEAD OF NOUNS**

Try to use verbs rather than noun forms whenever possible. Actions expressed as verbs are more easily understood than actions named as nouns.

Unnecessary Noun Form: <u>The decision was</u> to adjourn.

Revised: <u>They decided</u> to adjourn.

Some Noun Forms	Verbs to Use Instead
The determination of . . .	They determine
The approval of . . .	They approve
The preparation of . . .	They prepare
The discovery of . . .	They discover
The analysis of . . .	They analyze

18e MAKING THE INTENDED SUBJECT THE SENTENCE SUBJECT

Be sure that the real subject or the doer of the action in the verb is the grammatical subject of the sentence. Sometimes the real subject of a sentence can get buried in prepositional phrases or other less noticeable places.

Subject Buried in a Prepositional Phrase

For real music lovers, it is preferable to hear a live concert instead of a CD.

[The grammatical subject here is *it,* which is not the real subject of this sentence.]

A revision brings the real subject out of the prepositional phrase. The following example shows one possibility:

Revised: Music lovers prefer to hear a live concert instead of a CD.

Real Subject Buried in the Sentence

It seems like ordering online is something that Matthew does too much.

[If the real subject, *Matthew,* becomes the sentence subject, the entire sentence becomes clearer.]

Revised: Matthew seems to do too much ordering online.

18f USING ACTIVE INSTEAD OF PASSIVE VOICE

The active verb (see 21d and Chapter 34) is often easier to understand than the passive because the active voice explains who is doing the action.

Active: The committee decided to postpone the vote.
(ACTIVE)

Less Clear: The decision that was reached by the committee was to postpone the vote. (PASSIVE)

Exercise 18.1 Proofreading Practice

Each sentence that follows could be revised by using one or more of the suggestions in this chapter. List the section numbers of all the suggestions that could be followed to improve each of these sentences.

(1) Much attention was paid to "Y2K" in the late twentieth century when analysts began to think about how the year 2000 would affect computers. (2) The panic that was caused by Y2K revolved around the idea that systems won't hardly work right when the year turned from 1999 to 2000. (3) The 00 would be understood by the computer to be 1900 and could cause major chaos. (4) The majority of the problem was expected to affect bank accounts, telephone service, utilities, and food supply. (5) It seemed that crashing computers is something that most experts expected. (6) The discovery of this problem actually took place more than fifty years before the turn of the century, but nobody didn't want to address something that was fifty years in the future. (7) Consequently, companies raced against the clock to rid their systems of the Y2K problem.

Exercise 18.2 Pattern Practice

Look back through this chapter at the patterns for the changes you suggested in Exercise 18.1. Use those patterns to revise the paragraph in Exercise 18.1 so that it is clearer.

19

TRANSITIONS

Transitions are words and phrases that build bridges between sentences, parts of sentences, and paragraphs. These bridges show relationships and help blend sentences together smoothly. Several types of transitions are illustrated in this chapter.

19a REPETITION OF A KEY TERM OR PHRASE

Among the recent food fads sweeping America is the interest in **exotic foods.** While not everyone can agree on what **exotic foods** are, most of us like the idea of trying something new and different.

19b SYNONYMS

Because the repetition of a key word or phrase can become boring, use a synonym (a word or phrase having essentially the same meaning) to add variety and to avoid repeating.

One food Americans are not inclined to try is **brains.** A Gallup poll found that 41 percent of the people who responded said they would never try **brains.** Three years later, the percentage of those who wouldn't touch animals' **gray matter** had risen to 49 percent.

19c PRONOUNS

Pronouns such as *he, she, it, we,* and *they* are useful when you want to refer to something mentioned previously. Similarly, *this, that, these,* and *those* can be used as links.

In addition to brains, there are many other foods that some <u>Americans</u> now
                                                                    (1)
find more distasteful than <u>they</u> did several years ago. For example, more
                            (1)
people now say they would never eat <u>liver, rabbit, pig's feet, or beef kidneys</u>
                                                                          (2)
than said so three years ago. Even restaurant workers who are exposed to

<u>these delicacies</u> aren't always wild about <u>them.</u>
      (2)   (2)

19d TRANSITIONAL WORDS AND PHRASES

English has a huge storehouse of words and phrases that cue the reader to relationships between sentences. Without these cues, the reader may be momentarily puzzled or unsure of how sentences relate to each other. For example, read these two sentences:

Jules is very tall. He does not play basketball.

If it took you a moment to see the connection, try reading the same two sentences with a transitional word added:

Jules is very tall. However, he does not play basketball.

The word *however* signals that the second sentence contradicts or contrasts with the first sentence. Read the following:

The state government was determined not to raise taxes. Therefore, . . .

As soon as you reached the word *therefore,* you knew that some consequence or result would follow.

The transitions listed in the following table are grouped according to the categories of relationships they show.

TRANSITIONS

Adding	and, besides, in addition, also, too, moreover, further, furthermore, next, first, second, third, finally, last, again, and then, likewise, similarly
Comparing	similarly, likewise, in like manner, at the same time, in the same way
Contrasting	but, yet, however, still, nevertheless, on the other hand, on the contrary, in contrast, conversely, in another sense, instead, rather, notwithstanding, though, whereas, after all, although
Emphasizing	indeed, in fact, above all, add to this, and also, even more, in any event, in other words, that is, obviously
Ending	after all, finally, in sum, for these reasons
Giving examples	for example, for instance, to illustrate, that is, namely, specifically
Pointing to cause and effect, proof, or conclusions	thus, therefore, consequently, because of this, hence, as a result, then, so, accordingly
Showing place or direction	over, above, inside, next to, underneath, to the left, to the right, just behind, beyond, in the distance
Showing time	meanwhile, soon, later, afterward, now, in the past, then, next, before, during, while, finally, after this, at last, since then, presently, temporarily, after a short time, at the same time, in the meantime
Summarizing	to sum up, in brief, on the whole, as has been noted, in conclusion, that is, finally, as has been said, in general, to recapitulate, to conclude, in other words

Hint

USING *AND* AND *BUT* AS TRANSITIONS

Some people prefer not to begin a sentence with the word *and* or *but*. Others think these are useful words to achieve variety and smooth transitions between sentences.

Although jet lag is a nuisance for travelers, it can be a disaster for flight crews. **But** flight crews can reduce the effects of jet lag by modifying their sleep patterns. **And** airlines are beginning to recognize the need for in-flight naps.

19e   TRANSITIONS IN AND BETWEEN PARAGRAPHS

1. Transitions Between Sentences in a Paragraph

Your paragraphs are more easily understood when you show how every sentence in the paragraph is connected to the whole. As the following example shows, you can use *repetition, synonyms, pronouns*, and *transitional words* and *phrases* to signal the connections.

◯ = repetition	ⵔ = pronouns
▢ = synonyms	⬚ = transitional words and phrases

While drilling into Greenland's layers of ice, scientists recently pulled up evidence from the last ice age showing that the island's climate underwent extreme shifts within a year or two. This unexpected finding is based on evidence from ice cores that the climate often shifted from glacial to warmer weather in just a few years. In addition, other evidence indicates that the annual amount of snow accumulation also changed abruptly at the same time. As the climate went from cold to warm, the amount of snowfall jumped abruptly by as much as 100 percent. This change happened because more snow falls during warmer periods when the atmosphere holds more water. From this evidence, scientists therefore conclude that warming and cooling of the earth may be able to occur much faster than had been previously thought.

2. Transitions Between Paragraphs

As you start a new paragraph, you should also show the link to the previous paragraph, and an effective place to do this is in the first sentence of the new paragraph. Use the following strategies for including transitions between paragraphs.

Repetition

One way to make a connection is to reach back to the previous paragraph, referring to an element there in the beginning of your next paragraph. Some writers think of this as using a hook. They "hook" an element from above and bring it down—through the use of repetition—to the next paragraph, providing a connecting thread of ideas.

Suppose your paper discusses the changing role of women in combat. In a paragraph on the history of women's roles in warfare, you conclude with the example of Harriet Tubman, an African American who led scouting raids into enemy territory during the Civil War. In the next paragraph, you want to move to new roles for women in modern combat. Your opening sentence can "hook" the older use of women as scouts and tie that to their new role as pilots in the Iraq wars:

> Whereas a few women served in more limited roles as <u>scouts</u> in previous
> ("HOOK" TO PREVIOUS PARAGRAPH)
> wars, in the wars in Iraq, women took on more extensive roles as pilots flying
>
> supplies, troops, and ammunition into combat areas.

Transitional Words

Because every paragraph moves your paper forward, you can use the first sentence to point your readers in the direction of your whole essay. Think of the first sentence of every paragraph as being like a road sign, indicating to your readers where they are headed.

For example, suppose that your next paragraph in a paper on campaign reform presents a second reason in your argument against allowing large personal contributions to political candidates. Use a transitional word or phrase to show that you are building a list of arguments:

> <u>Another reason</u> political candidates should not receive large personal contributions is . . .

[The underlined words show that the writer is adding another element.]

Or suppose that your next paragraph is going to acknowledge that there are also arguments for the opposing side in this topic. You would then be going in the opposite direction or contrasting one side against the other.

> <u>Not everyone, however</u>, is in favor of making personal contributions to candidates illegal. Those who want to continue the practice argue that . . .

[The underlined words signal a turn in the opposite direction.]

Exercise 19.1 Proofreading Practice

Read the following paragraph, and highlight or underline the transitions. Categorize them by putting the appropriate numbers near the words you mark:

1. Repetition of key term or phrase
2. Synonyms
3. Pronouns
4. Transitional words or phrases

The largest ocean liner of its time set sail for New York in April 1912. This now-famous ship, the *Titanic,* never finished its voyage. It hit an enormous iceberg halfway through the trip and caused the 2,227 passengers to head for the lifeboats. Then, within hours, the mammoth vessel plunged beneath the icy Atlantic Ocean. Next, the *Titanic* broke in two and fell to the bottom of the ocean. It was seen by people in other ships only from a distance and was untouched until 1986, when a team of researchers entered the boat and explored it. Eventually, a small piece of steel brought back from one of the expeditions was examined to determine whether this material played a part in the sinking of the ship. Later, researchers tried raising a portion of the ship from the bottom of the ocean, but it was too heavy and fell beneath the water once again. In time, the ship itself will disintegrate, but the fascination with the *Titanic* will remain.

Exercise 19.2 Proofreading Practice

The connections or transitional links are missing in the following sample paragraph; they have been added in the revised version. Revise the practice paragraph, adding transitions where they are needed.

Sample Paragraph
I like autumn. Autumn is a sad time of year. The leaves turn to brilliant yellow and red. The weather is mild. I can't help thinking ahead to the coming of winter. Winter will bring snowstorms, slippery roads, and icy fingers. In winter the wind chill factor can make it dangerous to be outside. I find winter unpleasant. In autumn I can't help thinking ahead to winter's arrival. I am sad when I think that winter is coming.

Sample Paragraph (Revised)
Although I like autumn, it is a sad time of year. Of course, the leaves turn to brilliant yellow and red, and the weather is mild. Still, I can't help thinking ahead to the coming of winter with its snowstorms, slippery roads, and icy fingers. Moreover, in winter the wind chill factor can make it dangerous to be outside. Because I find these things unpleasant, in autumn I can't help thinking ahead to winter's arrival. Truly, I am sad when I think that winter is coming.

Practice Paragraph

Caring for houseplants requires some basic knowledge about plants. Every plant should be watered regularly. The plant's leaves should be cleaned. Spring and summer bring a special time of growth. The plant can be fertilized then. The plant can be repotted. The diameter of the new pot should be only two inches larger than the pot the plant is presently in. Some plants can be put outside in summer. Some plants cannot be put outside. If you are familiar with basic requirements for houseplants, you will have healthy plants.

20

SENTENCE VARIETY

Sentences with the same word order and length produce the kind of monotony that is boring to readers. To make your sentences more interesting, add variety by making some longer than others and by finding alternatives to starting every sentence with the subject and verb.

20a   COMBINING SENTENCES

■ You can combine two sentences (or independent clauses) into one longer sentence.

                                     , but the

Doonesbury cartoons laugh at contemporary politicians. ~~The~~ victims of the

satire probably don't read the cartoon strip.

■ You can combine the subjects of two independent clauses in one sentence when the verb applies to both clauses.

Original: During the flood, the Wabash River overflowed its banks. Wildcat Creek did the same.

Revised: During the flood, the Wabash River and Wildcat Creek overflowed their banks.

Hint

JOINING INDEPENDENT CLAUSES

To join an independent clause to another with *and, but, for, nor, or, so,* or *yet,* use a comma. Use a semicolon if you do not use connecting words or if you use other connecting words such as *therefore* or *however.* A comma is also required after a connecting word of more than one syllable.

- You can join two predicates when they have the same subject.

  Original: Karl often spends Sunday afternoons watching football on TV. He spends Monday evenings the same way.

  Revised: Karl often spends Sunday afternoons and Monday evenings watching football on TV.

20b ADDING WORDS

- You can add a description, a definition, or other information about a noun after the noun.

  , our family dentist,
  Dr. Dutta recently moved to Florida.
  ⌃

  , a city with a wide variety of ethnic restaurants
  I plan to visit New York.
  ⌃

  ,   ,
  Professor Nguyen ~~is~~ a political science teacher./~~She~~ gives lectures in the
  ⌃   ⌃

  community on current events.

- You can add a *who, which,* or *what* clause after a noun or turn another sentence into a *who, which,* or *what* clause.

  , who takes his job very seriously,
  Ed always arrives at his desk at 7:55 A.M.
  ⌃

  , which
  The experiment failed because of Murphy's Law./ ~~This law~~ states that buttered
  ⌃

  bread always falls buttered side down.

- Sometimes you can delete the *who, which,* or *what* words, as in the following example:

  The National Football League, ~~which is~~ popular with TV fans, is older than the American Football League.

- You can add phrases and clauses at the beginning of the sentence. For example, you can begin with a prepositional phrase. Some prepositions you might use include the following:

at	for	in addition to
because of	from	on
between	in	under

  <u>In addition to</u> soup and salad, she ordered breadsticks and coffee.

From an advertiser's point of view, commercials are more important than the TV programs.

■ You can begin with infinitives (*to* + verb) or with phrases that start with *-ing* and *-ed* verbs.

To attract attention, the hijackers ordered the plane to fly to Algeria.

Hearing her dog whining, she opened the door and let the cold, wet pooch in the house.

■ You can add transitional words (see Chapter 19) at the beginning of sentences.

However, I don't want to make a decision too quickly.

What's more, the new model for that sports car will have a turbocharger.

■ You can begin with dependent clauses that start with dependent markers such as the following words:

after	because	since	when
although	if	until	while

After the parade was over, the floats were quickly taken apart.

When spring comes, I'll have to start searching for a summer job.

20c CHANGING WORDS, PHRASES, AND CLAUSES

■ You can move adjectives after the *be* verb to the front of the sentence so that they describe the subject noun.

Original: The homecoming queen was surprised and teary-eyed. She waved enthusiastically to the crowd.

Revised: Surprised and teary-eyed, the homecoming queen waved enthusiastically to the crowd.

■ You can expand your subject to a phrase or clause.

Hunting is his favorite sport.

Hunting grouse is his favorite sport.

To hunt grouse in the early morning mists is to really enjoy the sport.

Whoever has hunted grouse in the early morning mists knows the real joys of the sport.

That grouse hunting is enjoyable is evident from the number of people addicted to the sport.

■ You can change a sentence to a dependent clause (see 28b) and put it before or after the independent clause.

> *Because he*   *, he*
> ~~He~~ overslept yesterday morning and missed class./ ~~He~~ did not hear the
>
> announcement of the exam.

> *Although*   *, scientists*
> ᴧAmerica is overly dependent on foreign oil./ ~~Scientists~~ have not yet found
>
> enough alternative sources of energy.

Exercise 20.1 Pattern Practice

The sample paragraph below (which you will probably find very choppy and boring) is composed of sentences in a very similar pattern. Its revision follows the strategies for achieving variety that are described in this chapter. Use these strategies to revise the practice paragraph.

Sample Paragraph
Whistling is a complex art. It involves your lips, teeth, tongue, jaw, rib cage, abdomen, and lungs. It occasionally also involves your hands and fingers. Whistling sounds are produced by the vibration of air through a resonating chamber. This resonating chamber is created by your mouth or hands. One factor is particularly crucial. This factor is the type of space produced in your mouth by your tongue. Whistling is usually thought of as a means of entertainment. It can also be a means of communication. Some people include whistling as part of their language. Others use whistling to carry messages over long distances.

Sample Paragraph (Revised)
Whistling is a complex art that involves your lips, teeth, tongue, jaw, rib cage, abdomen, lungs, and occasionally your hands and fingers. Whistling sounds are produced by the vibration of air through a resonating chamber created by your mouth or hands. One particularly crucial factor is the type of space produced in your mouth by your tongue. Although whistling is usually thought of as a means of entertainment, it can also be a means of communication. Some people include whistling as part of their language, and others use whistling to carry messages over long distances.

Practice Paragraph
Scientists neglect whistling. Amateurs and hobbyists do not neglect it. There are whistling contests all over the United States. Accomplished whistlers whistle classical music, opera, jazz, Broadway show tunes, polkas, and even rock and roll at these contests. People whistle very differently. Some people pucker their lips. Other people use their throat,

hands, or fingers to produce whistling sounds. These whistling sounds resemble the flute. Whistling has several advantages. One advantage is that it is a happy sound. Whistlers never lose their instrument. Their instrument doesn't need to be cleaned or repaired. Their instrument costs nothing. It is easily transported. Learning how to whistle is hard to explain. Whistling is something you pick up at a young age or not at all.

21
VERBS

A **verb** is a word or group of words that expresses action, shows a state of existence, or connects the subject (usually the doer of the action) to the rest of the sentence.

The first step in distinguishing complete sentences from incomplete ones is recognizing the verb. Many sentences have more than one verb, but they must have at least one. Verbs provide several kinds of essential information in a sentence.

Hint

UNDERSTANDING ENGLISH VERBS

Because languages differ in the types of information the verb conveys, it's helpful to remember that in English, the verb or verb phrase is very important. It always indicates (1) what the time is, (2) whether the subject is singular or plural, and (3) whether the subject is first person (*I* or *we*), second person (*you*), or third person (*he, she, it,* or *they*).

■ Some verbs express action.

Tonya **jogs** every day.   I **see** my face in the mirror.

■ Some verbs (called **linking verbs**) indicate that a subject exists or link the subject (the who or what) to the rest of the sentence.

She **feels** sad.   The shark **is** hungry.

■ Verbs indicate time.

They **went** home.   The semester **will end** in May.
[past time]   [future time]

■ Verbs indicate number.

Matt always **orders** anchovy pizza.
[singular—only one doer of the action, Matt]

Qun and Medhi always **order** cheese pizza.
[plural—two doers of the action, Qun and Medhi]

■ Verbs indicate the person for the subject (the who or what, usually the doer of the action).

First Person
I or *we*   I **love** to cook.

Second Person
you   You **love** to cook.

Third Person
he, she, it, or *they*   He **loves** to cook.

Try This

TO FIND THE VERB

You can find the verb (or part of it, when the verb has more than one word) by changing the time expressed in the sentence (from the present to the past, from the past to the future, and so on). In the following examples, the word that changes is the verb, and the sentence expresses something about the past or present because of the verb form.

Present
Tamar **jogs** every day.
I **see** my face in the mirror.
She **feels** sad.
The shark **is** hungry.

Past
Tamar **jogged** every day.
I **saw** my face in the mirror.
She **felt** sad.
The shark **was** hungry.

21a VERB PHRASES

A **verb phrase** is several words working together as a verb.

He **has gone** home.   I **am enjoying** my vacation.

They **should have attended** the movie with me.

21b VERB FORMS

Verb forms are words that are not complete verbs in themselves and may be part of a verb phrase or may appear elsewhere in the sentence.

1. *-ing* Verbs

Forms of the verb that end in *-ing,* called **gerunds,** are never complete verbs by themselves. To be part of the verb phrase, the *-ing* form needs a helping verb and is then part of a progressive tense verb (see 21c). The *-ing* form may also be used alone elsewhere in the sentence.

The software **is working** smoothly.

[*Working* is a verb form but it is only a part of the verb phrase. *Is working* is the whole verb phrase, which includes the helping verb *is.*]

Feeling guilty is one of his favorite pastimes.

[*Feeling* is part of the subject. It is a verb form but not a verb.]

Everyone enjoys **laughing.**

[*Laughing* is the direct object of the verb. The direct object completes the meaning or receives the action of the verb. *Laughing* is a verb form but not a verb.]

Hint

AVOIDING FRAGMENTS

Some incomplete sentences, called **fragments,** are caused by using only an -*ing* verb form with no helper.

Serina, with her fast track record yesterday, ~~showing~~ all the practice and effort of the last three months.
    is showing **(or)** shows

[*This was not a complete sentence because* showing *is not a complete verb.*]

For more information on fragments, see Chapter 12.

2. -*ed* Verbs

To show past tense, most verbs have -*ed* or -*d* added to the base form. (The base form is the main entry in the dictionary.) With no helping verb, the -*ed* or -*d* form is the simple past tense. When the -*ed* form has a helping verb such as *has* or *had,* it is part of one of the perfect tenses (see 21c). The -*ed* or -*d* form can also be used alone elsewhere in the sentence.

LaToya **has jumped** farther than any other contestant so far.

[*Jumped* is part of the verb phrase, and *has jumped* is the complete verb phrase.]

I read that chapter, the one **added** to last week's assignment.

[*Added* is not part of the verb phrase.]

3. *to* + Verb

Another verb form, called the **infinitive,** has *to* added to the base form. This infinitive form is used with certain verbs (see 52c).

I was supposed **to give** her the ticket.

[*Was supposed to give* is the whole verb phrase.]

To forgive is easier than **to forget.**

[*To forgive* and *to forget* are not part of the verb phrase.]

Exercise 21.1 Proofreading Practice

Underline the verbs and verb phrases in the following sentences. Highlight or circle the verb forms both in verb phrases and elsewhere in the sentence. As an example, the first sentence is already marked. Remember to ask yourself the following questions:

■ *To find a verb or verb phrase.* Which word or group of words expresses action, shows a state of existence, or links the subject, the doer of the action, to the rest of the sentence?

■ *To find a verb form.* Which words end in *-ing* or *-ed* or have *to* + verb? Which of these are not complete verbs in themselves?

(1) For a long time, psychologists have (wondered) what memories are

and where they are (stored) in the human brain. (2) Because it is the

basis of human intellect, memory has been studied intensely. (3) According to one psychologist, memory is an umbrella term for a whole range of processes that occur in the brain. (4) In particular, psychologists have identified two types of memory. (5) One type is called declarative memory, and it includes memories of facts such as names, places, dates, and even baseball scores. (6) It is called declarative because we use it to declare things. (7) For example, a person can declare that his or her favorite food is fried bean sprouts. (8) The other type is called procedural memory. (9) It is the type of memory acquired by repetitive practice or conditioning, and it includes skills such as riding a bike or typing. (10) We need both types of memory in our daily living because we need facts and we use a variety of skills.

Exercise 21.2 Pattern Practice

The following paragraph is in the present tense. Highlight or underline each verb and write the past tense form above it. As an example, the first sentence is already done for you.

(1) To learn more about memory, a psychologist studies [studied] visual memory by watching monkeys. (2) To do this, he uses a game that requires the monkey to pick up a block in order to find the food in a pail underneath. (3) After a brief delay, the monkey again sees the old block on top of a pail and sees a new block with a pail underneath it. (4) The new block now covers a pail with bananas in it. (5) The monkey quickly learns each time to pick up the new block in order to find food. (6) This demonstrates that the monkey remembers what the old block looks like and also what distinguishes the new block. (7) The psychologist concludes that visual memory is at work.

21c VERB TENSE

Verb tense indicates the time of the verb: past, present, or future.

The four tenses for the past, present, and future are as follows:

- Simple
- Progressive: *be* + *-ing* form of the verb
- Perfect: *have, had, will have,* or *shall have* + *-ed* form of the verb
- Perfect progressive: *have* or *had* + *been* + *-ing* form of the verb

The following table shows verb forms.

VERB FORMS			
	Present	**Past**	**Future**
Simple	I walk.	I walked.	I will walk.
Progressive	I am walking.	I was walking.	I will be walking.
Perfect	I have walked.	I had walked.	I will have walked.
Perfect progressive	I have been walking.	I had been walking.	I will have been walking.

1. Present Tense

Simple Present

- *Present action or condition:* She **counts** the votes. They **are** happy.
- *General truth:* States **defend** their rights.
- *Habitual action:* He **drinks** orange juice for breakfast.
- *Future time:* The plane **arrives** at 10 P.M. tonight.
- *Literary or timeless truth:* Shakespeare **uses** humor effectively.

Form: This is the form found in the dictionary and is often called the **base form.** For third person singular subjects (*he, she, it*), add *-s* or *-es.*

I, you, we, they **walk.**   I, you, we, they **push.**

He, she, it **walks.**   He, she, it **pushes.**

Hint

MEANING OF PRESENT TENSE VERBS

Students learning English as a second language may have difficulty in deciding when American culture determines that something is a general, literary, or timeless truth and should be expressed in simple present tense. If so, a teacher or writing center tutor can help.

Present Progressive

■ Activity that is in progress:

The committee **is studying** that proposal.

Form: This form has two parts: *am, is,* or *are* + *-ing* form of the verb.

We **are going.**   He **is singing.**

Present Perfect

■ Action that was completed in the past or began in the past and is still ongoing:

The company **has sold** that product since January.

■ Habitual or continued action started in the past and continuing into the present:

Ashley **has** not **smoked** a cigarette in three years.

Form: Use *have* or *has* + the *-ed* form of regular verbs (called the **past participle**).

I **have eaten.**   He **has** not **called.**

Present Perfect Progressive

■ Action that began in the past, continues to the present, and may continue into the future:

They **have been considering** that purchase for three months.

■ *Form:* Use *have* or *has* + *been* + the *-ing* form of the verb.

He **has been running.**   They **have been meeting.**

2. Past Tense

Simple Past

■ *Completed action:*   We **visited** the museum last summer.

■ *Completed condition:*   It **was** cloudy yesterday.

Form: Add *-ed* for regular verbs. For other forms, see the list of irregular verbs in 21c4.

I **walked.**   They **awoke.**

Past Progressive

■ Past action that took place over a period of time:

They **were driving** through the desert when the sandstorm hit.

■ Past action that was interrupted by another action:

The engine **was running** when he left the car.

Form: Use *was* or *were* + the *-ing* form of the verb.

She **was singing.**   We **were running.**

Past Perfect

■ Action or event completed before another event in the past:

When the meeting began, she **had** already **left** the building.

Form: Use *had* + the *-ed* form of the verb (the past participle).

He **had** already **reviewed** the list when Olivia came in.

Past Perfect Progressive

■ Ongoing condition in the past that has ended:

The diplomat **had been planning** to visit when his government was overthrown.

Form: Use *had* + *been* + the *-ing* form of the verb.

They **had been looking.**   She **had been speaking.**

3. Future Tense

Simple Future

■ Actions or events in the future:

The recycling center **will open** next week.

Form: Use *will* (or *shall*) + the base form of the verb. (In American English, *will* is commonly used for all persons, but in British English, *shall* is often used for first person.)

I **will choose.**   They **will enter.**

Future Progressive

■ Future action that will continue for some time:

I **will be expecting** your call.

Form: Use *will* (or *shall*) + *be* + the *-ing* form of the verb.

He **will be studying.**   They **will be driving.**

Future Perfect

- Action that will be completed by or before a specified time in the future:

By Thursday, we **will have organized** the whole filing cabinet.

Form: Use *will* (or *shall*) + *have* + the *-ed* form of the verb (the past participle).

They **will have walked.**   We **will have finished.**

Future Perfect Progressive

- Action or condition continuing until a specific time in the future:

In June, we **will have been renting** this apartment for a year.

Form: Use *will* (or *shall*) + *have* + *been* + the *-ing* form of the verb.

They **will have been paying.**   She **will have been traveling.**

4. Irregular Verbs

Some brief samples of irregular verb forms are shown in the following tables. Consult a dictionary for more verbs.

IRREGULAR VERB FORMS				
	Present		**Past**	
Verb	*Singular*	*Plural*	*Singular*	*Plural*
be	I am	we are	I was	we were
	you are	you are	you were	you were
	he, she, it is	they are	he, she, it was	they were
have	I have	we have	I had	we had
	you have	you have	you had	you had
	he, she, it has	they have	he, she, it had	they had
do	I do	we do	I did	we did
	you do	you do	you did	you did
	he, she, it does	they do	he, she, it did	they did

SOME IRREGULAR VERBS		
Base (Present)	**Past**	**Past Participle**
be (am, is, are)	was, were	been
become	became	become
begin	began	begun
bring	brought	brought
come	came	come
do	did	done
eat	ate	eaten
find	found	found
forget	forgot	forgotten
get	got	gotten
give	gave	given
go	went	gone
grow	grew	grown
have	had	had
know	knew	known
lay	laid	laid
lie	lay	lain
make	made	made
mean	meant	meant
read	read	read
say	said	said
see	saw	seen
sit	sat	sat
speak	spoke	spoken
stand	stood	stood
take	took	taken
teach	taught	taught
think	thought	thought
write	wrote	written

Exercise 21.3 Proofreading Practice

Choose the correct verbs from the options given in parentheses. Remember that the time expressed in the verb has to agree with the meaning of the sentence.

The way children (1. learn, will learn) to draw seems simple. But studies show that when given some kind of marker, young children (2. have begun, will begin, begin) by scribbling on any available surface. At first, these children's drawings (3. are, should be, had been) simple, clumsy, and unrealistic, but gradually the drawings (4. have become, should become, become) more realistic. One researcher who (5. will study, could study, has studied) the drawings of one- and two-year-olds concludes that their early scrawls (6. are representing, may represent, had represented) gestures and motions. For example, the researcher notes that one two-year-old child who was observed (7. took, has taken, had taken) a marker and (8. is hopping, hopped, had hopped) it around on the paper, leaving a mark with each imprint and explaining as he drew that the rabbit (9. was going, had gone, could have gone) hop-hop. The researcher (10. had concluded, has concluded, concludes) that the child was symbolizing the rabbit's motion, not its size, shape, or color. Someone who (11. had seen, sees, might see) only dots on a page (12. would not see, has not seen, had not seen) a rabbit and (13. should conclude, would conclude, had concluded) that the child's attempts to draw a rabbit (14. have failed, had failed, failed).

Exercise 21.4 Pattern Practice

At the beginning of the following paragraph below, add the words "Last year," and rewrite the rest of the paragraph so that it is in past tense.

St. John's wort is one of the many herbal supplements advertised in magazines and news reports as an alternative remedy for treating anxiety and depression. This herb has been around for hundreds of years, even before the dawn of antidepressants. Many depressed people take medications such as Prozac, but research reveals that herbal treatments are also effective. A person who experiences anxiety or depression may benefit more from an herbal remedy than from a drug that causes side effects. Antidepressants often cause side effects such as weight gain, lack of interest in sex, and insomnia. Herbal remedies such as St. John's wort may have no side effects. Many people who have tried this remedy say that they enjoy life more and are anxiety free. Experimenting with an herbal remedy is not harmless, however; like a drug, an herbal remedy is capable of causing unpleasant side effects or permanent damage.

21d   VERB VOICE (ACTIVE/PASSIVE)

Verb voice tells whether the verb is in the active or passive voice. In the **active voice**, the subject performs the action of the verb. In the **passive voice**, the subject receives the action. The doer of the action in the passive voice may either appear in a *by* phrase or be omitted.

Active: **Tameka** bought a new **car**.
    (SUBJECT)   (OBJECT)
[Tameka did the buying.]

Passive: The **car** was bought by **Tameka**.
    (SUBJECT)   (OBJECT)
[Here, Tameka is now the object, and there is a "by" phrase.]

Hint

USING PASSIVE VOICE

- In the passive voice, the verb phrase always includes a form of *be,* such as *is, are, was,* or *is being.* Also, if the doer of the action is named, it is in a *by* phrase.
- Many instructors prefer to read essays written in the active voice, but there are occasions when the use of passive is appropriate. To decide whether to use active or passive and to avoid unnecessary shifting between active and passive, see 15d.

21e VERB MOOD

The **mood** of a verb tells whether it expresses a fact or opinion (**indicative**); a command, a request, or advice (**imperative**); or a doubt, a wish, a recommendation, or something contrary to fact (**subjunctive**).

Indicative

Verbs in the indicative (or declarative) mood express a fact or opinion and have their subjects stated in the sentence.

He **needs** a computer to print out his résumé.

The environmentalists and loggers **could** not **reach** an agreement.

Imperative

Verbs in the imperative mood express a command or offer advice. The subject word is not included because the subject is understood to be the reader or listener (*you*).

Open that window, please.   **Watch** your step!

Next, **put** the wheel on the frame.

Subjunctive

In the subjunctive mood, verbs express a doubt, a wish, a suggestion, a recommendation, a request with a *that clause,* or something that is untrue or not likely to be true. In the subjunctive, present tense verbs stay in the simple base form and do not indicate the number or person of the subject.

It is important that she **be** (not *is*) here by 9 P.M.

The form requires that a passport photo **accompany** (not *accompanies*) the application.

For past subjunctive, the same form as simple past is used; however, for the verb *be, were* is used for all persons and numbers.

I wish she **had arrived** on time.

If I **were** (not *was*) he, I'd sell that car immediately.

If land **were** (not *was*) cheaper there, they could buy a farm.

Exercise 21.5 Proofreading Practice

Highlight or underline the verb phrases in each of the following sentences, and indicate the voice of the verb by writing "active" or "passive." Indicate whether the mood of each verb is declarative (factual), subjunctive (contrary to fact), or imperative (a command).

(1) Fun and unique training programs await many college graduates. (2) Interactive computer simulations are a good method for training the Nintendo generation. (3) The realization by corporate trainers that new employees in the 21-to-30 age group performed best when interacting with a computer or video game led to the invention of these special training programs. (4) Designers were informed that it is important for an employee to be comfortable when new material and methods are being presented. (5) "Play the game and learn the trade" is the motto of many companies recruiting young college graduates. (6) The transformation brought about by interactive training systems is just beginning.

Exercise 21.6 Sentence Practice

Combine the short sentences in the following paragraph into longer ones. Highlight or underline all verb phrases in your revised sentences, and label them as active or passive.

Corporate Gameware is an interesting company. It was founded by Marc Prensky. He noticed that younger employees performed well using interactive games. He thought they could learn skills through this method. Some skills are customer relations, company policies, and troubleshooting client problems. It is a better option than reading a training manual. Business schools adopted this idea. The military also uses interactive software. Studies show that this approach works. Employees like this method. Training employees takes less time. They are better trained. There is less turnover of staff. They feel confident. They like coming to work.

21f MODAL VERBS

Modals are helping verbs that express ability, a request, or an attitude, such as interest, expectation, possibility, or obligation.

The following table shows some common modal verbs.

COMMON MODAL VERBS		
Verb	**What It Expresses**	**Example**
shall, should	Intent, advisability	You **should** try to exercise more often.
will, would	Strong intent	I **will** return those books to the library tomorrow.
can, could	Capability, possibility, request	I **can** lend you my lecture notes.
may, might	Possibility, permission, request	She **may** buy a new computer.
must, ought to	Obligation, need	I **ought to** fill the gas tank before we drive to town.

22
NOUNS AND PRONOUNS

22a NOUNS

A **noun** is a word that names a person, place, thing, or idea.

The following words are nouns:

Julia Roberts	Des Moines	peace
Henri	bulb	justice
forest	pictures	French

(For proper and common nouns, see Chapter 55.)

1. Singular, Plural, and Collective Nouns

- A **singular noun** refers to one person, place, or thing and is the form you would look up in the dictionary.

- A **plural noun** is the form that refers to more than one person, place, or thing.
- A **collective noun** refers to a group acting as a unit, such as a committee, a herd, or a jury.

Exceptions: Some nouns do not fall into these categories because they refer to abstract or general concepts that cannot be counted and do not have plural forms. Examples are *homework, peace, furniture,* and *knowledge.* (See Chapter 55.)

Singular Nouns	Plural Nouns	Collective Nouns
box	boxes	family
child	children	senate

2. Noun Endings

Nouns have endings that show plural and possession. (See also xx and xx.)

Plural

Nouns in English indicate the plural in these five ways. The first way, adding *-s* or *-es,* is by far the most common.

PLURALS		
Indicator of Plural	**Singular**	**Plural**
1. -s or -es	one cup	many cups
	a box	two boxes
2. Changed form	one child	three children
	one man	some men
3. f or fe → ves	one half	two halves
	the life	nine lives
4. Other forms	one ox	a pair of oxen
	this medium	all media
5. No change	a deer	several deer
	one sheep	two sheep

Hint

FORMING NOUN PLURALS

1. The *-s* noun ending can be either the plural marker or the possessive marker. Don't make the mistake of putting an apostrophe in plural nouns.

   There was a sale on potato ~~chip's~~. *chips*

▶

2. Some writers do not use—or hear—plural forms in their speech, but standard English requires plural endings in writing. If you tend to omit written plurals, proofread your last drafts. To help your eye see the end of the word, point to the noun with your pen or finger to be sure that you see the plural ending. Some writers need repeated practice to notice the missing plural endings.

3. Although the *-s* marks the plural at the end of many nouns, it is also the ending for singular verbs with *he, she, it,* or a singular noun as the subject.

   He **walks.**   The shoe **fits.**

An *-s* ending may be needed either at the end of the *noun* for a *plural* or at the end of the *verb* for a *singular* form. Thus, both the subject and the verb cannot have an *-s* marker at the end.

Possession

The possessive form shows ownership or a close relationship. This is clear when we write *Maria's hat* because Maria owns or possesses the hat, but the possessive is less apparent when we write *journey's end* or *yesterday's news.* It is more helpful to think about the "of" relationship between two nouns when the first noun is in the possessive form. Replace the possessive ending with the word *of,* and place the second noun first.

Maria's hat —→ hat of Maria

two days' time —→ time of two days

Doing this not only clarifies the possessive relationship but also shows whether the word with the possessive marker is singular or plural. The possessive marker is either *'s* or *'.* When the plural *-s* or *-es* is added to the noun, only an apostrophe is added after the plural (see 39c). For singular nouns ending in *s,* such as *grass,* the *s* after the apostrophe is optional. It can be added if it doesn't make pronouncing the word more difficult. (See 39a.)

Singular
Miriam's hat

the glass's edge

James's story, James' story

Alexis' ZIP code

[Adding *'s* to *Alexis* would make pronunciation difficult.]

Plural
the girls' hats

all the glasses' edges

Try This

Incorrect: The shoe's don't fit.　　　There's a sale on sweatshirt's.

Revised: The shoes don't fit.　　　There is a sale on sweatshirts.

	Word	**Plural**	**Possessive Marker**
girls' gloves =	girl	s	'
baby's toe =	baby		's

22b PRONOUNS

A **pronoun** takes the place of a noun.

If we had no pronouns in English, we would have to write sentences like these:

Sanjay lost Sanjay's car keys.

When Tyrell went to the library, Tyrell found some useful references for Tyrell's paper.

1. Personal Pronouns

Personal pronouns refer to people or things.

Subject Case	Object Case	Possessive Case	
I	me	my	mine
you	you	your	yours
he	him	his	his
she	her	her	hers
it	it	its	its
we	us	our	ours
they	them	their	theirs

2. Demonstrative Pronouns

Demonstrative pronouns refer to things.

this	**This** cup of coffee is mine.
that	He needs **that** software program.

| these | Can I exchange **these** shoes? |
| those | No one ordered **those** soft drinks. |

3. Relative Pronouns

Relative pronouns show the relationship of a dependent clause (see 28b) to a noun in the sentence.

that	The statement **that** it was too soon to expect results delayed the project.
which	They took the television set, **which** was broken, to the dump.
who	Mrs. Bloom is the friend **who** helped me.
whom	That manager, **whom** I respect, was promoted.
what	Everyone wondered **what** the loud noise was.

Sometimes relative pronouns can be omitted when they are understood.

This isn't the sandwich **that** I ordered.

This isn't the sandwich I ordered.

Hint

AVOIDING PROBLEMS WITH PRONOUNS

Pronouns can cause problems when a writer shifts inappropriately from one person or number to another or uses a different person or number to refer to a noun (see 15a).

When ~~you~~ *we* watch television commercials, we should not believe all the

claims that are made.

When you watch television commercials, ~~we~~ *you* should not believe all the

claims that are made.

Many baseball players do not want to be tested for drugs. But if

~~he refuses~~ *they refuse*, the manager is unhappy.

4. Interrogative Pronouns

Interrogative pronouns are used in questions.

who	**Who** wrote that screenplay?
whose	**Whose** jacket is this?
whom	**Whom** do you wish to talk to?
which	**Which** movie do you want to see?
what	**What** will they do now?

5. Indefinite Pronouns

Indefinite pronouns make indefinite reference to nouns.

anyone, anybody	The notice said that **anyone** could apply.
some	May I have **some?**
everyone, everybody	She was delighted that **everybody** showed up.
everything	That dog ate **everything** on the table.
nothing	There is **nothing** he can't fix.
one	Please give me **one.**
someone, somebody	Would **somebody** show me how this works?

Hint

USING INDEFINITE PRONOUNS CORRECTLY

Indefinite pronouns are usually singular and require a singular verb.

Everyone is going to the game.

However, some indefinite pronouns, such as *both, few,* and *many,* require a plural verb. Other indefinite pronouns, such as *all, any, more, most, none,* and *some,* may be either singular or plural, depending on the meaning of the sentence.

Singular: Some of my homework is done.

[Here some refers to a portion or a part of the homework. Because a portion or a part is thought of as a single entity, the verb is singular.]

Plural: Some of these plates are chipped.

[Here some refers to more than one plate, so the verb is plural.]

Singular: All of the coffee is brewed.

Plural: All customers are pleased.

6. Possessive Pronouns

Possessive pronouns do not take an apostrophe.

its nose   [not *it's* nose]

that dog of **hers**   [not that dog of *her's*]

the house is **theirs**   [not the house is *theirs'*]

Some writers confuse the possessive pronouns with contractions.

It's a warm day.   = **It is** a warm day.

There's a shooting star. = **There is** a shooting star.

(See Chapter 39 on apostrophes.)

7. Reflexive Pronouns

Reflexive pronouns, which end in *-self* or *-selves,* intensify the nouns they refer to.

myself	I covered **myself** in sunscreen.
yourself	Please help **yourself.**
itself	The pig stuffed **itself** with feed.
themselves	They allowed **themselves** enough time to eat.

8. Reciprocal Pronouns

Reciprocal pronouns refer to individual parts of plural terms.

each other	They congratulated **each other.**
one another	The group helped **one another** prepare.

Exercise 22.1 Proofreading Practice

In the following paragraph, underline all the -s and -es endings that mark plural nouns, and highlight or circle all the 's, s', and ' possessive markers.

It is a sad fact of life that what some people call the "everyday courtesies" are disappearing faster than finger bowls and engineers' slide rules. People in movie theaters carry on loud conversations on cell phones, older people on buses rarely have anyone get up to offer them a seat, and few shoppers bother to offer thanks to a helpful salesperson. Some people say that courteous ways seem to have lingered longer in small towns than in big cities and that some regions—notably the South—cling more than others to some remaining signs of polite behavior. More often we hear complaints that courtesy is declining, dying, or dead. Says one New York executive, "There's no such thing as umbrella courtesy. Everybody's umbrella is aimed at eye level." A store owner in another city says that short-tempered waiters in restaurants and impatient salesclerks in stores make her feel as if she's bothering them by asking for service. Common courtesy may be a thing of the past.

Exercise 22.2 Pattern Practice

In the following paragraph, change the singular nouns to plural, add the appropriate noun endings, and change any other words or word endings that need to be altered.

The foreign tourist who travels in the United States often notices that the people in the United States are not as polite as a person from another country. The tourist from Europe, who is used to a more formal manner, is particularly offended by the American who immediately calls the tourist by his or her first name. Impoliteness in the United States extends even to an object. An English businessperson noted that in America a public sign issues a command: "No Smoking" or "Do Not Enter." In England, such a sign would be less commanding: "No Smoking Please" or "Please Do Not Enter." An American can also be rude without meaning to be. As a Japanese visitor noticed, the nurse who led him into the doctor's office said, "Come in here." In Japan, the visitor noted, a nurse would say, "Please follow me." The foreign tourist, unfortunately, has a variety of such stories to take back to his or her country.

23
PRONOUN CASE AND REFERENCE

23a PRONOUN CASE

Pronoun case refers to the form of the pronoun needed in a sentence. The following table shows the pronoun cases.

PRONOUN CASES					
	Subject		**Object**		**Possessive**
	Singular	*Plural*	*Singular*	*Plural*	*Singular*	*Plural*
First person	I	we	me	us	my, mine	our, ours
Second person	you	you	you	you	your, yours	your, yours
Third person	he	they	him	them	his	their, theirs
	she	they	her	them	her, hers	their, theirs
	it	they	it	them	it, its	their, theirs

1. Subject Case

Subject case of pronouns is used when pronouns are subjects. Subject case is also used after linking verbs such as *be*.

She won the lottery.   [*She* is the subject case pronoun.]

Who's there? It is **I.**   [In the second sentence, *I* is the subject case pronoun that comes after the linking verb *is*.]

2. Object Case

Object of the Verb

The **object case** of pronouns is used when pronouns are objects of verbs (receive the action of the verb).

I hugged **her.**   [object of the verb]

Seeing Dan and **me,** she waved.   [object of the verb]

Indirect Object

When pronouns are indirect objects of verbs (when they explain for whom or to whom something is done), use the object case.

I gave **her** the glass.   [indirect object]

The indirect object can often be changed to a *to + object pronoun* phrase.

I gave the glass **to her.**

Try This

TO CHOOSE THE CORRECT PRONOUN CASE

To be sure you use the correct pronoun case, try this:

1. Remember that *between, except,* and *with* are prepositions and take the object case.

   between you and ~~I~~ *me*   except Alexi and ~~she~~ *her*

   with ~~he~~ *him* and ~~I~~ *me*

2. Don't use *them* as a pointing pronoun in place of *these* or *those.* Use *them* only as the object by itself.

   He liked ~~them~~ *those* socks.   He liked them.

Object of a Preposition

Use the object case when a pronoun is the object of a preposition (completing the meaning of the preposition).

Al gave the money to **them.** [object of the preposition]

3. Possessive Case

Possessive case refers to pronouns used as possessives.

Is this **her** hat?	(*or*)	Is this **hers?**
We gave **him** our pens.	(*or*)	We gave him **ours.**

Hint

USING POSSESSIVE PRONOUNS CORRECTLY

1. Possessive case pronouns never take apostrophes.

 its
 The insect spread it's wings.
 ^

2. Use possessive case before -*ing* verb forms.

 his
 The crowd cheered him making a three-point basket.
 ^

4. Pronouns in Compound Constructions

When in doubt as to which pronoun case to use, some writers mistakenly choose the subject case because it sounds more formal or "correct." To find the right case when your sentence has two pronouns or a noun and a pronoun, temporarily eliminate the noun or one of the pronouns as you read it to yourself. You'll hear the case that is needed.

 he
Jon and him went to the store.
 ^

[If *Jon* is eliminated, the sentence would be "*Him* went to the store." It's easier to notice the wrong pronoun case this way.]

 me
Mrs. Weg gave the tickets to **Lutecia** and I.
 ^

[Once again, try the strategy of dropping the noun, in this case *Lutecia*. You'll be able to hear that the sentence sounds wrong. ("Mrs. Weg gave the tickets to *I*.") Because *to* is a preposition, the noun or pronoun that follows is the object of the preposition and should be in the object case.]

We
~~Us~~ **players** gave the coach a rousing cheer.

[When you drop the noun *players,* the original sentence would be "*Us* gave the coach a rousing cheer." The pronoun is the subject of the sentence and needs the subject case, the pronoun *we.*]

us
The lecturer told **we students** to quiet down.

[When you drop the noun *students,* the original sentence would be "The lecturer told *we* to quiet down." Instead, the sentence needs the pronoun in the object case, *us,* because it is the object of the verb.]

I
The newest members of the club, **Mahendi** and ~~me~~, were asked to pay our dues promptly.

[Because the phrase *Mahendi and me* explains the noun *members,* which is the subject of the sentence, the subject case of the pronoun, *I,* is needed.]

me
The usher had to find programs for the latecomers, **Mahendi** and **I.**

[The phrase *Mahendi and I* explains the noun *latecomers,* the object of the preposition *for.* Therefore, the pronoun has to be *me,* the object case.]

5. *Who/Whom*

In informal speech, some people may not distinguish between *who* and *whom.* But for formal writing, the cases are as follows:

Subject	Object	Possessive
who	whom	whose
whoever	whomever	

The subject case refers to pronouns used as subjects.

Who is going to the concert tonight?
[*Who* is the subject of the sentence.]

Give this to **whoever** wants it.
[When *who* introduces a dependent clause after a preposition, use *who* (or *whoever*) when it is the subject of the following verb.]

The object case refers to pronouns used as objects.

To **whom** should I give this ticket?
[*Whom* is the object of the preposition *to.*]

The possessive case refers to pronouns that show possession.

No one was sure **whose** voice that was.

Try This

TO CHOOSE BETWEEN *WHO* AND *WHOM*

If you aren't sure whether to use *who* or *whom,* turn a question into a statement or rearrange the order of the phrase:

Question: (Who, whom) are you looking for?

Statement: You are looking for **whom.**
     (OBJECT OF THE PREPOSITION)

Sentence: She is someone **(who, whom)** I know well.

Rearranged Order: I know **whom** well.
     (DIRECT OBJECT)

6. Omitted Words in Comparisons

In comparisons using *than* and *as,* choose the correct pronoun case by re-calling the words that are omitted.

He is taller than (**I, me**).

[The omitted words here are *am tall.*]

He is taller than I (am tall).

Our cat likes my sister more than (**I, me**).

[The omitted words here are *it likes.*]

Our cat likes my sister more than (it likes) **me.**

Exercise 23.1 Proofreading Practice

Highlight or underline the incorrect pronoun forms in the following para-graph and replace them with the correct forms.

Have you ever wondered how people in the entertainment industry choose what you and me will see on television, read in books, and hear on CDs? Some producers and publishers say that the executives in their companies and them rely on instinct and an ability to forecast trends in taste. But we consumers cannot be relied on to be consistent from one month to the next. So market researchers constantly seek our opinions. For example, they ask we moviegoers to preview movies and to fill out questionnaires. Reactions from we and our friends are then studied closely. Sometimes the market researchers merely forecast from previous experience what you and me are likely to prefer. Still, some movies fail for reasons that the market researchers cannot understand. When that happens, who does the movie studio blame? The producer will say that the director and him or her did all they could but that the leading actor failed to attract an audience. Sometimes, though, us moviegoers simply get tired of some types of movies and want more variety.

Exercise 23.2 Pattern Practice

Write a similar sentence of your own for each pattern that follows.

Pattern A: A sentence with an object case pronoun after the preposition *between, except,* or *with*

Everyone was able to hear the poster presentation **except her.**

Pattern B: A sentence with a compound object that includes a pronoun in the object case

The newspaper article listed Brittany and **him** as the winners of the contest.

Pattern C: A sentence with a comparison that includes a subject case pronoun

Everyone in the room was dressed more warmly than I.

Pattern D: A sentence with a comparison that includes an object case pronoun

The bird was more frightened of the dog than **me.**

Pattern E: A sentence with a compound subject that includes a subject case pronoun

During the festival, the announcer and **she** took turns thanking all the people who had helped organize the event.

23b PRONOUN REFERENCE

Pronoun reference is the relationship between the pronoun and the noun (antecedent) for which it is substituting.

Pronouns substitute for nouns. To help your reader see this relationship clearly, remember the following rules.

■ Pronouns should indicate which nouns they are referring to.

■ Pronouns should be reasonably close to their nouns.

Unclear Reference: Gina told Michelle that **she** took **her** bike to the library. [Did Gina take Michelle's bike or her own bike to the library?]

Revised: When Gina took Michelle's bike to the library, she told Michelle she was borrowing it.

Be sure your pronoun refers to a noun that has been recently mentioned and not merely implied.

Hint

AVOIDING VAGUE PRONOUNS

Watch out for the vague *they* that doesn't refer to any specific group and the vague use of *this, it,* or *which* that doesn't refer to any specific word or phrase (antecedent).

the screenwriters and producers
In Hollywood, ~~they~~ don't know what the American public really wants in movies.

[Who are the they *referred to here?]*

When the town board asked about the cost of the next political campaign,

the politicians
the board was assured that ~~they~~ would pay for **their** own campaigns.

[To whom do they *and their* refer? Most likely *they* refers to the politicians who will be campaigning, but *politicians* is only implied.]*

serving as a forest ranger
Martina worked in a national forest last summer, and ~~this~~ may be her career choice.

[What does this *refer to? Because no word or phrase in the first part of the sentence refers to the pronoun, the revised version has one of several possible answers.]*

Many people who have cell phones let their musical ringtones go off

and the loud ringing
loudly when sitting in movies or lectures, ~~which~~ bothers me.

[What does which *refer to here? The fact that many people have cell phones, that they let their phones go off in movies or lectures, or maybe that the ringtones are so loud?]*

1. Pronoun Number

For collective nouns, such as *group, committee,* and *family,* use either a singular or plural pronoun, depending on whether the group acts as a unit or acts separately as many individuals within the unit.

The committee reached **its** decision before the end of the meeting.
[Here the committee acted as a unit.]

The committee relied on **their** own consciences to reach a decision.
[Here each member of the committee relied separately on his or her own conscience.]

Be consistent in pronoun number. Don't shift from singular to plural or plural to singular.

After **someone** studies the violin for a few months, **she** may decide to try the

piano. Then ~~they~~ *she* can compare and decide which instrument ~~they~~ *she* likes better.

2. Compound Subjects

Compound subjects with *and* take the plural pronoun.

The **table** and **chair** were delivered promptly, but **they** were not the style I had ordered.

For compound subjects with *or* or *nor,* the pronoun agrees with the subject word closer to it.

The restaurant offered either regular **patrons** or each new **customer** a free cup of coffee with **his** or **her** dinner.

Neither this **house** nor the **others** had **their** shutters closed.

3. *Who/Which/That*

When *who, which,* or *that* begins a dependent clause, use the word as follows:

■ *Who* is used for people (and sometimes animals).

He is a person **who** can help you.

■ *Which* is used most often for nonessential clauses (see Chapter 29).

The catalog, **which** I sent for last month, had some unusual merchandise. [The *which* clause here is nonessential.]

■ *That* is used most often for essential clauses.

When I finished the book **that** she lent me, I was able to write my paper. [The *that* clause here is essential.]

4. Indefinite Words

Indefinite words such as *any* and *each* usually take the singular pronoun.

Each of the boys handed in **his** uniform.

5. Indefinite Pronouns

He was traditionally used to refer to indefinite pronouns ending in *-body* and *-one.* For current use of nonsexist pronouns, see Chapter 37c.

Everyone brought **his** coat.

Use the following strategies to avoid the exclusive use of the masculine pronoun when the reference is to both males and females (a practice seen by many people as sexist):

■ Use both the masculine and feminine pronoun.

Everyone brought **his** or **her** coat.   [Some people view this as wordy.]

■ Switch to the plural subject and pronoun.

All of the people brought **their** coats.

■ Use the plural pronoun.

Everyone brought **their** coats.   [Some people view this as incorrect. Others, such as the National Council of Teachers of English, accept this as a way to avoid sexist language.]

■ Use *a, an,* or *the* if the meaning remains clear.

Everyone brought **a** coat.

Exercise 23.3 Proofreading Practice

Rewrite each sentence in the following paragraph that has a problem with pronoun reference or clarity.

(1) More than three million children are homeschooled in the United States each year. (2) Parents who educate their children at home do so because home schooling is good for them. (3) Many parents believe that each child is an individual, and their educational needs are best met by them. (4) A mother who homeschools him claims it has brought the family closer and increased his self-confidence. (5) Other parents believe the public education system in this country is in need of repair, and they need to do something about it. (6) Some states have made it very easy for a parent to start educating them at home. (7) In Montana, a parent may remove their child from school simply by registering with the superintendent. (8) This is a cause for concern among educators. (9) Many school districts are in favor of a formal system of accountability for them when they take their children out. (10) Consequently, the increase in homeschooling will require a comprehensive study of the best method to monitor their achievement.

Exercise 23.4 Pattern Practice

Using each of the patterns shown, write a sentence of your own with pronouns that correctly and clearly refer to the noun.

Example: Everyone should put his or her jacket in the closet upon arriving at school. (indefinite pronoun)

Sentence Using the Same Pattern: Anybody can purchase his or her book at the sale price.

1. The girl and the boy walked arm in arm, and they seemed to be in love. (compound subject)
2. All people in the theater ate their popcorn. (indefinite pronoun)
3. He is a person who can do almost anything. (*who/which/that*)
4. After a student graduates from high school, she may wish to travel abroad for the summer before heading to college. (pronoun number)
5. Each of the girls wore her new dress to the prom. (indefinite words)

24
ADJECTIVES AND ADVERBS

24a ADJECTIVES AND ADVERBS

Adjectives and **adverbs** describe or add information about other words in a sentence. To distinguish adjectives from adverbs, locate the words they describe or modify. Adjectives modify nouns and pronouns. Adverbs modify verbs, verb forms, adjectives, and other adverbs.

Adjectives modify nouns and pronouns:

red   house
(ADJECTIVE)   (NOUN)

cheerful   smile
(ADJECTIVE)   (NOUN)

It   was **beautiful**.
(PRONOUN)   (ADJECTIVE)

They   were **loud**.
(PRONOUN)   (ADJECTIVE)

Adverbs modify verbs, verb forms, adjectives, and other adverbs:

danced   **gracefully**
(VERB)   (ADVERB)

very   tall
(ADVERB)   (ADJECTIVE)

ran   **very**   **quickly**
(VERB)   (ADVERB)   (ADVERB)

had   **barely**   moved
          (ADVERB)   (VERB FORM)

Many adverbs end in -*ly:*

Adjective	Adverb
rapid	rapidly
nice	nicely
happy	happily

However, the -*ly* ending isn't a sure test for adverbs because some adjectives have an -*ly* ending (*early, ghostly*), and some adverbs do not end in -*ly* (*very, fast, far*). To be sure, check your dictionary to see whether the word is listed as an adjective or adverb.

To use adjectives and adverbs correctly:

■ Use -*ed* adjectives (the -*ed* form of verbs, past participles) to describe nouns. Be sure to include the -*ed* ending.

used clothing   **painted** houses   **experienced** driver

■ Use adjectives following linking verbs such as *appear, seem, taste, feel,* and *look.*

The sofa seemed **comfortable.**   [sofa = comfortable]

The water tastes **salty.**   [water = salty]

Some verbs can be either linking or action verbs, depending on the meaning. Note the two different meanings of the verb *looked:*

The cat **looked** sleepy.   [cat = sleepy]

The cat **looked** eagerly at the canary.

[The cat is performing the action of looking.]

■ Use adverbs to modify verbs.

     quickly   suddenly   sweetly
He ran ~~quick~~.   The glass broke ~~sudden~~.   She sang ~~sweet~~.

■ Be sure to distinguish between the following adjectives and adverbs:

Adjective	Adverb
sure	surely
real	really
good	well
bad	badly

    surely   badly   well
She ~~sure~~ likes to dance.   The car runs ~~bad~~.   He sings ~~good~~.

■ When you use adverbs such as *so, such,* and *too,* be sure to complete the phrase or clause.

Hailey was so tired. *that she left the office early*

Malley's is such a popular restaurant. *that reservations are recommended*

Tran's problem was that he was too proud. *to ask for help*

Hint

USING *WELL*

Well is most common as an adverb, but *well* is an adjective when it refers to good health.

Despite her surgery, she looks **well.**

Exercise 24.1 Proofreading Practice

Rewrite the following paragraph so that all the adjectives and adverbs are correct. Highlight or underline the words you have changed.

What will life be like for the child born in the United States in the year 2040? Inform historians have diligent researched what will sure be in store for these youngsters. First, it is expected that children born in the year 2040 will live twice as long as those born in 1910. They will enjoy a more affluent lifestyle and better health than their baby-boomer grandparents. Convenient, children will be able to eat broccoli Jell-O instead of the actual despise vegetable. They will join an enormous inflated population of 475 million people, with the majority living in California, Texas, and Florida. Larger homes will be squeezed onto smaller lots, and an abundance of homes will be for sale as older homeowners begin to retire. The more academic inclined person born in the year 2040 will have to pay $320,000 for a year at Harvard. There will not be a real big change in methods of child rearing. Parents will struggle with the same child-rearing dilemmas that consumed the latter part of the twentieth century. In fact, a child is a child and faces the same challenges no matter what year he or she is born.

Exercise 24.2 Pattern Practice

Write a sentence of your own for each of the following patterns.

Pattern A: Sentence with an *-ed* adjective modifying a noun

The **fertilized** plant grew quickly on my windowsill.

Pattern B: Sentence with an adverb modifying another adverb

The sound echoed **very** clearly.

Pattern C: Sentence with the adverb *so, such,* or *too* that is complete

It was **such** a long concert that I was tempted to leave during intermission.

Pattern D: An *-ed* adjective after a linking verb

The old man seemed **pleased** when the child said hello.

Pattern E: Sentence with the adverb *well*

With some coaching, the game-show contestant answered the questions very **well.**

Pattern F: Sentence with the adverb *badly*

As the horse cleared the hurdle, it got caught on a bar, fell, and hurt its back leg **badly.**

24b *A / AN / THE*

The articles *a, an,* and *the* precede nouns. The choice between *a* and *an* is determined by the word that follows it.

■ Use *a* before a word that starts with a consonant sound.

a book	a horse	a very big house
a one-inch pipe	a youth	a PTA parent

a union   [Use *a* when the *u* sounds like the *y* in *you*.]

Hint

USING *A* AND *AN*

A is used before consonant **sounds,** not just consonants. In the phrase *a one-syllable word,* the word *one,* though spelled with a vowel, starts with a "wah" sound, which is a consonant sound. Similarly, in the phrase *a union,* the word *union* starts with a consonant "you" sound.

▶

Formerly, *an* was used before unaccented syllables beginning with *h,* as in the following:

an historian   an hotel   an habitual offender

However, this practice is becoming less frequent, and *a* is now considered preferable:

a historian   a hotel   a habitual offender

■ Use *an* when the word following it starts with a vowel or an un-sounded *h* (as in *honor, hour,* and *honest*).

an egg   an hour   an onion

an ancient coin   an eagle   an idea

an SOS signal   [the *S* here is sounded as "es"]

Exercise 24.3 Proofreading Practice

Underline any errors in the use of a *or* an *in the following paragraph. Highlight or circle* a *or* an *when it is used correctly.*

Maintaining a clear complexion, salvaging a unusually bad semester, and decorating a dorm room are among the topics treated in one of the magazine world's fastest-growing segments, magazines for college students. This market is fueled by advertisers eager to reach a untapped market of 14 to 16 million college students with an large disposable income and a earning potential of many billions of dollars after graduation. Most college magazines are quarterlies, distributed free at a campus newsstand or by direct mail as an insert in the college paper. While profits are high, there is some criticism that these magazines are merely a advertising vehicle and do not focus on substantive issues, such as taking a close look at student loan programs or attempting a honest appraisal of racism on campus.

Exercise 24.4 Pattern Practice

Write a sentence using the suggested nouns with a, an, *or* the.

Example: egg, piece of toast, cup

Sentence: For breakfast, I ordered **an** egg, **a** piece of toast, and **a** cup of coffee.

1. used car, salesperson, helpful
2. train, hour, Alaska, Yukon
3. yeast, bread, oven, cookbook
4. *A*'s, *F*'s (as letter grades in a college course), grade book
5. old barn, young chickens, wire fence

24c COMPARISONS

Adverbs and adjectives are often used to show comparison, and their forms indicate the degree of comparison. In comparisons, most adjectives and adverbs add *-er* and *-est* as endings or combine with the words *more* and *most* or *less* and *least*.

- **Positive form** is used when no comparison is made.

    a **large** box   an **acceptable** offer

- **Comparative form** is used when two things are being compared (with *-er, more,* or *less*).

    the **larger** of the two boxes

    the **more** (or **less**) **acceptable** of the two offers

- **Superlative form** is used when three or more things are being compared (with *-est, most,* or *least*).

    the **largest** of the six boxes

    the **most** (or **least**) **acceptable** of all the offers

ADJECTIVES AND ADVERBS IN COMPARISON		
Positive	Comparative	Superlative
(for one; uses the base form)	*(for two; uses -er, more, or less)*	*(for three or more; uses -est, most, or least)*
tall	taller	tallest
pretty	prettier	prettiest
cheerful	more cheerful	most cheerful
selfish	less selfish	least selfish
Curtis is **tall**.	Curtis is **taller** than Rachel.	Curtis is the **tallest** player on the team.

IRREGULAR FORMS OF COMPARISON		
Positive	Comparative	Superlative
(for one)	*(for two)*	*(for three or more)*
good	better	best
well	better	best
little	less	least
some	more	most
much	more	most
many	more	most
bad, badly	worse	worst

Hint

MAKING COMPARISONS CORRECTLY

1. Be sure to avoid double comparisons in which both the -er and more (or -est and most) are used.

the ~~most~~ farthest   ~~more~~ quicker

2. Be sure to complete your comparisons by using all needed words.

Driving down Hill Street is slower than ^driving down^ Western Avenue.

[The act of driving down one street is being compared to the act of driving down another street. The streets themselves are not being compared.]

The weather here is as warm as ^it is in^ Phoenix.

The results of the second medical test were more puzzling than ^those of^ the first test.

3. Remember to choose the correct pronoun case in comparisons with omitted words. (See 23a.)

Terrence jumps higher than **I** (do).
Terrence likes Aisha more than (he likes) **me.**

Following are some guidelines for choosing between -er and -est or more and most (or less and least).

■ With one-syllable words, the -er and -est endings are commonly used.

quick	quicker	quickest

■ With two-syllable words, some adjectives take -er and -est, and others use more and most (all use less and least). Check the dictionary to be sure.

happy	happier	happiest
thoughtful	more thoughtful	least thoughtful

■ For adverbs, more and most or less and least are commonly used.

smoothly	more smoothly	least smoothly

■ For words with three or more syllables, use more and most or less and least.

generous	more generous	least generous

Exercise 24.5 Proofreading Practice

Revise the paragraph to correct errors in the words used to show comparisons.

A new sport, already popular in Canada and sweeping across the United States, is indoor box lacrosse. It is a more faster, furiouser, and often more brutal version of the field game of lacrosse. Box lacrosse is indeed an exciting game because it is more speedy and more rougher than ice hockey but requires the kind of teamwork needed in basketball. Scores for box lacrosse are more high than those for field lacrosse because the indoor game has a more smaller playing area with the most opportunities for scoring. The team in box lacrosse is also more smaller than in field lacrosse; there are only six people on a side in the indoor game, instead of the ten people on a conventional field lacrosse team. In addition, box lacrosse is played on artificial turf in ice hockey rinks, and the sticks are more short and more thinner than conventional field lacrosse sticks. Almost anything goes in this rough-and-tumble indoor sport.

Exercise 24.6 Pattern Practice

Write sentences of your own using information provided. Try to include as many comparisons as you can.

Example: Write a sentence comparing the cost of the items listed here and using the word *expensive*.

bananas $0.65/pound

apples $1.29/pound

pears $1.59/pound

Sample Sentence: At the First Street Fruit Market, apples are more expensive than bananas, but bananas are less expensive than pears, which are the most expensive of these three fruits.

1. Write a sentence about magazines using the word *interesting*.

Today's Trends is very dull.
Home Magazine is somewhat interesting.
Now! is very interesting.

2. Write a sentence about teenagers using the words *old* and *young*.

Vinay is thirteen years old.
Michelle is fifteen years old.
Ethan is eighteen years old.

3. Write a sentence about movies using the word *scary*.

> *Terror at Night* is not a very scary movie.
> *Teen Horror* is a somewhat scary movie.
> *Night of the Avengers* is a very scary movie.

4. Write a sentence about car engines using the word *powerful*.

> The Hyundai engine is not very powerful.
> The Ford engine is fairly powerful.
> The Ferrari engine is very powerful.

5. Write a sentence about professors using the word *clear*.

> Professor Tischler's lectures are not very clear.
> Professor Liu's lectures are somewhat clear.
> Professor Gottner's lectures are very clear.

25
PREPOSITIONS

Prepositions connect nouns and pronouns to other words in a sentence.

They left **in** the morning.
[The preposition *in* connects *morning* with the verb *left*.]

25a COMMON PREPOSITIONS

The following is a list of common prepositions:

about	at	down
above	because of	during
according to	before	except
across	behind	except for
after	below	excepting
against	beneath	for
along	beside	from
along with	between	in
among	beyond	in addition to
apart from	by	in case of
around	concerning	inside
as	despite	in spite of

instead of	out of	toward
into	outside	under
like	over	underneath
near	past	unlike
next	regarding	until
of	round	up
off	since	upon
on	through	up to
onto	throughout	with
on top of	till	within
out	to	without

25b IDIOMATIC PREPOSITIONS

If choosing the right preposition is difficult, look up the word it is used with (not the preposition) in the dictionary. The following combinations can be troublesome:

Wrong	Revised
apologize about	apologize for
argue on	argue about
bored of	bored with
capable to	capable of
concerned to, on	concerned about, over, with
in search for	in search of
independent from	independent of
interested about	interested in, by
outlook of life	outlook on life
puzzled on	puzzled at, by
similar with	similar to
write over (a subject)	write about (a subject)

25c OTHER PREPOSITIONS

Selecting other prepositions can also be difficult. See the Glossary of Usage at the back of this book for help with the following combinations:

among, between	different from, different than
compared to, compared with	off (*not* off of)
could have (*not* could of)	should have (*not* should of)

Hint

USING PREPOSITIONS

In formal writing, avoid putting a preposition at the end of a sentence, if possible.

Informal: This is the argument he disagreed **with**.

Formal: This is the argument **with** which he disagreed.

Some prepositions, however, cannot be rearranged.

He wants to go **in**.

The mayor was well thought **of**.

The results may not be worth worrying **about**.

Exercise 25.1 Proofreading Practice

Highlight or underline the prepositions that are incorrectly used in the following paragraph, and then write in the correct words.

The next time you are stuck with traffic, look toward the sky. You might be puzzled on the birds flying south for the winter. The management of human traffic could of been solved hundreds of years ago if we had patterned our behavior on migratory birds. Researchers interested about migration have noted that due to the flocking system, birds do not crash into each other or go astray. This theory was published to *Physical Review* about four years ago. The theory refers of the behavior of gases and liquids and the idea that a bird flock behaves like a liquid being poured into a glass. If one drop of liquid or one bird deviates from the course, the rest remains intact. Researchers hope this information will help engineers design spaces that allow people to flow smoothly among one area to the next and avoid bottlenecks upon the road. Within the future, when you "flock" on the beach, spare a thought to those feathered friends.

Exercise 25.2 Pattern Practice

In the following sentences, supply an appropriate preposition in each blank.

(1) It has been proved that people's outlook _____ life can help them live longer. (2) A person who is bored _____ living tends to contract illnesses more often than a person who looks forward _____ every new day. (3) Someone who is always expecting the worst and is overly concerned _____ the negatives in life is more likely to become depressed. (4) All people are capable _____ living life _____ the fullest. (5) Don't spend your days in search _____ the answers to all of life's questions. (6) It is better to regard each new day _____ a challenge.

26

SUBJECTS

The **subject** of a sentence is the word or words that indicate who or what is doing the action of active verbs. The subject of a passive verb is acted on by the verb.

There are several complications to remember when finding subjects:

■ Some subjects have more than one word.

> Juan and Quo realized that despite being roommates, they really liked each other.
>
> **1.** Who *realized*? Juan and Quo.
>
> **2.** The subject is *Juan and Quo.*

> That roommates occasionally disagree is well known.
>
> **1.** What *is well known*? That roommates occasionally disagree.
>
> **2.** The subject is *That roommates occasionally disagree.*

Try This

TO FIND THE SUBJECT

To find the subject, first look for the verb (see Chapter 21), and then ask *who* or *what* is doing the action for active verbs. Ask *who* or *what* is acted on for passive verbs.

> Annie worked as an underpaid lifeguard last summer.

1. Locate the verb: *worked* (active).
2. Ask: Who or what *worked*?
3. The answer is "Annie worked," so *Annie* is the subject.

> Annie was paid less than minimum wage by the swimming pool manager.

1. Locate the verb: *was paid* (passive).
2. Ask: Who or what *was paid*?
3. The answer is "Annie was paid," so *Annie* is the subject.

■ Some subjects may be buried among describing words before and after the subject word.

The major **problem** with today's parents is their tendency to avoid being like their parents.

Almost **all** of his CDs were legally downloaded from the Internet.

Too many **farmers** in that area of the state planted soybeans last year.

■ Subjects in commands are not expressed in words because the person being addressed is the reader (*you*). "Turn the page" really means that you, the reader, should turn the page.

Close the door. [Who is being told to close the door? You are.]

Mix the eggs thoroughly before adding milk. [Who is being told to mix the eggs? You are.]

■ Most subjects come before the verb, but some come in the middle of the sentence or after the verb. For questions, the subject comes in the middle of the sentence or after the verb.

When is the **band** going to start?   Are **they** here yet?

■ For sentences that begin with *here, there,* or *it,* the subject comes after the verb.

Here comes the **rain** again.   Here come those **rain drops.**

There is a buzzing **sound** in my left ear.

Now there are buzzing **sounds** in both ears.

It is **one** of those medical mysteries, I guess.

■ For verbs in the passive voice, the doer of the action is expressed in a phrase beginning with *by,* and the subject receives the action. When we are not interested in who is doing the action or when it is obvious who did it, the *by* phrase is omitted.

The ball was hit by the boy.   (*or*)   The ball was hit.

The experiment was performed   (*or*)   The experiment was performed.
by several assistants.

Exercise 26.1 Proofreading Practice

Highlight or underline the subjects of all the verbs in the following sentences. As an example, the first sentence is already marked.

(1) <u>Humans</u> are unique in preferring to use the right hand. (2) Among other animals, each individual favors one hand or another, but in every species other than humans, the split between using the right or left hand is even. (3) Only humans seem to favor the right hand. (4) Even in studies

of prehistoric people, anthropologists have found this preference. (5) For example, in ancient drawings over five thousand years old, most people are shown using their right hands. (6) This evidence suggests that handedness is not a matter of cultural pressures but perhaps of some genetic difference. (7) Although left-handedness seems to run in families, it is not clear how hand preference is passed from one generation to the next.

Exercise 26.2　Pattern Practice

In each blank, write a subject that could fit the sentence. Try to add a word or phrase describing the subject.

(1) <u>Greedy credit card companies</u> keep finding new targets to plunge into debt. (2) These _____ have begun issuing credit cards to college students with little money and no credit history. (3) _____ are now walking around campus with the ability to accumulate thousands of dollars of debt. (4) Worst of all, _____ usually do not know about the cards until their children's bills arrive. (5) Some _____ have begun screening credit applications from college students more stringently. (6) _____ have found that it is difficult to squeeze blood from a stone, so they might as well not issue cards to college students.

27

PHRASES

A **phrase** is a group of related words without a subject and complete verb. The words in phrases act as the subject or verb in a sentence, or they can add information to other parts of the sentence.

Note how the related words in these phrases work together to offer information:

<u>A major earthquake</u> hit the area last night.
[This phrase is the subject of the sentence.]

<u>Listening to music</u> is one form of relaxation.
[This phrase is the subject of the sentence.]

Dr. Prada, <u>a famous brain surgeon</u>, will be on television this evening.
[This phrase tells us more about the subject, Dr. Prada.]

The bike leaning on its side fell over during the rainstorm.
[This phrase also tells us more about the subject.]

They may have been eating when I called.
[This phrase is the verb phrase.]

He always walks with his toes pointed out.
[This phrase gives added information about the verb.]

Her favorite pastime is visiting museums.
[This phrase comes after a linking verb and completes the subject.]

Jenny looks like Edna, a second cousin of mine.
[This phrase gives added information about another element in the sentence.]

Exercise 27.1 Proofreading Practice

Each one of the underlined phrases in the following paragraph performs one of the six functions listed. Identify the function of the phrase by writing the appropriate number near the phrase. The first sentence has been done as an example.

1. The phrase acts as the subject.
2. It tells something more about the subject.
3. It acts as the verb.
4. It tells something more about the verb.
5. It completes the subject of a linking verb.
6. It tells something more about another element in the sentence.

(1) Finding a place for our garbage ⁽¹⁾ is a problem as old as human beings. (2) Along the Pacific Coast, there are large, round shell mounds where for centuries people had been discarding the bones and clamshells that constituted their garbage. (3) When people gathered together in cities, they hauled their waste to the outskirts of town or dumped it into nearby rivers. (4) In the United States, the first municipal refuse system was instituted in Philadelphia, a well-organized city. (5) Slaves there were forced to wade into the Delaware River and toss bales of trash into the current. (6) Eventually, this dumping into rivers was outlawed, and people looked for new solutions to the garbage problem. (7) Municipal dump sites, unused plots of land far away from houses, were a frequent answer. (8) But the number of landfill sites is decreasing as many dumps are closed because of health hazards or because of cost. (9) America, a land of throwaway

containers and fancy packaging, clearly faces a garbage problem, <u>a prob-lem without any obvious answers</u>.

Exercise 27.2 Pattern Practice

In each of the following sentences, one of the phrases has been underlined. Describe the function of that phrase, and then make up your own sentence that has a phrase performing the same function. The first sentence has been labeled as an example.

1. America <u>is facing</u> a garbage crisis that gets worse each year.
   (VERB PHRASE)
2. In 1980, <u>the average American</u> sent 2.2 pounds of trash to the dump each day, but now it's 5.1 pounds a day.
3. We need new dump sites, but they are <u>hard to find</u> because no one wants a landfill next door.
4. Some cities, <u>the ones without potential new landfill space</u>, have given up looking for nearby sites.
5. These cities <u>have started</u> a new practice, exporting their garbage to other states.
6. For example, trash <u>from New Jersey</u> is sent to landfills in Ohio.
7. Exporting garbage is an answer, <u>a temporary one</u>, until other states start refusing to accept someone else's trash.

28

CLAUSES

A **clause** is a group of related words that (unlike a phrase) has both a subject and a complete verb. A sentence can have one or more clauses.

A sentence can have one clause:

Some <u>students see</u> themselves one day working in an office environment
    (SUBJECT) (VERB)

and wearing formal business clothes.

A sentence can have two clauses:

Although <u>it becomes</u> expensive to buy a wardrobe of business clothes, many
    (SUBJECT 1) (VERB 1)

<u>people enjoy</u> the opportunity to dress well every day.
(SUBJECT 2) (VERB 2)

A sentence can have one clause embedded in the middle of another clause:

Students   who   seek well-paying jobs often think of careers in
(SUBJECT 1) (SUBJECT 2) (VERB 2)   (VERB 1)
business and finance.

28a INDEPENDENT CLAUSES

An **independent clause** can stand alone as a complete sentence because it doesn't depend on anything else to complete the thought.

An independent clause has a complete verb and subject.

No one could understand the message written on the blackboard.
(SUBJECT) (COMPLETE VERB)

It expresses a complete thought and can stand alone as a sentence.

He never wanted to lend me any of his magazines.

Two different groups of connecting words can be used at the beginning of an independent clause:

■ *And, but, for, nor, or, so, yet* (coordinating conjunctions)

Detasseling corn is exhausting work, **but** she needs the money.

(For use of the comma with these connectors, see 38a.)

■ *Therefore, moreover, thus, consequently,* and so on (conjunctive adverbs)

Detasseling corn is exhausting work; **however,** she needs the money.

(For the use of the semicolon with these connectors, see Chapter 10 and 40a.)

An independent clause can be combined with another independent clause or with a dependent clause to form a sentence (see Chapter 30).

■ An independent clause can be its own sentence.

The popularity of some cartoon characters lasts for years.

■ Two independent clauses can form one sentence.

Mickey Mouse, Donald Duck, and Bugs Bunny are perennial favorites, but other once-popular characters such as Jiggs and Maggie have disappeared.

■ An independent clause can be joined with a dependent clause.

Because Homer Simpson and the *Peanuts* characters have become great favorites, perhaps they will last for several generations like Mickey Mouse.

Exercise 28.1 Proofreading Practice

In the following paragraph, groups of words are underlined. Identify each underlined group of words in the following paragraph as a phrase or a clause. The first sentence has been done as an example.

(1) For years, strange noises, <u>which would start in June and last until</u>
                                        (CLAUSE)
<u>September</u>, filled the air around the waters of Richardson Bay, <u>an inlet</u>

<u>of water near Sausalito, California</u>. (2) The noise was heard in the house-
                    (PHRASE)
boats, <u>especially those with fiberglass hulls</u>, moored along the southwestern shore of the bay. (3) <u>The noise was usually described as a deep</u>
<u>hum like an electric foghorn or an airplane motor</u>. (4) The noise, <u>which</u>
<u>would start in late evening</u>, would continue until morning, <u>ruining people's</u>
<u>sleep</u>. (5) <u>During the summer of 1994</u>, the hum was unusually loud and
<u>stirred investigations</u>. (6) Suspicion initially centered on a nearby sewage
plant, <u>which was suspected of dumping sewage at night when no one would</u>
<u>notice</u>. (7) Other people thought there were <u>secret Navy experiments going</u>
<u>on</u>. (8) An acoustical engineer, <u>studying the mystery sound for months</u>,
kept thinking he would find the answer, <u>but he didn't</u>. (9) Finally, a marine ecologist identified the source of the hum as the sound of the plain-
fin midshipman, <u>a fish also known as the singing toad</u>. (10) <u>The male's</u>
<u>singing</u> was the sound everyone heard, he said, <u>though some people still</u>
<u>suspect the sewage plant</u>.

Exercise 28.2 Pattern Practice

Each sentence in the following paragraph has one of these patterns:

1. Some sentences have one clause.
2. Some have two clauses separated by punctuation.
3. Some have one clause in the middle of another.

Identify the pattern by its number, and then write your own paragraph of five or more sentences. Identify the pattern of clauses in each of your sentences using these same numbers. As a subject for your paragraph, you may want to describe other types of pollution.

(1) One type of pollution that the government tries to eliminate is the visual pollution of billboards along our highways. (2) In 1965, Congress passed
the Highway Beautification Act to outlaw those ugly signs, but the law
didn't work. (3) While the federal government paid for the removal of 2,235
old billboards in 1983, the billboard industry was busy putting up 18,000
new signs in the same year. (4) Since then the situation has gotten worse.
(5) The 1965 act had all kinds of loopholes; however, the real problem is a
requirement in the law to pay billboard companies for removing the signs.

(6) Because some communities don't have the funds for this, too many old signs are still standing along with all the new ones going up.

28b DEPENDENT CLAUSES

A **dependent clause** cannot stand alone as a complete sentence because it depends on another clause in the sentence to complete the thought.

Try This

TO FIND DEPENDENT CLAUSES

1. Dependent clauses have conjunctions such as *after, when,* or *if* at the beginning of the clause (see the explanation of adverb clauses in 28b2) or relative pronouns such as *who, that,* or *which* (see 28b1).

   after the advertisement included a small child tossing a car

   that he stated the major reason for the rise in crime

   [Each of these dependent clauses needs an independent clause before or after it to make a complete sentence.]

2. Say the dependent clause aloud, and you'll hear that you need to add more information.

   "When I got up this morning . . ."

   [What happened when you got up this morning? We need more information.]

3. To recognize dependent clauses punctuated as sentences, try proofreading your paper backward from the last sentence to the first.

There are two kinds of dependent clauses: adjective and adverb clauses.

1. Adjective Clauses (*Who/Which/That* Clauses)

An **adjective clause** gives additional information about a noun or pronoun in the sentence and starts with *who, which, that, whose,* or *whom.*

The singer, **who used to play lead guitar,** now lets the other band members play while she sings.

The group tried a concert tour, **which was a financial disaster.**

The rumor **that the poor ticket sales were due to mismanagement** never appeared in print.

2. Adverb Clauses (*Because* / *If* / *When* Clauses)

An **adverb clause** gives more information about other verbs, adjectives, or adverbs in a sentence or another clause. Adverb clauses start with joining words such as the following:

after	before	though	when
although	even if	unless	whenever
as	even though	until	whether
as if	if	what	while
because	since	whatever	

Try This

TO FIND ADVERB CLAUSES

You can recognize adverb clauses by marker words at the beginning. The meaning of each of these words creates the need for another clause to complete the thought. Think of the relationship as follows:

After *X, Y.*   *[After X happens, Y happens.]*

After I eat lunch tomorrow . . .   *[What will happen?]*

After I eat lunch tomorrow, I will call you.

Because *X, Y.*   *[Because X happens, Y happens.]*

Because it was so dark out . . .   *[What happened?]*

Because it was so dark out, she tripped on the steps.

If *X, Y.*   *[If X happens, Y will happen.]*

If I win the lottery . . .   *[What will happen?]*

If I win the lottery, I'll quit my job and retire.

When *X, Y.*   *[When X happens, Y happens.]*

When it began to rain . . .   *[What happened?]*

When it began to rain, the game was canceled.

Dependent clauses may appear at the beginning of a sentence, before the independent clause, or at the end of the sentence, where they are harder to recognize.

I will call you **after I eat lunch tomorrow.**

She tripped on the steps **because it was so dark out.**

The game was canceled **when it began to rain.**

Hint

PUNCTUATING DEPENDENT CLAUSES

■ When an adverb clause appears at the beginning of a sentence, it is followed by a comma.

Until gas prices come down, I will buy only compact cars.

■ When an adverb clause follows an independent clause, no punctuation is needed before the adverb clause if it is essential (see 29a), but include a comma before the adverb clause if it is nonessential.

I will buy only compact cars **until gas prices come down.**

[essential adverb clause]

I buy only compact cars, **though I was tempted to consider an SUV.**

[nonessential adverb clause]

Exercise 28.3 Proofreading Practice

In the following paragraph, highlight or underline each dependent clause, and identify it as an adjective or adverb clause.

(1) The tiny lichen is an amazing plant. (2) It can survive in an incredibly difficult environment because it can do things no other plant can do. (3) The lichen, which can anchor itself on a bare rock by etching the rock's surface with powerful acids, grows into the pits that it burns out. (4) Because lichens grow in cold climates above the tree line, they are frozen or covered by snow most of the year. (5) Unlike the cactus in the desert, the lichen has no way to retain moisture. (6) Because of this, the sun dries lichens into waterless crusts during the day. (7) When there is a drought, lichens may dry out completely for several months. (8) Even under ideal conditions, their total daily growing period may last only for an hour or two while they are still wet with morning dew. (9) The lichen, which may take twenty-five years to grow to a diameter of one inch, can live for several thousand years. (10) These amazing plants are able to live in all sorts of difficult places but not in cities because the pollution may kill them.

Exercise 28.4 Pattern Practice

Write your own paragraph with sentences that include dependent clauses. As in Exercise 28.3, identify the dependent clauses by highlighting or underlining them and labeling them as either adjective or adverb clauses. As a subject for your paragraph, you may wish to describe an animal, a person, or another plant like the lichen that manages to survive under difficult conditions.

Exercise 28.5 Proofreading Practice

Identify the independent clauses in this paragraph by highlighting or underlining them. If an independent clause is interrupted by a dependent clause, put parentheses around the dependent clause. The first sentence has been done as an example.

Kwanzaa, (which is an African American holiday celebrated from December 26 through January 1), did not originate in any one of the fifty-five African countries. When the festival was first introduced in 1966, it was designed as a ritual to welcome the first harvests to the home. Dr. Maulana Karenga, who created the festival, was reacting against the commercialism of Christmas. Similar to Hanukkah, Kwanzaa uses candles as symbols of the holiday. The seven principles that the candles represent are unity, self-determination, responsibility, cooperative economics, purpose, creativity, and faith. The seven candles, which are red, black, and green, remind participants of the seven principles and the colors in flags of African liberation movements. Gifts are exchanged, and on December 31, participants celebrate with a banquet reflecting the cuisine of various African countries. Kwanzaa has become an important American celebration.

29

ESSENTIAL AND NONESSENTIAL CLAUSES AND PHRASES

29a ESSENTIAL CLAUSES AND PHRASES

An **essential clause** or **phrase** (also called a *restrictive* or *necessary* clause or phrase) appears after a noun and is essential to complete the meaning of the sentence. An essential clause or phrase cannot be moved to another sentence or omitted because the meaning of the sentence would change.

Compare the meaning of the following two sentences with and without the clause after the noun *people:*

People who can speak more than one language are multilingual.

People are multilingual.

[The second sentence seems odd because not all people are multilingual. The *who* clause is essential because we need it to understand the meaning.]

Please repair all the windows <u>that are broken</u>.

[If the *that* clause is taken out, the sentence is a request to repair all the windows, not just those that are broken. Because the meaning of the sentence is changed when the *that* clause is removed, the *that* clause is essential to the sentence.]

Tom Hanks's movie *Forrest Gump* will be on TV tonight.

[The movie title *Forrest Gump* is necessary because Tom Hanks has appeared in many movies. If *Forrest Gump* is taken out of the sentence, it then says that Hanks made only one movie, and that's the one that will be on TV.]

Try This

TO IDENTIFY ESSENTIAL CLAUSES

Essential clauses and phrases are not set off by commas. To see if you have an essential clause, try this:

■ If the clause or phrase starts with *that,* it is almost always essential.

Example: U.S. corn that is genetically modified cannot be sold in most countries in Europe.

■ Read the sentence without the clause in question. Does the sentence still have the same meaning?

Example: The CD that showed the effects of glacial melt was shown in the geology class.

[Without the that *clause, the sentence doesn't explain which CD was shown in class.]*

29b NONESSENTIAL CLAUSES AND PHRASES

A **nonessential clause** or **phrase** (also called a *nonrestrictive* or *unnecessary* clause or phrase) adds extra information but can be removed from a sentence without disturbing the meaning. The information can be put in another sentence.

Compare the following two sentences to see whether the primary meaning of the sentence remains the same after the clause is removed:

My cousin Jim, <u>who lives in Denver</u>, is coming for a visit over Thanksgiving vacation.

My cousin Jim is coming for a visit over Thanksgiving vacation.

[The *who* clause is nonessential because it adds information about where Jim lives but is not necessary to the meaning of the sentence. The assumption here is that the writer has only one cousin named Jim. If the writer had two cousins named Jim, one who lives in Denver and another in Saint Louis, then *who lives in Denver* would be essential.]

Sandwich Supreme, <u>one of the first of a new chain of gourmet sandwich shops</u>, serves six different types of cheese sandwiches with a choice of three different types of bread.

[If the phrase describing Sandwich Supreme as a part of a chain of gourmet shops is removed from the sentence, the meaning of the main clause remains intact. The phrase is therefore not essential.]

Forrest Gump, <u>starring Tom Hanks</u>, will be on TV tonight.

[In this sentence, the phrase noting who stars in the movie can be removed because it merely adds information about the name of one of the actors. Compare this sentence with the example of *Forrest Gump* as an essential clause in 29a.]

Hint

PUNCTUATING NONESSENTIAL CLAUSES

Nonessential clauses and phrases are set off by a pair of commas when they appear within a sentence. Only one comma is needed when they appear at the end of a sentence. (See 38c.)

The compact disc, <u>a revolutionary advance in high-fidelity recording</u>, has made records and tape cassettes obsolete.

[Here the nonessential phrase appears in the middle of the sentence and needs two commas.]

Records and tapes are now obsolete, thanks to the compact disc, <u>a revolutionary advance in high-fidelity recording</u>.

[Here the nonessential phrase appears at the end of the sentence and needs only one comma.]

Some sentences will be punctuated differently, depending on the meaning.

Maia's daughter <u>Maeve</u> is playing in the soccer match.

[This sentence states that Maia has more than one daughter, and the daughter named Maeve is playing in the soccer match.]

Maia's daughter, <u>Maeve</u>, is playing in the soccer match.

[This sentence states that Maia has only one daughter and an extra bit of information is that her name is Maeve.]

The bank offered loans to the farmers, <u>who were going to plant soybeans</u>.

[This sentence states that all farmers received loans.]

The bank offered loans to the farmers <u>who were going to plant soybeans</u>.

[This sentence states that the bank offered loans only to the farmers planting soybeans, not to those planting other crops.]

Exercise 29.1 Proofreading Practice

Identify each underlined phrase in the following paragraph as either essential (E) or nonessential (N).

(1) Art fraud, <u>a widespread problem</u>, is probably as old as art itself. (2) Fourteenth-century Italian stonecarvers <u>who wanted to deceive their buyers</u> copied Greek and Roman statues and then purposely chipped their works so they could peddle them as antiquities. (3) Today forgers, <u>who have become specialists in different kinds of fraud</u>, produce piles of moderately priced prints, paintings, statues, and pottery. (4) The people <u>whom they defraud</u> are usually beginning or less knowledgeable collectors. (5) These people, <u>who usually can afford to spend only a modest amount of money for a work of art</u>, have not developed a skilled eye for detecting fraud.

29.2 Proofreading Practice

In the following paragraph, some of the underlined clauses and phrases are essential; others are nonessential. Practice using clauses and phrases like these in your writing by composing your own sentences in the same patterns. As your topic, you may want to describe another common kind of fraud or deception that exists today.

(1) Thomas Hoving, <u>a former director of the Metropolitan Museum of Art</u>, estimates that 40 percent of the art <u>that is on the market today</u> is fake. (2) However, much of this fraudulent art is not detected because even buyers <u>who suspect fraud</u> find it difficult to prove that the seller knowingly unloaded a fake on them. (3) Thus, collectors <u>who get stuck with dubious pieces of art</u> usually don't go to court. (4) Instead, they attempt to return the piece to the person <u>from whom they bought it</u>. (5) If that isn't possible, some collectors, <u>particularly the less honest ones</u>, pass the piece of art on to another unsuspecting buyer.

30

SENTENCES

A **sentence** is a group of words that has at least one independent clause and expresses a relatively complete thought.

Although a sentence is said to express "a complete thought," sentences normally occur in the context of other sentences that explain the meaning more fully. Therefore, a sentence may seem to need more information because it will refer to other sentences.

He was able to do it.

[This is a complete sentence because it is an independent clause. We don't know who *he* is or what *he* was able to do, but when this sentence appears with others, the sentences around it will make the meaning clear.]

The following characteristics of sentences help distinguish them from fragments:

- Sentences can start with any word.

  1. *And* and *but* are connecting words that can start an independent clause.

     But the dog did not bark.

     [This sentence may not seem complete because it needs a context of other sentences to explain the whole situation.]

  2. *Because, since,* and other markers that begin adverbial clauses can open a sentence as long as an independent clause follows.

     Because she did not lock her bike, it was stolen.

     [dependent clause first, then an independent clause]

  3. Dependent clauses and phrases can start a sentence as subjects.

     That it was hot did not bother the athletes.

     [dependent clause as subject]

  4. Transitional words and phrases, such as *first, to sum up,* and *meanwhile,* can begin a sentence.

     Next, she lifted the window.

     [We don't know what she did first, but again, the context of other sentences will help.]

- Sentences can have pronouns as subjects.

  He was proud of his accomplishments.

- Sentences don't have to have any specified length. They can have only a few or many words.

  Go away!

  [short complete sentence]

31
STYLE VERSUS GRAMMAR

Some writers tend to confuse style with grammar, but these terms apply to very different topics. *Grammar* refers to the rules of standard edited English, such as the correct tense for verb endings and the need to write complete sentences instead of fragments. The rules writers generally need are explained in this book in the sections entitled Revising Sentences, Parts of Sentences, Punctuation, and Mechanics and Spelling. But "style" refers to choices writers make. Is it better to use the abstract noun *beverage* or a specific word, such as *lemonade*? Neither is correct or incorrect. However, given the goal, purpose, and audience for a specific piece of writing, one choice may be better than another. What about using a cliché, such as "white as snow"? It's not *wrong*, but it is a tired, overused comparison. Writing that pays attention to stylistic matters is fresher, more vivid, more appropriate. Stylistically effective writing is also pleasing to read. Which of the sentences below do you prefer? Why? (They are both grammatically correct.)

1. That short girl plays basketball very well, and she makes a lot of successful jump shots. There is very loud cheering by her teammates who are watching when she accomplishes these shots.

2. When that 5′4″ female races past her opponents in basketball, she jackrabbits up to sink her shots. Her teammates, their eyes glued to the ball, cheer wildly and enthusiastically as the ball sinks in.

32
GENERAL AND SPECIFIC LANGUAGE

32a GENERAL VERSUS SPECIFIC STATEMENTS

When we make a general statement, we are thinking broadly. For example, the statement "stopping violence is important" is very general. It applies widely to many instances, but it can be too vague when details or specifics are needed. For example, we don't know whether the writer is writing about abuse that harms children or perhaps driveby shooters who kill others in addition to their intended victims. A statement using more specific language could be the following: "Violence in the form of crimes committed with the use of high-power machine guns harms not only the people involved but also the whole city because violence provokes more violence." When we see a movie and say, "It was a good movie," that doesn't tell the reader much about the movie. To write more specific statements, we need to provide the details and examples using language that conveys more information.

32b GENERAL VERSUS SPECIFIC WORDS

General words refer to whole categories or large classes of items. **Specific words** identify items within the group.

Tree is more general than *maple,* and *maple* is more general than *sugar maple,* a particular kind of maple tree.

General	Specific	More Specific
animal	dog	cocker spaniel
plant	flower	rose
clothing	shoes	flip-flops
visual media	movie	animated full-length feature

Sometimes a general word is adequate or appropriate for the occasion. For example, *car* is a more general word than *Ford,* and it is more appropriate in the following brief account of a trip:

This year we visited several parts of the country that we had not seen before. Last fall we flew to New Mexico for a week, and during spring vacation we traveled by car from New York to Chicago.

General terms are appropriate in some contexts, but specific words are often better choices because they are more precise and vivid and can help the reader's imagination in seeing, hearing, feeling, and smelling what is described (if that is the writer's purpose). Compare these examples.

General: He walked across the street to see the merchandise in the store window.

More Specific: He ambled across Lexington Avenue to see the velvet ties in the window at Bloomingdale's.

General: To help our economy, the United States needs to sell more products on the world market.

More Specific: To decrease our trade deficit, U.S. industries should develop their best high-tech products, such as high-definition television and communications satellites, to sell to growing markets in China and Europe.

Some general words are too vague to convey a writer's meaning.

bad child [Is the child rude? evil? ungrateful?]

bad food [Is the food contaminated? tasteless? unhealthy?]

good movie   [Is the movie funny? Is it well acted? Does it have unusual visual effects? Does it feature someone you like to see onscreen?]

nice person   [Is he polite? interesting to talk to? friendly and outgoing?]

Exercise 32.1 Pattern Practice

Following are some general terms. What are more specific words that could be used instead? An example is provided.

General	Specific	More Specific
food	vegetable	carrot

1. music
2. book
3. animal
4. clothes
5. field of study
6. machine
7. car
8. plant
9. place of business
10. athlete

32c CONCRETE VERSUS ABSTRACT WORDS

Concrete words refer to people and things that can be perceived by the senses. We are able to form images in our minds of concrete terms: *the thick white foam in the glass, dog, garden gate, smoke.* **Abstract words** refer to qualities, concepts, conditions, and ideas: *truth, economics, slow, happy, ethical.*

We need both abstract terms to communicate complex ideas and concrete words to communicate what we see, hear, taste, touch, and feel. However, dull writing tends to be unnecessarily abstract and overuses words such as *aspects, factors,* and *means.*

Abstract
Rainforest trees account for more than 20 percent of the industrial world's consumption of wood. The crop harvest from rainforest trees is valuable because of the trees' resistance to disease and insect infestations. In addition,

wood from these trees has special properties that are useful in particular types of structures. Their characteristic colors and growth patterns make rainforest trees well suited for use in furniture and other wooden products in which color is a prized commodity. This explains why global demand for tropical hardwoods has increased dramatically in recent years.

Concrete
More than 20 percent of the wood used throughout the world is cut from rainforests. The trees from these forests are valued for their ability to resist termites, fungi, and other common diseases of wood. In addition, rainforest hardwoods have qualities that make them especially useful for certain purposes. For example, teak resists water damage, so it is used on sailboats. The dark reddish color and interesting grains of rosewood are particularly attractive when made into chairs, tables, and beds; dark brown or black ebony wood is used in billiard balls and for the black keys of pianos. Over the past five years, countries throughout the world have ordered and imported more tropical wood than they used in the preceding fifty years.

Exercise 32.2 Revision Practice

Rewrite the following paragraph so that it is more specific and concrete. You may make up details or find them by doing some quick research.

Traveling to the Bahamas, a group of islands fifty miles across the water from the United States, is an easy trip for private boats. Because gambling is a popular pastime, people go on weekends to gamble and to enjoy a number of sports. Tourism is the nation's leading industry, and Bahamian planners predict a sharp rise in the future. Because of this expectation, developers are building more housing of different types. The Bahamian capital, Nassau, which has suffered from increased crime, is no longer the primary location for tourist development, but boats continue to stop there to let people look around.

33

CONCISENESS AND WORDINESS

Be concise when writing. You will be communicating to your reader more clearly and are more likely to keep your reader's interest. Many readers don't have time for excess words. To keep your paper concise, eliminate what your readers do not need to know, what they already know, and whatever doesn't further the purpose of your paper. That often means resisting the impulse to include everything you know about a subject.

Here are some suggestions for eliminating unnecessary words:

■ Avoid repetition. Some phrases, such as the following, say the same thing twice:

first beginning	6 P.M. in the evening
final completion	beautiful and lovely
circular in shape	true facts
green in color	prove conclusively
really and truly	each and every
positive benefits	connected together

■ Avoid fillers. Some phrases, such as the following, say little or nothing:

there is	there are
in light of the fact that	I am going to explain
what I want to say is	I am going to discuss

He said ~~that there is~~ a storm approaching. *is*

The mayor said that ~~in view of the fact that~~ the budget was overspent, no more projects could be started. *because*

~~It seems to me that it~~ is getting dark out. *It*

~~I am going to discuss artificial~~ intelligence/ ~~which~~ is an exciting field of research. *Artificial*

■ Combine sentences. When the same nouns or pronouns appear in two sentences, combine the two sentences into one.

The data will be entered into the reports/ ~~It will also be~~ included in the graphs. *and*

■ Eliminate *who, which,* and *that.*

The book ~~that is~~ lying on the piano belongs to her.

■ Turn phrases and clauses into adjectives and adverbs.

the player who was very tired	=	the tired player
all applicants who are interested	=	all interested applicants
spoke in a hesitant manner	=	spoke hesitantly
the piano built out of mahogany	=	the mahogany piano

- Turn prepositional phrases into adjectives.

  an employee with ambition = an ambitious employee

  the entrance to the station = the station entrance

- Use active rather than passive.

  research department   the figures
  The ~~figures were~~ checked ~~by the research department~~.

- Remove excess nouns and change them to verbs whenever possible.

  He ~~made the statement that he~~ agreed ~~with the concept~~ that inflation could be controlled.

          stores
  The ~~function of the~~ box ~~is the storage of~~ wire connectors.

- Replace cumbersome words and jargon with clearer, shorter words.

Avoid	Use
advantageous	beneficial, positive
extraordinarily	very
implement	carry out
procure	acquire, buy
utilize	use
effectuate	carry out
ascertain	find out
impact	affect

Exercise 33.1 Proofreading Practice

In the following paragraph, eliminate as many words as you can without losing clarity. You may need to add a few words, too.

It has been noted by researchers that there is a general concern among psychologists that because many parents who are working entrust the responsibility for caring for their infants of a very young age to day-care centers, some of these babies may face harm of a psychological nature. The research findings of the researchers in this field focus on children who are younger than eighteen months of age who are left in day-care centers more than twenty hours a week. For children who are at that most formative age, say the researchers, day care seems to increase the feeling of insecurity. One of the foremost leading researchers in this field says that she isn't sure how the increase in the feeling of insecurity happens, but it is her guess that the stress that a child undergoes each and every day as a result of the separation from the parent can be a contributing causal factor here. Studies of the infants who are in day care for long periods of time each week have shown that more of these infants exhibit feelings of anxiousness and also hyperactivity. These findings definitely and strongly challenge the view that day care does not harm or hurt a young child.

Exercise 33.2 Pattern Practice

Make up a wordy sentence and then a more concise revision following the patterns and examples given.

Pattern A: Reducing a *who, which,* or *that* clause

Wordy: The cook who was flipping hamburgers . . .

Revised: The cook flipping hamburgers . . .

Pattern B: Eliminating fillers

Wordy: It is important that we agree that . . .

Revised: We must agree that . . .

Pattern C: Changing a passive verb to active

Wordy: The car was started by the driver.

Revised: The driver started the car.

Pattern D: Combining sentences

Wordy: The cereal box had pictures of famous athletes on one side. The box had recipes for candy and snacks on the other side.

Revised: The cereal box had pictures of famous athletes on one side and recipes for candy and snacks on the other side.

Pattern E: Turning a phrase or clause into an adjective or adverb

Wordy: The salesperson who sold used cars starred in the TV commercial.

Revised: The used-car salesperson starred in the TV commercial.

Pattern F: Eliminating repetition

Wordy: When she was first beginning to drive her car, she never drove more than 30 miles per hour.

Revised: When she began to drive her car, she never drove more than 30 miles per hour.

Pattern G: Turning a prepositional phrase into an adjective

Wordy: Use the paper with the red lines.

Revised: Use the red-lined paper.

34

PASSIVE VERSUS ACTIVE VOICE

The passive voice is sometimes necessary (see page 131), but in general, it can lessen a document's effectiveness because it may cause the writing to be flat, uninteresting, and wordy. The passive voice may also leave out the doer of the action and cause confusion. Consider these sentences:

Passive: When the children stepped off the bus, the front door was opened by their mother.

[wordy]

(vs.)

Active: Their mother opened the door when the children stepped off the bus.

Passive: It was clear that the voting machine was incorrectly handled by the supplier.

[dull, flat]

(vs.)

Active: The supplier clearly handled the voting machine incorrectly.

Passive: After the car was seen speeding away, the police arrived.

[Who saw the car? The police? Someone else?]

(vs.)

Active: The police arrived after a neighbor saw the car speeding away.

35

UNNECESSARY AND INAPPROPRIATE LANGUAGE

35a CLICHÉS

Clichés are overused expressions that have lost their ability to communicate effectively.

When you read phrases such as *busy as a beaver* or *a crying shame*, you aren't likely to think about a beaver busily working or someone actually crying in shame. Avoid expressions such as the following, which are worn out from too much repetition and are no longer vivid:

white as snow	rat race
beat around the bush	have a screw loose
suits me to a T	add insult to injury
in a nutshell	calm before the storm
crack of dawn	better late than never
clear as mud	green with envy
playing with fire	stubborn as a mule
at the drop of a hat	selling like hotcakes

Exercise 35.1 Proofreading Practice

Highlight or underline the clichés in the following paragraph.

The Ford Motor Company has developed a method of testing automobiles for different age groups. In a nutshell, Ford has designed a suit that makes the crash tester feel as old as the day is long. In order for the tester to experience empathy for aging customers, the suit dims vision, weakens muscles, and makes the tester feel stiff as a board. One tester states, "I'm thirty-two years old, but this gear suits me to a T because it helps me do my job." Testers wear the suit while getting in and out of vehicles, buckling the seat belt, and driving in reverse. Ford hopes that vehicles designed for aging consumers will sell like hotcakes. Many senior citizens feel that they are ignored in the competitive market of automobile sales. One senior says, "We are virtually ignored in the car market, so it is good to see cars designed for senior citizens. It's better late than never." With the success of Ford's designing techniques, many other manufacturers will be jumping on the bandwagon.

Exercise 35.2 Revision Practice

Revise the paragraph in Exercise 35.1 by using more precise language in place of the clichés.

35b PRETENTIOUS LANGUAGE

Pretentious language is too showy; it calls attention to itself by the use of overly complex sentences and ornate, polysyllabic words used for their own sake.

The following sentence is an example of overblown, pompous language that makes the writer sound pretentious and affected. Plain English that communicates clearly is far better than such attempts at showing off.

Pretentious: The specificity with which she formulated her questions as she interrogated the indigenous population of the rustic isle drew gasps of admiration from her cohorts engaged in anthropological studies.

Revised: Other anthropologists admired her ability to be specific when she questioned the island's inhabitants.

35c OFFENSIVE LANGUAGE

Language that may potentially offend readers has no place in academic writing, the business world, and most social situations. Offensive language falls into several categories. *Profanity* is disrespectful of God or religion. *Vulgarity* refers to certain body parts or functions or sexual practices. Other objectionable language is contemptuous of people's racial background, physical appearance, mental abilities, sexual orientation, or political beliefs. Although many of these offensive terms have crept into modern American culture, it is important that you recognize and avoid them in your schoolwork, business life, and social encounters.

36

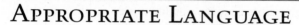

APPROPRIATE LANGUAGE

Choosing among words is a matter of selecting the word that is right in a given writing situation. Some choices are matters of grammatical correctness. For example, whether an essay is formal or informal, you should always write "between you and *me*" (not "between you and *I*"). Other word choices are not so clear-cut. Instead, good writers select appropriate words for the subject, audience, and purpose of a particular piece of writing.

36a STANDARD ENGLISH

Standard English (sometimes called *Standard Edited English*) is the generally accepted language of people in academia, the business world, and other contexts where correct usage is expected. It is "standard" because it conforms to established rules of grammar, sentence structure, punctuation, and spelling and because people are often judged by how well their writing conforms to this level of English.

Standard English, the language used in respected magazines, newspapers, and books, is the language you are expected to use in academic writing. If you are not sure a particular word is standard, check the dictionary.

Nonstandard words such as *ain't* are labeled to indicate that they are not acceptable in these types of writing. In addition, the abbreviations used in instant messaging are unacceptable in college-level writing, as are the abbreviated spellings of words such as *donut* instead of *doughnut,* *tho* instead of *though,* and *lite* instead of *light.*

36b LEVELS OF FORMALITY

The level of formality is the **tone** in writing; it reflects the attitude of the writer toward the subject and audience. The tone may be highly formal or very informal or somewhere in between.

Informal tone uses words and sentence constructions close to ordinary speech and may include slang, colloquialisms, and regionalisms. Like everyday speech, informal writing tends not to have the most precise word choices. It uses contractions; it uses first and second person pronouns such as *I* and *you* (see 23a); it uses simple verbs such as *get, is,* and *have*; and it may include sentence fragments for effect. Speakers and writers use an informal tone for everyday communication, and it is acceptable in informal writing.

Informal: He was *sort of* irritated because he *couldn't* find his car keys and *didn't* have *a whole lot of* time to get to his office.

Medium/Semiformal tone is not too casual but not too scholarly. It uses standard vocabulary, conventional sentence structures, and few or no contractions. This is often the level you are generally expected to use for college papers and public writing.

Medium/Semiformal: He was *somewhat* irritated because he *could not* find his car keys and *did not* have *much* time to get to his office.

Formal tone is scholarly and contains sophisticated, multisyllabic words in complex sentence structures not likely to be used when speaking. It often uses the third-person pronouns *he or she* or *one* (see 23a) instead of *I* or *you.* Some readers prefer formal writing, but others find that it is not as easy to read or understand. Many businesses, as well as government and other public offices, encourage employees to maintain a higher level of formality.

Formal: Unable to locate his car keys and lacking sufficient time to find alternative transportation to his office, he was agitated.

In the following extended example, the same information is presented at three levels of formality.

Informal

Someone who wants to have a bill passed in this state should start the process by getting it presented in the General Assembly or the Senate. The next thing that happens is that there's a committee that looks at it. The committee meets to decide on changing, accepting, or killing the bill. Usually, there's a lot of discussion when the bill comes back to the General Assembly and Senate. Both places have to OK the bill. If they don't like it, then a committee gets together with people from both the General Assembly and the Senate. They pound out a version that will make both houses happy. When the bill gets passed in both houses, it moves on to the governor. If the governor signs the bill or doesn't do anything, it becomes a law. If the governor says no, it either dies or goes back to the Senate and General Assembly. It's got to get a two-thirds vote in both houses to become a law.

Medium/Semiformal

For a bill to become a law in this state, the first step is to have it introduced in the General Assembly or the Senate. Next the bill goes to a committee that holds hearings to change, approve, or reject the bill. When the bill returns to the General Assembly and Senate, members debate it, often at great length, before a vote is taken. If both houses do not pass the bill, a joint committee is appointed, with representatives from both the General Assembly and the Senate. This committee then draws up a bill that is acceptable to both houses. When both houses approve and pass the bill, it moves to the governor's office. For the bill to become a law, the governor can either sign it or take no action. The governor may, however, veto the bill. In this case, it either dies or goes back to both houses, where it must be accepted by a two-thirds majority. If it passes, it becomes a law despite the governor's veto.

Formal

The procedure for passage of legislation in this state originates in either the General Assembly or the Senate. From there the bill is forwarded to a committee, which conducts hearings to determine whether the bill will be endorsed, altered, or terminated. The committee returns the bill to the General Assembly and Senate, where extensive debate occurs before voting is completed. If the bill fails to pass both houses, a joint committee is charged with formulating a compromise bill acceptable to both the Senate and the General Assembly. Approval by both houses advances the bill to the governor's office; the bill will then become law when the governor signs it or takes no action. Should the governor veto the bill, however, it is no longer viable, but it can be resuscitated through a two-thirds favorable vote in both houses, which then constitutes passage into law.

Once you set the level of formality in an essay, keep it consistent. Mixing levels can be distracting and indicates that the writer lacks adequate control (see 15c).

The economist offered the business executives a lengthy explanation for the

                                                    quite
recent fluctuation in the stock market. It was ~~pretty~~ obvious from their ques-
                                                      ^
                              did not understand
tions afterward, however, that they ~~didn't get~~ it.
                                        ^

For an example of a paragraph with an inconsistent level of formality, see the following exercise.

Exercise 36.1 Proofreading Practice

The following paragraph was intended to be written in a medium / semiformal to formal tone, but the writer used some informal words and phrases. Rewrite the paragraph so that the wording is consistently at a medium / semiformal to formal level.

The technology called MP3 has altered the way consumers buy their favorite music. Companies sell music and musicians use this thing to market songs directly to consumers, bypassing agents, recording companies, and distributors. You need a special recording device to download the best stuff off the computer. Consumers are able to copy and store music on home computers or on a portable music player, such as iPod. Music industry bosses are sweating this out. These dudes are afraid they won't get their cut. The Recording Industry of America Association (RIAA) warns that many illegal copies of certain artists' work are floating around, and they are suing some of the little guys who download music for free, especially on peer-to-peer networks. The RIAA is concerned for the artists and the royalties they lose because of this technology. The artists, consumers, and record companies can all get a pretty good deal from this technology if they cool it at the get-go and get more imaginative about how they sell music. The old days of buying CDs are almost gone.

Exercise 36.2 Pattern Practice

In the following exercise, if the sentence is informal, change it to a more formal tone. Similarly, if the sentence is formal, change it to a more informal tone. A sample sentence has been changed.

Original: Scientists are issuing warnings that one procedure for alleviating the menace of global warming is to reduce carbon dioxide emissions.

Informal Tone: Scientists warn that one way to reduce the threat of global warming is to cut down on carbon dioxide exhaust.

1. A step in the right direction would be to lean on automobile makers and make them raise the fuel efficiency of the gas-guzzling cars they are turning out.
2. An even quicker way to drop fuel use would be to hike gas taxes.
3. Environmentalists are also requesting stricter limitations on smokestack emissions of sulfur dioxide, a major contributor to acid rain.
4. However, states now producing high-sulfur coal aren't happy about the damage this will do to their economies.

36c **EMPHASIS**

When you want to be sure your readers are paying attention and are more likely to remember your message, you can add emphasis to your writing in several ways:

- *Use parallelism.* When you have two or more items in a group, each item in that group should be in the same parallel form, such as all verbs, all clauses, or all phrases (see Chapter 14). An example of a memorable use of parallelism was John F. Kennedy's statement: "Ask not what your country can do for you; ask what you can do for your country." Groucho Marx used parallelism for many of his humorous one-liners: "Politics is the art of looking for trouble, finding it, misdiagnosing it, and then misapplying the wrong remedies."

- *Use strong adverbs.* Adverbs such as *certainly* or *definitely* add emphasis. Compare the two sentences here, and decide which one is more emphatic:

  1. She is talented.

  2. She is definitely talented.

- *Use striking language.* To add emphasis, you can use an interesting metaphor, concrete details, or an unusual way of stating something.

   The mind is hungry, feasting on ideas and digesting them carefully.

   Web browsers are portals because they open doors to the whole world.

- *Use visual design.* When you design a document and think carefully about its visual impact, you are more likely to draw readers' attention to the document. See Chapter 6 for principles of visual design that will help you emphasize the content of your writing.

36d **DENOTATION AND CONNOTATION**

The **denotation** of a word is the dictionary meaning or definition. The **connotation** is the group of ideas implied but not directly indicated by the word. The connotation conveys attitudes and emotional overtones, either positive or negative, beyond the direct definition. Although connotations may vary among individuals, a large group of shared connotations exists.

A pig is an animal (the denotation), but there are also negative connotations of sloppiness, dirt, and fat associated with pigs. *Elected official* and *politician* have similar denotative meanings, but *elected official* connotes a more positive quality. While *fat, plump*, and *obese* describe the same condition, *fat* has a more negative connotation than *plump*, and *obese*, a medical term, is more neutral.

Exercise 36.3 Pattern Practice

The following groups of words have similar denotative meanings, but their connotations differ. Arrange each group so that the words go from most positive to most negative.

Most Positive	Neutral	Most Negative
Slender	lean	scrawny

1. canine, mutt, puppy
2. law enforcement officer, police officer, cop
3. cheap, inexpensive, economical
4. ornate, embellished, garish
5. counterfeit, replica, copy
6. scholar, geek, intellectual
7. determined, stubborn, uncompromising
8. scared, apprehensive, paranoid
9. explanation, excuse, reason
10. gabby, talkative, chatty

36e COLLOQUIALISMS, SLANG TERMS, AND REGIONALISMS

Colloquialisms are the language of casual conversation and informal writing.

kids (*instead of* children)
sci-fi (*instead of* science fiction)
flunk (*instead of* fail)

Slang terms consist of terms that are made up (such as *ditz* or *zonked out*) or are given new definitions (such as *suits* for business executives) to be novel or unconventional. Distinguishing between colloquialisms and slang is often difficult, and experts who are consulted when dictionaries are compiled do not always agree.

diss ("show disrespect")

bling (jewelry or expensive accessory)

boo (boyfriend or girlfriend)

wicked ("exceedingly")

tight ("cool" or "close friendship")

shout out (to recognize publicly)

po (police officer)

crib ("house")

blow off ("ignore" or "dismiss")

chops ("skill" or "expertise")

hit on ("make advances toward")

no worries

hit me up ("pick me up")

snarky ("sarcastic" or "mean")

scoop me up ("pick me up")

jack ("to steal" or "betray")

Regionalisms (also called *localisms* or *provincialisms*) are words and phrases more commonly used in one geographical area than in others.

pail	(*or*)	bucket					
bag	(*or*)	sack	(*or*)	poke	(*or*)	tote	
porch	(*or*)	veranda	(*or*)	lanai			
seesaw	(*or*)	teeter-totter	(*or*)	teeterboard			

Although colloquialisms, slang, and many regionalisms are not necessarily substandard or illiterate, most readers consider them inappropriate for formal academic writing. Colloquial language is acceptable for informal writing and dialogue, but slang may be unfamiliar to some readers. Slang terms are appropriate for very informal conversations among a group familiar with the current meanings of the terms. After a period of usage, many slang terms become outdated and disappear (for example, *the cat's pajamas, twenty-three skiddoo,* and *a real cool cat*), but some, such as *bug, dropout, fan, job,* and *phone,* have become accepted as standard. Slang that is becoming dated (for example, *mall rat* and *classic*) may also make the writer appear to be behind the times.

Some writers are able to use an occasional colloquialism or slang term for effect when the writing is not highly formal.

The arts and humanities should be paid for by the private sector, not by government grants. Freedom of artistic expression is in danger when government has its paws where they should not be.

The National Park Service is fighting back at people who say it doesn't know beans about keeping up the ecological health of our national parks. To stand up for its recent actions, the service has sent out some reports that show its policies have had beneficial effects.

Exercise 36.4 Dictionary Practice

Look up the following colloquialisms and slang terms in two or three different dictionaries. What labels and usage suggestions are given for these terms?

1. yo (meaning "hello")
2. cheesy (meaning "of poor quality")
3. face time (meaning "to spend time in the presence of another person")
4. diss (meaning "put a person down verbally")
5. nerd (meaning "a person who is not popular")
6. flame (meaning "to argue emotionally or violently against a person or opinion, usually on the Internet")
7. airhead (meaning "someone lacking in common sense")

8. rip-off (meaning "something overpriced")
9. dude (meaning "guy")
10. crash (meaning "to fall asleep somewhere")
11. dot gone (meaning "an unsuccessful Internet company")
12. geek (meaning "socially awkward person who is knowledgeable about computers")

Exercise 36.5 Writing Practice

List five slang words that you know. Use the words in sentences, and then rewrite each sentence using a standard word with the same definition.

Example: gross out

Slang: He was so grossed out by the biology experiment that he was unable to finish it.

Revised: He was so disgusted by the biology experiment that he was unable to finish it.

36f JARGON AND TECHNICAL TERMS

Jargon is the specialized language of various trades, professions, and groups, such as lawyers, plumbers, electricians, horse racers, biologists, and pharmacists. Specialists within the group use these terms to communicate with each other in a concise way when referring to complex concepts, objects, techniques, and so on. **Jargon** also refers to the use of unnecessarily inflated expressions, including *euphemisms*, which are terms used to disguise unpleasant realities.

Specialized Language: subcutaneous hemorrhage, metabolic disorders, exhaust manifold, beta decay

Inflated Expressions: learning facilitator (teacher), monetary remuneration (pay)

Euphemisms: revenue enhancement (taxes), preowned (used), nonmilitary collateral damage (dead civilians)

When you are writing about a specialized subject for a general audience and need to use a technical term, define the term in easily understandable language the first time you use it. You can then use the word later on and not lose the reader.

One of the great challenges for the computer industry is the manufacture and continued development of superconductors, metallic ceramics that, when cooled below a certain critical temperature, offer no resistance to the flow of an electric current. Presently, research on superconductors is resulting in some major breakthroughs, but research continues.

Unnecessary jargon reflects the writer's inability to write clearly. Note the wordiness and pompous tone of this example:

Original: Utilize this receptacle, which functions as a repository for matter to be disposed of.

Revised: Deposit litter here.

37

NONSEXIST LANGUAGE

It was once usual in English, as in many other languages, to use male pronouns and even such nouns as *man* as "universals" that were understood to include members of both sexes. The fairness of such usage has come into question, and it is wise to avoid offending readers by using language that seems to favor one sex over the other. The guidelines and suggestions in this chapter should help you check to see that your writing is gender free. This may be a special challenge for those ESL students whose first language uses male "universal" pronouns or has pronouns that do not indicate gender.

37a ALTERNATIVES TO *MAN*

As noted, the word *man* was formerly understood to refer not only to a male individual but also collectively to all humans, male and female. Because the word has become closely associated with adult males only, it is best to avoid it in contexts where the reference is to both genders or where gender is irrelevant.

Sexist Term	Neutral Alternatives
man	person, individual
mankind	people, human beings, humanity
man-made	machine-made, synthetic, artificial
the common man	the average person, the ordinary person
manpower	staff, workforce
to man	to staff, to run, to work at

37b ALTERNATIVE JOB TITLES

Many job titles suggest that only men or only women hold or can hold those jobs. To avoid this implication, use a neutral or inclusive term.

Sexist Term	Neutral Alternatives
chairman	chairperson, chair, coordinator
mailman	letter carrier, postal worker
policeman, patrolman	police officer
steward, stewardess	flight attendant
congressman	congressional representative, member of Congress
businessman	business professional
Dear Sir	Dear Editor, Dear Service Representative, Dear Sir or Madam
saleswoman/salesman	salesperson, salesclerk, sales specialist

Note that we don't indicate the marital status of men when using *Mr.*, so when addressing women professionally, it is best to use *Ms.*, which does not indicate whether the woman is married.

37c ALTERNATIVES TO THE MALE OR FEMALE PRONOUN

When you want to convey a general meaning or refer to both sexes, avoid the masculine pronoun *he* or the feminine pronoun *she*; use one of the following alternatives instead.

- Use the plural.

   Sexist: Give the customer a receipt with his change.

   Revised: Give customers receipts with their change.

   Sexist: A nurse is trained to understand her patients' emotions as well as physical symptoms.

   Revised: Nurses are trained to understand their patients' emotions as well as physical symptoms.

- Eliminate the pronoun or reword to avoid using a pronoun.

   Sexist: The average citizen worries about his retirement benefits.

   Revised: The average citizen worries about retirement benefits.

   Sexist: The secretary kept her cell phone on her desk.

   Revised: The secretary kept a cell phone on the desk.

   Sexist: If the taxpayer has questions about the new form, he can call a government representative.

   Revised: A taxpayer who has questions about the new form can call a government representative.

■ Replace the pronoun with *one, he or she,* or an article (*a, an, the*). If this becomes awkward, switch to the plural.

Sexist: The pet owner who can afford it takes his pet to a veterinarian.

Revised: The pet owner who can afford it takes his or her pet to a veterinarian.

(*or*)

The pet owner who can afford it takes the pet to a veterinarian.

Sexist: The parent who reads to her infant helps increase the infant's sound discrimination.

Revised: The parent who reads to an infant helps increase the infant's sound discrimination.

Sexist: When a student applies for admission to the nursing program, she will need to submit her transcripts to her advisor.

Revised: When students apply for admission to the nursing program, they will need to submit their transcripts to their advisors.

■ Repeat a title rather than using a pronoun.

Sexist: See your doctor first, and he will explain the prescription.

Revised: See your doctor first, and the doctor will explain the prescription.

■ Address the reader directly in the second person.

Sexist: Each applicant must mail his form by Thursday.

Revised: Mail your form by Thursday.

Regarding the indefinite pronouns *everybody, anybody, everyone,* and *anyone,* there are different views on their use. Some people prefer to continue using the male pronoun (*everyone . . . he*) or consider the plural *they* to be wrong. The use of the plural pronoun (*everyone . . . they*) has become acceptable in many informal contexts. In formal writing, it is still advisable to avoid using either gender-specific or plural pronouns with these words.

Exercise 37.1 Proofreading Practice

Revise the following paragraph so that nonsexist language is used consistently.

In the curricula of most business schools, the study of failure has not yet become an accepted subject, yet the average business student needs to know what he should do when a business strategy fails and how he can learn from his mistakes. Even the chairman of one Fortune 500 company says that the average businessman can learn more from his mistakes than from his successes, but the concept of studying failure has been slow to catch on. However, a few business schools and even engineering management majors at one university in California now confront the question of how anyone can recover from his mistakes. Student papers analyze how a typical failed entrepreneur might have managed his problems better. Sometimes a perceptive student can even relate the lessons to his own behavior. One of the typical problems that is studied is that of escalating commitment, the tendency of a manager to throw more and more of his financial resources and manpower into a project that is failing. Another is the tendency of the hapless executive not to see that his idea is a bomb. For this reason, computers are being enlisted to help him—and his superiors—make decisions about whether he should bail out or stay in. The study of failure clearly promises to breed success, at least for future businessmen now enrolled in business schools.

Exercise 37.2 Pattern Practice

Write a short paragraph about people in a particular profession or group, such as parents, chefs, doctors, or teachers. Try to include various options for using nonsexist language.

NOTES

NOTES

38

COMMAS

Commas are signals to help readers understand the meaning of written sentences. In the same way as our voices convey meaning by pausing or changing in pitch, commas indicate pauses to help readers understand writing. Thus, the sound of your sentences may help indicate where commas are needed. Sound isn't always a dependable guide, however, because not every voice pause occurs where a comma is needed, and not every comma needs a voice pause. The rules in this section, along with clues you get from pauses in your voice, will indicate where you'll need commas.

COMMAS AND SEMICOLONS IN SENTENCES

- For simple sentences, use pattern 1.
- For compound sentences, use patterns 2, 3, and 4.
- For complex sentences, use patterns 5, 6, and 7.

1. | Independent clause | | . |

2. | Independent clause | | , | | **coordinating conjunction:**
and   or
but   so
for   yet
nor | | independent clause | | . |

3. | Independent clause | | ; | | independent clause | | . |

4. | Independent clause | | ; | | **independent clause marker:**
however,
nevertheless,
therefore,
consequently,
(etc.) | | independent clause | | . |

5. | **Dependent clause marker:**
Because
Since
If
When
While
After
(etc.) | | dependent clause | | , | | independent clause | | . |

▶

COMMAS AND SEMICOLONS IN SENTENCES *(continued)*

6. | Independent clause | **dependent clause marker:** because since if when while after (etc.) | dependent clause | . |

7. | Subject | dependent clause | verb/predicate | . |

[Use commas before and after the dependent clause if it is nonessential.]
(See 29b.)

38a   COMMAS IN COMPOUND SENTENCES

There are three ways to join independent clauses in a compound sentence.

1. Use the comma with one of the seven coordinating conjunctions:

| and | for | or | yet |
| but | nor | so | |

(*Clause*), **and** (*clause*).

The television program was dull, but the commercials were entertaining.

After the storm, we collected seashells along the beach, and we all found some interesting specimens, but the conservationists asked us not to take the shells home.

Exception: A comma may be omitted if the two independent clauses are short and there is no danger of misreading.

We were tired so we stopped the game.

Romilly smiled and we all smiled back.

Try This

TO REMEMBER COORDINATING CONJUNCTIONS

To remember the seven coordinating conjunctions, think of the phrase "**fan boys**":

| **f**or | **a**nd | **n**or | |
| **b**ut | **o**r | **y**et | **s**o |

2. Join independent clauses with a semicolon and a connecting word such as the following:

however,	therefore,	consequently,
moreover,	nevertheless,	furthermore,

(Clause); **therefore,** *(clause)*.

The camping sites were all filled; however, the park ranger allowed latecomers to use empty spaces in the parking lot.

David's new sports car was designed for high-speed driving; moreover, it was also designed to be fuel efficient.

Hint

USING COMMAS IN COMPOUND SENTENCES WITH SEMICOLONS

Use a comma after the connecting word. Some writers prefer to omit the comma after one-syllable connective words, such as "thus" or "hence."

3. Join the independent clauses with a semicolon and no joining words.

(Clause); *(Clause)*.

Everyone in the room heard the glass shattering; no one moved until it was clear that there was no danger.

Exercise 38.1 Proofreading Practice

The following paragraph contains compound sentences that need commas or semicolons. Add the appropriate punctuation.

An inventor working on a "flying car" says that traveling several hundred miles by commercial airplane is a fairly inefficient way to get around. First you have to drive through traffic to the airport and then you have to park your car somewhere in order to board a plane. You fly to another crowded airport outside a city but then you have to rent another automobile to drive to your final destination in town. A more practical solution would be a personal commuter flying vehicle. The inventor, working in a company supported by several government agencies, has developed a vertical-takeoff-and-landing vehicle that has the potential to allow everyone to take to the air. The vehicle can take off and land vertically and it travels five times faster than an automobile. The most recently developed model looks more like a car than a plane however, it operates more like a cross between a plane and a helicopter. Above 125 mph in flight, it flies like a conventional plane and below 125 mph, it maneuvers like a helicopter. It has a number of safety features, such as six engines therefore it can recover if it loses an engine while hovering close to the ground.

Exercise 38.2 Sentence Combining

Combine the following short sentences into longer compound sentences. Remember that commas in compound sentences follow this pattern:

(*Clause*), conjunction (*and, but, for, nor, or, so,* or *yet*) (*clause*).

1. The personal commuter flying vehicle now being designed has room for four passengers.
2. It can fly roughly 850 miles per tank of fuel at a cruising speed of 225 mph.
3. The vehicle can rise above 30,000 feet.
4. It can also hover near the ground.
5. According to the inventor, it has taken two decades of theoretical studies to design the vehicle's shape.
6. It has also taken ten years of wind tunnel tests to achieve the aerodynamic shape.
7. Government officials foresee an entire transportation network in the future based on the personal flying vehicle.
8. Using flying vehicles will require an automated air traffic control system.
9. The technology for controlling these vehicles already exists.
10. The technology will create electronic highways in the sky.

38b COMMAS AFTER INTRODUCTORY WORDS, PHRASES, AND CLAUSES

A comma is needed after introductory words, phrases, and clauses that come before the main clause.

Introductory Words

Yes,	No,	However,
Well,	In fact,	First,

Well, perhaps he meant no harm. **In fact,** he wanted to help.

Introductory Phrases

■ Long prepositional phrases (usually four words or more):

In the middle of a long, dull movie, I decided to get some popcorn.

With the aid of an Internet connection in his residence hall room, he finished all of the homework quickly.

For very short introductory phrases, the comma can be omitted if there is no danger of misreading.

> In the campground no pets were allowed.

■ Phrases with *-ing* verbals, *-ed* verbals, and *to* + verb:

> Having finished the exam before the bell rang, he left the room.

> Tired of never having enough money, she took a second job.

> To get a seat close to the stage, you'd better come early.

Hint

USING COMMAS WITH INTRODUCTORY WORDS

When dependent clauses come after the main clause, there is no comma.

> When the telephone rang, the dog started to bark.

> The dog started to bark when the telephone rang.

Use commas after introductory clauses, phrases, and words in the following cases:

■ If the introduction is four or more words

■ If there is a distinct voice pause after the introductory part

■ If the comma is necessary to avoid confusion

> **Possibly Confusing:** As I stated the rules can be broken occasionally.

> **Revised:** As I stated, the rules can be broken occasionally.

When your sentence starts with an *-ing* verbal, *-ed* verbal, or *to* + verb, be sure you don't have a dangling modifier (see 13a).

Introductory Clauses

■ Introductory dependent clauses that begin with adverbs such as these:

After	Because	Until
Although	If	When
As	Since	While

> While I was eating, the cat scratched at the door.

Exception: The comma may be omitted when the introductory phrase or clause is short and there is no danger of misreading.

> While eating I read the newspaper.

> After they retired they moved to Mexico.

Exercise 38.3 Proofreading Practice

The following paragraph contains introductory words, phrases, and clauses that require commas. Add commas where needed.

(1) A recent study showed that small cars are tailgated more than bigger ones, such as SUVs and vans. (2) Moreover the drivers of subcompact and compact cars also do more tailgating themselves. (3) In the study traffic flow at five different locations was observed, and various driving conditions were included, such as two-lane state roads and four-lane divided highways. (4) In all more than 10,000 vehicles were videotaped. (5) Although subcompact and compact cars accounted for only 38 percent of the vehicles on the tape their drivers were tailgating in 48 percent of the incidents observed. (6) In addition to having done all of this tailgating these drivers were the victims of tailgating 47 percent of the time. (7) Midsize cars made up 31 percent of the cars on the tapes but accounted for only 20 percent of the tailgaters and 24 percent of the drivers being tailgated. (8) Having considered various reasons for this difference the researchers suggest that drivers of other cars may avoid getting close to midsize cars because of the cars' contours. (9) Because midsize cars have more curves in their sloping backs and trunks people have more trouble seeing around them.

Exercise 38.4 Pattern Practice

The following sentences illustrate some of the rules for using commas with introductory expressions. Identify the rule by selecting the appropriate letter from the list given here, and then write your own sentence in this pattern.

Pattern A: Comma after an introductory word

Pattern B: Comma after an introductory phrase

Pattern C: Comma after an introductory clause

1. Because tailgating is a road hazard that is known to cause many accidents, other studies have searched for causes of tailgating.
2. For example, one study examined how drivers judge distances.
3. Puzzled by the question of why small cars are tailgated so often, researchers studied other drivers' perceptions of how far away small cars appear to be.
4. Despite the fact that many people were generally able to guess distances accurately, they sometimes perceived small cars to be more than 40 feet farther away than they actually were.
5. If drivers tend to think that small cars are really farther away than they actually are, this may explain why small cars are tailgated so often.
6. However, researchers continue to study this problem.

38c COMMAS WITH ESSENTIAL AND NONESSENTIAL WORDS, PHRASES, AND CLAUSES

Nonessential word groups (see 29b) require a pair of commas, one before the nonessential element and the other afterward (unless there is a period). Essential word groups do not have commas to set them off from the rest of the sentence.

Hint

RECOGNIZING ESSENTIAL AND NONESSENTIAL WORD GROUPS

- When an essential clause is removed, the meaning is lost because it's too general.

  Students who cheat harm only themselves.

  [With the word group who cheat removed, the sentence would say that students harm themselves. That's too general and does not convey the intended meaning of the sentence.]

- When a nonessential clause is removed, the meaning is the same.

  The restaurant, which serves only breakfast and lunch, was closed.

  [With the word group which serves only breakfast and lunch removed, the sentence still says that the restaurant was closed. The meaning of the main clause is the same.]

- When the word group interrupts the flow of words in the original sentence, it's a nonessential element and needs commas. Some people can hear a slight pause in their voice or a change in pitch as they begin and end a nonessential element.

- When you can move the word group around in the sentence or put it in a different sentence, it is a nonessential element.

  No one, however, wanted to tell her she was wrong.

  No one wanted, however, to tell her she was wrong.

  However, no one wanted to tell her she was wrong.

- When the clause begins with *that,* it is always essential.

  I'll return the sweater that I borrowed after I wear it again tonight.

  That clauses following verbs that express mental action are always essential.

  I think that . . .   She believes that . . .   He dreams that . . .

  They wish that . . .   We concluded that . . .

  ▶

■ Word groups (called *appositives*) following nouns that identify or explain the nouns are nonessential and need commas.

Uncle Ike, a doctor, smoked too much even though he continued to warn his patients not to smoke.

[Uncle Ike = a doctor]

The movie critic's review of *Heartland*, a story about growing up in Indiana, focused on the beauty of the scenery.

[Heartland = a story about growing up in Indiana]

When this word group is the last element in the sentence, keep it attached to the sentence and set it off with a comma. Some fragments are appositives that became detached from the sentence.

She is a good friend. A person whom I trust and admire.
 ^, a^

Exercise 38.5 Proofreading Practice

Some of the sentences in the following paragraph have essential and nonessential clauses, words, or phrases. Underline these elements, write N for nonessential or E for essential, and add commas where they are needed.

(1) The television rating system is designed to provide parents with a method of monitoring the shows that children watch. (2) The system which was introduced in 1999 operates using a rating scale that flashes in an upper corner of the television screen. (3) However, the parent is responsible for watching carefully when a child is viewing television programs. (4) For example a very young child would not know what the symbols represent. (5) An older child who knows what the symbols represent may choose to ignore them if a parent is not present. (6) Experts agree that the system is not without faults. (7) Many parents feel that the television industry should forgo the rating system and remove much of the sex and violence from television shows. (8) Proponents of the system mainly directors of television networks state that parents have the option of restricting television viewing for their children. (9) The subject matter of television programming is not a new debate. (10) However, the rating system adds another dimension to this topic which will continue to concern parents and the owners of television networks.

Exercise 38.6 Pattern Practice

Write your own sentences following each pattern.

Pattern A: Subject + comma + nonessential clause + comma + verb + object

Pattern B: Subject + essential clause + verb + object

Pattern C: Introductory phrase + comma + nonessential word + comma + subject + verb + object

Pattern D: Subject + verb + object + comma + nonessential phrase

38d COMMAS IN SERIES AND LISTS

Use commas when three or more items are listed in a series.

- A series of words:

Would you prefer the poster printed in yellow, blue, green, or purple?

- A series of phrases:

He first spoke to Julio, then called his roommate, and finally phoned me.

- A series of clauses:

She never dreamed she'd be in the movies, she hadn't even tried out for a part, and she was sure she didn't have enough talent to act.

There are some variations in using commas in lists. The comma after the last item before *and* or *or* is preferred, but it may be omitted if there is no possibility of misreading.

Americans' favorite spectator sports are football, baseball and basketball.

[The comma after *baseball* is optional.]

However, the comma before *and* cannot be omitted in sentences where *and* is preceded or followed by terms that belong together, such as *bread and butter*, or where misreading is possible.

He talked about his college studies, art, and history.

[This sentence means he talked about three things: his college studies, art, and history.]

He talked about his college studies, art and history.

[This sentence means his college studies were in art and history.]

If one or more of the items in a series have commas, semicolons should be used between items.

The group included Bill Packo, guitar; Arlo Pavelites, drums; and Art Clutz, electronic keyboard.

Exercise 38.7 Proofreading Practice

The following paragraph contains some series of three or more items that need punctuation. Add commas where they are needed.

(1) Imagine not being able to recognize the face of your sister your boss or your best friend from high school. (2) Imagine looking into a mirror seeing a face and realizing that the face you see is totally unfamiliar. (3) Though this may sound impossible, a small number of people do suffer from a neurological condition that leaves them unable to recognize familiar faces. (4) The condition is called *prosopagnosia* and results from brain damage caused by infection or stroke. (5) Many people with this problem who have been studied have normal vision reading ability and language skills. (6) They know that a face is a face they can name its parts and they can distinguish differences between faces. (7) But only through other clues—hearing a familiar voice remembering a specific feature like a mustache hearing a name or recalling a particular identifying mark such as an unusual scar—can the people who were studied call up memories of people they should know. (8) Researchers studying this phenomenon have found evidence suggesting that the step leading to conscious recognition of the face by the brain is somehow being blocked.

Exercise 38.8 Pattern Practice

The following sentences have items in a series. Using these sentences as patterns, write your own sentences with correctly punctuated items in series.

1. His favorite pastimes are sleeping late on weekends, drinking too much beer, and watching game shows on television.
2. Marta plans to work hard when she's young, save her money, and then spend it all when she retires.
3. Do you prefer jogging shoes with leather, canvas, or mesh tops?
4. Some people try to forget their birthdays, some like to have big celebrations, and others don't have any strong preference.

38e COMMAS WITH ADJECTIVES

Use commas to separate two or more adjectives that describe the same noun equally.

cold, dark water   happy, healthy baby

However, not all adjectives in front of a noun describe the noun equally. When they are not equal (or coordinate) adjectives, do not use commas to separate them.

six big dogs

bright green sweater

Try This

TO USE COMMAS CORRECTLY WITH ADJECTIVES

Can you add *and* between the adjectives? Can the adjectives be written in reverse order? If so, separate the adjectives with commas:

a greedy, stubborn child

[Either of the following is acceptable: a greedy, stubborn child *or* a stubborn, greedy child.]

an easy, happy smile

[Either an easy, happy smile *or* a happy, easy smile *would be fine.]*

In contrast, notice the following examples, which do not describe the noun equally:

a white frame house

[A frame white house is not acceptable.]

two young men

[Young two men is not acceptable.]

Exercise 38.9 Proofreading Practice

The following paragraph contains sentences with missing commas. Add them where they are needed, and highlight or circle them.

(1) Online shopping is the easiest fastest way to shop! (2) If you are a person who hates noisy crowded stores, especially during the holidays, go online to browse, comparison shop, and even bid on hard-to-find items. (3) Among the best buys on the Internet are fine vintage wines, some clothing, CDs, popular books, and children's electronic toys. (4) Mail-order retailers such as Eddie Bauer, L.L. Bean, and Lands' End all have informative interesting shopping sites. (5) The sites provide colorful realistic illustrations of merchandise along with stock availability of colors and sizes. (6) For example, instead of running from store to store to price a white cotton shirt in your size, you can quickly obtain this information by checking online sites. (7) However, buyer beware! (8) You must know prices to be able to determine whether you are getting a fair deal. (9) Add in the shipping and handling fees to find out whether you are getting a bargain. (10) If the total price equals the price at your local mall, an online purchase saves you the time spent traveling to the store and waiting in line with tired cranky shoppers, only to find a tired cranky salesperson at the register. (11) Now you can be tired and cranky from shopping in the privacy of your own home.

Exercise 38.10 Pattern Practice

For each pattern, write two phrases of your own, correctly punctuated with commas.

1. Twelve angry jurors (use a number and another describing word)
2. A shiny gold ring (use a color and another describing word)
3. A tall, lean man (use at least two body features)
4. Loving, compassionate eyes (use at least two emotions)
5. A solid steel shed (use a material and another describing word)

38f   COMMAS WITH DATES, ADDRESSES, GEOGRAPHICAL NAMES, AND NUMBERS

1. Commas with Dates

If a date is given in the order month-day-year, set off the day and year with commas.

June 12, 2007,

The order was shipped out on September 2, 2006, and not received until May 12, 2007.

No commas are needed if the order is day-month-year or month-year.

12 June 2007   June 2007

The application deadline was 15 August 2007 for all students.

2. Commas with Addresses

In a letter heading or on an envelope, use a comma between the city and the state name.

Jim Johnson Jr.
1436 Westwood Drive
Birlingham, ID 83900

In a sentence, use a comma at the end of each element as well.

You can write to Jim Johnson Jr., 1436 Westwood Drive, Birlingham, ID 83900, for more information.

3. Commas with Geographical Names

Put commas after each item in a place name.

The planning committee has chosen Chicago, Illinois, as the site for this year's conference and Washington, D.C., for next year's meeting.

4. Commas with Numbers

Separate long numbers into groups of three going from right to left. Commas with four-digit numbers are optional.

4,300,150   27,000   4,401   (*or*)   4401

Exercise 38.11 Proofreading Practice

Add commas in the following paragraph where they are needed.

(1) In addition to its Web site (http://www.gpo.gov), the United States Government Printing Office has a paper catalog of thousands of popular books that it prints. (2) If you'd like a copy of this catalog, write to the Superintendent of Documents Government Printing Office Washington DC 20402. (3) Books on agriculture, business and industry, careers, computers, diet and nutrition, health, history, hobbies, space exploration, and other topics are available. (4) To pay for the books, you can send a check or money order, but more than 60000 customers every year set up deposit accounts with an initial deposit of at least $50. (5) Future purchases can then be charged against this account. (6) The Government Printing Office also has bookstores all around the country where you can browse before buying. (7) They do not stock all 16000 titles in the inventory, but they do carry the most popular ones. (8) For example, if you live in Birmingham, you can find the Government Printing Office bookstore in Roebuck Shopping City 9220-B Parkway East Birmingham AL 35206. (9) Other bookstores are in Cleveland Ohio and Jacksonville Florida.

Exercise 38.12 Pattern Practice

For each pattern, write two sentences of your own, correctly punctuated with commas.

Pattern A: Sentence with a date

July 4, 1776, was a memorable day in U.S. history.

Pattern B: Sentence with an address

His business address is Fontran Investments, 3902 Carroll Boulevard, Indianapolis, IN 46229.

Pattern C: Sentence with a geographical name

Talika enjoyed her car trip to Santa Fe, New Mexico, and plans to go again next spring.

Pattern D: Sentence with two numbers of five digits or more

The police estimated that more than 50,000 people took part in the demonstration, but the event's organizers said they were sure that at least 100,000 had shown up.

38g OTHER USES FOR COMMAS

Commas have a number of other uses.

- To prevent misreading:

  Confusing: To John Harrison had been a sort of idol.

  Revised: To John, Harrison had been a sort of idol.

  Confusing: On Thursday morning orders will be handled by Jim.

  Revised: On Thursday, morning orders will be handled by Jim. (*or*)

  Revised: On Thursday morning, orders will be handled by Jim.

- To set off sharply contrasted elements at the end of a sentence:

  He was merely ignorant, not stupid.

- To set off a question:

  You're one of the senator's closest aides, aren't you?

- To set off phrases at the end of the sentence that refer to the beginning or middle of the sentence:

  Shaundra waved enthusiastically at the departing boat, laughing happily.

- To set off direct quotations and after the first part of a quotation in a sentence:

  Becky said, "I'll see you tomorrow."

  "I forgot," Serkan explained, "to complete the apparatus and materials section of my lab report."

- To set off the opening greeting and closing of a letter:

  Dear David,   Sincerely yours,

Exercise 38.13 Proofreading Practice

Add commas where they are needed in the following paragraph.

(1) There is hope for infertile couples who want to have a child with genetic material from both parents to have a baby. (2) A fertility specialist who does research at New York University has developed a technique that adds an infertile woman's genetic material to a donor egg. (3) Says one woman undergoing fertility treatments "This gives hope to women who want a natural child." (4) Dr. Jamie Grifo talked about the procedure called *oocyte nuclear transfer* with reporters. (5) "The purpose of this is to give more options to infertile women" he said "but the procedure remains expensive." (6) Not many pregnancies have occurred yet, but the doctor tries

the process on women who are willing to pay for it. (7) Previously, a woman using a donor egg to become pregnant would have no genetic link to the child. (8) "Now" says the doctor "a child conceived using this procedure would actually contain genetic material from three people—the father the mother and the donor." (9) That the genes will come from the mother's nucleus and will determine how the child looks and acts is comforting for an infertile woman. (10) As with all research ethical questions have been raised, but the research team maintains that this process is for infertility purposes not for cloning purposes. (11) The process continues to promise to be a major breakthrough in the area of infertility research.

Exercise 38.14 Pattern Practice

For each pattern, write two sentences of your own, correctly punctuated with commas.

Pattern A: To prevent misreading

After eating, the cat stretched out near the fire and fell asleep.

[If the comma is left out, there is a possible misreading.]

Pattern B: To set off sharply contrasted elements at the end of the sentence

Everyone thought the car had stopped, not broken down.

Pattern C: To set off a question

They were at the game, weren't they?

Pattern D: To set off a phrase at the end of a sentence that refers to the beginning or middle of the sentence

Hannah decided not to go out in the evening, preferring to enjoy the quiet in her apartment.

Pattern E: To set off direct quotations

Professor Bendini said, "Don't call me tonight to ask about your grade."

38h UNNECESSARY COMMAS

Putting in commas where they are not needed can mislead readers because unnecessary commas suggest pauses or interruptions not intended as part of the meaning. (Remember also that not every pause needs a comma.)

■ Don't separate a subject from its verb.

Unnecessary Comma: An eighteen-year-old in most states, is now considered an adult.

■ Don't put a comma between two verbs that share the same subject.

Unnecessary Comma: We laid out our music and snacks, and began to study.

■ Don't put a comma in front of every *and* or *but*.

Unnecessary Comma: We decided that we should not lend her the money, and that we should explain our decision.

[The *and* in this sentence joins two *that* clauses.]

■ Don't put a comma in front of a direct object. (Remember that clauses beginning with *that* can be direct objects.)

Unnecessary Comma: He explained to me, that he is afraid to fly on airplanes because of terrorists.

■ Don't put commas before a dependent clause when it comes after the main clause except for extreme or strong contrast.

Unnecessary Comma: She was late, because her alarm clock was broken.

Extreme Contrast: The movie actor was still quite upset, although he did win an Academy Award.

■ Don't put a comma after *such as* or *especially*.

Unnecessary Comma: There are several kinds of dark bread from which to choose, such as, whole wheat, rye, oatmeal, pumpernickel, and bran bread.

Exercise 38.15 Proofreading Practice

In the following paragraph, highlight or circle the commas that should be removed.

Although the dangers of alcohol are well known, and have been widely publicized, there may be another danger that we haven't yet realized. Several controlled studies of drunken animals have indicated to researchers, that in an accident there is more swelling and hemorrhaging in the spinal cord, and in the brain, if alcohol is present in the body. To find out if this is true in humans, researchers studied the data on more than 1 million drivers in automobile crashes. One thing already known is, that drunks are more likely to be driving fast, and to have seat belts unfastened. Of course, their coordination is also poorer than that of sober people, so drunks are more likely to get into serious accidents. To compensate for this, researchers grouped accidents according to type, speed, and degree of vehicle deformation, and found that alcohol still appears to make people more vulnerable to injury. The conclusion of the study was, that the higher the level of alcohol in the person's body, the greater the chance of being injured or killed. In minor crashes, drunk drivers were more than four times as likely to be killed as sober ones. In average crashes, drunk drivers were more than three times as likely to be killed, and in the worst ones, drunks were almost twice as likely to die. Overall, drunks were more than twice as likely to die in an accident, because of the alcohol they drank.

Exercise 38.16 Pattern Practice

For each pattern, write two sentences of your own, correctly punctuated with commas.

Pattern A: Subject + verb + object + and + verb + object

Before the test <u>Midori</u> <u>studied</u> the botany <u>notes</u> from the lectures and
        (SUBJECT) (VERB)   (OBJECT)

<u>reread</u> the <u>textbook</u> several times.
(VERB)   (OBJECT)

Pattern B: Independent clause + dependent clause

<u>He decided not to live in the dorm</u> <u>because it was so expensive.</u>
   (INDEPENDENT CLAUSE)   (DEPENDENT CLAUSE)

Pattern C: A sentence with a *that* clause or phrase as a direct object

My high school physical education teacher often told me <u>that eating a</u>
                                       (*THAT* CLAUSE)

<u>good breakfast</u> was an important part of keeping in shape.

Pattern D: A sentence with a subject that has many words modifying it

Almost <u>everyone</u> attending the recent meeting of the union <u>decided</u>
    (SUBJECT)   (VERB)

not to vote for the strike.

39

APOSTROPHES

39a APOSTROPHES WITH POSSESSIVES

Use the apostrophe to show possession (see Chapter 22).

- For singular nouns, use *'s.*

  the book**'s** author   a flower**'s** smell

- For a singular noun ending in *-s,* the *s* after the apostrophe may be omitted, especially if it would make the pronunciation difficult, as often happens when the next word starts with *s* or *z.*

  James**'s** car   (*or*)   James**'** car

  the grass**'s** color   (*or*)   the grass**'** color

  Euripides**'** story   [Trying to say *Euripides's story* is a bit difficult.]

- For plural nouns ending in -*s,* add only an apostrophe.

    both teams' colors   six days' vacation

- For plural nouns not ending in -*s* (such as *children, men,* or *mice*), use *'s.*

    the children's game   six men's coats

- For indefinite pronouns (pronouns ending in -*body* and -*one,* such as *no one, someone,* and *everybody*), use *'s.*

    no one's fault   someone's hat

- For compound words, add *'s* to the last word.

    brother-in-law's job   everyone else's preference

- For joint ownership by two or more nouns, add *'s* after the last noun in the group.

    Lisa and Vinay's house   the bar and restaurant's parking lot

- For individual ownership when several nouns are used, add *'s* after each noun.

    Lisa's and Vinay's houses   [This indicates that there are two houses, one belonging to Lisa and the other to Vinay.]

Try This

TO USE APOSTROPHES CORRECTLY

1. When you aren't sure if you need the apostrophe, turn the phrase into an *of the* phrase.

   the day's effort = the effort **of the** day

   (*Note*: Occasionally, you'll have both the *of the* phrase and the apostrophe.)

   The painting **of** Cesar's

   [*Without* 's, *this phrase would mean that Cesar was pictured in the painting.*]

2. When you aren't sure whether the word is plural or not, remember this sequence:

   - First, write the word.
   - Then write the plural.
   - Then add the possessive apostrophe marker.

   ▶

Thus everything to the left of the apostrophe is the word and its plural, if needed.

Word	Possessive Marker	Result
cup	's	cup's handle
cups	'	cups' handles

3. Ask yourself whether the first word is a descriptive word rather than the owner. These phrases can often (but not always) be turned into a "for . . ." phrase. When they can, don't use an apostrophe.

teachers college = college for teachers

clothes store = store for clothes

the Bulls quarterback = quarterback for the Bulls

39b APOSTROPHES WITH CONTRACTIONS

Use the apostrophe to mark the omitted letter or letters in contractions.

it's = it is   don't = do not   that's = that is

o'clock = of the clock   '79 = 1979

Jeff's going = Jeff is going   [informal usage]

39c APOSTROPHES WITH PLURALS

Use apostrophes to form the plurals of lowercase letters, abbreviations with periods, and capital letters whose plural could otherwise be mistaken for a word (*As, Is,* or *Us*). For other capital letters, abbreviations without periods, numbers, symbols, and words used as words, the apostrophe before the -s is optional if the plural is clear. In all cases, *'s* is neither italicized nor underlined.

- Necessary apostrophes:

  a's   B.A.'s   *A's*

- Optional apostrophes:

9s	(*or*)	9's
UFOs	(*or*)	UFO's
ands	(*or*)	and's
&s	(*or*)	&'s

Be consistent in choosing one or the other of these options.

39d UNNECESSARY APOSTROPHES

Don't use the apostrophe with possessive pronouns or with the regular plural forms of nouns. Possessive pronouns don't need apostrophes.

his	hers	its
ours	yours	theirs	whose

Is that umbrella ~~yours'~~ *yours* or mine?   I think ~~it's~~ *its* leg is broken.

Remember, *it's* and *who's* are contractions, not possessives.

it's = it is   **It's** a good time to clean out the closet.

who's = who is   **Who's** going to run for vice president?

Don't use the apostrophe with regular plural forms of nouns that do not show possession.

The ~~Jacksons'~~ *Jacksons* went to Disney World for vacation.

Gift ~~certificate's~~ *certificates* are available.

We sell an assortment of ~~tea's~~ *teas*.

Exercise 39.1 Proofreading Practice

The following paragraph contains some words that should show possession. Add apostrophes where they are needed.

Although teachers commonly use tests to grade their students learning, taking a test can also help students learn. Peoples memories seem to be more accurate after reading some material and taking a test than after merely reading the material with no testing. In fact, studies have shown that students who take several tests learn even more than those who take only one test after reading material. Although everyones ability to memorize material generally depends on how well the material was studied, scientists research does indicate that test taking aids memory. The type of test is also important because multiple-choice exams help us put facts together better while fill-in-the-blank questions promote recall of specific facts. These questions ability to test different types of learning suggests that teachers ought to include different types of tests throughout the semester.

Exercise 39.2 Pattern Practice

For each pattern, write two sentences of your own, correctly punctuated with apostrophes.

Pattern A: Two singular nouns with *'s*

If **Daniel's** car doesn't start, we can borrow **Alicia's** van.

Pattern B: A singular noun ending in -*s* with '

Does anyone know Mr. **Myconos'** ZIP code?

Pattern C: Two plural nouns ending in -*s* with '

Although the **girls'** coats were on sale, all of the **boys'** coats were regular price.

Pattern D: A sentence with *its* and *it's*

Whenever **it's** raining, our cat races inside to keep **its** fur dry.

Pattern E: A plural noun not ending in -*s* with '*s*

We helped collect money for the **Children's** Fund.

Pattern F: An indefinite pronoun with '*s*

I would really appreciate **someone's** help right now.

Pattern G: A sentence with *who's* and *whose*

I wonder **whose** skates those are and **who's** going with us to the rink.

Pattern H: One compound word with '*s*

It was the **president-elect's** decision not to campaign on TV.

Pattern I: One example of joint ownership with '*s*

The next morning, he felt the **pizza and beer's** effects.

Exercise 39.3 Proofreading Practice

In the following paragraph, add the apostrophes needed to mark plurals, even if they are optional.

In the 1990s, the use of standardized tests, such as the SATs for high school juniors, came under scrutiny. Critics said that these commonly used tests did not reflect a student's ability, nor did they project a level of success in college. In the 1970s and 1980s, the SATs were the primary factor for entrance to college. A movement to consider other factors such as GPAs, activities, and the interview began after educational leaders explored the merits of alternative assessment. Alternative assessment evaluates the whole student and frowns on ranking the number of As on a transcript and GPAs. However, the SATs are a U.S. institution, and thousands of high school students are still subjected to this procedure each spring. Perhaps in the future the SATs will be a thing of the past.

Exercise 39.4 Pattern Practice

For each pattern, write your own sentence correctly punctuated with apostrophes.

Pattern A: The plural of two lowercase letters

In the note he wrote, the **e's** and **c's** looked alike.

Pattern B: The plural of two abbreviations without periods

The electronics stores sold their **CDs** at a better discount than their **DVDs.**

Pattern C: The plural of a number and a capital letter

Her new license plate number had several **3's** and some **M's** too.

Pattern D: The plural of a date and a word

He dressed like a **1960s** hippie and sprinkled lots of **"far out's"** and other outdated expressions in his speech.

Exercise 39.5 Pattern Practice

For each pattern, write your own correctly punctuated sentence.

Pattern A: A sentence with two possessive pronouns

I can never remember whether that car is **hers** or **his.**

Pattern B: A sentence with *it's* and *its*

It's never clear whether that dog wants **its** ears scratched or **its** water dish filled.

Pattern C: A sentence with a plural noun that does not show possession and a plural noun that does show possession

That magazine has six pages of **ads** with different **dealers'** prices.

40

SEMICOLONS

The semicolon is a stronger mark of punctuation than a comma. It is almost like a period but does not come at the end of a sentence. Semicolons are used only between closely related equal elements—that is, between independent clauses and between items in a series. See the box "Commas and Semicolons in Sentences" on pages 233–34.

40a SEMICOLONS IN COMPOUND SENTENCES

Use the semicolon when joining independent clauses not joined by the seven connectors that require commas: *and, but, for, nor, or, so, yet.*

Two patterns for using semicolons are the following:

■ Independent clause + semicolon + independent clause

He often watched TV reruns; she preferred to read instead.

- Independent clause + semicolon + joining word or transition + comma + independent clause

He often watched TV reruns; however, she preferred to read instead.

Some joining words or transitional phrases that connect two independent clauses must be preceded by a semicolon. They are also ordinarily followed by a comma.

after all,	finally,	in the second place,
also,	for example,	instead,
as a result,	furthermore,	meanwhile,
at any rate,	hence,	nevertheless,
besides,	however,	on the contrary,
by the way,	in addition,	on the other hand,
consequently,	in fact,	still,
even so,	in other words,	therefore,

Variations in Compound Sentences

A semicolon can be used instead of a comma with two independent clauses joined by *and, but, for, nor, or, so,* or *yet* when one of the clauses has its own comma. The semicolon thus makes a clearer break between the two independent clauses.

- Independent clause with commas + semicolon + independent clause:

Congressman Dow, who headed the investigation, leaked the story to the
(INDEPENDENT CLAUSE WITH COMMAS)
press; but he would not answer questions during an interview.

A colon can be used between two independent clauses when the second clause restates the first (see 28a).

Her diet was strictly vegetarian: she ate no meat, fish, poultry, or eggs.

Exercise 40.1 Proofreading Practice

The following paragraph contains compound sentences that need punctuation. Add semicolons and commas where needed.

Even before children begin school, many parents think they should take part in their children's education and help the children develop mentally. Such parents usually consider reading to toddlers important moreover they help the children memorize facts such as the days of the week and the numbers from one to ten. Now it is becoming clear that parents can begin helping when the children are babies. One particular type of parent communication, encouraging the baby to pay attention to new things, seems especially promising in helping babies' brains develop for example handing the baby a toy encourages the baby to notice something new. Some studies seem to indicate that this kind of activity helps children score higher on intelligence tests several years later. Parents interested in helping their babies' brain development have been encouraged by this study to point to new things in the babies' environment as part of the parents' communication with their babies thus their children's education can begin in the crib.

Exercise 40.2 Pattern Practice

For each pattern, write two sentences of your own, correctly punctuated with semicolons.

Pattern A: Independent clause + semicolon + independent clause

<u>I didn't know which job I wanted;</u> <u>I was too confused to decide.</u>
    (INDEPENDENT CLAUSE)   (INDEPENDENT CLAUSE)

Pattern B: Independent clause + semicolon + joining word or transitional phrase + comma + independent clause

<u>Three friends recommended that movie;</u> <u>however,</u> <u>I was bored by it.</u>
    (INDEPENDENT CLAUSE)   (JOINING WORD) (INDEPENDENT CLAUSE)

Pattern C: Independent clause + comma + *and* (or) *but* + independent clause

                  (COMMA)
<u>The shirt is a little small,</u>   <u>but</u>   <u>he has nothing else to wear.</u>
  (INDEPENDENT CLAUSE)   (JOINING WORD)   (INDEPENDENT CLAUSE)

40b SEMICOLONS IN A SERIES

For clarity, use semicolons to separate a series of items in which one or more of the items contain commas. Semicolons are also preferred if items in the series are especially long.

■ Items with their own commas:

Among her favorite Netflix rentals were old Cary Grant movies, such as *Arsenic and Old Lace;* any of Woody Allen's movies; and children's classics, including *The Sound of Music, Willy Wonka and the Chocolate Factory,* and *The Wizard of Oz.*

■ Long items in a series:

When planning the bus schedule, they took into consideration the length of travel time between cities where stops would be made; the number of people likely to get on at each stop; and the times when the bus would arrive at major cities where connections would be made with other buses.

40c SEMICOLONS WITH QUOTATION MARKS

If a semicolon is needed, put it after the quotation marks.

> Her answer to every question I asked was, "I'll have to think about that"; she clearly had no answers to offer.

40d UNNECESSARY SEMICOLONS

Don't use a semicolon between unequal parts of a sentence, such as between a clause and a phrase or between an independent clause and a dependent clause. Don't use a semicolon in place of a dash, comma, or colon.

Unnecessary Semicolon: They wanted to see the government buildings; especially the courthouse and the post office.   [should be a comma]

Unnecessary Semicolon: He kept trying to improve his tennis serve; because that was the weakest part of his game.   [should be no punctuation]

Unnecessary Semicolon: When Mike kept spinning his car wheels to get out of the sand, I realized he was really just persistent; not stupid. [should be a dash or a comma]

Incorrect Semicolon: The office clearly needed several more pieces of equipment; a faster computer, another fax machine, and a larger paper shredder.   [should be a colon]

Exercise 40.3 Proofreading Practice

The following paragraph contains some unnecessary semicolons and lacks some necessary semicolons. Highlight or circle semicolons that are incorrect, and add semicolons and other punctuation where needed.

In the not-too-distant future, when airline passengers board their flights, they will be able to enjoy a number of new conveniences; such as buying their snacks and drinks from onboard vending machines, being able to take showers, use exercise machines, and sleep in beds, and making hotel and car-rental reservations from an onboard computer. Such features are what aircraft designers envision within the next few years for passenger jets. Their plans, though, may not be realized until much further in the future, if ever, but the ideas reflect the airline industry's hopes. If fare hikes continue and ticket prices stabilize, passengers may begin choosing different airlines on the basis of comfort, not cost; if that happens, airlines will have to be ready with new and better in-flight features. A Boeing Company executive says that "cabin environment will be a major factor;" that is, designers must make the cabin so attractive that it will offset lower fares on other airlines. The problem, however, is added weight caused by some of the suggested features; such as; showers, exercise areas, and more elaborate kitchens. Added weight will mean that the plane consumes more fuel; thus driving up the price of the ticket. Still, some carriers, determined to find answers, are studying ways to use the new services to generate more passengers and more income; particularly in the area of advertising-supported or pay-per-use high-definition entertainment.

Exercise 40.4 Pattern Practice

For each pattern, write your own sentence correctly punctuated with semicolons.

Pattern A: Semicolons with a series of items that have their own commas

Boeing's wide-body jet has refrigerators to hold fresh food; aisles wide enough so that passengers, even heavyset people, can walk past a serving cart; and a high-definition video monitor for every seat.

Pattern B: A comma before the phrase *such as*

Planes are being built with other changes sought by passengers, such as more overhead storage, handrails above the seats, and fresher air.

Pattern C: A semicolon after quotation marks

One airline executive says that for now, it is "hard to justify the costs of some innovations"; however, airlines must be ready to respond if more passengers start choosing their carrier on the basis of comfort.

41

COLONS

The colon is used to call attention to words that follow it.

41a   COLONS TO ANNOUNCE ELEMENTS AT THE END OF A SENTENCE

Use the colon at the end of a sentence to introduce a list, an explanation (or intensification) of the sentence, or an example.

The university offers five majors in engineering: mechanical, electrical, civil, industrial, and chemical engineering.

After weeks of intensive study, she really wanted only one thing: a vacation.

[A dash could also be used here, though it is more informal.]

USING COLONS CORRECTLY

Think of the colon as the equivalent of the expression *that is*. For most elements at the end of the sentence, you could say "that is" where the colon is needed.

When the company president decided to boost morale among the employees, the executive board announced an improvement that would please everyone: pay raises.   *[: = that is]*

41b COLONS TO SEPARATE INDEPENDENT CLAUSES

Use the colon instead of a semicolon to separate two independent clauses when the second amplifies or restates the first clause. Again, think of the colon as the equivalent of *that is*. An independent clause following a colon may begin with a capital or lowercase letter, although the lowercase letter is preferred.

Some people say that lobbying groups exert too much influence on Congress: they can buy votes as a result of their large contributions to the right senators and representatives.

41c COLONS TO ANNOUNCE QUOTATIONS

Use the colon to announce a quotation that follows an independent clause.

The head of the company's research department, Ms. Cohen, made a surprising announcement: "We recommended budgeting $1 million for the development of that type of software, but we were turned down. We regrouped and tried to think of a new approach to change their minds. We got nowhere."

The CEO of the company offered an apology to calm her down: "I'm truly sorry that we were not able to fund your project."

41d COLONS IN SALUTATIONS AND BETWEEN ELEMENTS

Use the colon in the salutation of a formal or business letter, in scriptural and time references, between a title and subtitle, with proportions, and between city and publisher in bibliographical format.

Dear Mayor O'Daly:	6:15 A.M.
Genesis 1:8	a scale of 4:1
"Jerusalem: A City United"	(New York: Midland Books, 1998)

41e **COLONS WITH QUOTATION MARKS**

If a colon is needed, put it after the closing quotation mark.

"To err is human; to repeat an error is stupid": that was my chemistry teacher's favorite saying in the lab.

41f **UNNECESSARY COLONS**

Don't use the colon after a verb or a phrase like *such as* or *consisted of.*

Unnecessary Colon: The people who applied were: Mr. Al Shaha,
(NO PUNCTUATION NEEDED)
Mr. Pappagonus, and Ms. Lassiter.

Unnecessary Colon: She preferred a noncontact sport such as: tennis,
(NO PUNCTUATION NEEDED)
swimming, or golf.

Hint

REPLACING UNNECESSARY COLONS

When you revise for unnecessary colons before a list, you can either omit any punctuation or add a word or phrase such as *the following* after the verb.

The committee members who voted for the amendment were the following: Mia Lungren, Sam Heffelt, and Alexander Zubrev.

Exercise 41.1 Proofreading Practice

The following paragraph contains some colons that are used incorrectly and lacks some needed punctuation. Add colons and any other needed punctuation, and highlight or circle any incorrect punctuation.

When the Apollo astronauts brought back bags of moon rocks, it was expected that the rocks would provide some answers to a perennial question; the origin of the moon. Instead, the moon rocks suggested a number of new theories. One that gained supporters is called: the giant impact theory. Alan Sabata, a lunar scientist, offers an explanation of the giant impact theory "Recently acquired evidence suggests that the moon was born of a monstrous collision between a primordial, just-formed Earth and a protoplanet the size of Mars." This evidence comes from modeling such a collision on powerful supercomputers. The theory proposes the following sequence of events (1) as Earth was forming, a projectile the size of Mars struck it with a glancing blow; (2) a jet of vapor then spurted out, moving so fast that some of it escaped from Earth and the rest condensed into pebble-sized rock fragments; and (3) gravitational attraction fused this cloud of pebbles into the moon. Several reasons make some scientists favor this theory, for example it dovetails with what is known about the moon's chemistry, and it explains why the moon's average composition resembles Earth's. Another lunar scientist says, "We may be close to tracking down the real answer."

Exercise 41.2 Pattern Practice

For each pattern, write your own sentence correctly punctuated with colons.

Pattern A: Sentence with a list following a colon

The coffeeshop offered samples of five new coffee flavors: mocha java, chocolate fudge, Swiss almond, cinnamon, and French roast.

Pattern B: Independent clause + colon + second independent clause that restates or explains the first clause

That cat has only one problem: she thinks she is a human.

Pattern C: Sentence with a quotation not introduced by words such as *said, remarked,* or *stated*

Jun clarified his views on marriage: "It should be a commitment for a lifetime, not a trial run for a relationship."

42

QUOTATION MARKS

42a QUOTATION MARKS WITH DIRECT AND INDIRECT QUOTATIONS

Use quotation marks with direct quotations of prose, poetry, and dialogue.

1. Quotation Marks with Prose Quotations

Direct quotations are the exact words said by someone or the exact words you saw in print and are recopying. Use a set of quotation marks to enclose direct quotations included in your writing.

Indirect quotations are not the exact words said by someone else but a rephrasing or summary of someone else's words. Don't use quotation marks for indirect quotations. (For more information on quoting directly and indirectly, see 64e.)

If a quotation is longer than four lines on a page, set the quotation off as a block quotation by indenting one inch or ten spaces from the left margin. Use the same spacing between lines as in the rest of your paper. Do not use quotation marks around this indented material.

- Direct quotation of a whole sentence: Use a capital letter to start the first word of the quotation.

  Mr. and Mrs. Yoder, owners of a 300-acre farm, said, "We refuse to use that pesticide because it might pollute the nearby wells."

- Direct quotation of part of a sentence: Don't use a capital letter to start the first word of the quotation.

  Mr. and Mrs. Yoder stated that they "refuse to use that pesticide" because of possible water pollution.

- Indirect quotation:

  According to their statement to the local papers, the Yoders will not use the pesticide because of potential water pollution.

- Quotation within a quotation: Use single quotation marks (' at the beginning and ' at the end) for a quotation enclosed inside another quotation.

  The agricultural reporter for the newspaper explained, "When I talked to the Yoders last week, they said, 'We refuse to use that pesticide.'"

If you leave some words out of a quotation, use an ellipsis (three spaced periods) to indicate omitted words. If you need to insert something within a quotation, use brackets [ ] to enclose the addition. (See 45d and 45e.)

- Full direct quotation:

  The welfare agency representative said, "We are unable to help this family whom we would like to help because we don't have the funds to do so."

- Omitted material with ellipsis:

  The welfare agency representative said, "We are unable to help this family . . . because we don't have the funds to do so."

- Added material with brackets:

  The welfare agency representative explained that the agency is "unable to help this family whom [it] would like to help."

2. Quotation Marks in Poetry

When you quote a single line of poetry, write it like other short quotations. Two lines of poetry can be run in as part of your text with a slash (/) inserted to indicate the end of the first line. Leave a space before and after the slash. If the quotation is three lines or longer, set it off, indented one inch or ten spaces, just like a longer quotation. (Some people prefer to set off even two-line quotations.) Quote the poem line by line as it appears on the original page, and do not use quotation marks. (See 45b.)

- Poetry quoted in your writing:

> In his poem "Mending Wall," Robert Frost writes, "Something there is that doesn't love a wall, / That sends the frozen-ground-swell under it."

- Longer quotation from a poem set off from the sentence:

> In his poem "Mending Wall," Robert Frost questions the building of barriers and walls:
>
>> Before I built a wall I'd ask to know
>> What I was walling in or walling out,
>> And to whom I was like to give offense.

3. Quotation Marks in Dialogue

Write each person's speech, however short, as a separate paragraph. Use commas to set off *he said* or *she said.* Closely related bits of narrative can be included in the paragraph. If one person's speech goes on for several paragraphs, use quotation marks at the beginning of each paragraph but not at the end of any paragraph except the last one. To signal the end of the person's speech, use quotation marks at the end of the last paragraph. (See 64e.)

> "May I help you?" the clerk asked as she approached the customer.
> "No, thanks," responded the woman in a quiet voice.
> "We have a special sale today on sweaters," persisted the salesperson. She continued to stand next to the customer, waiting for the woman to indicate why she was there.
> "How nice for you," the customer replied as she walked out.

42b QUOTATION MARKS FOR MINOR TITLES AND PARTS OF WHOLES

Use quotation marks for the titles of parts of larger works (titles of book chapters, magazine articles, and episodes of television and radio series) and for short or minor works (songs, short stories, essays, short poems, and other literary works that are shorter than book length).

For longer works, see Chapter 49. Neither quotation marks nor italics are used for the titles of most religious texts and legal documents.

> Whenever he did hard work in his garden, he'd hum his favorite song, "Ol' Man River."

> Mark Twain's short story "The Celebrated Jumping Frog of Calaveras County" made frog-jumping contests wildly popular.

> She wanted to memorize the first eighteen chapters of Genesis.

42c QUOTATION MARKS FOR WORDS

Use quotation marks for words used in special ways, such as for irony (when the writer means the opposite of what is being said), and for expressions being cited as expressions rather than for their meaning. Words used as words are usually italicized but can be enclosed in quotation marks. Definitions of words are also enclosed in quotation marks.

The three-year-old held up his "work of art" for the teacher to admire.

"Why not?" is a phrase I wish she'd omit from her vocabulary.

The word "accept" is often confused with "except."

Per capita means "for each person."

42d USE OF OTHER PUNCTUATION WITH QUOTATION MARKS

Put commas and periods inside quotation marks. When a reference follows a short quotation, put the period after the reference. For long quotations that are set off from the paragraph, put the period before the reference that is enclosed in parentheses. (For more information, see 64e.)

"The Politics of Hunger," a recent article in *Political Quarterly,* discussed the United Nations' use of military force to help victims of hunger.

He said, "I may forget your name, but I never remember a face."

Junius said, "Moshenberg's style of writing derives from his particular form of wit" (252).

Put a colon or semicolon after the quotation marks.

The critic called the movie "a potential Academy Award winner"; I thought it was a flop.

Put a dash, a question mark, or an exclamation point inside the quotation marks when these punctuation marks are part of the quotation and outside the quotation marks when the marks apply to the whole sentence.

He asked, "Do you need this book?"

[The quotation here is a question.]

Does Dr. Lim tell all her students, "You must work harder"?

[The quotation here is a statement, but it is part of a sentence that is a question.]

42e UNNECESSARY QUOTATION MARKS

Don't put quotation marks around the titles of your essays (though someone else will use quotation marks when referring to your essay), and don't use quotation marks for common nicknames, bits of humor, technical terms, and trite or well-known expressions.

Unnecessary Quotation Marks: The crew rowed together like "a well-oiled machine." [No quotation marks are needed.]

Unnecessary Quotation Marks: He decided to save his money to buy "the latest DVD burner." [No quotation marks are needed.]

Exercise 42.1 Proofreading Practice

Add quotation marks where needed in the following paragraph, and delete any that are incorrect, unnecessary, or inappropriately placed.

Remember Silverton wine coolers? Silverton, like hundreds of other products that appeared in the same year, was pulled from the shelf after it failed to gain a market. Silverton didn't seem to have any connotation as a cooler, explains G. F. Strousel, the company's vice-president in charge of sales. Every year new products appear briefly on the shelf and disappear, and established products that no longer have "customer appeal" are canceled as well. "Either way," experts say, "the signs that point to failure are the same." Companies looking to cut their losses pay attention to such signs. In a recent newspaper article titled Over 75 Percent of Business Ideas Are Flops, T. M. Weir, a professor of marketing, explains that products that don't grow but maintain their percentage of the market are known as *cash cows*, and those that are declining in growth and in market share are called *dipping dogs*. Says Weir, "Marketers plot the growth and decline of products, especially of the dipping dogs, very closely." According to several sources at a New York research firm that studies new product development, "The final decision to stop making a product is a financial one." When the "red ink" flows, the product is pulled.

Exercise 42.2 Pattern Practice

For each pattern, write two correctly punctuated sentences of your own.

Pattern A: Direct quotation with a whole sentence being quoted

The president of the university stated, "It is my fervent hope that next year there will be no tuition increase."

Pattern B: Direct quotation with a part of a sentence being quoted

The president of the university vowed that next year "there will be no tuition increase."

Pattern C: A quotation within a quotation

The announcer said, "You heard it live on this station, Coach Montenegra predicting that his team 'will run away with the game tomorrow.'"

Pattern D: Dialogue between two speakers

"Can you help me with the chem lab report?" Ivan's roommate asked.

"I'll try, but my notes aren't very complete," Ivan said as he ambled off to turn up the stereo.

"That's OK. They have to be better than mine."

Pattern E: Quotation marks with a minor title or a title of a part of a work

In his autobiography, Hsao titled his first chapter "In the Beginning."

Pattern F: Quotation marks with an expression cited as an expression

I can't believe that any grown person really says "awesome."

43

HYPHENS

43a   HYPHENS TO DIVIDE WORDS

Use the hyphen to indicate that part of a word appears on the next line. Be sure to divide words between syllables. Check your dictionary to see how words are split into syllables. When you split words, do so in a way that is most helpful to your reader. Follow these guidelines:

■ Don't divide one-syllable words.

■ Don't leave one letter at the end of the line. Instead, put the whole word on the next line.

Wrong: Nils took the big package a-
     part very carefully.

Revised: Nils took the big package
     apart very carefully.

■ Break only at the end of a syllable. In compound words, break between the parts of the compound.

     Twila was so hungry she ordered pan-
     cakes, eggs, and sausage.

■ Don't put fewer than three letters on the next line.

> **Wrong:** Musa asked for some much need-
> ed funds for buying books.

> **Revised:** Musa asked for some much
> needed funds for buying books.

■ Don't divide the last word in a paragraph or the last word on a page.

43b HYPHENS TO FORM COMPOUND WORDS

Use the hyphen to form compound words. Hyphens are used in compounds of all kinds, including all spelled-out fractions and spelled-out numbers from twenty-one to ninety-nine. Some non-numerical compounds are written separately, as one word, and others are connected by hyphens; check your dictionary to determine the preferred form.

> two-thirds   thirty-six   clear-cut   mother-in-law

For hyphenated words in a series, use hyphens as follows:

> mother-, father-, and sister-in-law
>
> four-, five-, and six-page essays

43c HYPHENS TO JOIN WORD UNITS

Use the hyphen to join two or more words that work together and serve as a single descriptive before a noun. When the words come after the noun, they are usually not hyphenated. Don't use hyphens with *-ly* adverb modifiers.

The office needed up-to-date copiers.	The office needed copiers that were up to date.
The repair involved a six-inch pipe.	The repair involved a pipe that was six inches long.
They brought along their nine-year-old son.	They brought along their son, who was nine years old.

43d HYPHENS TO JOIN PREFIXES, SUFFIXES, AND LETTERS TO A WORD

Use hyphens between words and the prefixes *self-*, *all-*, and *ex-*. For other prefixes, such as *anti-*, *non-*, *pro-*, and *co-*, no hyphen is ordinarily required except to prevent misreading; use the dictionary as a guide. Use the hyphen when you add a prefix to a capitalized word (for example, *mid-August*) and when you add the suffix *-elect* to a word. In addition, use the hyphen to join single letters to words.

self-supporting	co-opt	president-elect
all-encompassing	non-union	T-shirt
ex-senator	pro-American	U-turn

The hyphen is also used to avoid double vowels (especially *aa* or *ii*) and triple consonants.

anti-itch   [*not* antiitch]

bell-like   [*not* belllike]

43e HYPHENS TO AVOID AMBIGUITY

Use the hyphen to avoid confusion between words that are spelled alike but have different meanings.

re-creation (making again)	recreation (fun)
re-cover (cover again)	recover (regain health)
co-op (something jointly owned)	coop (cage for fowl)

Exercise 43.1 Proofreading Exercise

Add hyphens where they are needed in the following paragraph, and delete any that are incorrect.

For health conscious people who cringe at the thought of using a toothpaste with preservatives and dyes, there are alternative toothpastes made entirely from plants. One brand of these new, all natural toothpastes advertises that its paste includes twenty nine different herbs, root and flower-extracts, and seaweed. Some of these toothpastes have a pleasant taste and appearance, but the owner of a San Francisco health food store decided not to carry one brand because it is a reddish brown paste. "When squeezed from a tube, it resembles a fat earthworm," she explained. She prefers a brand made of propolis, the sticky stuff bees use to line their hives, and myrrh. The hard core macrobiotic group favors another brand, a black paste made of charred eggplant powder, clay, and seaweed. This interest in natural toothpastes may be cyclical, explains the director of an oral health institute. He recalls a gray striped, mint flavored paste from the Philippines that sought to capitalize on a spurt of interest several years ago. It was a big-seller for a few months and then disappeared.

Exercise 43.2 Pattern Practice

For each pattern, write your own correctly hyphenated sentence.

Pattern A: Hyphen that splits a word at the end of a line

Pattern B: Hyphen with at least two compound words

My great-grandmother worked in a garment factory for twenty-seven years.

Pattern C: Hyphen with two words serving as a single descriptive in front of a noun (and, if possible, the same two words after the noun)

The plastic-trimmed suitcases were promptly returned by unhappy customers, who said the plastic trim fell off within several weeks.

Pattern D: Hyphen with a prefix or suffix

Some rap artists have been accused of being anti-intellectual.

44

END PUNCTUATION

At the end of a sentence, use a period, a question mark, or an exclamation point.

44a PERIODS

1. Periods at the End of a Sentence

Use the period to end sentences that are statements, mild commands, indirect questions, or polite questions to which an answer is not really expected.

He's one of those people who don't like pets.

[statement]

Hand in your homework by noon tomorrow.

[mild command]

She asked how she could improve her golf game.

[indirect question]

Would you please let me know when the bus arrives.

[polite question]

2. Periods with Abbreviations

Use the period after most abbreviations.

Mr.	Mrs.	etc.	9 P.M.
Ms.	Ave.	A.D.	Ph.D.
R.S.V.P.	Inc.	U.S.A.	Dr.

Don't use a second period if the abbreviation is at the end of the sentence.

> She studied for her R.N.

Periods are not needed after certain abbreviations (acronyms) made up of the initial letters of the names of companies, organizations, or other entities. Periods are not used with the state abbreviations used by the U.S. Postal Service.

> NATO   NBA   CIA   YMCA
>
> TV   NFL   FBI   DNA
>
> Tampa, FL 33601

3. Periods with Quotation Marks

Put periods that follow quotations inside the quotation marks.

> As she said, "No one is too old to try something new."

However, if there is a reference to a source, put the period after the reference.

> Hemmings states, "This is the best example of Renaissance art" (144).

Exercise 44.1 Proofreading Practice

Add periods where they are needed in the following paragraph. Take out any periods used incorrectly.

Several years ago, the nation's print and broadcast media joined with advertising agencies to launch a massive media campaign against drugs. Some, like ABC-TV, announced that they would donate prime-time T.V. spots, but CBS Inc, while agreeing to cooperate, announced its intention to continue to commit funds for campaigns for other public issues such as AIDS prevention. James R Daly, a spokesman for the antidrug campaign, said, "We are glad to see other companies joining in to help the campaign". For example, the Revlon Co. donated the film needed for TV spots, and in Washington, DC, a group of concerned parents volunteered to do additional fund-raising. In the first two years of this media campaign, more than $500 million was raised Says Dr Harrison Rublin, a leading spokesperson for one of the fund-raising groups, "One thirty-second ad aired at 8 PM is ten times more effective than a hundred brochures on the subject".

Exercise 44.2 Pattern Practice

For each pattern, write two correctly punctuated sentences of your own.

> **Pattern A:** Statement (with a period at the end)
>
> > Luis started guitar lessons at the age of six.

Pattern B: Mild command (with a period at the end)

Return that pencil to me when you have finished.

Pattern C: Indirect quotation (with a period at the end)

Jennifer asked the gas station attendant whether he had a wrench.

Pattern D: Polite question (with a period at the end)

Would you please send the material I am requesting as soon as possible.

Pattern E: Containing an abbreviation with periods

He couldn't decide whether to enroll for a B.S. or a B.A. degree.

Pattern F: Containing an abbreviation without periods

The computer shop featured IBM and Apple computers.

Pattern G: Containing a quotation

His father announced, "If you want to use the car tonight, you'd better fill it with gas."

Pattern H: Containing a quotation and a parenthetical reference

According to this article, "Smokers can no longer demand rights that violate the air space of others" (Heskett 27).

44b QUESTION MARKS

1. Question Marks at the End of a Sentence

Use a question mark after direct quotations but not after indirect quotations.

Direct Quotation: "Do you have another copy of this book in stock?"

Indirect Quotation: She asked the salesperson whether he had another copy of the book in stock.

Use the question mark in statements that contain direct quotations.

"Did Henri ever pay back that loan?" she wondered.

Place the question mark inside the quotation marks only if the question mark is part of the quotation.

Uki said, "Who's that standing by the door?"

Did Jon really say, "Get lost"?

2. Question Marks in a Series

Question marks may be used between parts of a series.

Would you prefer to eat at a restaurant? go on a picnic? cook at home? order out?

3. Question Marks to Indicate Doubt

Question marks can be used to indicate doubt about the correctness of the preceding word, figure, date, or other piece of information.

The city was founded about 1837 **(?)** but did not grow significantly until about fifty years later.

4. Unnecessary Question Marks

Don't use a question mark in parentheses to indicate sarcasm. Instead, rewrite the sentence so that the meaning is clear.

Unnecessary Question Mark: She thought it was her intelligence **(?)** that charmed him.

Revised: She thought it might have been her intelligence that charmed him.

Exercise 44.3 Proofreading Practice

In the following paragraph, add question marks where they are needed and delete any that are incorrect, unnecessary, or inappropriate.

Recent research has found that the heat can kill you? Two meteorologists exploring weather patterns for the second half of the twentieth century found that the frequency of heat waves increased substantially from 1949 (?) to 1995. The deaths of 600 people in a 1995 Chicago heat wave prompted the researchers to examine the effects of heat on society. The researchers' main question was whether hot and humid weather that occurs at night is dangerous? Subsequently, the team did find that prolonged periods of hot weather that last through several nights have the most profound effects on people, especially the elderly. A nursing home administrator asked the researchers, "What precautions should be taken when the heat is extreme." These knowledgeable (?) researchers responded, "Extreme summer heat affects people's health more than other types of severe weather. The elderly should drink plenty of fluids and remain indoors during the hottest part of the day?" With proper precautions, the deaths of countless people from extreme heat can be avoided. With all of the TV campaigns, though, is it really necessary to keep repeating these warnings in the twenty-first century.

Exercise 44.4 Pattern Practice

For each pattern, write two correctly punctuated sentences of your own.

Pattern A: Sentence ending with a question mark
Which way should I turn this knob?

Pattern B: Statement containing a direct question
"Can you speak Swahili?" he asked.

Pattern C: Quotation with a question mark inside the quotation marks

> Lukas kept demanding, "Did she really ask my name?"

Pattern D: Quotation with a question mark outside the quotation marks

> Why did the coach say, "No more practice this week"?

Pattern E: Question mark to indicate doubt about a piece of information

> The cavalry unit had about 1,000 (?) horses before the battle.

44c EXCLAMATION POINTS

1. Exclamation Points at the End of a Sentence

Use an exclamation point after strong commands, statements said with great emphasis, interjections, and sentences intended to express surprise, disbelief, or strong feeling.

> What a magnificent surprise!
>
> I am not guilty!
>
> Definitely!

Don't overuse the exclamation point, and don't combine it with other end punctuation as shown here:

> Wow! What a party! There was even a live band! [The first exclamation point is enough.]
>
> I won $5! [The exclamation point seems overly dramatic.]
>
> Is he for real?! [The question mark alone is enough.]

2. Exclamation Points with Quotation Marks

Enclose the exclamation mark inside quotation marks only if it is part of the quotation.

> He burst into the room and yelled, "We are surrounded!"
>
> Then, at the end of the meeting, Sarah admitted, "My committee has already vetoed this motion"!

Exercise 44.5 Proofreading Practice

Add exclamation points where they are needed in the following paragraph, and delete any that are incorrect, unnecessary, or inappropriate.

At the end of winter, when gardeners are depressed from the long months indoors, plant catalogs start flooding the mail! In large type, the catalogs blare out their news to hungry gardeners. "Amazing!!" "Fantastic!!!" "Incredible!!!!" The covers always belong to some enormous new strain of tomatoes. "Bigger than Beefsteaks" or "Too Big to Fit on This Page"! they yell. Even the blueberries are monsters. "Blueberries as big as quarters!" the catalogs promise. All you do, according to these enticing catalogs, is "Plant 'em and stand back!?!" On a gloomy February afternoon, many would-be gardeners are probably ready to believe that this year they too can have "asparagus thicker than a person's thumb"!!!

Exercise 44.6 Pattern Practice

For each pattern, write your own correctly punctuated sentence.

Pattern A: Sentence with an exclamation point

This is the happiest day of my life!

Pattern B: Quotation with an exclamation point inside the quotation marks

After the ballots were counted, Dan yelled, "I won!"

Pattern C: Quotation with an exclamation point outside the quotation marks

Every time we try to study, Uri always says, "Let's go out instead"!

45

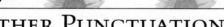

OTHER PUNCTUATION

45a   DASHES

Dashes, considered somewhat informal, can add emphasis and clarity. But they shouldn't be overused, especially as substitutes for commas or colons. When you are writing on a computer, you most likely have the dash available, but if the font set you are using doesn't have the dash, use two hyphens to form one. Don't leave a space before or after the hyphens. For anything written by hand, draw a dash as an unbroken line, at least twice as long as a hyphen.

1. Dashes at the Beginning or End of a Sentence

Use the dash at the beginning or end of the sentence to set off an explanation or illustration or to add emphasis or clarity. Near the beginning of a sentence, the dash usually comes after a series of items that are explained in the rest of the sentence, which often begins with *these, all,* or *none.* Toward the end of the sentence, it may be used to set off some clarifying information. If this added explanation is of less importance than the rest of the sentence, use parentheses instead.

> Fame, fortune, and a Ferrari—these were his goals in life.

> Her acting gave an extra touch of humor to the play—some badly needed pizzazz.

2. Dashes to Mark an Interruption

Use the dash as an interrupter to mark a sudden break in thought, an abrupt change or surprise or a deliberate pause and to show in a dialogue that the speaker has been interrupted.

> According to her way of looking at things—but not mine—this was a worthwhile cause.

> The small child stood there happily sniffing a handful of flowers—all the roses from my garden.

> Of course, Everett was willing to work to get good grades—but not too hard.

> Leshaun announced, "I'm going to clean up this room so that—"
> "Oh, no, you don't," yelled her little brother.

3. Dashes to Set Off a Phrase or Clause Containing a Comma

When a phrase or clause already has commas in it, you can use dashes to set off the whole word group.

> Hildy always finds interesting little restaurants—such as Lettuce Eat, that health food place, and Ho Ming's Pizza Parlor—to go to after a concert.

Exercise 45.1 Proofreading Practice

Add dashes where they are needed in the following paragraph.

If you love to shop for clothes but hate fitting rooms, you might be interested in a new invention that can eliminate trying on clothing in stores. Surprisingly, scientific researchers not tailors have developed a body scanner that measures a person's body. Going to stores to try on clothes may soon be an outdated practice; you could do it all at home. The body scanner is shaped like a photo booth and contains infrared lights that measure more than 300,000 points on the body. This invention, which is really an electronic tailor, is in the development stage. The team expects that the scanner will be ready for use soon but not in the next year. Potential customers such as the leading London fashion designers are anxious for the product to gain final approval. The prediction is that custom clothing will really fit like a glove. Online shopping for clothes may also become easier but not soon.

Exercise 45.2 Pattern Practice

For each pattern, write two sentences of your own with dashes.

Pattern A: Near the beginning or end of the sentence for explanation or illustration

Those leather boots cost about $400—almost half a week's salary.

Pattern B: To mark an interruption or break in thought

Ricardo borrows—but never returns—everyone else's class notes.

Pattern C: To set off phrases and clauses that contain commas

There were several exercise programs—including aerobic dancing, gymnastics, Pilates, and aquatic exercises in the pool—to choose from in the students' recreational program at the gymnasium.

45b SLASHES

1. Slashes to Mark the End of a Line of Poetry

When you quote two or three lines of poetry within a paragraph, indicate the end of each line with a slash (with a space before and after the slash). Don't use the slash when you indent and quote three or more lines of poetry.

Andrew Marvell's poem "To His Coy Mistress" begins by reminding the lady that life is indeed short: "Had we but world enough, and time / This coyness, lady, were no crime." And as the poem progresses, the imagery of death reinforces this reminder of our brief moment of life:

> But at my back I always hear
> Time's winged chariot hurrying near;
> And yonder all before us lie
> Deserts of vast eternity.

2. Slashes to Indicate Acceptable Alternatives

Use the slash, with no space before or afterward, to indicate that either of two terms can apply. The slash on a computer keyboard is the slanting line / (also known as the forward slash used in Web addresses).

pass/fail   and/or   yes/no

Exercise 45.3 Proofreading Practice

Add slashes where appropriate in the following paragraph.

I have kept a journal since I entered college. In this journal, I have recorded my favorite poems and or their significance in my life at the time I read them. I enrolled in a poetry course for fun because I was a biology major and poetry was not often recited in lab. Of course, I opted for the pass fail grading system because I feared that my scientific mind would not yield memorable poetry. I think the poem that I will remember forever is "I Never Saw a Moor" by Emily Dickinson. The first stanza is familiar to almost everyone:

> I never saw a Moor—
> I never saw the Sea—
> Yet know I how the Heather looks,
> And what a Billow be.

I have heard these lines again and again since taking the college poetry course. It is the second stanza that is less familiar. The first two lines of the second stanza contain the theme of the poem: "I never spoke with God, Nor visited in Heaven." These are the two lines I wrote about in my journal. In fact, the journal is filled with lines from the poetry of Emily Dickinson.

Exercise 45.4 Pattern Practice

For each pattern, write your own sentence with slashes.

Pattern A: With poetry quoted within a sentence

Whenever she was asked to discuss her ability to cope with great difficulties, she quoted John Milton: "The mind is its own place, and in itself / Can make a Heaven of Hell, a Hell of Heaven."

Pattern B: With two terms when either is acceptable

Because the reading list for History 227 was so long, he decided to register for it on a pass/fail option.

45c PARENTHESES

A dash gives emphasis to an element in the sentence, whereas a pair of parentheses indicates that the element enclosed is less important. *Parentheses* is the plural form of the word *parenthesis* and refers to both the parenthesis at the beginning and the parenthesis at the end of the enclosed element.

1. Parentheses to Set Off Supplementary Matter

Use parentheses to enclose supplementary or less important material that you include as further explanation or as added detail or examples. The added material does not need to be part of the grammatical structure of the sentence. If the material is inside the sentence, any punctuation needed for the rest of the sentence is outside the closing parenthesis. If a whole sentence is enclosed in parentheses, not part of another sentence, put the end punctuation for that sentence inside.

The officers of the fraternity **(the ones elected last month)** called a meeting just before the dance to remind everyone of the new parking regulations.

2. Parentheses to Enclose Figures or Letters

Use parentheses to enclose figures or letters that number items in a series in a sentence or paragraph.

The three major items on the agenda were **(1)** the budget review, **(2)** the construction permits, and **(3)** the evaluation procedure.

Exercise 45.5 Proofreading Practice

Add parentheses as needed to the following paragraph.

Medical researchers have announced a new finding that Alzheimer's patients are demonstrating remarkable abilities in painting. Alzheimer's also known as *dementia* is a degenerative brain disorder that affects the part of the brain responsible for several functions: 1 social skills, 2 verbal communication, and 3 physical orientation. Neuropathologists doctors who study brain disorders have found that this disease may not affect visual thinking. Some famous artists including Willem de Kooning and Vincent van Gogh may have suffered from Alzheimer's disease. This study could lead to new and innovative treatments for Alzheimer's patients.

Exercise 45.6 Pattern Practice

For each pattern, write your own sentence with parentheses.

Pattern A: To enclose less important material

The sixth-grade teacher decided to offer his students an opportunity to try out different drawing materials (such as pastel chalks and charcoal) that they hadn't used before.

Pattern B: To enclose figures or letters in a numbered list

The job offer included some very important fringe benefits that similar positions in other companies did not include: (a) a day-care center in the building, (b) retirement benefits for the employee's spouse also, and (c) an opportunity to buy company cars after they have been used for a year or so.

45d BRACKETS

1. Brackets to Add Comments Within a Quotation

When you are quoting material and have to add your own explanation, comment, or addition within the quotation, enclose your addition within brackets [ ].

Everyone agreed with Phil Brown's claim that "this great team [the Chicago Bears] is destined for next year's Super Bowl."

The Latin word *sic* ("thus, so") in brackets means that you copied the original quotation exactly as it appeared, but you think that the word just before *sic* may be an error or a questionable form.

After the town meeting, the newspaper's lead story reported the discussion: "The Town Board and the mayor met to discuss the mayor's proposal to raise parking meter rates. The discussion was long but not heated, and the exchange of views was fiendly [*sic*] despite some strong opposition."

2. Brackets to Replace Parentheses Within Parentheses

When you need to enclose something already within parentheses, use brackets instead of a second set of parentheses.

"Unlike children born after 1985, baby busters—the children born between 1965 and 1980—had more choices in the job market and better prospects for advancement than the previous 'baby boom' generation and the generation born slightly after the baby busters," says John Sayers in his study (*The Changing Face of Our Population* [New York: Merian, 1994] 18).

Exercise 45.7 Proofreading Practice

In the following paragraph, brackets are needed in several places. Insert the missing brackets, replacing parentheses if necessary.

One medieval Christian celebration was called the Feast of the Ass. According to John Smith, a Middle Ages scholar, "At one time this was a solemn celebration reenacting the flight of the Holy Family (Mary, Joseph, and Jesus) into Egypt. It ended with a Mast *sic* in the church" (*Christian Celebrations* (New York: United Press, 1995) 23). The festival (started in the fourteenth century by the tribune, a group of church elders) became very popular as it became transformed into a humorous parody in which the ass was led into the church and treated as an honored guest. Historians claim that the members of the congregation all brayed like asses. The church abandoned the celebration in the fifteenth century, but it remained popular for years.

Exercise 45.8 Pattern Practice

For each pattern, write your own sentence containing brackets.

Pattern A: Brackets around comments within a quotation

The lab assistant explained that "everyone [who has finished the lab experiment] should hand in notebooks by Friday."

Pattern B: Brackets to replace parentheses within parentheses

Two famous battlefield nurses, Florence Nightingale (in the Crimean War [1854–1856]) and Clara Barton (in the American Civil War [1861–1865]), transformed nursing into a true profession.

45e ELLIPSIS (OMITTED WORDS)

Use an ellipsis (a series of three spaced periods) to indicate that you are omitting words or a part of a sentence from material you are quoting.

Original: "In 1891, when President Benjamin Harrison proclaimed the first forest reserves as government land, there were so many people opposed to the idea that his action was called undemocratic and un-American."

Some Words Omitted: "In 1891, when President Benjamin Harrison proclaimed the first forest reserves . . . his action was called undemocratic and un-American."

If you are omitting a whole sentence or paragraph, add a fourth period with no space after the last word preceding the ellipsis:

"Federal lands quickly increased. . . . They were designated as government property."

An ellipsis is not needed if the omission occurs at the beginning or end of the sentence you are quoting, but if your sentence ends with quoted words that are not the end of the original sentence, use an ellipsis mark. Add your period (the fourth one) with no space after the last word if there is no documentation included. If there is documentation, such as a page number, add the last period after the closing parenthesis.

"the National Forest System. . . ."

"the National Forest System . . ." (Smith 27).

If you omit words immediately after a punctuation mark in the original, include that mark in your sentence.

"because of this use of forests for timbering, mining, and grazing, . . ."

Three ellipsis points are also used to show hesitation or an unfinished statement.

The lawyer asked, "Did you see the defendant leave the room?"

"Ah, I'm not sure . . . but he might have left," replied the witness.

46
CAPITALS

Capitalize words that name one particular thing, most often a person or place (known as *proper nouns*), rather than a general type or group of things (known as *common nouns*). Names that need capitals can be thought of as legal titles that identify a specific entity. For example, you can take a course in history (a word not capitalized because it is a general field of study), but the course is offered by a particular department with a specific name, such as History Department or Department of Historical Studies. The name of that specific department is capitalized. However, if you take a course in French, *French* is capitalized because it is the name of a specific language. (For more on common and proper nouns, see Chapter 55.)

Listed here are categories of words that should be capitalized. If you are not sure about a particular word, check your dictionary.

- Persons

Vincent Baglia	Rifka Kaplan	Masuto Tatami

- Places, including geographical regions

Indianapolis	Ontario	Midwest

- Peoples and their languages

Spanish	Swahili	English

- Religions and their followers

Buddhist	Judaism	Christianity

- Members of national, political, racial, social, civic, and athletic groups

Democrat	African American	Chicago Bears
Danes	Friends of the Library	Olympics Committee

- Institutions and organizations

Supreme Court	Legal Aid Society	Lions Club

- Historical documents

Declaration of Independence	Magna Carta

- Periods and events, but not centuries

Middle Ages	Boston Tea Party	eighteenth century

- Days, months, and holidays, but not seasons

Monday	Thanksgiving	winter

- Trademarks

    Coca-Cola   Sony   Ford

- Holy books and words denoting the Supreme Being (pronouns referring to God may be capitalized or lowercased)

    Talmud   Bible   Lord

    God   His creation (*or*) his creation

- Words and abbreviations derived from specific names, but not the
  names of things that have lost that specific association

    Stalinism   Freudian   NATO   CBS

    french fries   pasteurize   italics   panama hat

- Place words, such as *street, park,* and *city,* that are part of specific
  names

    New York City   Wall Street   Zion National Park

- Titles that precede people's names, but not titles that follow names

    Aunt Sylvia   Sylvia, my aunt

    Governor Lionel Washington   Lionel Washington, governor

    President John Taft   John Taft, president

- Words that indicate family relationships when used as a substitute
  for a specific name

    Here is a gift for Mother.   Li Chen sent a gift to his mother.

- Titles of books, magazines, essays, movies, plays, and other works,
  but not articles (*a, an, the*), short prepositions (*to, by, on, in*), or short
  joining words (*and, but, or*) unless they are the first or last word.
  With hyphenated words, capitalize the first and all other important
  words.

    The Taming of the Shrew   "The Sino-Soviet Conflict"

    The Ground Beneath Her Feet   "A Brother-in-Law's Lament"

[For APA style, which has different rules, see Chapter 67.]

- The pronoun *I* and the interjection *O,* but not the word *oh*

    "Sail on, sail on, O ship of state," I said as the canoe sank.

- The first word of every sentence and the first word of a comment in
  parentheses if the comment is a complete sentence, but not in a series of questions in which the questions are not full sentences

    The American Olympic ski team (which receives very little government
    support) spent six months training for the elimination trials, whereas the

German team trained for over two years. (Like most European nations, Germany provides financial support for all team members.)

What did the interviewer want from the rock star—gossip from the music world? personal information? inside news about her next CD?

■ The first word of directly quoted speech but not a continuation of an interrupted direct quotation or a quoted phrase or clause that is integrated into the sentence

She answered, "No one will understand."

"No one," she answered, "will understand."

When Bataglio declined the nomination, he explained that he "would try again another year."

■ The first word in a list after a colon if each item in the list is a complete sentence or if each item is displayed on a line of its own

The rule books were very clear: (1) No player could continue to play after committing two fouls. (2) Substitute players would be permitted only with the consent of the other team. (3) Every eligible player had to be designated before the game.

(*or*)

The rule books were very clear:

1. No player could continue to play after committing two fouls.

2. Substitute players would be permitted only with the consent of the other team.

3. Every eligible player had to be designated before the game.

The rise in popularity of walking as an alternative to jogging has led to commercial successes of various kinds: (1) better designs for walking shoes, (2) an expanding market for walking sticks, and (3) a rapid growth in the number of manufacturers selling a variety of models of walking shoes.

(*or*)

The rise in popularity of walking as an alternative to jogging has led to commercial successes of various kinds:

1. Better designs for walking shoes

2. An expanding market for walking sticks

3. A rapid growth in the number of manufacturers selling a variety of models of walking shoes

■ Words placed after a prefix that are normally capitalized

un-American   anti-Semitic

Exercise 46.1 Proofreading Practice

The following paragraph contains some errors in capitalization. Underline the first letter of any word that needs a capital, and highlight or circle the first letter of any word that should not be capitalized.

Melbourne, a City in Australia, is the site of one of the World's tallest buildings. The Building has 120 stories and contains offices and apartments. Construction started in the Spring of last year. The Building surpassed petronas towers in Malaysia as the world's tallest Building. The Malaysian Building became the Tallest Building in 1996 when it took the title from the Sears Tower in chicago. The melbourne building is now twice the size of the city's previous tallest structure, but developers assured citizens that it did not look out of place. The developers' aim was to build a "Beautiful and appropriate building" for the city of Melbourne. "We created a new landmark for our city," Said the chief developer. He also claimed "the people of the City are proud of this accomplishment."

Exercise 46.2 Pattern Practice

For each pattern, write a sentence of your own that uses capitals correctly.

Pattern A: A sentence with the name of a national, political, racial, social, civic, or athletic group; the name of a season of the year; and a person's name and title

When Matthew Given, superintendent of the Monticello School Corporation, suggested a summer program for additional study, many parents vigorously supported his idea.

Pattern B: A sentence with a quotation interrupted by other words in the sentence

"You know," said the customer, "this is just what I was looking for."

Pattern C: Two place names and a holiday

On the Fourth of July, Chicago hosts an art and food fair in Grant Park.

47

ABBREVIATIONS

In the fields of social science, science, and engineering, abbreviations are used frequently, but in other fields and in academic writing in the humanities, only a limited number of abbreviations are generally used.

47a ABBREVIATING NUMBERS

■ Write out numbers that can be expressed in one or two words.

nine   twenty-seven   135

■ The dollar sign is generally acceptable when the written-out phrase would be three words or more.

$2 million

■ For temperatures, use figures, the degree symbol, and F (for Fahrenheit) or C (for Celsius).

−10°F   25°C

47b ABBREVIATING TITLES

■ *Mr., Mrs.,* and *Ms.* are abbreviated when used as titles before a name.

Mr. Tanato   Ms. Whitman   Mrs. Ojebwa

■ *Dr.* and *St.* ("Saint") are abbreviated only when they immediately precede a name; they are written out when they appear after the name.

Dr. Marlen Chafonanda   Marlen Chafonanda, doctor of internal medicine

■ *Prof., Sen., Gen., Capt.,* and similar abbreviated titles can be used when they appear in front of a full name or before initials and a last name but not when they appear before the last name only.

Gen. R. G. Brindo   General Brindo

■ *Sr., Jr., J.D., Ph.D., M.F.A., C.P.A.,* and other abbreviated academic titles and professional degrees can be used after the name.

Leslie Lim, Ph.D., . . .   Charleen Takamota, C.P.A.

■ *Bros., Co.,* and similar abbreviations are used only if they are part of the exact name.

Bass & Co.   Warner Bros.

47c ABBREVIATING PLACE NAMES

In general, spell out names of states, countries, continents, streets, rivers, and so on. Here are two exceptions:

■ Use the abbreviation *D.C.* in Washington, D.C. Use *U.S.* only as an adjective, not as a noun.

U.S. training bases   training bases in the United States

■ If you include a full address in a sentence, you must use the postal abbreviation for the state.

> For further information, write to us at 100 Peachtree Street, Atlanta, GA 30300, for a copy of our free catalog.

> The company's headquarters, on Peachtree Street in Atlanta, Georgia, will soon be moved.

47d ABBREVIATING MEASUREMENTS

Spell out units of measurement, such as *acre, meter, foot,* and *percent* when you use them infrequently and the accompanying numbers can be written as three or fewer words. But use abbreviations for measurements in tables, graphs, and figures.

47e ABBREVIATING DATES

Spell out months and days of the week. With dates and times, the following are acceptable:

57 B.C.   57 B.C.E.   329 C.E.   A.D. 329

[The abbreviations B.C., B.C.E. (before the common era), and C.E. (common era) are placed after the year, while A.D. is placed before.]

A.M., P.M. *(or)* a.m., p.m.   EST *(or)* E.S.T.

47f ABBREVIATING INITIALS USED AS NAMES

Use abbreviations for names of organizations, agencies, countries, and things usually referred to by their initials.

IBM	NAACP	NASA	NOW
PTA	UNICEF	the former USSR	VCR

If you are using the initials for a term that may not be familiar to your readers, spell it out the first time and give the initials in parentheses. From then on, you can use the initials. (Regarding the use or omission of periods, see 44a.)

> The study of children's long-term memory (LTM) has been difficult because of the lack of a universally accepted definition of childhood LTM.

47g ABBREVIATING LATIN EXPRESSIONS

Some Latin expressions always appear as abbreviations.

Abbreviation	Meaning	Abbreviation	Meaning
cf.	compare	et al.	and others
e.g.	for example	etc.	and so forth

Abbreviation	Meaning	Abbreviation	Meaning
i.e.	that is	vs. (*or*) v.	versus
n.b.	note carefully		

47h ABBREVIATING DOCUMENTATION

Because the format for abbreviations may vary from one style manual to another, use the abbreviations listed in the particular style manual you are following. (See Chapters 66, 67, and 68.)

Abbreviation	Meaning
abr.	abridged
anon.	anonymous
b.	born
©	copyright
c. (*or*) ca.	about—used with dates
ch. (*or*) chap.	chapter
col., cols.	column, columns
d.	died
ed., eds.	editor (*or*) edited by, editors
esp.	especially
f., ff.	and the following page, pages
illus.	illustrated by
ms., mss.	manuscript, manuscripts
no.	number
n.d.	no date of publication given
n.p.	no place of publication given
n. pag.	no page number given
p., pp.	page, pages
trans. (*or*) tr.	translated by
vol., vols.	volume, volumes

Exercise 47.1 Proofreading Practice

Proofread the following paragraph, and correct the errors in use or omission of abbreviations and symbols.

The fluctuations in the stock market affect investors and job hunters alike. In times of high unemployment, business school graduates find that the MBA may not guarantee a job after graduation. The volatile stock market often causes downsizing in investment firms such as Merrill Lynch,

Prudential, and Morgan Stanley. But some graduates have no problem landing a position starting at 64,500 dollars a year on average. The recruitment process is fairly constant at prestigious schools such as Georgetown University in Washington, D.C.. However, if employment opportunities are down, students from less highly ranked schools most likely still obtain positions but at a lower salary than previously offered. Students in schools in the US ranked at the bottom are more worried about finding a position. There can be two or three positions to fill in a company where in the past there would be ten or twelve positions. Worried students network to find internships that may lead to positions. An unpredictable market is a sign that not every MBA student can automatically expect a lucrative job.

Exercise 47.2 Pattern Practice

For each pattern, write a sentence of your own that correctly uses abbreviations.

Pattern A: A sentence that contains a number that can be written as one or two words, a name with a degree after it, and the names of a city and state

Cleon Martin, C.P.A., rented an office on the thirty-sixth floor of a high-rise building in Rochester, New York.

Pattern B: A sentence with the abbreviation for the United States used correctly and the names of a month and a day of the week

Elections for many positions in the U.S. government are held on the first Tuesday in November.

Pattern C: A sentence with a unit of measurement and a specific dollar amount

The luxurious yacht, more than sixty feet long, cost $750,000.

48

NUMBERS

Style manuals for different fields and companies vary. The suggestions for writing numbers given here are generally useful as a guide for academic writing.

Spell out numbers that can be expressed in one or two words, and use figures for other numbers.

Words	Figures
two pounds	126 days
six dollars	$31.50

Words	Figures
thirty-one years	6,381 bushels
eighty-three people	4.78 liters

Use a combination of figures and words for numbers that are close together when such a combination will make your writing clearer.

The club celebrated the birthdays of six 90-year-olds born in the city.

Use Figures for the Following

■ Days and years

December 12, 2003	(or)	12 December 2003
A.D. 1066		
in 1971–1972	(or)	in 1971–72
the 1980s	(or)	the 1980's

■ Time of day

8:00 A.M. (or) a.m.	(or)	eight o'clock in the morning
4:30 P.M. (or) p.m.	(or)	half past four in the afternoon

■ Addresses

15 Tenth Street		
350 West 114 Street	(or)	350 West 114th Street
Prescott, AZ 86301		

■ Identification numbers

Room 8	Channel 18
Interstate 65	Henry VIII

■ Page and division of books and plays

page 30	Book I
Act 3, sc. 2	Ch. 3

■ Decimals and percentages

2.7 average	13½ percent
0.037 metric ton	

■ Numbers in series and statistics

two apples, six oranges, and three bananas

115 feet by 90 feet

Be consistent, whichever form you choose.

■ Large round numbers

$4 billion	(or)	four billion dollars
16.5 million	(or)	16,500,000

■ Repeated numbers (in legal or commercial writing)

   Notice must be given at least ninety (90) days in advance.

Do Not Use Figures for the Following

■ Numbers that can be expressed in one or two words

   in his forties   the twenty-first century

■ Dates when the year is omitted

   June sixth

■ Numbers beginning sentences

   Thirty-one percent of the year's crop was harvested.

Exercise 48.1 Proofreading Practice

Proofread the following paragraph, and correct any numbers that are written incorrectly.

In the 21st century, many historians are reflecting on the events that shaped the latter half of the 20th century. The center of many important events of that century was Sixteen Hundred Pennsylvania Avenue, Washington, D.C. Baby boomers remember President John F. Kennedy, who was assassinated in the year nineteen hundred and sixty-three. Another former resident of the White House, Richard M. Nixon, will be remembered for the Watergate hearings, which dominated television programming for a long, hot 70's summer. Many people recall turning on Channel 2, 4, 5, 7, or 11 and finding Watergate on every station. Ronald Reagan brought the country "Reaganomics" and a new sense of patriotism. George H. W. Bush promised a "kinder, gentler nation" and promised not to raise taxes. Then came William Jefferson Clinton. Even more than those before him, the 42nd president of the United States gave historians much to argue about in trying to evaluate his accomplishments.

Exercise 48.2 Pattern Practice

For each sentence given here, compose a sentence of your own using that model for writing numbers. One sentence is given as an example.

Example: There was a 7.2 percent decrease in sales of cigarettes after the Surgeon General's speech.

Possible Answer: The study showed that 16.7 percent of the population in the country did not have running water.

1. The plane was due at 4:15 P.M. but arrived at 5:10 P.M.
2. That book was volume 23 in the series.
3. The astronomer calculated that the star is 18 million light-years from our planet.

4. In the 1960s, during the height of the antiwar movement, the senator's political actions were not popular, but by the time of the 1972 election, more people agreed with him.

5. The television commercial warned buyers that there were only 123 days until Christmas.

49
UNDERLINING/ITALICS

You can use either underlining or an italic font style to indicate italics. Be consistent in using whichever one you choose.

49a   UNDERLINING FOR TITLES

Use underlining (or italics) for titles and names of books, magazines, newspapers, pamphlets, films, works of art, plays, long musical works (operas, concertos, CDs), radio and television programs, and long poems. (For the use of quotation marks for titles of minor works and parts of whole works, see 42b.)

Underlining	(*or*)	**Italics**
The Catcher in the Rye		*The Catcher in the Rye*
U.S. News and World Report		*U.S. News and World Report*
New York Times		*New York Times*

Try This

TO CHOOSE BETWEEN UNDERLINING/ITALICS AND QUOTES

Think of the difference between *whole* and "part." For example, the title of a book is underlined or italicized, but the title of a chapter, which is just part of the book, goes in quotation marks. Sometimes you can make the distinction between whole and part by considering whether you can hold the item in your hand. You can hold a printed book in your hands, but you can't hold a chapter of that book. You can hold a whole CD but not just one song. For other titles, such as television series, the specific episodes are parts of the whole series and therefore go in quotation marks. However, for a movie series (for example, *Spider-Man*), each movie in the series is a separate whole and is therefore underlined or set in italics. Similarly, the parts of Dante's *Divine Comedy* are also underlined or italicized because each is a separate book.

Dead Man's Chest is Tran's favorite film in the *Pirates of the Caribbean* series.

The assignment was to read not all of Dante's The Divine Comedy but only the first book, The Inferno, by next week.

Do not use underlining, italics, or quotation marks for references to the Bible and other religious works, the Internet or World Wide Web, and legal documents.

Genesis	Bible	Upanishads
Torah	U.S. Constitution	Internet
World Wide Web	Web site	Google

49b UNDERLINING FOR OTHER USES

Use Underlining (or Italics) for the Following

■ Names of ships, airplanes, trains, and spacecraft

<u>Queen Mary</u>   <u>Concorde</u>   <u>Orient Express</u>   <u>Challenger</u>

■ Foreign words and phrases and scientific names of plants and animals

<u>in vino veritas</u>   <u>Canis lupus</u>

■ Words used as words or letters used as examples or terms

Some words, such as <u>Kleenex</u>, are brand names for products.

In English, the letters <u>ph</u> and <u>f</u> often have the same sound.

■ Words being emphasized

It <u>never</u> snows here at this time of year.

[Use italics or underlining for emphasis only sparingly.]

Do Not Use Underlining (or Italics) for the Following

■ Words of foreign origin that are now part of English

alumni	cliché	karaoke
hacienda	chutzpah	Realpolitik

■ Titles of your own papers

Exercise 49.1 Proofreading Practice

Add underlining or italics where it is needed in the following paragraph, and delete any incorrect underlining or quotation marks.

The <u>Internet</u> is considered a mass medium, according to articles in magazines like "Time" and "Newsweek." In elections, the <u>Internet</u> became a new <u>genre</u> to lasso voters when candidates established <u>Web</u> sites. A poll of voters for the television show "20/20" revealed that 82 percent of voters regularly use a computer at home or work. The New York Times reported that California was the first state to use the Internet for political purposes and was quickly imitated by "Florida," "Texas," "South Dakota," and "Wisconsin." The sites generally include information on a candidate, photos from the campaign trail, and methods for sending contributions. Voters obtain addresses for the sites from campaign literature and television commercials. While some political experts conclude that this is a less costly campaign method and highly effective for raising funds, others think that having to access a site is a deterrent. The fact remains that print and television advertisements still reach more voters and may not be replaced by the Internet. One political consultant observed, "There are more people watching Good Morning America and listening to the radio on the way to the office than visiting political Web sites." Voters feel the Internet provides options. A voter interviewed about these sites stated, "Vive la différence!"

Exercise 49.2 Pattern Practice

For each pattern, write two sentences of your own with correctly underlined (or italicized) words, names, and titles.

Pattern A: Underlining (or italics) with titles of books, magazines, newspapers, and long creative works

After surveying its recently checked-out materials, the library concluded that the most popular items on the shelves were murder mysteries, such as The Da Vinci Code by Dan Brown; current big-city newspapers, such as the New York Times; and CDs of old movies, such as North by Northwest and Gone with the Wind.

Pattern B: Underlining (or italics) with names of ships, airplanes, trains, and spacecraft

The Challenger, with a crew of seven astronauts, exploded during its launch in 1986.

Pattern C: Underlining (or italics) with foreign words or phrases and scientific names

Dr. Zagody diagnosed the cause of his illness: infection with a combination of Candida albicans and Giardia lamblia.

Pattern D: Underlining (or italics) with words used as words or examples

If she would stop overusing empty words such as great and nice in her composition class papers, she would probably be able to get an A.

Pattern E: Underlining (or italics) for emphasis

Is there a difference between acting up and acting out?

50

SPELLING

English spelling can be difficult because many words have been imported from other languages that have different spelling conventions. But it is important to spell correctly. Some misspelled words can cause confusion, and any misspelled word can signal that the writer is careless. It is wise therefore to spend some time on spelling, doing one or more of the following:

- Learn some spelling rules that are useful for you.

- Make up your own memory aids.

- Make up some rules or letter associations that will help you remember particularly troublesome words. For example, if you have trouble choosing between *e*'s and *a*'s in *separate,* it may help to remember that there's a *pa* in *separate.*

- Learn your own misspelling patterns.

- Learn how to proofread.

- Use a dictionary to check the spelling of words you are not sure of. If you don't have a dictionary in book form or a digital dictionary included with your word-processing software, consult an online dictionary on the World Wide Web.

50a PROOFREADING

Proofreading means reading your final written work slowly and carefully to catch misspellings and typographical errors. Proofreading is best done after you have finished writing and are preparing to turn your paper over to your readers.

The following are some useful proofreading strategies.

- *Slow down.* Proofreading requires slowing down your reading rate so you will see all of the letters in each word. In normal reading, your eyes skip across the line and you notice only groups of words.

- *Zoom in.* If you proofread on your computer, set the display at 125 percent or more so that you can clearly see each word.

- *Focus on each word.* One way to slow yourself down is to point a pencil or pen at each word as you say it aloud or quietly to yourself.

- *Read backward.* Move backward through each line from right to left. In this way, you won't be listening for meaning or checking for grammatical correctness.

- *Cover up any distractions.* Hold a sheet of paper or a notecard under the line being read. This way you won't be distracted by other words on the page.

- *Watch for patterns of misspellings.* Remember to look for groups or patterns of misspellings that occur most frequently in your writing.

- *Read forward.* End-to-beginning proofreading will not catch problems with omitted words or sound-alike words. To check for those, do a second proofreading moving from left to right, so that you can attend to the meaning of your sentences.

- *Run the spell-checker.* As a final step, run the spell-checking program and review each word it flags. (See 50b.)

Exercise 50.1 Proofreading Practice

Proofread the following paragraph, which has a number of typos, misspellings, and omitted words. Strike through each word that is spelled incorrectly, and correct the spelling. Insert any words that are missing.

Turkish people do'nt think of St. Nicholas as having reindeer or elfs, living at North Pole, or climbing down chimneys with gifts on Christmass Eve. Accept for a twist of history, Santa Claus might well speak Turkish, ride a camel, dress for a warmmer climate, bring gifts of oranges and tomatoes, and appear on December 5 instead of Christmas Eve. According to the story of the Turkish church about his backround, Nicholas was the frist bishop of Myra, on the coast Turkey. Turkish scholars say he was known far and wide for his peity and charity. He was killed around A.D. 245, and after his martyrdom, on December 6, tails of his good deeds lived on. His faime was so great that in the eleventh centruy, when the Italian branch of the Catholic church began a drive to bring to Italy the remains of the most famous saints, theives stole most of Nicholas's bones from the church tomb in Turkey and took them to a town in southren Italy. "Nicholas" was abbreviated to *Claus,* and "St. Nick" became *Santa.* Because there are no dociuments or records of the original Nicholas of Myra, some sholars doubt his existance, but others are convinced there really was a St. Nicholas, even if he didn't have reindeer or live at North Pole.

50b SPELL-CHECKERS

Spell-checkers on computers are useful tools, but they can't catch all spelling errors:

- *Missing words.*

- *Sound-alike words (homonyms).* The spell-checker will not flag a word if it is a correctly spelled homonym of the one you want. For example, if you mean *"They're* going to the tennis match" but write *"Their* going to the tennis match," the spell-checker will not highlight *Their* for you.

■ *Many proper nouns.* Some well-known proper nouns, such as *Washington,* may be in the spell-checker dictionary, but many will not be.

■ *Misspellings that the spell-checker can't match to an appropriate word.* For example, if you mean to write *phenomena* but instead type *phinomina,* spell-checkers will highlight the word as not matching any word in their dictionary, but many won't be able to suggest the correct spelling.

50c   SOME SPELLING GUIDELINES

1. *ie/ei*

Write *i* before *e* / except after *c* / or when sounded like "ay" / as in *neighbor* and *weigh.*

This rhyme reminds you to write *ie* except under two conditions:

■ When the two letters follow a *c.*

■ When the two letters sound like *ay* (as in *day*).

Some *ie* Words

believe	field	relief
chief	niece	yield

Some *ei* Words

ceiling	deceive	receive
conceit	eight	vein

The following common words are exceptions to this rule:

conscience	forfeit	seize
counterfeit	height	sheik
either	leisure	species
financier	neither	sufficient
foreign	science	weird

Exercise 50.2 Proofreading Practice

Proofread the paragraph, and correct any misspellings by highlighting or circling the incorrect word and writing the correct spelling.

Diwali is a five-day Hindu festival often referred to as the Festival of Lights. During this time, homes are cleaned from ceiling to floor and the windows are opened to recieve Lakshmi, a Hindu goddess. The Hindu people beleive that Lakshmi is the goddess of wealth. The cheif beleif is that wealth is not a corruptive power but is considered a reward for good deeds in a past life. The festival begins with a day set aside to worship Lakshmi. On the second day, Kali, the goddess of strength, is worshiped. The third day is the last day of the year in the lunar calendar. On this day, lamps are lighted and shine brightly in every home. Participants are encouraged to remove anger, hate, and jealousy from their lives on the fourth day. On the final day of the festival, Bali, an anceint Indian king, is recalled. The focus of this day is to see the good in others.

Exercise 50.3 Pattern Practice

Use each of the following words in a sentence of its own.

ei words

eight	vein	receive	conceit	deceive

ie words

relief	yield	field	believe	niece

2. Doubling Consonants

A few rules about doubling the last consonant of the base word will help you spell several thousand words correctly.

One-Syllable Words

If the word ends in a consonant preceded by a single short vowel, double that last consonant when you are adding a suffix beginning with a vowel.

shop	shopped	shopping	shopper
wet	wetted	wetting	wettest

Two-Syllable Words

For words with two or more syllables that end with a consonant preceded by a single vowel, double the consonant when both of the following conditions apply:

- You are adding a suffix beginning with a vowel.
- The last syllable of the base word is accented.

occur	occurred	occurring	occurrence
regret	regretted	regretting	regrettable

Exercise 50.4 Proofreading Practice

Highlight or underline the words that are misspelled in the following paragraph, and write the correct spelling.

Last week, Michael planed to have his bicycle repaired, though he admitted that he was hopping he had stopped the leak in the front tire with a patch. Even though he concealled the patch with some heavy tape, he found that he had to keep tapping the patch back onto the tire. Yesterday, when Michael looked at the bicycle on the way to his first class, he could see that the front tire had become flatter than it should be because it was lossing air. With no time to spare, he joged off to class, resolving that he would take the bicycle to a shop that afternoon.

3. Prefixes and Suffixes

A **prefix** is a group of letters added at the beginning of a base word. A **suffix** is a group of letters added to the end of the word.

The following prefixes are used in many English words.

Prefix	Meaning	Examples
ante-	before	anteroom
anti-	against	antidote
auto-	self	automobile
bene-	good	benefit
bi-	two, twice	bicycle, biweekly
bio-	life	biography, biology
de-	away, down	defer, depress
dis-	not, no longer, away	disappear
ex-	out, former	exclude, expel, ex-wife
inter-	between, among	interact, interstate
intra-	within, among members of the same group	intramural, intrastate
mis-	wrong, bad	misspell, misdeed
per-	entirely, through	perfect, pertain
post-	after	postgame, postdate
pre-	before	pregame, prefix
pro-	before, forward, in favor of	prohibit, produce, pro-American
re-	again, back	retell, redo, readmit
semi-	half, partly	semicircle, semiautomatic
un-	not, contrary to	unhappy, unable

The -*ly* Suffix

If a word ends in *l*, don't drop the *l* when adding the suffix -*ly*, but if the word already ends with two *l*'s, add only the -*y*.

chill	chilly
formal	formally

Suffixes with Words Ending in *ic*

When a word ends in *ic*, add a *k* before suffixes starting with *i, e,* or *y.* Some words that end in *ic* add the suffix -*ally,* not -*ly.*

logic	logically
public	publicly
traffic	trafficking

Exercise 50.5 Pattern Practice

Using your dictionary, look up three examples of words that include each of the prefixes listed here. Then use each one in a sentence.

1. ante-	**7.** dis-	**13.** post-
2. anti-	**8.** ex-	**14.** pre-
3. auto-	**9.** inter-	**15.** pro-
4. bene-	**10.** intra-	**16.** re-
5. bio-	**11.** mis-	**17.** semi-
6. de-	**12.** per-	**18.** un-

4. Changing *y* to *i*

When adding a suffix to words ending with *y*, change the *y* to an *i*. To avoid a double *i* in a word, keep the *y* before the -*ing* suffix.

apply	applies, applied	(*but*)	applying
carry	carries, carried	(*but*)	carrying
study	studies, studied	(*but*)	studying

Exception: If there is a vowel before the final *y*, keep the *y* before adding -*s* or -*ed:*

stay	stays, stayed
enjoy	enjoys, enjoyed

Exercise 50.6 Pattern Practice

Using your dictionary to check the correct spelling, add the suffixes in parentheses to the words listed here.

1. tray + (-s)
2. apology + (-s)
3. ally + (-ed)
4. steady + (-ing)
5. accompany + (-ing)
6. study + (-ing)

7. mercy + (-ful)
8. funny + (-er)
9. monkey + (-s)
10. bury + (-al)
11. likely + (-er)
12. story + (-s)

13. lonely + (-ness)
14. vary + (-ed)
15. ninety + (-eth)
16. study + (-ous)
17. pretty + (-ness)
18. employ + (-er)

50d PLURALS

■ Most plurals are formed by adding -s. Add -es when words end in s, sh, ch, x, or z because another syllable is needed to make the ending easy to pronounce.

| one apple | two apples |
| one box | two boxes |

■ With phrases and hyphenated words, pluralize the last word unless another word is more important.

one systems analyst   two systems analysts
one sister-in-law   two sisters-in-law
one attorney general   other attorneys general

■ For some words that end in *f* or *fe,* change the *f* to *ve* and add -s. For other words that end in *f,* add -s without any change in the base word.

one thief   six thieves
a leaf   some leaves
a roof   two roofs
his belief   their beliefs
the chief   two chiefs

■ For words ending in a consonant plus *y,* change the *y* to *i* and add -es. For words ending in a vowel plus *y,* add -s.

one company   four companies
a monkey   two monkeys

■ For words ending in a vowel plus *o,* add *-s.* For words ending in a consonant plus *o,* add *-s* or *-es* (some words may be pluralized both ways).

a radio	some radios
one potato	bag of potatoes
one zero	two zeros (*or*) zeroes

■ For some words, the plural is formed by changing the base word.

one child	several children
one woman	two women
one goose	nine geese
one mouse	some mice

■ Some words have the same form for both singular and plural.

| deer | sheep | pliers |

■ Some words from other languages keep their original plural endings.

one alumnus	some alumni
one antenna	two antennae
an appendix	three appendices
a criterion	some criteria
a crisis	two crises
a medium	all media
one memorandum	two memoranda

Note, however, that some of these words appear now with an English plural, such as *antennas, appendixes,* and *memorandums.*

Exercise 50.7 Proofreading Practice

Correct the spelling of each incorrect word. Use a dictionary if needed.

1. foxs	**6.** stereos	**11.** womans
2. papers	**7.** tariffs	**12.** freshmans
3. companys	**8.** brother-in-laws	**13.** passer-bys
4. latchs	**9.** bushes	**14.** heroes
5. analyses	**10.** windows	**15.** hoofs

50e SOUND-ALIKE WORDS (HOMONYMS)

English has a number of words that sound alike but are spelled differently and have different meanings. These are called **homonyms.**

For the correct meanings of these words, consult the Glossary of Usage.

accept/except	a while/awhile
affect/effect	its/it's
all ready/already	than/then
all together/altogether	their/there/they're
any more/anymore	who's/whose
any one/anyone	your/you're

Exercise 50.8 Proofreading Practice

Highlight or underline the correctly spelled word for each of the following sentences. Use a dictionary if needed.

1. The weather always (affects, effects) my moods.
2. She was (to, too) tired to join in.
3. It was a (quite, quiet) summer evening.
4. Would (anyone, any one) of these shirts be acceptable?
5. I need another (envelop, envelope) for these letters.
6. Her tardiness was an (every day, everyday) occurrence.
7. The coach offered some useful (advice, advise).
8. It seemed that (any way, anyway) he threw the basketball, it landed in the hoop.
9. It is always cooler in the woods (than, then) in the city.
10. I often drive (by, buy) the Smiths' house.
11. When (it's, its) snowing, the street sounds seem muffled.
12. The table remained (stationary, stationery) when the wind shook the room.
13. When the teacher asked a question, the students answered (all together, altogether).
14. The dictionary (maybe, may be) helpful in deciding which word you want.
15. Whenever the train (passed, past) the station, the conductor waved to the stationmaster.
16. The salesclerk asked the supervisor for some (assistants, assistance) with the computer.

17. The committee agreed that it was (alright, all right) to table the motion being discussed.

18. The football game was nearing the end of the (forth, fourth) quarter.

19. The teacher asked everyone to (sight, cite, site) all the sources used in the term paper.

20. What does (there, their, they're) car horn sound like?

51
AMERICAN STYLE IN WRITING

If your first language is not English, you may have writing style preferences that are different from American style and questions about English grammar and usage. Some of these matters are discussed here. If you are a student at an institution with a writing center, talk with a tutor in the writing center.

Your style preferences and customs will depend on what languages you are most familiar with, but in general, consider the following differences between the languages you know and academic style in American English.

	Language Styles of Other Cultures	American Academic Language and Style
Conciseness	In some cultures, writers strive for a style marked by a rich profusion of words and phrases, and ideas can be repeated in a variety of ways.	Effective academic and public writing style in American English is concise, eliminating extra or unnecessary words.
Introduction of topic	In some languages, the topic is not immediately announced or not specifically stated at all. Instead, suggestions lead readers to develop the main ideas themselves.	In American English, there is a strong preference for announcing the topic in the opening paragraph or near the beginning of the paper.
Organizational style	Digressions, or moving off the main topic into related matters, are encouraged in some cultures because they add to the richness of ideas.	In American English, there is a preference for staying on the topic and not moving away, or digressing, from it.
Pattern of reasoning	Writers in some cultures prefer inductive reasoning, moving from specifics to the more general conclusion.	American academic writing is usually deductive, beginning with general ideas and moving to more specific reasons or details.
Citation of sources	In some cultures, there is less attention to citing sources, ideas, or the exact words used by others. Ideas of great scholars, for example, can be used without citation because it is assumed that readers know the sources.	In American academic writing, writers are expected to cite all sources of information that are not generally known by most people. A writer who fails to credit the words or ideas of others is in danger of being viewed as a plagiarist.

www.eslcafe.com

Dave Sperling's ESL Café provides discussion forums, links to jobs, help with pronunciation and slang, useful books, and many other aids.

owl.english.purdue.edu/handouts/esl/eslstudent.html

Purdue University's Online Writing Lab page includes links to handouts on ESL issues as well as other resources, such as online courses, quizzes, vocabulary, e-mail, and listservs.

www.1-language.com

1-Language.com offers free English courses, an audio listening center, forums, real-time chat, job listings, and more.

www.englishforum.com/00

Aardvark's English Forum includes dictionaries, interactive exercises, re-sources for teachers, world weather and news, and links to other useful sites.

http://a4esl.org

Quizzes, tests, exercises, and puzzles to help with ESL issues (a project of *The Internet TESL Journal*)

home.gwu.edu/~meloni/eslstudyhall

Professor Meloni's ESL Study Hall at George Washington University lists re-sources for ESL students working on their reading, writing, vocabulary, grammar, and listening skills, as well as a section on U.S. culture.

52
VERBS

Verbs are very important parts of English sentences because they indicate time and person as well as other information (see Chapter 21).

52a HELPING VERBS WITH MAIN VERBS

Helping or **auxiliary verbs** combine with other verbs to form all of the tenses except the simple present and simple past. The following table shows the forms of three major helping verbs, and 21c explains when to use a form of *be* and *have* and what the meanings are when these helping verbs are added.

FORMS OF HELPING VERBS		
be	be am is are was were + *-ing* form:	I am going.
	with modal verb:	I may be going.
	passive (with past participle):	I was given the title.
have	have has had	I have started.
		He had started.
do	do does did + base form	Did she buy that?

1. Modals

Modal verbs are helping verbs with a variety of meanings.

can	may	must	should	would
could	might	shall	will	ought to

A modal + a base form of the verb: Use this for the present or future.

Your car battery can die if you leave your headlights on all night.

A modal + a present perfect form: Use this for past events.

You could have lost your keys at the restaurant yesterday.

Modals are used to indicate the following:

Permission: May I take this?   [Is it all right if I take this?]

Advisability:

In present time: I ought to take this.   [It's a good idea to take this.]

In past time: I ought to have taken this before class.

Necessity: Must I take this class?   [Am I required to take this?]

Ability:

In present time: Can I take this?   [Am I able to take this?]

In past time: I could have done that when I was young.

Uncertainty or request for advice: Should I take this?   [I'm not certain whether I should take this.]

Possibility:

In present time: Even an expert can make mistakes. (*or*) Even an expert might make a mistake.

[It is possible for experts to make mistakes.]

In past time: The experiment could have failed because of the lack of air conditioning.

2. Conditionals

In conditional sentences, clauses after *if, when,* and *unless* show whether the result is possible or real, depending on other circumstances. Conditionals also show the time of the event.

Prediction

The sentence predicts something based on some condition.

Present	Future (Usually Modal + Base Form)
If you eat more fresh fruit,	you will be healthier.
Unless she arrives soon,	we will be late for the concert.

Fact

Something usually happens when something else happens.

Present	Present
When that dog barks at night,	he wakes us up.
Past	**Past**
When that dog barked at night,	he woke us up.

Unreality

Use *would* in the result clause to show that the result is possible only if the conditions of the *if* clause happen.

Past Tense for Hypothetical Present Action	*Would* + Base Form
If she drove more slowly,	she would get fewer speeding tickets.

To show that something is not reality, use *were* instead of *was.*

If I were rich,	I would travel to Tahiti.

Speculation

To show that something is unlikely or not real, use *were* instead of *was.*

Past Tense to Indicate Present	*Would, Could, Might* + Base Form
If he weren't so busy,	he could come with us to the restaurant.
If I were better prepared,	I might be less nervous about this test.

> ### Hint
>
> **USING *WOULD, COULD, MIGHT,* AND OTHER MODALS**
>
> When *would, could, might,* and other modals are used with the base form, *-s* is not added to the base form for third person singular present.
>
>   *drive*
> If he had a car, he could ~~drives~~ us to the restaurant.

52b TWO-WORD (PHRASAL) VERBS

Two-word (phrasal) verbs have one or sometimes two words known as *particles* following the verb that help indicate the meaning.

Because the additional word or words often change the meaning of the verbs, phrasal verbs can be idioms (see Chapter 58).

look over ("examine")	She **looked over** the terms of the contract.
look up ("search for")	I need to **look up** that phone number.

Some particles, such as *up*, can have many meanings when they follow different verbs, so it is best to check a dictionary to be sure of the meaning.

We "call up" our friends.	We "lock up" our car.	We "warm up" leftover food.
We "line up" for tickets.	We "wake up" in the morning.	We "tear up" a piece of paper.

We "open up" a clogged drain, but "close up" our offices at night. Topics "come up" in conversation.

Something can "take up" a lot of your time when you "look up" a word in the dictionary, but don't "give up."

In some cases, a noun or pronoun can be inserted so that the verb is separated from its additional word or words. In other cases, there can be no separation.

Separable: count in ("include")

Manuel told the team to count **him** in.
                              (INSERTED PRONOUN)

Inseparable: count on ("rely on")

The team could count on **him** to help.
                        (PRONOUN NOT INSERTED)

Some Common Two-Word (Phrasal) Verbs

If the second word can be separated from the verb, a pronoun is included in parentheses.

add (it) up	call (her) up	drop (it) off
back out of	carry (it) out	fall behind
bring (it) on	clean (it) up	get around
bring (it) up	come across	get by
burn (it) down	cross (it) out	get out of
burn (it) up	cut (it) off	get through
call for	cut (it) out	give (it) away
call (it) off	cut (it) up	go over

hand (it) in	look out for	show up
keep on	pass (them) out	stay up
keep (it) up	put (it) off	take (it) off
leave (it) out	put (it) on	take (it) up
look ahead	run across	try (it) out
look into	run into	turn (it) up
look like	show (it) off	use (it) up

52c VERBS WITH -*ING* AND *TO* + VERB FORMS

Some verbs combine only with the -*ing* form of the verb (the gerund); some combine only with the *to* + verb form (the infinitive); some can be followed by either form.

Verbs Followed Only by -*ing* Forms (Gerunds)

admit	enjoy	practice
appreciate	finish	quit
avoid	keep	recall
consider	keep on	risk
deny	postpone	suggest

He <u>admits spending</u> that money.
   (VERB) + (GERUND)

To show past action, change the verb to past tense, but leave the gerund as it was.

         reading
I recalled ~~to read~~ that book.
        ^

Verbs Followed Only by *to* + Verb Forms (Infinitives)

agree	have	offer
ask	hope	plan
claim	manage	promise
decide	mean	wait
expect	need	want

We <u>agree to send</u> an answer soon.
   (VERB) + (INFINITIVE)

       to go
They planned ~~going~~ on vacation.
       ^

Verbs That Can Be Followed by Either Form

begin	intend	prefer
continue	like	start
hate	love	try

They begin to sing.   *(or)*   They begin singing.

Some verbs that can be followed by either form change meaning:

| forget | remember | stop | try |

She stopped talking.   [She finished speaking and remained silent.]

She stopped to talk.   [While going somewhere, she paused to speak with someone.]

Exercise 52.1 Proofreading Practice

The following paragraph contains some errors with verbs. Highlight or underline the errors, and write in your corrections.

When people from other countries will visit the United States, they find a bewildering variety of words that can be used for the same thing. In some parts of the United States, a salesperson will asked the customer if she would want the item in a *sack*. In other places, the salesperson might ask, "Did you wanted this in a *bag?*" It is hard for tourists who don't understand to bring up it when they don't know whether there is a difference. A tourist may ask, "May I take this *metro* to First Avenue?" in a city where the underground train is called the *subway*. If I was one of those tourists, I could always keep a dictionary in my pocket to use when the situation calls it for.

Exercise 52.2 Pattern Practice

In the following paragraph, highlight or underline the correct form of the verb.

In schools in the United States, teachers hope (1. to encourage, encouraging) students to ask questions. They think that if students (2. talk, will talk) about a subject and ask questions, they (3. will learn, learn) more about the subject. In some other countries, students avoid (4. to ask, asking) questions because that may be a sign of rudeness in their country. The culture of the country has a very important influence on how teachers want (5. talking, to talk) to the class and how the class continues (6. to respond, responding) to the teacher. In the United States, some teachers like (7. to have, having) their students call them by their first name. This often surprises students from other countries, where they (8. might be, must be) very formal with their teachers in order to show respect.

Exercise 52.3 Pattern Practice

Use each of the following verb forms in a sentence of your own.

1. may + *verb*	**5.** look like	**9.** begin + *verb*
2. can + *verb*	**6.** hope + *verb*	**10.** do + *verb*
3. If she were	**7.** try (it) out	**11.** could + *verb*
4. hand (it) in	**8.** forget + *verb*	**12.** have + *verb*

53

OMITTED WORDS

53a VERBS

Verbs are necessary parts of English sentences and must be included. Verbs such as *am, is,* and *are* and other helping verbs are needed and cannot be omitted.

> is
> Luis ⌃ studying to be a computer programmer.

> has
> She ⌃ been studying ancient Mayan ruins in Mexico for many summers.

> is
> Mr. Pandurahgan maintains it ⌃ necessary to recharge his laptop twice a day.

53b SUBJECTS AND *THERE* OR *IT*

In some languages, such as Spanish, the subject can sometimes be omitted, but in English, the subject is left out only when expressing a command (*Put that box here, please.*). Particularly troublesome are *there* and *it* as subjects. Even when *there* seems to be the subject word and the real subject is elsewhere in the sentence, *there* must be included. *It* is sometimes needed as a subject in sentences about the weather, distance, time, and other aspects of the world around us.

> there
> Certainly, ⌃ are many confusing rules in English spelling.

> it
> I think ⌃ is about 10 miles from here to the shopping mall.

54

REPEATED WORDS

54a SUBJECTS

In some languages, the subject can be repeated as a pronoun before the verb. In English, the subject is included only once.

Bones in the body ~~they~~ become brittle when people grow older.

[*Bones* is the subject of the verb *brittle,* and *they* is an unnecessary repetition of the subject.]

The plane that was ready for takeoff ~~it~~ stopped on the runway.

[*Plane* is the subject of the verb *stopped,* and *it* is an unnecessary repetition of the subject.]

54b PRONOUNS AND ADVERBS

When relative pronouns such as *who, which,* and *that* or relative adverbs such as *where* or *when* (see 28b) are the object of the verb, no additional word is needed.

The woman tried on the hat that I left ~~it~~ on the seat.

[*That* is the object of the verb *left,* and *it* is unnecessary repetition.]

The city where I live ~~there~~ has two soccer fields.

[*Where* is the object of the verb *live,* and *there* is unnecessary repetition.]

Exercise 54.1 Proofreading Practice

The following paragraph has omitted words. Add the missing words. Where words are unnecessarily repeated, draw a line through them.

(1) When students looking for part-time work, one difficulty is that they want the job to be after class hours. (2) Another difficulty for students is that want the job to be near their school so that don't have far to travel. (3) That means are many students who want to work at the same time and in the same area of town. (4) The competition for the jobs that exist it causes too many students to be unable to find work. (5) Some counselors they tell their students to try looking for jobs that have flexible hours or for work that it can be done at home. (6) Is also worth trying to look farther away from the campus.

55
COUNT AND NONCOUNT NOUNS

Proper nouns name specific things and begin with capital letters; all other names are **common nouns.** There are two kinds of common nouns, count and noncount nouns. English dictionaries for speakers of other languages mark nouns as count or noncount.

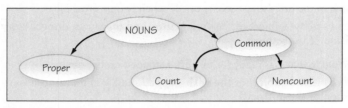

Figure 55.1 Types of Nouns

A **count noun** names something that can be counted because it can be divided into separate and distinct units. Count nouns have plurals (see 22a) and usually refer to things that can be seen, heard, touched, tasted, or smelled. Count nouns have a plural form when they are used to indicate plurals, and the verb and all words that refer to the noun, such as *a/some, this/these,* or *that/those,* are also plural.

A **noncount noun** names something that cannot be counted because it is an abstraction, a substance that is thought of as a whole, or something that cannot be cut into parts. Noncount nouns do not have plurals and may have a collective meaning. Noncount nouns are used with singular verbs and pronouns. They are never used with *a* or *an,* but they can be used with *some.*

Count Nouns

book   (one book, two books)

chair   (a chair, several chairs)

child   (the child, six children)

Noncount Nouns

air	humor	oil
furniture	literature	weather

The names of many foods and materials are noncount nouns.

bread	corn	electricity
coffee	spaghetti	steel

To indicate the amount for a noncount noun, use a count noun first. If you use *some*, use a singular verb.

a pound of coffee   a loaf of bread

an ear of corn   a gallon of oil

Nouns That Can Be Both Count and Noncount Nouns

Some nouns in English have both a count and a noncount meaning, depending on the context in which the noun is used. The count meaning is specific, and the noncount meaning is abstract.

Count: The **exercises** were difficult to do.

Noncount: Exercise is good for our health.

Count: There were bright **lights** in the sky.

Noncount: Those plants need more **light.**

Count: She ate five **chocolates** from the box.

Noncount: Chocolate is fattening.

Hint

IDENTIFYING COUNT AND NONCOUNT NOUNS

Knowing whether a noun is a count or noncount noun is important in determining whether or not to use a, an, or the (see 56c).

■ Singular count nouns need an article: *She returned **the book.***

■ Noncount nouns usually do not need an article: *Plants enjoy **water.***

Exercise 55.1 Proofreading Practice

In the parentheses in the following paragraph, underline the correct choice between count and noncount nouns.

(1. American, Americans) love browsing and shopping for consumer (2. good, goods). In our (3. society, societies), a shopper has choices that include shopping in (4. mall, malls), (5. outlet, outlets), department (6. store, stores), or discount (7. club, clubs). A (8. consumer, consumers) must know prices and return (9. policy, policies) to get the best deal. For shoppers in a (10. mall, malls), the prices and return policies vary. Malls have some chain (11. store, stores) that can be overpriced unless items are on sale. Most stores in a mall allow customers to return an item with the (12. receipt, receipts). An outlet store offers reduced (13. price, prices) on discontinued and irregular items. However, (14. shopper, shoppers) must know that most items are "final sale" and cannot be returned in outlet (15. store, stores). Department stores offer a large variety of items and

have weekly sales. Returning items is usually not a problem, but some stores require that the item be returned within a (16. week, weeks) of purchase. If an item is a gift, a shopper can receive store (17. credit, credits) so that the shopper can select another item of equal value. Discount clubs look like warehouses and carry large quantities of (18. item, items) at reduced prices. The shopper must know prices to get the best bargain. Many items, especially food, appear to be discounted but may be less expensive to purchase in a regular (19. supermarket, supermarkets). Discount clubs allow (20. return, returns) within thirty days of purchase as long as the customer has a receipt. Consumers should always check prices and policies before purchasing items.

Exercise 55.2 Pattern Practice

Make up sentences of your own using the underlined count and noncount nouns in the following sentences.

1. The insect had four wings.
2. They walked down many streets to the river.
3. Some bones in the skeleton were broken, but the museum had no bone to use in repairing the exhibit.
4. The coat was made of cotton.
5. She picked some roses from the garden.
6. He knew six languages and wanted to learn another one because language is a fascinating thing to study.
7. She likes to eat rice with a lot of sugar on it.
8. The rain caused some mud to splash on my car.
9. The clothing was on sale in the store.
10. After the snow melted and froze again, the street was like a sheet of ice.

56

ADJECTIVES AND ADVERBS

56a　ORDER OF ADVERBS

The ordering of adverbs in relation to adjectives in English is as follows:

Adverb	→	Adjective	→	Noun
very		large		gate

Adverbs are placed first when they describe adjectives. Then adjectives are placed next because they describe nouns.

Adverbs that indicate frequency, such as *sometimes* and *usually*, describe verbs and can move around in the sentence and appear in the following places:

- At the beginning of the sentence.

    Sometimes Noam can find great bargains.

- At the end of the sentence.

    Noam can find great bargains **sometimes.**

- Before the verb.

    Noam **sometimes** can find great bargains.

- Between the helping and main verb.

    Noam can **sometimes** find great bargains.

- After the verb.

    Jana types **quickly** on her laptop computer.

Do not place adverbs between verbs and objects.

> **Wrong:** She picks quickly the fruit.

> **Revised:** She quickly picks the fruit.   (*or*)   She picks the fruit quickly.

56b ORDER OF ADJECTIVES

Putting adjectives in the accepted English order can be confusing to speakers of other languages. Follow the order of these categories, but it is best not to pile up more than two or three adjectives between the article (or other determiner) and the noun.

Determiner	**Evaluation or Opinion**	**Physical Description**				**Nationality**	**Religion**	**Material**	**Noun**
		Size	**Shape**	**Age**	**Color**				
a one her	lovely	big	round	old	green	English	Catholic	silk	purse

- the quiet Japanese rock garden
- a square blue cotton handkerchief
- my lazy old Siamese cat
- six excellent new movies
- many difficult physics problems
- every big green plant

Exercise 56.1 Pattern Practice

Reorder the adjectives and nouns in these clusters; then incorporate them into your own sentences.

1. old   famous   six   sports stars
2. Hispanic   favorite   her   song   old
3. steel   German   new   a   knife
4. square   small   strange   a   box
5. large   nine   balls   yellow

56c   *A/AN/THE*

A and *an* identify a noun in a general or indefinite way and refer to any member of a group. *A* and *an*, which mean "one among many," are generally used with singular count nouns (see Chapter 55).

> She likes to read **a** book before going to sleep.

[This sentence does not specify which book but refers to any book. *Book* is a singular count noun.]

The identifies a particular or specific noun in a group or a noun already identified in a previous phrase or sentence. *The* may be used with singular or plural nouns.

> She read **the** book that I gave her.

[This sentence identifies a specific book.]

> Give the coins to **the** boys at that table.

[This sentence identifies a specific group.]

> **A** new model of computer was introduced yesterday. **The** model will cost much less than **the** older model.

[*A* introduces the noun the first time it is mentioned, and then *the* is used afterward whenever the noun is mentioned.]

1. *A, An,* and *The* with Proper Nouns

Singular: Usually no article   Mrs. Samosha

Plural: Usually use *the*   **the** United States

2. *A, An,* and *The* with Common Nouns

Count Nouns

Singular: Use an article or pronoun for singular count nouns.

> a tree   **her** wrist

Plural: Use *the* when naming a specific representative of a category.

the committee

Do not use *the* when the meaning is "all" or "in general."

Chairs were provided.   People are creatures of habit.

Noncount Nouns

Never use *a* or *an* with noncount nouns.

3. Other Uses of *The*

■ Use *the* when an essential phrase or clause follows the noun (see Chapter 29).

The man who is standing at the door is my cousin.

■ Use *the* when the noun refers to a class as a whole.

The ferret is a popular pet.

■ Use *the* with names that combine proper and common nouns.

the British Commonwealth   **the** Gobi Desert   **the** University of Illinois

■ Use *the* when names are plurals.

the Netherlands   **the** Balkans

■ Use *the* with names that refer to rivers, oceans, seas, points on the globe, deserts, forests, gulfs, and peninsulas.

the Nile   **the** Pacific Ocean   **the** Persian Gulf

■ Use *the* when points of the compass are used as names.

the South   **the** Midwest

■ Use *the* when points of time are indicated.

the beginning   **the** present   **the** afternoon

■ Use *the* with superlatives.

the best reporter   **the** most expensive car

■ Use *the* with adjectives used as nouns.

The homeless are in need of health care.

■ Use *the* with gerunds or abstract nouns followed by *of* phrases.

The meaning of that word is not clear.

4. No Articles

Articles are not used with names of streets, cities, states, countries, continents, lakes, parks, mountains, languages, sports, holidays, universities and colleges without *of* in the name and with academic subjects.

He traveled to Botswana.	She is studying Mandarin.
That shop is on Fifth Avenue.	Pollution in Lake Erie has been reduced.
He prefers to watch volleyball.	My major is political science.
They celebrated Thanksgiving.	She applied to Brandeis University.

5. Summary: Uses of *A, An,* and *The*

A/An

■ Unspecified singular count nouns.

> **A** computer is **a** useful tool.

The

■ Particular or specific singular count nouns and specific plural count nouns.

> I ate **the** pizza, but she wanted **the** pretzels.

■ Noncount nouns that are specific members of a general group.

> **The** sunlight in the late afternoon sky cast interesting shadows.

■ Plural proper nouns.

> They sailed to **the** Virgin Islands.

No Articles

■ Singular proper nouns.

> He moved to Salt Lake City.

■ Unspecified plural count nouns meaning "all" or "in general."

> Bats are night feeders.

■ Noncount nouns.

> Trina does not like beer.

Exercise 56.2 Proofreading Practice

In the following paragraph, add a, an, *or* the *where needed.*

One of most interesting physicists of twentieth century was Richard Feynman. He wrote best-selling book about his own life, but he became even more famous on television as man who was member of team that investigated after accident happened to *Challenger*, space shuttle that crashed in 1986. People watched on television as he demonstrated that faulty part in space shuttle probably caused accident. Feynman's greatest achievement in science was theory of quantum electrodynamics, which described behavior of subatomic particles, atoms, light, electricity, and magnetism. Field of computer science also owes much to work of Feynman. Many scientists consider Feynman to be one of geniuses of twentieth century.

56d *SOME/ANY, MUCH/MANY, LITTLE/FEW, LESS/FEWER, ENOUGH, NO*

Some, any, enough, and *no* modify count and noncount nouns (see Chapter 55).

She brought **some** fresh flowers.	There is **some** water on the floor.
Do you have **any** erasers?	Do you have **any** food?
I have **enough** glasses for everyone.	There is **enough** money to buy a car.
There are **no** squirrels in the park.	There is **no** time to finish now.

Some is used in positive statements.

They ate **some** fruit.

Any is used in negative statements and in questions.

They did not eat **any** fruit.	Did they eat **any** fruit?

Used with Noncount Nouns	**Used with Count Nouns**
(not) much	(not) many
little	few
less	fewer
They have **much** money in the bank.	**Many** Americans travel to Asia.
He had **little** food in the house.	There are a **few** doctors here.
Use **less** oil in the mixture.	We ordered **fewer** books this year.

57

PREPOSITIONS

For a list of idiomatic prepositions, see 25b. The following guide will help you choose among *on, at, in, of,* and *for* to indicate time, place, and logical relationships.

Prepositions of Time

on   Use with days (**on** Monday).

at   Use with hours of the day (**at** 9 P.M.) and with *noon, night, midnight,* and *dawn* (**at** midnight).

in   Use with other parts of the day: *morning, afternoon, evening* (**in** the morning); use with months, years, seasons (**in** the winter).

They are getting married **on** Sunday **at** four o'clock **in** the afternoon.

Prepositions of Place

on   Indicates a surface on which something rests

The car is **on** the street.

She put curtains **on** the windows.

at   Indicates a point in relation to another object

My sister is **at** home.

I'll meet you **at** Second Avenue and Main Street.

in   Indicates an object is inside the boundaries of an area or volume

The sample is **in** the bottle.

She is **in** the bank.

Prepositions to Show Logical Relationships

of   Shows relationship between a part (or parts) and the whole

One **of** her teachers gave a quiz.

of   Shows material or content

They gave me a basket **of** food.

for   Shows purpose

We bought a new hose **for** our garden.

Exercise 57.1 Proofreading Practice

The following paragraph contains some errors in the use of the prepositions in, on, *and* at *and in the use of* some/any/much/many/little/few. *Highlight or underline the errors, and write in your corrections.*

(1) Table tennis used to be a minor pastime at America, but a little years ago it began to develop into an important sport. (2) Newcomers to the United States from countries such as Nigeria, Korea, and China, where table tennis is a major sport, have helped the United States become a respectable contender at world competition. (3) Much new residents who are very good in this sport have brought their skills to this country. (4) Now there are specialized table tennis parlors where players play in tables

with special hard surfaces. (5) Players no longer use some sandpaper paddles. (6) Instead, much paddles are made of carbon fiber and have special
coatings in the hitting surface. (7) At the past, the United States was often
on last place in international competitions. (8) Now, with many strong
players, often born at China, the United States is beginning to win.

Exercise 57.2 Pattern Practice

Make up sentences of your own that use the following words.

1. some
2. any
3. few
4. less
5. many

6. in (with a time expression)
7. on (a place)
8. in (a place)
9. of (showing a relationship)
10. at (a place)

58

IDIOMS

An **idiom** is an expression that means something beyond the literal meaning
of the words.

An idiom such as *kick the bucket* (meaning "die") cannot be understood
by examining the meanings of the individual words. Many idioms are used
only in informal English. Most dictionaries indicate the meanings of idioms
and label as "colloquial" or "informal" those that are considered appropriate only for informal writing or speaking. You can also consult dictionaries of idioms. Here are some typical idioms:

bottom line the last figure on a financial balance sheet; the result or
final outcome or ultimate truth

The **bottom line** is that he will not admit his mistake.

eager beaver someone who is very enthusiastic or works hard

The team's new coach is an **eager beaver** who can't wait to start spring
training.

hand over fist very rapidly, with rapid progress

Mina made money on that investment **hand over fist**.

hold water adequate to be proved, be correct

The excuse she gave did not **hold water** with her instructor.

on one's toes eager, alert

The new computer system keeps us **on our toes**.

on the table open for discussion

Put that plan **on the table** and see if anyone objects.

see the light understand something clearly at last, realize one's mistake

After working on the homework problem for several hours, he finally **saw the light** and answered the question correctly.

throw one's hat in the ring announce that one is a candidate, take up a challenge

Before the election, three people announced they would **throw their hats in the ring.**

toe the line do what is expected or required, follow the rules, especially unwillingly or under pressure

The new rules were designed to see whether the employees would **toe the line.**

For a list of idiomatic prepositions that follow certain words, see 25b. Because the meanings of two-word (phrasal) verbs (see 52b) change according to the prepositions that follow the verbs, these verbs are also idiomatic. Note the difference in the meanings of the two-word (phrasal) verbs *look after* and *look over:*

look after take care of

Could you **look after** my dog while I am away on vacation?

look over examine something (briefly)

I'll **look over** the report you gave me.

www. **Online Dictionaries for ESL**

dictionary.cambridge.org

Cambridge Dictionaries Online features several dictionaries. Try the *Cambridge International Dictionary of Idioms* to search for meanings of idioms and the *Cambridge International Dictionary of Phrasal Verbs* for idiomatic two-word (phrasal) verbs.

59

FINDING A TOPIC

When you have a research paper to write, the task may seem over-whelming and perhaps confusing, but completing a research paper is an excellent way to sharpen skills you already have. Perhaps you have already searched for information on a health problem or did some investigating before making a large purchase or looked for a solution to a business concern. A research paper follows similar procedures and helps you become an even better researcher. A useful way to begin such a project is to break it into small, manageable steps. That gives you an idea of how to allot your time and lets you see how the larger task of completing the assignment will be accomplished. A working list can include the following steps:

1. Choose a purpose and working topic (see 59a and 59b).
2. Decide on some keywords or phrases you'll use when searching for information.
3. Compile a list of materials you'll read by going to library catalogs, databases, indexes, Web sites, government documents, newspaper archives, newsgroups, and other resources, and make a list of people you might interview about your topic (see Chapters 60 and 61).
4. Eliminate materials that you decide won't be very useful (see Chapter 62).
5. Take notes from your reading of the remaining material on your working bibliography (see Chapter 63).
6. Organize your notes and make a plan for the paper (see 65a). Check to see if you need any more information (see 2c and 65b).
7. Write a draft and get feedback from your teacher, a writing center tutor, or a classmate (see 2d, 65c, and 65d).
8. Revise and edit (see 2e, 2f, and 65e).

Finding a topic for a research paper includes the following steps:

- Deciding on a purpose
- Deciding on a general topic that interests you
- Narrowing that topic to fit the assignment
- Formulating a research question about your topic
- Formulating a thesis statement that answers your research question

59a DECIDING ON A PURPOSE AND AUDIENCE

Research papers are complex projects that tend to be longer than others. They include two broad tasks—researching and writing, each of which can be broken into several smaller tasks. Because research leads to discovery, the very point or main idea of a research paper is likely to shift as you learn more about the topic. You may find that you are adding to the general knowledge about that topic, and what you learn and present in a research paper can be a discovery for you as well as useful information for your readers.

1. Thinking About Your Purpose

An important first step in this process is to think about the purpose of the research project. What is the goal you want to accomplish or are assigned to complete? If you are assigned a topic (or a task you have to accomplish when writing at your job), your goal will be stated. In either case, consider these activities.

- *Summarizing.* Are you being asked to summarize what is known about a topic? For example, you might be finding what the recent developments are in the ways reading is taught in grades one through five, or you might be asked which software tools a company needs to buy in order to redesign a product.

- *Analyzing.* Are you looking at how something is put together? how it works? how or why it came about? For example, you might be seeking the causes of the recent decrease in the polar bear population or why some software product isn't working properly. Perhaps you may be thinking about why college students don't vote in large numbers or why Hamlet waits so long to seek revenge for the murder of his father.

- *Evaluating.* Is your goal to make a judgment about something, to evaluate it? For example, you might be asked not what is known about reading instruction but which method of instruction you would recommend. Perhaps you might be asked not to list the software needed for a company to redesign a product but which software would be best to buy. You might also be asked to choose between two points of view on something and then explain the reasons for your choice. For example, you might want to decide whether it is better for the college to raise tuition or to ask students to pay separate fees in addition to tuition. For another assignment, you might be asked to evaluate the merits of a movie, television show, book, video game, blog, or CD.

- *Informing.* Is your goal to inform people about a topic and add to their knowledge? For example, you might be writing a brochure about how to select a motorcycle or what the advantages of high-definition television are. You would gather important considerations that a buyer needs to know.

■ *Researching.* Are you going to search for new knowledge? For example, you might want to conduct a survey on how students on your campus are financing their education. Perhaps you might want to find out how well drivers are obeying the speed limits on a major thoroughfare in your area.

■ *Persuading.* Are you trying to convince others that your viewpoint is the one to adopt? For example, you might want to argue that driving while smoking should be against the law in your state. Another option is to persuade others that the campus newspaper does not adequately report on important campus events.

For all of these assignments, you might consult the same sources, though what you look for in them could differ according to the different purposes of your assignment. If your assignment includes no indicated purpose— "Write a research paper on recent developments in reading instruction"— it will help you later if you create a tentative purpose for yourself.

Try This

TO DECIDE ON A PURPOSE FOR YOUR PAPER

If your topic is assigned, you can find the purpose or goal by looking at keywords, usually the verbs, in the assignment (see Chapter 21).

■ **Decide** asks you to make an evaluation.

■ **Explain** asks you to inform your readers.

■ **Argue for** (or **against**) calls for a persuasive paper.

■ **Review** asks you to summarize what is known.

■ **Survey** requires you to research and describe several aspects of a topic.

If you are not sure you know the purpose or goal of the assignment, ask your instructor or a writing center tutor to help clarify it.

2. Thinking About Your Audience

As you plunge into the research paper project, think about who your audience will be (see 1c). When you write in college, your audience may be your instructor. However, considering the audience as part of your early planning can lead you to some useful observations about what your instructor is emphasizing in the assignment. Does she want you to include information from readings assigned in class? Is he helping you learn how to make informed judgments? Such questioning isn't a way of figuring out how to tell your instructor what she or he wants to hear; instead, it is a useful exercise in learning what different audiences want to know. (If you become a teacher someday, you will write one way for an audience of parents of your students and a quite different way, with a different goal and different kinds of information, for an administrator in your school system. Similarly, if you become an information technology professional, you will write one way for other IT people you work with and a different way for nontechnical readers.)

You may find that your instructor has indicated an audience other than herself. Perhaps you are writing to students in your class to convince them of something. Maybe you are writing to persuade skeptical readers who aren't likely to agree with you unless you present strong arguments and acknowledge that they have some good arguments on their side. Perhaps you are writing to someone with whom you work who needs some information from you.

You may also be asked to write to a "general educated audience." This would be a group of educated people who may be somewhat aware of your general topic but uninformed about the specific details and undecided about their position on the issue. You'll have to write persuasively to convince them to adopt your viewpoint. All of these factors will influence the kinds of information you seek out.

59b   DECIDING ON A TOPIC

If you aren't assigned a specific topic, you can begin by looking for information about any subject that interests you. This can be an opportunity to learn about some aspect of your major field, future career, or another subject you would like to learn more about. Do some explorative thinking about your hobbies, the world around you, interesting topics that have come up in conversation, or something you're studying in a course. For example, have you recently heard something interesting about genetically modified food? technological developments in the cell phone industry? the effects of globalization? stem cell research? airline security? earthquake predictions? the future of car design? treatments for Alzheimer's disease? the confusing options in health care insurance? pollution in the ocean? the history of hip-hop? the rise of independently produced movies? America's changing preferences in sports? What news items do you read or hear on television that you'd like more background on?

One way to find an interesting subject is to browse through any book or catalog of subject headings. For example, the *Library of Congress Subject Headings* and the *Readers' Guide to Periodical Literature* are thick volumes of headings and subheadings. Another way to choose a fresh subject is to skim through the table of contents of a magazine you read regularly or one in your library's collection. More likely, though, you'll be starting your search for a topic with your computer in front of you. Use a well-known search engine such as Google or Yahoo!, a library database such as InfoTrac or LexisNexis, or an electronic card catalog, and type in a broad search term for a topic that comes to mind. Perhaps you're interested in the history of rap music or what the newest developments are in multiplayer online gaming or what volunteers for political campaigns do. Suppose you choose "airline security" as your search term and type that in. You'll find that search engines' ability to survey millions of sources quickly may give you some different avenues to consider. If an overwhelming list of sources ("hits") turns up (as is likely when you start with a broad term), you may realize the need to choose some smaller subdivision of your topic and from there to start narrowing it to a limited selection of all the suggested directions. At this point, you've made a start by identifying a large topic that now needs to be narrowed or limited.

59c NARROWING THE TOPIC

Once you've identified a general subject, you'll need to narrow it into a topic that is more specific and manageable. How much time will you have to do the research? How long will the paper be? The answers to these questions will determine how much you need to narrow your topic. A topic you can spend six to eight weeks researching can be larger or more complex than one you only have two weeks to investigate. Similarly, you will be able to cover more about a topic if you are to write a twenty-page paper than if you are to write an eight-page paper.

1. Topics That Are Too Broad

To narrow your topic, begin by thinking of it as a tree with many branches or a blanket covering many subtopics or smaller aspects. What are some of those branches or subtopics? List some, then choose one, and think of some aspects of that subtopic that might be topics in themselves. For example, suppose you had decided on the topic of world hunger. What might some subtopics of that be? It might help to also think about your purpose. Do you want to know about aid provided by the United Nations? Or what crops could be grown in drought-stricken areas? Or how extensive the problem is? You could subdivide each of those subjects into even narrower subtopics. If you want to research the extent of the problem, you could subdivide into various nations. If you choose one nation to investigate, you can look more closely at statistics or a period of time (such as the past twenty years) or progress being made in that country or contributing causes such as conflict between groups. You're now getting closer to a more reasonably limited topic.

2. Topics That Are Too Narrow

Sometimes a topic may be too narrow. This is especially the case when little information or mostly specialized information exists on the topic. Suppose you want to learn more about jobs at some company you hope to work for. It's hard to find more than a page or two of information about that. It's too narrow. Similarly, if you want to know if the iPhone is a successful product, you can find some sales figures, but there isn't much more you can research.

3. Topics That Are Too Well Known or Trivial

There are also topics that are no longer interesting because we know the answers, such as "smoking is harmful to our health." This is a topic that is no longer controversial, but you can think about a purpose and audience to revise the topic. Perhaps you want to investigate the export of cigarettes to other countries to alert your readers if tobacco companies are finding new markets by selling more cigarettes overseas. That's a topic that readers will want to read about.

Try This

TO DECIDE ON A TOPIC FOR YOUR PAPER

- **Change your point of view.** Think about a topic from the perspective of someone very different from you—someone much older, younger, richer, poorer, from a different place, of a different race or gender, or with a different religious, ethnic, or class background.

- **Take some pictures.** Walk around your campus or your neighborhood and snap some pictures of buildings, graffiti, or vacant spaces. When you review the pictures, think about why they are the way they are. Do the pictures raise questions about urban planning? For example, why is that grocery store in the middle of a block of houses? Perhaps the pictures will raise questions about the habits of people who live there. Why are all the windows covered? What does the graffiti mean?

- **Think historically.** For example, when was your campus built? How has it changed? Why has it changed? What economic or cultural issues influenced its change? What plans are in place right now to change your campus, and how might they be related to the past?

- **Imagine your perfect world.** What things in the present world would have to change to bring it to reality? What one thing could realistically be changed right now?

Exercise 59.1 Pattern Practice

In the following example, a broad topic is subdivided into a few smaller topics, which are in turn narrowed into even smaller topics. The narrowed topics that seem most promising are followed by a research question. Using this pattern, do the same with each of the suggested topics listed here.

Topic: Low-carbohydrate diet

Subtopic 1: Benefits of such a diet

- Lowers cholesterol: Does reducing carbohydrate intake lower cholesterol?
- Reduces cravings for sweets: Do dieters stay off sweets after stopping the diet?
- Decreases risk of diabetes: What data exist to indicate whether low-carb diets do reduce the incidence of diabetes?

Subtopic 2: Influences on the food industry

- Diminishes bakery sales
- Lowers sales of breakfast cereals
- Trims sales of snack foods
- Reduces customer use of fast-food chains

Subtopic 3: Research on effectiveness of such a diet

- Reports on FDA research
- Claims made by commercial diet book

1. Comic books
2. George W. Bush's foreign policy
3. Gabriel García Márquez's magical realism
4. The "smart" house of the future
5. Genetically modified food
6. Use of surveillance equipment in public places
7. Decreases in the number of males enrolled in college
8. Global warming
9. Outsourcing information technology services
10. The increasing shortage of nurses

59d FORMULATING A RESEARCH QUESTION

After you have selected a general topic and narrowed it sufficiently, you need to formulate a question your research is going to answer. This process will lead to your thesis, but before you formulate a thesis, collect some information and see what you find. The research question will help you decide what information is relevant and what additional information you need. Suppose you're writing about the benefits to your community of recycling paper, glass, and aluminum. What will your research question be? Are you interested in knowing whether the local government saves money by recycling? Or are you interested in the effect recycling might have on the cost of dumping garbage or buying land for landfills? Or are you interested in the community's support for this program? You can also ask yourself the reporter's questions (*who, what, when, where, why,* and *how*). It may help to formulate a thesis, a statement that you think might be true but might change as you do your research. In fact, it's very likely that your thesis will change as you research and learn more about your topic.

The reporter's questions will help you consider what you and your audience do not yet know about your topic. You can refine those questions by asking at least three more: Is my topic valid? How would I define my key terms? Why is my topic important?

Suppose you choose the topic of the increased number of children diagnosed with learning disabilities such as attention-deficit/hyperactivity disorder and treated with medication. The key terms are *children, learning disability, attention-deficit/hyperactivity disorder,* and *medication*. To answer the question about validity ("Did such an increase in diagnoses really happen?"), you might consult a medical encyclopedia or reference book. To define your terms, you might turn to a dictionary; there you'll see the basic two-part pattern of definition: the term being defined is first put into a class, and the term is then distinguished from all other members of the class. For example, the word *desk* might be defined as "a piece of furniture [class] at which one sits to read or write" [distinction]. The pattern of the definitions you find or write for yourself will help you see that the terms in your topic are members of a class (class: attention-deficit/hyperactivity disorder is a learning disability) but that they differ from other members of the class (distinction: attention-deficit/hyperactivity disorder is characterized by an individual's difficulty in concentrating on tasks and the exercise of impulsive behavior). Definitions will help you clarify what the terms of your topic are and are not, within a reasonable frame of reference.

The question "Why is my topic important?" will help you move closer to a thesis and a purpose. To do so, break this question into two parts:

How is my topic important to me?
How might I make it important to my reader?

If attention-deficit/hyperactivity disorder is an important topic to you because you want to be an elementary school teacher and are concerned about how the disorder affects students, you might formulate this research question: "How can knowing the symptoms of the disorder help teachers adjust their teaching styles to meet the educational needs of their students?" If you think attention-deficit/hyperactivity disorder will matter to your readers because they are concerned about the increased number of children being diagnosed with this disorder, you might formulate a different question: "Why are more children being diagnosed with this disorder now than twenty years ago?"

In these examples, you can see how asking questions about a topic can lead you toward an answer that ultimately becomes the thesis of your research paper. The thesis will be specific enough to be covered in an essay, and the essay will have a purpose that will draw your reader into reading it.

59e FORMULATING A THESIS

After completing your research and reviewing your information, you will be able to formulate a tentative thesis or main point that is the result of your investigation. This main point will answer your research question and will make a statement about one aspect of the general topic you started with. It may need to be revised as you write and revise the paper. The thesis is more than a summary of the information, however. It states your position or the point that you are arguing or researching and should synthesize the information into a unified whole that conveys what you, the knowledgeable writer, have learned.

Topic:	Alternative health treatments
Subtopic:	Herbal medicines
Original Research Question:	What are herbal medicines being used for? (too broad, had to be narrowed)
Revised Research Question:	What herbal remedies are investigators learning about that fight colds?
Thesis:	Investigators are finding that elderberry root has the potential to reduce or stop the spread of flu viruses.

A good thesis sentence will have two important parts:

1. *The essay's main idea.* Most often this is your opinion, judgment, or interpretation. Occasionally, though, a thesis can also be factual and inform readers of something they didn't know before, such as "Beginners at weight training should lift only every other day."
2. *The essay's purpose.* In addition to the main idea, your thesis should also suggest your purpose, one that is going to interest your readers. In the examples about elderberry root and its ability to fight viruses, the purpose—"reducing or stopping the spread of flu viruses"—is clear. We all want to know how to get over colds. However, when you research an artistic or cultural topic, such as a period in musical history, your purpose may be less practical. Perhaps you want your audience to understand the important influence of political events in the development of punk music. Your thesis might then say something like this: "The Vietnam War, the Watergate scandal, and rising unemployment rates among young people in the 1970s had an important influence on the themes and messages expressed in punk music."

For more on formulating a thesis, see 1f.

60

Searching for Information

60a CHOOSING PRIMARY AND SECONDARY SOURCES

Finding information is an art, not a science. Just as a good angler learns where the best fishing spots are located, a skilled researcher learns where the best sources are, depending on the kinds of information being sought. Even though many people nowadays begin their search for information on the Internet, some information is best found in print sources. In addition to the Internet and the library, you might be able to obtain information from knowledgeable people around you. For example, if you're interested in health care for the elderly, numerous articles are available in printed sources, on library databases, and on the Internet, but don't overlook local hospitals and nursing home administrators or local government agencies that are designed to provide such health care. Perhaps a faculty member at your school does research in this area or a nonprofit organization in the community is dedicated to providing information.

As you start searching for information, it is helpful to think about the types of sources you can consult. There are print sources, such as books, articles, and magazines; electronic sources, such as Web pages, online library databases, and e-mail; and other sources, such as interviews, lectures, films, and works of art. There are also experts and resource people who can share their knowledge and experience with you. All of these can be divided a different way, into "primary" and "secondary" sources. Looking at the advantages and disadvantages of primary and secondary sources helps you decide which is appropriate for the types of information you are seeking.

1. Primary Sources

Primary sources are original or firsthand materials.

If you read a novel or a poem by an author, you are reading the original or primary source; if you read a study or review of that writing, you are reading secondary material *about* that work of fiction or poetry, not the work itself. Primary sources include the following:

- Words written or spoken by the original author, such as essays, novels, or autobiographies (but not, for example, biographies *about* that person), speeches, e-mails, blogs (journals that a person writes and posts on the Web for others to read), or discussion group postings

- Surveys, studies, or interviews that you conduct

- Any creative works by the original author (poems, plays, Web pages, art forms such as pictures and sculpture)

- Accounts of events by people who were present

Primary sources may be more accurate because they have not been distorted by others. Primary sources are not always unbiased, however, because some people present pictures of themselves and their accomplishments that may not be objective. In general, though, primary sources are preferred if you can find them. Some primary sources, however, are not always available and may be difficult to access. For example, you might not be able to view an old movie that is no longer publicly available and may have to settle for reading reviews of it. The reviews will be secondhand reports, filtered through someone else's mind and interpreted from that person's viewpoint. Similarly, a Web site may disappear, but you find references to it from people writing about it. Again, their reports of it may not accurately reflect what was actually there. Secondary sources, then, may be all you can get, but you can't count on them as totally reliable. Whenever possible, use primary sources if they are appropriate for your topic.

2. Secondary Sources

Secondary sources are secondhand accounts, information, or reports about primary sources written or delivered by people who weren't direct participants in the events or issues being examined.

Typical secondary sources include the following:

- News articles about events

- Reviews

- Biographies

- Documentaries

- Encyclopedia entries

- Other material interpreted or studied by others

Although reading secondary sources may save time, we need to remember they are *interpretations* and may be biased, inaccurate, or incomplete. Because good research does not depend solely on analyses or evaluations done by others, use secondary sources to support your own thinking and conclusions you have reached on the basis of primary sources.

Note that the same source can be a primary source for one topic and a secondary source for another. For example, a biography written in 2000 about the first President Bush, who was president from 1989 to 1993, would be a secondary source if you are researching some aspect of his life. However, if you're researching public opinion and reactions to President

Bush after he left office, that biography would be a primary source of the writer's opinions about him.

Checklist

PLANNING YOUR RESEARCH

To search efficiently, begin by making a systematic plan and a schedule for finding the materials you want. Ask yourself the following questions:

- *Given the deadline I have, how much time can I devote to searching for materials?* Remember that you'll need time for reading sources, taking notes, and organizing your material as well as for writing drafts of the paper. Allow for delays in getting resources, especially if you are requesting materials through interlibrary loan.

- *How current do the materials need to be?* Periodicals (newspapers, magazines, and journals) often have more current materials than books do.

- *Can I find sources that don't agree with my point of view?* This is especially important if you're building an argument.

- *Does the assignment specify how many or what types of sources I should consult?*

As you search, start a working bibliography of materials to read—an initial list of sources that seem promising, even though some will not turn out to be helpful and will be dropped before you put together your final list of works cited. (See 63c for help putting together a working bibliography.) Build your working bibliography by doing some or all of the following:

- Look for sources in your library or on library databases (see 60b).

- Access information through Internet search engines (see 60c).

- Consult knowledgeable people, organizations, newspapers, libraries, and other resources in your own community (see 60d).

Hint

EMPHASIZING THE WRITER'S VIEWS

While some cultures place more value on student writing that primarily brings together or collects the thoughts of great scholars or experts, readers of research papers in American institutions value the writer's own interpretations and thinking about the subject, based on the information found.

60b SEARCHING LIBRARIES AND LIBRARY DATABASES

1. Types of Sources

Many students don't know what a wealth of resources libraries have because they are so used to using the World Wide Web as their major search tool. To avoid limiting yourself, get to know your library. It has the types of scholarly resources your instructor will most probably want you to use. You'll be pleasantly surprised by how much is in the library and by how helpful reference librarians can be. You may also be surprised at the ease with which you can find information using your library's online databases and subscription services. They are often as easy as using Internet search engines (such as Google) but with a much higher probability of finding relevant, fact-checked information.

Before you begin searching, spend some time learning about your library—what resources it has, where they are located, and how they are used. Libraries have various printed guides for users and an information desk where those helpful librarians will answer your questions. Information desk librarians really do want to answer questions (that's what they have been trained to do). Library catalogs—which list all of the library's materials by author, title, and subject—are often online, but they may be in a card catalog or on microfiche. Many library online catalogs are also connected to thousands of other library catalogs so that you can locate materials in other libraries. You may or may not be able to access databases of other libraries if they limit use to students at that institution. If your library doesn't have the sources you find in databases and other library catalogs, you may be able to ask for the materials on interlibrary loan, which means borrowing them from other libraries. You may want to start your library search with general or broad surveys of a topic to help you gain both an overview and suggestions for further reading before you go on to more specific sources. In addition to books, journals, and databases, libraries have collections of pamphlets and brochures, government documents, special collections of materials, and audio and video materials, and most offer interlibrary loan services.

General Reference Sources

The library's reference section includes encyclopedias such as the *Encyclopaedia Britannica* and the *Encyclopedia Americana,* as well as encyclopedias for specific areas of study such as anthropology, computer science and technology, American history, and American literature. Other general sources include collections of biographies, yearbooks and almanacs such as the *World Almanac and Book of Facts,* dictionaries, atlases, and government publications such as *Statistical Abstract of the United States.* When you read an entry in a subject encyclopedia and other scholarly sources, you know you're reading information from authors who are selected because of their expertise.

Library Indexes and Catalogs

Your library will have book indexes such as *Books in Print,* periodical indexes such as the *Readers' Guide to Periodical Literature,* and online indexes. Most library catalogs are computerized, so you can also do online searches of the library's holdings by author, title, keyword, and subject heading. When you request a *keyword search,* the search engine will look for the word in any part of the entry in the catalog (title, subtitle, abstract, etc.), whereas the *subject heading* has to match, word for word, the Library of Congress headings (listed in the *Library of Congress Subject Headings*). When doing a keyword search, you can also try synonyms for your topic or broader terms that might include it. For example, when searching for information about electric cars, you might also try **"battery-operated cars"** or **"alternative energy sources"** as keywords.

Library Databases and Subscription Services

Many libraries subscribe to periodical databases and other services that provide access to electronic versions of articles from journals, magazines, and newspapers. Sometimes these materials are available on CD-ROM in a library, but more often they can be located online through links on a library's Web page. These services make it easier than ever for you to locate reliable academic research. For research projects on current events and issues, library databases are often the best starting points for research. Unlike general Internet sources, which require users to spend additional time determining whether the Web sites they find are for commercial or entertainment purposes or if they are reliable and credible sources of information, resources in library databases are generally considered scholarly or newsworthy, don't contain advertisements, and have already been fact-checked and edited. Some of the most widely used databases include:

- *Academic Search Premier*—includes a wide range of newspaper, magazine, and journal articles.

- *Expanded Academic ASAP*—provides a wide range of newspaper, magazine, and journal articles.

- *General Business File ASAP*—offers articles on business news and research.

- *InfoTrac Custom Newspapers*—provides access to newspaper articles.

- *InfoTrac Health and Wellness Resource Center*—provides information on medical and health-related topics.

- *JSTOR*—contains full-text articles from a number of academic journals.

- *LexisNexis*—offers news articles, including transcripts of speeches, news shows, and other events.

- *MLA International Bibliography*—provides bibliographic information for literary criticism and research.

- *NewsBank*—contains newspaper articles.

- *OCLC FirstSearch*—contains a wide variety of articles on general academic subjects.

- *Project Muse*—provides full-text articles from several academic journals.

- *PsycARTICLES*—offers access to psychology research.

- *ScienceDirect*—specializes in science, technical, and medical articles.

Because your library or school pays for subscription services such as these, their use may be limited to students at your school, so you may need to use a school password or your student ID to access these materials. You should check on your library's Web page or with your reference librarians to find what other types of database resources your library offers as well as how to log in and access these materials.

Hint

UNDERSTANDING TERMS FOR LIBRARY DATABASES AND SUBSCRIPTION SERVICES

- **Library database:** a collection of bibliographic citations, abstracts, full-text articles, and PDF-formatted articles from newspapers, magazines, and journals that can be accessed through a library's Web site or on a CD-ROM. Colleges and libraries usually subscribe to these databases and very often permit access only to their own students or patrons.

- **Subscription service:** a service to which colleges, libraries, or individuals pay a fee to access research materials. Library databases are usually subscription services. Institutional or individual access to other resources, such as specific Web sites that offer periodical articles, reference materials, images, music, or videos, may also be acquired through subscription services.

- **Service provider:** the company that hosts the database or subscription service (e.g., the Expanded Academic ASAP database is hosted by Thomson Gale, and the MLA International Bibliography is hosted by EBSCOhost)

- **Abstract:** a short summary of an article

- **Bibliographic citation:** the information needed to retrieve the source, including the name of the source, volume number, issue number, date of publication, and page numbers

▶

- **Full-text article:** an article located on a library database or subscription service that provides the entire article text in electronic format
- **PDF-formatted article:** an electronic image of the entire article as it originally appeared in a print source, such as a newspaper, magazine, or journal
- **Periodical:** a publication that is published at regular intervals (such as on a daily, weekly, monthly, or annual basis), including newspapers, magazines, or journals

You can start an efficient database search by familiarizing yourself with the directions for using the database's search engine. Some databases allow you to search by subject. This means that when you enter a broad search term like **"AIDS,"** the database will connect you to a list of subdivided topics that allow you to narrow your search. Many search engines also allow you to search by keywords. If you have a more narrow or specific topic, such as the laws needed to protect the nesting grounds of loggerhead turtles on the South Carolina coast, you might enter a list of relevant keywords (**"loggerhead turtles," "nesting," "South Carolina,"** and **"law"**) to find relevant hits in the title or full text of articles. The use of Boolean operators can also sometimes help you narrow your search. For example, words like "AND" can add items to your search, "OR" can provide choices between search terms, and "BUT" can exclude certain items from your search (see 60c for more information on Boolean operators). Check the help section of your selected database to find the ways the program allows you to narrow your search. When you begin your research, consider whether a subject search or keyword search would be most helpful for finding information on your topic.

Many "full-text" databases provide the entire text of articles that originally appeared in journals, magazines, or newspapers. In many cases, you'll be able to see a Web page that shows the digitized text of the entire article. In other cases, you may be able to view a PDF file of the document. This allows you to see the article as it originally appeared in a journal, magazine, or newspaper with the same layout, colors, and photographs. In other cases, databases may provide just the bibliographic citations needed to locate relevant articles or an abstract, which is a brief summary of the article. To locate the full text of these materials, you should check in your library's catalog to see whether the library has these resources in print form or on microfiche. You can also ask your reference librarians to see whether these materials are available through its interlibrary loan service.

2. Search Strategies to Use

Many libraries have online tutorials that show you how to use the library effectively. Once you are familiar with using the library and what resources it has, you can start by checking reference books, databases, and card catalogs. People who work at the information desk may also be able to suggest other ways to start searching. See Exercise 60.2 for Web sites that explain how to search through libraries.

Checklist

DOING RESEARCH IN YOUR LIBRARY AND ON YOUR LIBRARY'S WEB SITE

These are some useful points to remember when you're in the library or on a library's Web site searching for materials.

- **Be prepared to make copies and printouts.** You may want to photocopy or print materials. Your school may allow you to put money on your ID card so you can swipe it in the copy machine to cover charges. If not, bring along a pocketful of coins or purchase a copy card.

- **Bring a flash drive or other storage device if you'll be using a library computer.** That enables you to transfer drafts or downloadable materials from a public computer to your personal computer.

- **Get a map of the library.** From this, you can learn where to look for what you want. Such maps are usually available at the entrance or the information or reference desk. Check to see whether there are other libraries on campus.

- **Look at your library's Web site when you are at your own computer.** Get to know some of its resources. Check the menu on the home page for links to online databases. If you can't access your library's online databases from an off-campus computer, ask the reference librarians if they can provide you with an access code or alternative electronic address (URL) to use.

- **Join a library tour, try a tutorial on using the library (if your library has one), or go to a workshop.** Doing so will save you time when you start your searches.

Exercise 60.1 Library Visit

Visit your library, and talk with a reference librarian. Ask the following questions (or questions of your own).

1. What are the most useful subject indexes you recommend when students are looking for material on space exploration?

2. What advice do you have about using databases to find material on Civil War battles?

3. What's your favorite tip or hint to suggest when students first start searching for material?

Exercise 60.2 Library Practice

If your library has a tutorial on its Web site on how to search the library, use it to provide answers to the following questions. If not, you can go to any of the following university libraries' tutorials. (Tutorials for other libraries, however, will not be as useful because they are providing information about specifics of their library, not yours.)

Cornell University: www.library.cornell.edu/olinuris/ref/research/tutorial.html

New York University: library.nyu.edu/research/tutorials

Purdue University: www.lib.purdue.edu/rguides/tutorials.html

Stanford University: www-sul.stanford.edu

University of Minnesota: tutorial.lib.umn.edu

Then answer the following questions.

1. Is there more than one library on campus? If so, where?
2. In the card catalog, what are two or three sources on Native American folklore?
3. What types of information do you find in the catalog entry for a book?
4. What is a periodical index? What is the title of one periodical index that would be helpful in finding material about your topic?
5. How long can you keep books after you check them out?
6. Why do you need the date of an article you are looking for?
7. What are the names of five databases in your library?
8. How do you request a book that is not in the library's collection?
9. What are two online journals to which the library subscribes?
10. What are two indexes or reference series you might want to use?

60c   SEARCHING THE INTERNET

Much information is available on the Internet, but you don't want to rely solely on what you find there because vast stores of knowledge are not (yet) available online. Your library is a rich resource for materials, many of which are quite different from what you'll find on the Internet. For help with searching libraries and library databases, see 60b, and for doing community research, see 60d.

1. Types of Information Available

The Internet is particularly useful when searching for the kinds of sources and information listed here. But be cautious and remember that the Internet is open to anyone who wants to post anything there, including biased, false, or distorted information and claims intended to entice people into buying products, changing their views, or donating money. For help with evaluating what you find on the Internet, see 62b, and for specific Internet sites to use, see Chapter 61. Despite the ocean of information you can access online, you are less likely to find older books, collections of reference works, the content of some journals, old archives of newspapers, and many other materials. For current events topics, searching your library's online or CD-ROM databases can be a better first research step than starting with the Internet. So you are likely to find yourself using both the Internet and your library resources (see 60b). For the Internet part of your search, you can find the sources described here.

Government Sources

The U.S. government maintains numerous sites on the Internet with huge quantities of information produced by various bureaus and agencies, in addition to that produced by legislative action. You can also check for references to appropriate government publications your library may have on the shelves. For a list of government sites on the Internet, see Chapter 61. There are also online city and state sites with information of local concern, and governments outside the United States also post information on the Web about their countries, including news, photos, reports, and information for tourists and investors. Some of the international sites offer the option of reading their material in either English or the local language.

Online Library Catalogs and Databases

You can search many libraries online, especially the Library of Congress, to find other materials on your topic, and your library may be able to borrow these resources for you. You can also read titles and abstracts to get a sense of what's available on the topic. Online catalogs are very useful for compiling a working bibliography to start your search (see 63c). Some of the major libraries online also have searchable databases and lists of resources in various areas that may be useful.

Your library may also subscribe to full-text databases or online journals (see 60b for a list of popular library databases).

Current News and Publications

Most newspapers (including nationally circulated papers such as the *New York Times* and your local newspapers), television networks (such as ABC, CBS, CNN, Fox, and NBC), and print publications (such as *Time, Wired, The New Republic,* and some scholarly journals) maintain online databases of information that include excerpts from current articles and news stories from their print sources or television programs. See the addresses listed in Chapter 61. Some of these archives charge for copies of their materials, but you may be able to request copies through your library's interlibrary loan service. You may also be able to access full-text articles from these sites if you enter them through your university library.

Newsgroups and Listservs

Newsgroups are open forums on the Usenet network where anyone can post a message on the topic of the forum. Listservs are e-mail discussion groups in which participants subscribe to the list. Any message from any member of the listserv goes to all subscribers. The listserv owner may or may not moderate what appears by controlling which messages get through to the list. Many newsgroups and listservs have very useful FAQs that may answer your questions, and some have archives of past discussions.

Blogs

Web logs or "blogs" are Web sites with dated entries listed in reverse chronological order so the most recent post is first. Some blogs are personal and informally written, but others are a form of editorial writing or independent journalism. Blogs may also have themes, such as politics, health care, education, or other topics. Some blogs are widely read and very influential because they are written by knowledgeable people whose writing is respected; other blogs have only a few visitors. Reading about the blog owner and writer(s) can help you determine the blog's credibility.

Older Books

Several sites, including Bartleby.com and Project Gutenberg, are dedicated to making available online older books whose copyrights have expired. Other projects are dedicated to making rare or hard-to-find older resources available online. See the addresses listed in Chapter 61.

Other Online Sources

In addition, you'll find sites maintained by public interest groups (such as environmental groups or consumer safety organizations) and nonprofit organizations (such as museums and universities) with information about their areas of interest; directories that help you locate companies and people; and company sites with information about their services and products (and discussion groups on the company site about its products and services). There are also biased sites that post propaganda to influence others to adopt their views. To sort out such sites from more trustworthy sites, evaluate your sources carefully (see Chapter 62).

Hint

EVALUATING THE RELIABILITY OF WIKIPEDIA

Wikipedia (www.wikipedia.com) is a collaboratively written online encyclopedia. According to its Web site, its name comes from "wiki," an interactive software program that allows multiple users to add, revise, and delete posted material. Registered users of the site can add new articles, and virtually any visitor can edit and change the information posted.

▶

Because Wikipedia is controlled by users rather than by a strict process of expert review, as most encyclopedias and academic journals are, its reliability is frequently questioned. Furthermore, posts on Wikipedia are limited to the interests of its readers. Therefore, the most relevant information about a topic may not be present in some of the entries posted by the site. However, some scholars have argued that because the entries in Wikipedia are written and reviewed by all users, it imitates the way all knowledge is constructed: people with varying degrees of expertise post information and exchange opinions about it through the community's ongoing editing process. Some also point out that experts are among those adding and revising material on Wikipedia, and for this reason, the information on some topics is kept very current.

You should be aware that many instructors do not consider Wikipedia a reliable source. It's best to check first with your instructor, and, if you do use it, always evaluate the credibility of information you find there as you would evaluate the credibility of any other information (see Chapter 62 for information about evaluating sources). Check the currency of posts on the topic, as well as the references cited in the entry. Also try to confirm the information you find in Wikipedia in other sources you consider reliable.

2. Search Strategies to Use

When people go into a huge mall without an idea of what they want to buy, they can spend unnecessary time browsing aimlessly. That's why it is so helpful when you begin your search to have refined your topic, formulated your research questions, and followed other strategies explained in Chapter 59. You will also need to evaluate your sources as you proceed. This is particularly true of Web sources because the Internet is open to any person who wants to post information. Not all sources on the Internet are fact-checked and edited before they are posted. Furthermore, information is posted on the Internet for a variety of purposes—to inform, to persuade, to entertain, or to encourage you to buy something. Therefore, a great deal of what you find may be irrelevant to your research topic, incorrect, or written with purposes that skew the quality and content of the information. (See 62b on evaluating Internet sources.) As we know, the Web is constantly changing, so a lot of information will disappear rapidly. What is available one day when you surf the Web may be different or gone when you return.

Search Engines

Just as we need different types of tools (hammers, saws, screwdrivers, and so on) to construct or fix things, we also need different types of search tools online for various projects. Often researching starts with using search engines. Search engines on the World Wide Web scan huge numbers of (but not all) Web sites, and they find materials from a vast variety of resources, such as discussions of your topic on newsgroups, listservs, and blogs. Different search engines also allow you to specify whether you want to search the Web, images, groups, news, audio, and so on (see Chapter 61 for a list of search engine addresses). Google is the most powerful and most widely used search engine; it allows users to search the full text of Web sites, articles, and books, as well as images and video. Yahoo!, MSN, AOL, and Ask.com are other commonly recognized search engines. Many search engines include sponsored links (links that advertisers pay for) listed prominently on the first page of results. Google, Yahoo!, and others identify their paid links, but some search engines do not. It's important to keep in mind that different search engines will turn up both similar and different links. You can also use metasearch engines, such as Dogpile and Mamma, to comb multiple search engines and view a limited number of the combined results.

Try This

TO USE INTERNET SEARCH ENGINES EFFECTIVELY

Keeping these suggestions in mind will make your search more efficient.

■ Use phrases instead of single words to define your search more specifically.

■ Think of a variety of keywords that apply to your topic. If your keyword doesn't turn up much that is useful, switch to a different one.

■ Enclose the whole term (as a unit) in quotation marks to ensure that the entire term is the object of the search.

■ Talk with a tutor in your writing center. Explain what your questions are, and ask about how you ought to search. If the writing center has computers connected to the Internet, you and the tutor may work together as you search.

■ Keep a search log or journal. Include terms you come across to use, terms you found useful, sites you visited, and other relevant information so that you don't find yourself forgetting where you have already looked. You can also record new links you want to check out later. It's handy to keep this log on your laptop or desktop.

■ When you find a useful site, look for links that connect you to related sites.

■ Be sure your terms are spelled correctly.

■ Use search engine directories or categories when they exist.

Search engines work by searching the content of public sites on the Internet for keywords that you indicate. The search engine returns a list of sites that include the search terms you used. Some sites also have their own search engines to help you find information on various parts of that site. Search engines differ in the way they suggest entering your key terms. They also offer a variety of options for narrowing your search. For example, Google can search images, video, news, maps, and other categories. By using the "Advanced Search," you can locate results in book texts, government documents, and other languages. Most search engines no longer need quotation marks around a group of words to indicate that you want to search the whole keyword or phrase as a unit, but if you want to combine two keywords to be more specific, use quotation marks around the entire phrase. When you have two sets of keywords or phrases, combine them with some terms (known as *Boolean terms*) in combination with your topic or keywords that will limit the results to what you are looking for. The following Boolean terms are especially useful when searching databases.

Hint

USING BOOLEAN TERMS FOR INTERNET SEARCHES

Each search engine has its own rules for the use of Boolean terms. Check the help section to understand how to use these terms effectively in your favorite search engines.

− (*or*) NOT

The minus sign or NOT can tell the database or search engine to find a reference that contains one term but not the other. For example, suppose you'd like some information about coaches who have worked with the Chicago Bulls basketball team. If you type in **"Chicago Bulls coaches"**, you'll also find links to sites that sell "coaches series women's watches." To narrow that search and weed out links where such watches can be bought, you can include a minus sign directly in front of the word you want to exclude: **"Chicago Bulls coaches" −"watches."**

OR

OR can help you combine terms in your search or find a search term that may appear two different ways. For example, if you want information on sudden infant death syndrome, try **"sudden infant death syndrome" OR "SIDS"**. Use OR if the comparative terms will help you find what you need more efficiently.

+ (*or*) AND

Many search engines, such as Google, Yahoo!, and MSN, automatically search for every keyword you list, so the word AND or a plus sign is often not needed for this purpose. For some search engines and library databases, however, the plus sign or AND tells the search engine to find your first word or term *and* your second word or term (and perhaps a third

▶

word or term if it's relevant). That helps narrow the results list closer to what you want.

In some search engines like Google, however, the plus sign immediately in front of a word means that it is essential for the search. For example, if you are looking up the film *Rocky IV*, you can type in **Rocky +IV** to narrow your results.

Using Directories or Categories

Some search engines, such as Google and Yahoo!, have materials arranged by general subjects in directories (such as "business and economy," "education," "government," "health," and "society and culture"). Within each subject, you can find numerous related sites. For example, under "health," you may find the subheadings "diseases," "drugs," and "fitness." These can be very helpful to browse through when you are looking for a topic for a paper. The categories are also helpful when you don't yet have specific information on a topic you are just learning about. For example, suppose you want to look into the effects of El Niño and know that you can consult government agencies, but you aren't sure which government agency will have useful information. One of the categories in the Google search engine directory (http://directory.google.com) is "science." Within it are numerous subcategories, including "earth sciences." Under "earth sciences" is a subcategory for "meteorology," and under this is a category for "El Niño and La Niña." Here you will find several links to sites, including some on research done by the agency you were searching for, the National Oceanic and Atmospheric Administration.

Thinking Creatively of Ways to Search

Use your detective skills to think about different ways to start and which leads to follow. When you use some creative thinking, you'll find that you begin to think of a variety of sites besides the ordinary or expected ones. Suppose your assignment is to research your major, and you want to learn more about job opportunities related to that major. Here are some different ways to approach your online search.

- Go to general job search sites to see what they list.

- Try the resource lists and directories in your selected academic field (see Chapter 61). These Web sites may list relevant job opportunities.

- Go to college and university Web sites. You may find that departments in your field list job opportunities. (For an extensive list of links to college and university home pages, go to www.google.com/universities.html.)

- Look at U.S. census reports online to see employment data. Other federal government sites list prospects for various fields.

- Try Web sites of large companies in your field to see what job openings they list. (Some search engines list company Web addresses in addition to street and city locations.)

- Tune in to listservs, newsgroups, discussion forums, and blogs of people in your area of work to see what they are discussing.

- Use a few search engines to see what they turn up. (Some listings will overlap, but each engine's list will be different. Most search engines turn up more items than you will want to read.)

Exercise 60.3 Practice with Internet Search Engines

Working in a small group, select a topic, decide on a few keywords, have each person look it up on a different search engine, and see what you find. When the group meets again, share your answers to the following questions:

1. Did the results differ? If so, in what ways?

2. Which search engine seemed most useful?

If you can't think of a topic for your group, here are a few suggestions.

Reality television	Alternative energy sources
Women in college wrestling	Avian flu
Reviews of a particular current film	Teen drug use
Embedded reporting in the Iraq War	Separation of church and state in the United States

Exercise 60.4 Practice in Searching the Internet

Try at least five of the Web sites listed in Chapter 61, using the same search term. Write a short paragraph about (1) what you found, (2) how the site would be useful in doing research, and (3) why you think that site would be helpful or why it isn't as helpful as you think it should be.

60d SEARCHING OTHER SOURCES

The Internet and your library will have useful information for you, but your topic may also offer opportunities to search other kinds of sources, such as those discussed here.

1. Community Sources

Your community has a variety of resources that can be tapped. If you're seeking public records or other local government information, your city hall or county courthouse can be a good place to search. Other sources of information are community service workers, social service agencies, teachers and school administrators, community leaders, and religious leaders and institutions, as well as coordinators in nonprofit groups. The local newspaper is another storehouse of useful information. If there is a chamber of commerce or a visitors and convention bureau nearby, its list of local organizations may be helpful. You can also check the phone book or the local public library for lists of community resources and people to contact. Local history can be studied at a historical museum or the library, and the newspaper may have useful archives. Don't forget your campus community; faculty and administrators can be good sources of information.

Checklist

PLANNING AND CONDUCTING AN EFFECTIVE INTERVIEW

- Before the interview, do some research so that you are informed about the person's field in relation to your topic.

- When you request an interview, explain the purpose. Be sure you've found the right person. Suggest the amount of time you'll need. Make sure that the person you interview is aware that his or her words will be used in your research paper. If you will be eventually publishing your research paper in a newspaper or on the Internet, let the person know that others will read his or her words in a public forum.

- Think about the information you want, and make a list. Formulate the questions you'll be asking. Include some open-ended questions by thinking of questions that begin with the reporter's *who, what, when, where, why,* and *how* starters.

- Be prepared for the conversation to veer off into other, perhaps more relevant and interesting, directions.

- Bring along some means of taking notes. If you want to record the conversation on tape, ask the person's permission first.

- Note the date, the place, and the name of the person you're interviewing.

- When you leave, thank the person and, if appropriate, follow up with a note of thanks.

- Read your notes after the interview, and if you have questions, contact the person for clarification.

- When you include quoted or paraphrased material from your interview in your paper, make sure you represent the person's viewpoints fairly, accurately, and respectfully.

2. Interviews and Surveys

You can do field research and seek information firsthand by interviewing people, exchanging e-mail messages, conducting surveys, and taking notes on your own observations. These forms of information gathering need to be undertaken thoughtfully. You need to be sure that you ask good questions (politely, of course) and that you know how to collect information without distorting it. You should always be aware of your own filtering of material. You can also try e-mailing scholars in the field; many are very willing to communicate with you.

Checklist

CONSTRUCTING YOUR QUESTIONNAIRE

- Think about your purpose, topic, and research question. What do you want the people answering the questionnaire to tell you?

- Make a list of more questions than you need, and then narrow it by whatever constraints are necessary (number of people, time it will take to answer the questions, and so on). Ask yourself how you would respond to each question. That helps you see any problems with phrasing or with the type of information people are likely to offer.

- Decide on the appropriate pool of people that you will draw from. How will you contact them? Why should they take time to answer your questionnaire?

- Ask a small sample of the appropriate people to try out the questionnaire to see what revisions are needed. Ask for their input on how to improve the questionnaire, and then revise accordingly.

- Design the questionnaire so that it is easy for others to read and has adequate space for answers. Don't make it too long or time-consuming because that reduces the number of people who will complete the questionnaire. Offer to share the results if they'd be interested.

- If you are sending out the questionnaire, provide an envelope and postage for people to return it. Include a date by which you'd like the questionnaire returned.

3. Government Sources

In addition to what you find on the Internet and in your library, the Government Printing Office has a searchable Web site of its catalog of print and electronic publications at www.gpoaccess.gov. In addition, local, county, and state government agencies have information you may find useful, depending on your topic.

61
USING WEB RESOURCES

This chapter provides you with a list of particularly useful Web sites to search. As you search, you'll need to collect bibliographic information about the Web sites you visit so you can locate them later as well as create entries for your Works Cited page (see 66c for MLA citation information) or References page (see 67c for APA citation information).

 Web Resources

Writers' Resources

These sites offer a variety of resources writers use, such as dictionaries, a thesaurus, instructional handouts, reference books, style guides, and a biographical dictionary. The Online Writing Labs (OWLs) are links to dozens of college and university writing centers with writing skills materials online.

Bartlett's Familiar Quotations	www.bartleby.com/100
Biographical Dictionary	www.s9.com
Dictionary.com/Writing Resources	dictionary.reference.com/writing
Indispensable Writing Resources	www.quintcareers.com/writing
IWCA Resources for Writers	writingcenters.org/writers.htm
Merriam-Webster Online Dictionary	www.m-w.com
OWLs (Online Writing Labs)	writingcenters.org/owcdb
Purdue Online Writing Lab	owl.english.purdue.edu
Roget's New Thesaurus	www.bartleby.com/62
Strunk's *Elements of Style*	www.bartleby.com/141
Thesaurus.com	thesaurus.reference.com

Academic Databases and Online Resources

Databases, as explained in 60b, are searchable indexes that offer either citations or the complete text of materials on a vast array of topics. Most academic libraries subscribe to some or all of these databases, and you can search your own library's databases. However, often you can't search most other academic libraries because they pay for many of the databases they have and therefore limit use of their databases to students on their campus. In that case, they require a password or student identification to access the material. The sites listed here, however, are available to all users. Public libraries also subscribe to databases but are usually open for public use.

Academic Info	www.academicinfo.net/digital.html
Directory of Open Access Journals	www.doaj.org
ERIC: Educational Resources Information Desk	www.eric.ed.gov
Google Books	books.google.com
Google Scholar	scholar.google.com
LookSmart Find Articles	www.findarticles.com
Project Muse	muse.jhu.edu
Questia Online Library of Books and Journals	www.questia.com

Search Engines

Search engines, as explained in 60c, search millions of Web sites to find sites that match your search terms. To read news and evaluations of search engines and to find specialized search engines, go to Search Engine Watch at www.searchenginewatch.com. Google is a very powerful search engine and is also a good starting point for most searches.

Google	www.google.com
Yahoo!	www.yahoo.com
Ask	www.ask.com
MSN	www.msn.com

Metasearch Engines

Metasearch engines, as explained in 60c, collect the results of multiple search engines. As search engines such as Google have expanded their search capabilities, metasearch engines have generally become more limited in their coverage, but they can still provide useful results.

| Dogpile | www.dogpile.com |
| Mamma | www.mamma.com |

Libraries and Subject Directories

These online libraries can be searched by subject. Some also have the complete text of literary works online.

Academic Information Index	www.academicinfo.net
English Server	eserver.org
Internet Public Library	www.ipl.org
Libcat: A Guide to Library Resources on the Internet	www.librarysites.info
Library of Congress	www.loc.gov
Library Spot	www.libraryspot.com
Online Literary Resources	andromeda.rutgers.edu/~jlynch/Lit

U.S. Government Publications (GPO) Catalog	www.gpoaccess.gov
Voice of the Shuttle	vos.ucsb.edu/index.asp
WWW Virtual Library	www.vlib.org

Online Books (E-Books)

These Web sites offer the complete text of previously printed books. See also the list of libraries and subject directories.

Bartleby.com	www.bartleby.com
Complete Works of William Shakespeare	thetech.mit.edu/shakespeare
Electronic Text Center	etext.lib.virginia.edu
Google Books	books.google.com
Online Books Page	onlinebooks.library.upenn.edu
Project Gutenberg	www.gutenberg.org
Read Print	www.readprint.org
Victorian Women Writers Project	www.indiana.edu/~letrs/vwwp

Magazines, Journals, and News Media

These Web sites are maintained by the major print, television, and online magazines, journals, and news media.

ABC News	abcnews.go.com
Arts and Letters Daily *(searches newspapers, magazines, columnists, etc.)*	www.aldaily.com
ArtsJournal.com	www.artsjournal.com
BBC News	news.bbc.co.uk
CBS News	www.cbsnews.com
CEO Express *(searches newspapers, magazines, online television news, etc.)*	www.ceoexpress.com
Chicago Tribune	www.chicagotribune.com
CNN News	www.cnn.com
Fox News	www.foxnews.com
Google News	news.google.com
London Times	www.thetimes.co.uk
Los Angeles Times	www.latimes.com
Metalinks.com *(search engine for journalists and has links to major national and international news media)*	metalinks.com/usmedia.htm
MSNBC News	www.msnbc.com

New York Times Online	nytimes.com
NPR (National Public Radio) News	www.npr.org
Reuters	www.reuters.com
Roper Center for Public Opinion	www.ropercenter.uconn.edu
Salon	www.salon.com
SciTechDaily	www.scitechdaily.com
Slate	www.slate.com
United Press International	www.upi.com
USA Today News	www.usatoday.com
Washington Post	www.washingtonpost.com
Washington Times	www.washtimes.com
Yahoo! News	news.yahoo.com

Government and Public Information

American Civil Liberties Union	www.aclu.org
Bureau of Labor Statistics	www.bls.gov
Census Bureau	www.census.gov
Census Bureau Fact Finder	factfinder.census.gov/home/saff/main.html?_lang=en
Census Bureau State and County QuickFacts	quickfacts.census.gov/qfd
Center for Urban Studies	www.cus.wayne.edu
Center on Budget and Policy Priorities	www.cbpp.org
Centers for Disease Control and Prevention	www.cdc.gov
Central Intelligence Agency	www.cia.gov
Childstats.gov	www.childstats.gov
CountryWatch	www.countrywatch.com
C-SPAN	www.c-span.org
Department of Commerce, Bureau of Economic Analysis	www.bea.gov
Department of Health and Human Services	www.hhs.gov
Department of Homeland Security	www.dhs.gov
Department of Housing and Human Development	www.hud.gov
Department of Justice, Bureau of Justice Statistics	www.ojp.usdoj.gov/bjs

Department of Transportation, Bureau of Transportation Statistics	www.bts.gov
Environmental Protection Agency	www.epa.gov
Federal Bureau of Investigation	www.fbi.gov
Fedstats	www.fedstats.gov
FedWorld.gov	www.fedworld.gov
Government Printing Office	www.gpoaccess.gov
National Aeronautics and Space Administration	www.nasa.gov
National Atlas.gov	www.nationalatlas.gov
National Bureau of Economic Research	www.nber.org
National Center for Education Statistics	nces.ed.gov
National Institutes of Health	www.nih.gov
National Oceanic and Atmospheric Administration	www.noaa.gov
NATO	www.nato.int
Smithsonian Institution	www.si.edu
Stat-USA	www.stat-usa.gov
Supreme Court of the United States	www.supremecourtus.gov
THOMAS: Legislative Information	thomas.loc.gov
United Nations	www.un.org/english
White House	www.whitehouse.gov
World Health Organization	www.who.int/en

Online Media, Images, Art, and Photographs

Hundreds of Web sites, including news media archives, museums, historical sites, and libraries, have photographs. The following list of links is a good place to start searching for images to use in educational projects.

One note of caution: before you use any images you find online, check the Web site's permissions and copyright information. Some Web sites allow the use of their photos and images free of charge. Many other Web sites, however, have copyrighted images that can't legally be reproduced in other work without permission from the image provider. If an image will be reproduced on a Web site or in a multimedia program, some image providers will request that a hyperlink be added to that site to lead readers back to the original online source. In any case, you must always cite your image sources, just as you would cite your use of text sources.

Artcyclopedia	www.artcyclopedia.com
CDC Public Health Image Library	phil.cdc.gov/Phil/home.asp
FreeDigitalPhotos.net	www.freedigitalphotos.net

FreeFoto.com	www.freefoto.com
Free Public Domain Photo Database	pdphoto.org
FreeStockPhotos.com	www.freestockphotos.com
Images of American Political History	teachpol.tcnj.edu/amer_pol_hist
Library of Congress American Memory Map Collections	memory.loc.gov/ammem/gmdhtml/gmdhome.html
Metropolitan Museum of Art	www.metmuseum.org
MorgueFile	www.morguefile.com
NASA Image Gallery	www.nasa.gov/multimedia/imagegallery/index.html
NOAA Photo Library	www.photolib.noaa.gov
Openphoto.net	www.openphoto.net
U.S. Government Photos and Multimedia	www.usa.gov/Topics/Graphics.shtml
Wikimedia Commons	commons.wikimedia.org/wiki/Main_Page

Universities

This site provides links to colleges and universities in the United States and Canada.

Google's University Search	www.google.com/universities.html

62

EVALUATING SOURCES

We live in an age of such vast amounts of information that we can't know everything about a subject. All information that comes streaming at us from newspapers, magazines, the media, books, journals, brochures, Web sites, and so on is also of very uneven quality. People want to convince us to depend on their data, buy their products, accept their viewpoints, vote for their candidates, make donations to their causes, agree with their opinions, and rely on them as experts.

We make decisions all the time about which information we will use, based on our evaluation of it. Evaluating sources, then, is a skill we rely on constantly, and applying that skill to research papers is equally important. Discussed next are some stages in the process of evaluating sources for research papers.

62a   GETTING STARTED

To begin, ask yourself what type of information you are looking for and where you're likely to find appropriate sources for it. You want to be sure that you are headed in the right direction as you launch into your search.

■ *What kind of information are you looking for?* Do you want facts? opinions? news reports? research studies? analyses? historical accounts? personal reflections? data? public records? scholarly essays reflecting on the topic? reviews?

■ *Where would you find such information?* Which sources are most likely to be useful: the Internet? online library databases and subscription services? libraries with scholarly journals, books, and government publications? public libraries with popular magazines? newspapers? community records? people on your campus?

For example, if you're searching for information on some current event, a reliable newspaper such as the *New York Times* will be a useful source, and it is available on the Web (see Chapter 61) and in a university or public library. If you need some statistics on the U.S. population, government census documents on the Web (see Chapter 61) and in libraries will be appropriate places to search. If you want to do research into local history, however, the archives and Web sites of local government offices and the local newspaper are better places to start. Consider whether there are organizations that gather and publish the types of information you are seeking. For example, if you are seeking information about teen drinking and driving, a useful source would be a local office of Mothers Against Drunk Driving (MADD) if you want to know about local conditions. If you want national or regional information, the MADD Web site is also likely to be helpful. Be sure to ask yourself whether the sponsoring organization's goal for the site is to be objective, to gain support for its viewpoint, or to sell you something. For example, a tobacco institute, funded by a large tobacco company, is not likely to be an unbiased source of information about the harmfulness of cigarettes.

Exercise 62.1 Practice in Getting Started

Listed here are several topics you might want to research. Think about where you might start looking for sources. What books, indexes, databases, Web sites, search engines, newspapers, and so on would be likely places to start? Might you need to do some field research?

1. Is it worth the price to pay for bottled water rather than drinking tap water? (*Hint:* Think about how this depends on where you live, what bottled water is available locally, what the city water supply health standards are, and what the federal government guidelines are.)

2. Is your institution providing adequate personal counseling for students with a particular problem you are interested in researching, such as drugs, AIDS awareness, poor time management skills, inadequate housing or parking, student health care, or student representation in major institutional decisions that affect students? (*Hint:* Think about how you would find out what's available on campus—counseling offices? Web site? school directory of services? How would you gather information about student attitudes?)

3. What is the economic outlook for jobs in a field you are either majoring in or hope to work in after you graduate? (*Hint:* What federal government sources would help you locate statistics on current employment and future outlook for this area of work? See Chapter 61 for government resources on the Web. What databases in your library would help you locate information in journals or newspapers?)

4. Choose a manufacturer of some major American product (such as athletic shoes, jeans, or cell phones) that has been accused of sending manufacturing overseas to be done in sweatshop conditions. Is the protest valid, or are the people (or children) overseas eager to have such work? (*Hint:* How would you find out about a company's suppliers? Would the library have databases or business directories that would help you learn about the company? Would the company be likely to post information about this on its Web site? If so, would the information be completely truthful? Would Web sites for groups that protest unfair working conditions be useful? Would their sites be biased?)

62b EVALUATING INTERNET SOURCES

Many of the things to remember while you evaluate Internet sources are similar to considerations for evaluating sources found elsewhere, but there are also some special matters to consider when deciding whether to use Internet materials. The Internet is a worldwide medium where anyone can post anything from anywhere. No monitors, evaluators, or fact-checking organizations regulate or review what is posted on the Web. In addition, the sponsor or organization name on the site can be misleading. Although excellent sources of information exist on the Web, many sites or pages on sites can lead unsuspecting readers into accepting as fact whatever biased, false, stolen, or fake information turns up in a search.

Hint

CHECKING THE DOMAIN NAME AND REGISTRANT

The domain is the last part of the URL or basic Web address, consisting of two or three letters that appear after the last dot. (Information after the domain name starts with a slash and links to pages on the site.) The domain can sometimes (though not always) give you clues about the Web site's source.

.gov	government sites (These are usually dependable.)
.edu	educational institutions (These are dependable, though personal student Web sites may not be.)
.org	organizations (These include nonprofit or public service organizations that may have their own bias.)
.com, .biz, .net	commercial sites (Business Web sites are likely to have a profit motive. Individuals, however, may also post their personal Web sites and blogs on corporate servers.)
.uk, .de, .ca, .jp	foreign sites (.uk = England; .de = Germany, .ca = Canada, .jp = Japan; there are two-letter abbreviations for all countries of the world.)

It is quite easy for businesses and individuals, however, to purchase most types of domain names (except .gov) for their corporate or personal Web sites. To check the names of people or groups who have registered their Web site domains, conduct a "whois" search at the following Web site:

www.networksolutions.com/whois

Some organizations and people pay to hide their names, so you won't find every Web site listed there, but it's worth a try because this search may help you learn more about who has created a particular Web site.

If you were looking for more information about the Individuals with Disabilities Education Act, consider how different types of Web sites might provide you with different types of information. For example, how might information on a .gov site (such as a U.S. senator's page) differ from that on an .org site (such as a Web site for a parent-teacher association), an .edu site (such as a Web site for a school for deaf children), and a .com site (such as a Web site for a company that specializes in cochlear implants). Use the checklist of questions to evaluate the differences in purpose and audience between such sites.

www.   Internet Resources for Evaluating Web Sites

"Evaluating Web Pages: Techniques   www.lib.berkeley.edu/TeachingLib/
to Apply & Questions to Ask"   Guides/Internet/Evaluate.html

"Evaluating Web Pages"	www.lib.duke.edu/libguide/evaluating_web.htm
"Criteria for Evaluating Web Pages"	web.library.emory.edu/services/ressvcs/howguides/internet.html#Criteria
"Evaluate Web Pages"	www3.widener.edu/Academics/Libraries/Wolfgram_Memorial_Library/Evaluate_Web_Pages/659
"Evaluating Web Sites: Criteria and Tools"	www.library.cornell.edu/olinuris/ref/research/webeval.html
"Thinking Critically About World Wide Web Resources"	www.library.ucla.edu/libraries/college/help/critical

Checklist

EVALUATING A WEB SITE

▪ Who is the site's author, organization, or sponsor? Try to find out through a link to the home page or by deleting all of the URL after the domain name (all of the information after the first slash) to bring you to the home page. Then search the Web for references to this author or organization to learn more. Are the authors clearly identified? Is there a way to contact them? Be very suspicious of an author or organization that wants to remain anonymous.

▪ What are the author's or organization's credentials? Why should you consider this a reliable source? If the domain name is .edu, be sure you are reading information the college or university posted. If you are reading a student's page, be aware that student pages are not always monitored by the institution.

▪ What evidence is there of the accuracy of the information? Are there any references cited or links provided to other sites or publications known to be reliable? Is there evidence that the information has been verified? Is there any evidence of bias? If a viewpoint is offered, are other viewpoints considered too?

▪ Is the information current? Is there a date of origin and any sign of the site's being maintained and revised in the recent past? If there are links to other sites, are they live links or links that no longer work? Does the information sound dated, referring to "recent" events that actually occurred several years ago?

▪ Does the site have any credentials or ratings by a reliable rating group? (The attractiveness of the site is not a reason for accepting the information as reliable.)

▶

- Is there advertising (or pop-up windows) on the site? Does that interfere with the site's credibility? (Sites with .gov as the domain will not have advertising.)

- What is the site's goal? to inform? to persuade? to provide information or disinformation? Is there an "About Us" link to an explanation about the organization? Who is the intended audience?

- How did you access the site? Did you link to it from a reliable site? If you find the site through a search engine result, that means only that the site contains your search keywords; it says nothing about the trustworthiness or value of the site.

- How good is the coverage of the topic? Does the site have uniquely useful information? Does the site offer in-depth information?

Exercise 62.2 Practice in Evaluating Web Sites

Assume you are researching information about avian flu, and you find the Web sites shown in Figures 62.1 and 62.2 (see p. 363). As you study the two Web sites, consider the following questions.

1. Consider Figure 62.1. Who is the sponsoring organization? Is it likely to be impartial? Why? What types of information are available on the site? Is there any bias evident?

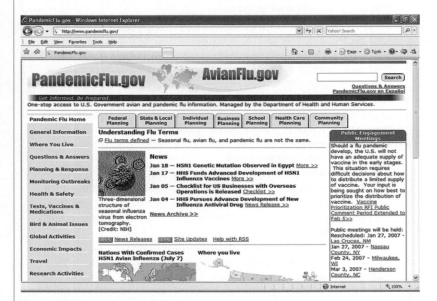

Figure 62.1 www.PandemicFlu.gov

2. Consider Figure 62.2. Who is the sponsor or organization? Is it likely to be impartial? Why? What kinds of information are available on the site? Is there any bias evident? What word choices and graphics lead you to that conclusion?

Figure 62.2 www.FluArmour.com
Reprinted by permission of Flu Armour, West Berlin, NJ.

You may have concluded in Exercise 62.2 that the Department of Health and Human Services's bird flu site is a useful, reliable source because it offers specific information and links to additional information. Because the Web site is sponsored by a government agency, its goal is to provide information for the public's health and well-being. The Flu Armour home page, by contrast, is sponsored by a company that sells supplies it claims will protect people in a bird flu pandemic. Notice the link to the shopping cart in the upper right corner. This site stresses the safety and usefulness of the products and has colorful graphics that add to its marketing appeal and user-friendliness.

Exercise 62.3 Small Group Practice

Form a small group, and have each member consult one or two of the sites on the list of Internet resources for evaluating Web sites. Compile the suggestions found on the various sites into a comprehensive list of things to remember when evaluating a Web site. Were there differences in the advice offered on the sites? Which sites were most useful? Why?

62c EVALUATING BIBLIOGRAPHIC CITATIONS

Before you spend time searching for any type of source or reading it, look at the following information in the citation to evaluate whether it's worth your time. These suggestions apply to all types of sources, including those you find on the Web, in your library, and in your community.

1. Author

Credentials

- How reputable is the person listed as the author?

- What is the author's educational background? Is it appropriate for the type of expertise you want?

- What has the author written in the past about this topic? If this is the author's first publication in this area, perhaps the author isn't yet an expert.

- Why is this person considered an expert or a reliable authority? Who considers this person an expert? Would that source have any bias?

- If the author is an organization, what can you find out about it? How reputable is it?

You can learn more about an author by checking the Web and the Library of Congress catalog to see what else this person has written, and the *Book Review Index* and *Book Review Digest* may lead you to reviews of other books by this author. Your library may have citation indexes in the field that will lead you to other articles and short pieces by this person that have been cited by others.

For organizations, you can check databases or the Web to see what the organization publishes or who links to it. You don't want to spend time searching for a source from an organization that may be biased, have a profit motive, or be considered unreliable.

For biographic information about people, you can read the online *Biographical Dictionary* (see Chapter 61) or, in the library, *Who's Who in America* or the *Biography Index*. There may also be information about the person in the publication, such as a list of previous works, awards, and notes about the author. Your goal is to get some sense of who this person is and why it's worth reading what the author wrote before you plunge in and begin reading. That may be important as you write the paper and build your case. For example, if you are citing a source to document the spread of AIDS in Africa, which of these sentences strengthens your argument?

> Dr. John Smith notes that the incidence of AIDS in Africa has more than doubled in the last five years.

> (or)

> Dr. John Smith, head of the World Health Organization committee studying AIDS in African countries, notes that the incidence of AIDS in Africa has more than doubled in the last five years.

References

- Did a teacher, librarian, or other knowledgeable person about the topic mention this person or organization?

- Did you see the person or organization listed in other sources that you've already determined to be trustworthy?

When a person or group is an authority, you may find other references to the person or group. Decide whether this sources's viewpoint or knowledge of the topic is important to read.

Institution or Affiliation

- With what organization, institution, or company is the author associated? If the name is not easily identified, perhaps the group is less than reliable.

- What are this group's goals? Is there a bias or reason for the group to slant the truth in any way?

- Does the group monitor or review what is published under its name?

- Why might this group be trying to sell you something or convince you to accept its views? Do its members conduct objective, disinterested research? Are they trying to be sensational or attention-getting to enhance their own popularity or ratings?

2. Timeliness

- When was the source published? (For Web sites, look at the "last revised" date at the end of the page. If no date is available, are all the links still live?)

- Is that date current enough to be useful, or might the site contain outdated material?

- Is the source a revision of an earlier edition? If so, it is likely to be more current, and a revision indicates that the source is sufficiently valuable to revise. For a print source, check a library catalog or *Books in Print* to see whether you have the latest edition.

3. Publisher, Producer, or Sponsor

■ Who published or produced the material?

■ Is that publisher or sponsor reputable? For example, a university press or a government agency is likely to be a reputable source that reviews what it publishes.

■ Is the group recognized as an authority?

■ Is the publisher or group an appropriate one for this topic?

■ Might the publisher be likely to have a particular bias? (For example, a brochure printed by a right-to-life group is not going to contain much objective material on abortion.)

■ Is there any review process or fact-checking? (If a pharmaceutical company publishes data on a new drug it is developing, is there evidence of outside review of the data?)

4. Audience

■ Can you tell who the intended audience is? Is that audience appropriate for your purposes?

■ Is the material too specialized or too popular or brief to be useful? (A three-volume study of gene splitting is more than you need for a five-page paper on some genetically transmitted disease. In contrast, a half-page article on a visit to Antarctica won't tell you much about research into the melting of glaciers going on there.)

62d EVALUATING CONTENT

When you have decided to find the source and have it in hand or are linking to the Web site, you can evaluate the content by considering the following important criteria:

Accuracy. What reasons do you have to think that the facts are accurate? Do they agree with other information you've read? Are there sources for the data given?

Comprehensiveness. Is the topic covered in adequate depth, or is it too superficial or limited to only one aspect that overemphasizes only one part of the topic?

Credibility. Is the source of the material generally considered trustworthy? Does the source have a review process or do fact-checking? Is the author an expert? What are the author's credentials for writing about this topic? For example, is the article about personal perceptions of how bad this season's flu epidemic is, or is it a report by the Centers for Disease Control and Prevention?

Checklist

EVALUATING CONTENT

- Read the preface, introduction, or summary. What does the author want to accomplish?

- Browse through the links to other pages on the site or the table of contents and the index. Is the topic covered in enough depth to be helpful?

- Is there a list of references to show that the author has consulted other sources? Can the sources lead you to useful material?

- Are you the intended audience? Consider the tone, style, level of information, and assumptions the author makes about the reader. Are they appropriate to your needs? If there is advertising in the publication or on the Web site, it may help you determine the intended audience.

- Is the content of the source fact, opinion, or propaganda? If the material is presented as factual, are the sources of the facts clearly indicated? Do you think enough evidence is offered? Is the coverage comprehensive? (As you learn more about the topic, answering these questions will become easier.) Is the language emotional or objective?

- Are there broad, sweeping generalizations that overstate or simplify the matter?

- Does the author use a mix of primary and secondary sources (see 60a)?

- To determine accuracy, consider whether the source is outdated. Do some cross-checking. Do you find some of the same information elsewhere?

- Are there arguments that are one-sided with no acknowledgment of other viewpoints?

Fairness. If the author has a particular viewpoint, are differing views presented with some sense of fairness, or are opposing views presented as irrational or silly?

Objectivity. Is the language objective or emotional? Does the author acknowledge differing viewpoints? Are the various perspectives presented fairly? If you are reading an article in a magazine or in an online publication, do other articles in that source promote a particular viewpoint?

Relevance. How closely related is the material to your topic? Is it really relevant or merely related? Is it too general or too specific? too technical?

Timeliness. Is the information current enough to be useful? How necessary is timeliness for your topic?

Exercise 62.4 Evaluating Sources

Form a small group, and choose a controversial subject or one that you know causes people to feel strongly one way or another. If you wish, you may select from the following list:

Should high schools remove vending machines that sell junk food?

Should companies in the United States transfer jobs overseas so that they can pay workers less?

Are some U.S. goods produced under sweatshop conditions?

Should immigration to the United States be restricted?

Should people who download music without paying for it be prosecuted?

Is organic food really healthier than other food?

Should institutions have honor codes to curb cheating?

Should the minimum miles-per-gallon rates required for automobiles sold in the United States be increased?

Should fast-food restaurants be required to put ingredient and nutrition labels on their food containers?

Find several print sources, Web sites, and other online sources (such as material in a database) that discuss the subject you have selected, and use the suggestions and guidelines in this chapter to evaluate each source.

63

COLLECTING INFORMATION

When you find useful sources, you'll want to collect the information in a way that permits you to have an overview of what has been gathered, organize and use the information later as you write, and have the bibliographic information you'll need to document your sources. You can choose from several ways to do this:

■ Keep notes on a computer.

■ Annotate pages you print out or photocopy from sources.

■ Collect a working bibliography.

■ Write notecards.

This chapter describes all of these ways, but because everyone organizes and writes in different ways, you may find one or two of these methods more useful than the others.

Checklist

KEEPING YOUR RESEARCH NOTES ORGANIZED

When collecting information, you don't want to wind up with piles of disorganized notes, computer files, or printouts. The following strategies will help you keep your notes organized as you proceed.

- Divide your major topics into subtopics.

- Save researched articles from library databases or Web sites on a USB key, flash drive, disk, CD-ROM, or hard drive of your computer.

- Clearly label the name of each file to keep your articles organized. Save your research in separate file folders labeled by subtopic.

- Have some highlighters or colored pens handy so you can assign a color for each subtopic, and then color-code your printouts or card margins related to that subtopic.

- Be prepared to find that you need to add, change, or modify your subtopics as you learn more about the topic.

- Keep a "researcher's notepad" as ideas come to you, perhaps as you read various sources of information or while you're doing something entirely different (such as walking to class or waiting at a stoplight).

63a KEEPING NOTES

Many library databases allow you to download copies of articles directly to your computer or storage device (a flash drive or CD-ROM). You may also be able to download copies of Web pages or other materials that will be helpful as you construct your project. If you keep notes on your computer, consider creating different folders for each subtopic or issue. You may find that you'll need subfolders within various folders. When you find a potentially useful source that may not seem immediately relevant or doesn't fall into any of your subcategories, create another folder to collect such possible information. Try bookmarking Web sites that you want to come back to later.

Even if you don't keep your notes in computer files, consider organizing your topics and subtopics in a file that outlines the topics you plan to have. That will help as you sort out the piles of paper you collect, and if your topics or subtopics change, you can easily revise on the computer. As always, make a backup copy (on a CD-ROM, flash drive, USB key, or your iPod) of all work kept on your computer so that a computer crash won't cause you to lose all your work.

As you take notes about your research, clearly identify which passages are quoted, paraphrased, or summarized from your original sources to avoid accidental problems with plagiarism (see 64a and 64b for information about plagiarism).

As you write drafts of your paper, make new files or folders for each version (perhaps labeled "Draft 1—March 14" and "Draft 2—March 18"). This can help you monitor your progress as well as retrieve information from earlier drafts that might be useful later.

63b   PRINTING AND ANNOTATING PHOTOCOPIES AND PRINTOUTS

1. Printing Your Sources

A good way to keep track of your information is to print out Web pages and articles from library databases or photocopy pages from books and magazines. There are several advantages to having your own copies:

- You don't have to spend time in the library taking notes or writing notecards.
- Web sites can change or disappear; keeping copies permits you to refer to the source for more information as you write.
- You can annotate the pages and color-code the margins (a useful strategy for more efficient organizing later as you write).
- You can check the accuracy of a quotation, summary, or paraphrase when you edit a later draft.
- You can check the source to be sure you are not plagiarizing.
- Your instructor may ask you to submit copies of your research with your final draft.

2. Collecting Bibliographic Information

When you collect research material from print or online sources, record the following information so that you'll have it handy when you prepare your bibliography.

From a Book (see Figure 63.1)
- Library call number (or other information needed to locate the entry)
- Name of authors, editors, or translators
- Chapter title
- Title and subtitle of book
- Edition
- Publication information (city, publishing company name, date)
- Page numbers

CITING A BOOK

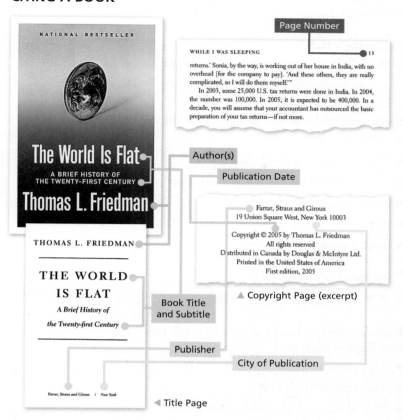

Page Number

WHILE I WAS SLEEPING   13

returns.' Sonia, by the way, is working out of her house in India, with no
overhead [for the company to pay]. 'And these others, they are really
complicated, so I will do them myself.'"
   In 2003, some 25,000 U.S. tax returns were done in India. In 2004,
the number was 100,000. In 2005, it is expected to be 400,000. In a
decade, you will assume that your accountant has outsourced the basic
preparation of your tax returns—if not more.

Author(s)

Publication Date

Farrar, Straus and Giroux
19 Union Square West, New York 10003

Copyright © 2005 by Thomas L. Friedman
All rights reserved
Distributed in Canada by Douglas & McIntyre Ltd.
Printed in the United States of America
First edition, 2005

▲ Copyright Page (excerpt)

THOMAS L. FRIEDMAN

THE WORLD
IS FLAT
A Brief History of
the Twenty-first Century

Book Title
and Subtitle

Publisher

City of Publication

Farrar, Straus and Giroux   /   New York

◀ Title Page

MLA Works Cited Format

Friedman, Thomas L. The World Is Flat: A Brief History of the Twenty-First
     Century. New York: Farrar, 2005.

APA References Format

Friedman, T. L. (2005). *The world is flat: A brief history of the twenty-first
     century.* New York: Farrar, Straus & Giroux.

MLA Parenthetical Citation Example

The growing number of American tax returns prepared in India each year is
reshaping the U.S. accounting industry (Friedman 13).

APA Parenthetical Citation Example

The growing number of American tax returns prepared in India each year is
reshaping the U.S. accounting industry (Friedman, 2005, p. 13).

Figure 63.1

Jacket design and excerpts from The World Is Flat: A Brief History of the Twenty-First Century [Updated and Expanded] *by Thomas L. Friedman. Copyright © 2005, 2006 by Thomas L.
Friedman. Reprinted by permission of Farrar, Straus and Giroux, LLC.*

Example in MLA Style

Mandelmann, Arthur. "Tomorrow's Ecological Needs." Living on Earth. Ed.

Steven Koppel and Anita Flanner. Boston: Stillman, 2002. 126-45.

From an Article in a Periodical (see Figure 63.2)

- Author's name
- Title and subtitle of article
- Title of magazine, journal, or newspaper
- Volume and issue numbers
- Date
- Page numbers

Example in MLA Style

Scheiber, Noam. "Race Against History." New Republic 31 May 2004: 18-24.

From an Article Located on a Library Database (see Figure 63.3)

- Author's name
- Title and subtitle of article
- Title of magazine, journal, or newspaper
- Volume and issue numbers
- Date
- Page numbers
- Name of database
- Name of corporate provider of database
- Name of library or library system, city, and state
- Date you accessed the article
- Home page or online access point for the database (usually the Web address up to the first slash)

Example in MLA Style

Rawe, Julie. "Why Teens Are Obsessed with Tanning." Time 7 Aug. 2006: 54.

Expanded Academic ASAP. Thomson Gale. Francis Marion U, Rogers

Lib., Florence, SC. 20 Jan. 2007 <http://find.galegroup.com>.

CITING A MAGAZINE ARTICLE

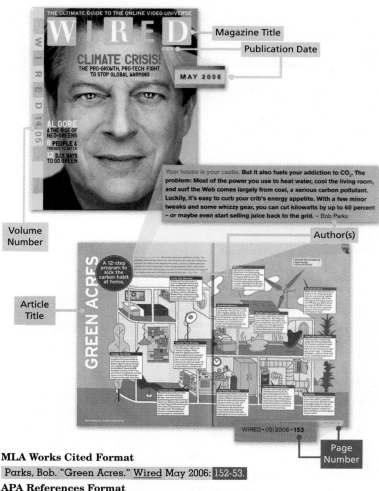

Magazine Title

Publication Date

Volume Number

Author(s)

Article Title

Your house is your castle. But it also fuels your addiction to CO_2. The problem: Most of the power you use to heat water, cool the living room, and surf the Web comes largely from coal, a serious carbon pollutant. Luckily, it's easy to curb your crib's energy appetite. With a few minor tweaks and some whizzy gear, you can cut kilowatts by up to 60 percent – or maybe even start selling juice back to the grid. – Bob Parks

WIRED · 05|2006 · 153

Page Number

MLA Works Cited Format

Parks, Bob. "Green Acres." Wired May 2006: 152-53.

APA References Format

Parks, B. (2006, May). Green acres. Wired, 14, 152–153.

MLA Parenthetical Citation Example

With some simple adjustments in power usage, homeowners "can cut kilowatts by up to 60 percent—or maybe even start selling juice back to the grid" (Parks 152).

APA Parenthetical Citation Example

With some simple adjustments in power usage, homeowners "can cut kilowatts by up to 60 percent—or maybe even start selling juice back to the grid" (Parks, 2006, p. 152).

Figure 63.2

Wired *May 2006 cover with coverlines, photo by Martin Schoeller and pp. 152–153 "Green Acres" illustration by Steen Guarnaccia, text by Robert Parks, corner graphic by Marcel Laverdet. Originally published in* Wired. *Copyright © 1996 by The Condé Nast Publications Inc. Reprinted by permission.*

CITING A MAGAZINE ARTICLE FROM A LIBRARY DATABASE

Service Provider | URL | Database Title | Article Title | Library and Library System

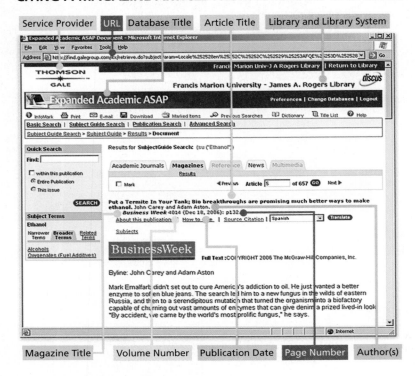

Magazine Title | Volume Number | Publication Date | Page Number | Author(s)

MLA Works Cited Format

Carey, John, and Adam Aston. "Put a Termite in Your Tank: Bio Breakthroughs
Are Promising Much Better Ways to Make Ethanol." Business Week 18 Dec.
2006: 132. Expanded Academic ASAP. Thomson Gale. Francis Marion U,
Rogers Lib., Florence, SC. 28 Jan. 2007 <http://find.galegroup.com/>.

▲ Date of Access

APA References Format

Carey, J., & Aston, A. (2006, December 18). Put a termite in your tank: Bio
breakthroughs are promising much better ways to make ethanol.
Business Week, 4014, 132.

MLA Parenthetical Citation Example
One researcher was looking for a way to make denim softer and ended up finding
a possible means of relieving our dependence on foreign oil (Carey and Aston).

APA Parenthetical Citation Example
One researcher was looking for a way to make denim softer and ended up finding
a possible means of relieving our dependence on foreign oil (Carey & Aston, 2006).

Figure 63.3
Screen shot of Thomson/Gale product Expanded Academic ASAP *database for libraries used
here with the permission of Thomson/Gale, a division of Thomson Learning. All rights reserved. Text and images may not be cut, pasted, altered, revised, modified, scanned, or
adapted in any way without the prior permission of the publisher: www.thomsonrights.com;
Courtesy of Paul Dove, Dean of the Library, Francis Marion University; Courtesy of Amy
Duernberger, DISCUS Program Director.*

From an Internet Source (see Figure 63.4)

- Author
- Title of document
- Information about any version of this in print form
- Title of the project, database, periodical, or Web site
- Date of electronic publication or last revision or update
- Name of organization that sponsors the site
- Date you accessed the site
- Exact Web address

Example in MLA Style

Oko, Dan. "Super Hot Skiing." <u>Salon</u> 26 Jan. 2007. 28 Jan. 2007 <http://
www.salon.com/news/feature/2007/01/26/skiing/index.html>.

3. Annotating Your Pages

When you print or photocopy a page, write notes on the page so that you
don't have to reread or shuffle through a stack of pages later when you are
trying to find information. You can note the bibliographic information by
circling or highlighting it if it's on the page or writing it in the top margin, and you can underline, highlight, or write short notes about the content. Across the top, you can also include a brief phrase to indicate the
information available on that page.

Hint

FORMATTING AS YOU GO

As you record bibliographic information, put it in the format you'll be
using for your bibliography. That way, as you finish your research paper
(especially if time is short), preparing your bibliography won't be a time-
consuming, stress-inducing task and you will avoid missing needed
information. (See Chapters 66, 67, and 68 for bibliographic formats.) If
you're taking notes or drafting on your computer, open a second window
to start a list of your Works Cited or References page entries.

CITING AN ARTICLE FROM AN INTERNET SOURCE

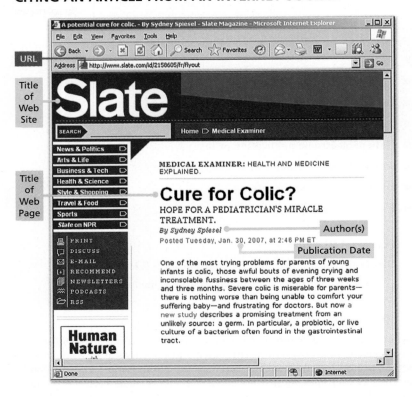

MLA Works Cited Format

Spiesel, Sydney. "Cure for Colic?" Slate 30 Jan. 2007. 1 Feb. 2007
   <http://www.slate.com/id/2158605/fr/flyout>.   ▲ Date of Access

APA References Format

Spiesel, S. (2007, January 30). Cure for colic? Slate. Retrieved from
   http://www.slate.com/id/2158605/fr/flyout

MLA Parenthetical Citation Example
One recent study suggests that probiotic bacteria may be effective in treating
colicky infants (Spiesel).

APA Parenthetical Citation Example
One recent study suggests that probiotic bacteria may be effective in treating
colicky infants (Spiesel, 2007).

Figure 63.4
*"Cure for Colic: Hope for a Pediatrician's Miracle Treatment" by Sidney Spiesel, Slate,
1/30/07. Reprinted by permission of Slate.com and Washington Post. Newsweek Interactive.
All rights reserved.*

63c STARTING A WORKING BIBLIOGRAPHY

As you begin to collect sources, build a working bibliography, a list of materials you plan to read. As you find additional suggestions for sources, add them to the list. This working list can include Web sites, books, magazines, journals, and other sources you may find. Then, as you write a draft of your paper, you can include the ones you're using in your final bibliography. Some of the materials listed in the working bibliography may not be used in your paper, so your working bibliography will be longer than your final bibliography. Use the suggestions in Chapter 62 to help evaluate the sources as you decide which you will read and use. See 63b2 for a list of the information you need for a bibliographic entry.

To keep your information organized, you can write each entry on a separate notecard and sort the cards alphabetically (see 63d), or you can build computer files of the entries you type in. As you print out Web pages, you may find they don't contain all of the information you will need for your working bibliography. If that is so, plan to spend some time searching for the missing information while you are looking at each Web page, such as the date of publication or last revision, the sponsoring organization, or whatever else is missing from the printout (see 63b). This will save you time later, and you won't have to hunt for a site that may have a new URL or may even have disappeared.

63d WRITING NOTECARDS

If your instructor asks you to keep notecards or you choose to do so, record your information on 3-by-5-inch or 4-by-6-inch cards. Note whether you're summarizing (see 64c), paraphrasing (see 64d), or recording a quotation (see 64e). Use brackets or parentheses or different-colored ink for your own comments on the significance of a source and your thoughts as to how you might use this source in your paper. It is best to limit each notecard to one short aspect of a topic so that you can rearrange the cards later as you organize the whole project. One way is to decide what the heading or subheading for this notecard will be. You can use the headings and subheadings of your outline or master list of all of your sources, and as you take more notes, new subheadings may occur to you.

On each notecard, record the last name of the author in the upper right-hand corner with a shortened form of the title. You can write the heading for the card's topic in the upper left-hand corner. As you write information on the card, include the exact page reference. If the note refers to more than one page in your source, indicate where the new page starts. For quotations, be sure that you've copied the original exactly. For information on how to document your sources for summaries, paraphrases, and quotations, see Chapters 66 through 68.

64
USING SOURCES AND AVOIDING PLAGIARISM

64a UNDERSTANDING WHY PLAGIARISM IS WRONG

Plagiarism results when a writer fails to document a source and presents the words and ideas of someone else as the writer's own work.

1. Plagiarism Is Stealing

To plagiarize is to include someone else's writing, information, or ideas in a paper and fail to acknowledge what you took by indicating whose work it is. By citing sources, we lead readers to the source of our information, but when we take information and don't indicate whose work it is that we are using, we are stealing. Plagiarism, then, is an unethical act. Students who present someone else's work as their own destroy the trust their audience members have in them.

2. Plagiarism Defeats the Purposes of Education

Professors assign papers because they want students to learn through the research and writing process. When we skip parts of the research and writing process and fail to cite sources, we have lost an opportunity to learn how and when to cite sources. Readers who want to find the information included in papers need correct documentation to help them locate what they want to know more about; therefore, they also lose when those citations are missing. It's a complicated process to document a source and smoothly integrate that source into our writing. So the more practice we have writing research papers, the better equipped we are to handle such writing later on.

Hint

UNDERSTANDING CULTURAL DIFFERENCES ABOUT PLAGIARISM

In some cultures, documenting sources is not very important. In other cultures, documenting something, particularly from a well-known work of literature, can be interpreted as an insult because it implies that the reader is not familiar with that work. In U.S. academic writing, however, it is very important to document sources. This may be a skill that is new or needs sharpening, but it is a vital skill.

3. Documenting Sources Responsibly Helps Writers Avoid Plagiarism and Build Credibility

Using another person's words or ideas in our writing is appropriate in writing research papers. Citing expert sources helps build both our credibility and the persuasiveness of our arguments, but we do have to let readers know where we found those words, ideas, and information during our research. A good writer is not indicating any weakness or lack of knowledge by citing a source. On the contrary, finding and combining information from other sources with our own comments on a topic is one of the primary goals of research writing.

Especially rewarding for writers who do not plagiarize is the sheer enjoyment—and sometimes a sense of triumph—of discovering new information or putting known information together in new ways. That's a personal type of growth. Moreover, when you add or create knowledge about a subject, you as a researcher and writer are contributing to the larger community's pool of knowledge. When you experience both the personal pleasure of discovery and the larger sense of sharing what you know, need to know, and want to know, you will realize that you have grown in important ways.

Hint

TERMS ASSOCIATED WITH PLAGIARISM

- **bibliography**—a list of all sources consulted during a research project
- **common knowledge**—a body of general ideas we share with our readers that does not have to be documented (see 64b1)
- **copyright**—a provision in U.S. law that protects original literary, artistic, musical, and intellectual work from unauthorized copying or distribution (see the Web site for the U.S. Copyright Office for more information: www.copyright.gov/circs/circ1.html)
- **parenthetical references**—in MLA and APA format, short citations in parentheses located throughout the body of a research paper to indicate (1) that certain words in the paper have been quoted, paraphrased, or summarized from other sources and (2) the sources in which the original words or ideas are located (see Chapter 66 for MLA format and Chapter 67 for APA format)
- **plagiarism**—the act of taking someone else's words, images, ideas, or intellectual property and presenting them as one's own (see 64a and 64b)
- **public domain**—phrase used to refer to works that are not granted or are no longer granted exclusive protection by copyright law

▶

- **References page**—in APA format, the bibliography page at the end of a research paper that lists every source quoted, paraphrased, or summarized in the body of the paper (see Chapter 67)
- **Works Cited**—in MLA format, the bibliography page at the end of a research paper that lists every source quoted, paraphrased, or summarized in the body of the paper (see Chapter 66)

4. Plagiarism Has Serious Consequences

The consequences of plagiarism are many (and very unpleasant). Some people regard plagiarism as a form of fraud, passing off as ours what is really someone else's work. Plagiarism can have legal consequences if the person who wrote the work you copied decides to sue you for violation of copyright or misuse of intellectual property. At colleges and universities, plagiarism is considered a violation of academic honesty and may result in a variety of penalties, including expulsion. Check your student handbook or campus policies to learn about penalties for plagiarism at your academic institution. The worst aspect of plagiarism, however, is what we lose in the process. When we plagiarize, we lose an important opportunity to learn something we need to know.

It is becoming ever easier to detect plagiarism on college campuses because in addition to instructors checking on phrases, sentences, and paragraphs on Google or another search engine, research paper software programs can easily detect bought or copied documents. Some universities purchase these software programs for use by instructors (some of whom may use the software in class to help students learn about plagiarism and to learn how to quote, summarize, and paraphrase from sources).

After college, plagiarism can cost you your job. A New England college president who did not acknowledge his sources in some of his public writing was forced to resign. In another case, a well-known journalist was fired when he copied the writing of others into his news reports without acknowledging the sources of that material. His reputation—as well as his job—was lost. His editor was also forced to step down for having permitted the fraud. In another situation, an applicant to Harvard Law School was denied admission when the admissions committee learned that she had once failed to document sources for an article in her local paper.

In the article "Market Widens for Tools to Uncover Plagiarism" in the *Houston Chronicle* on April 8, 2004, May Wong reports that "a growing number of newspapers, law firms, and other businesses are using data sorting tools that can cross-check billions of digital documents and swiftly recognize patterns in just seconds." Even military and police agencies, reports Wong, check officers' applications for promotions. In short, learning how to document is a very necessary skill we all need to have. We need to learn how to document sources while it's still an exercise we learn from—

before we lose a job, a reputation, or an opportunity because of a problem with plagiarism.

Plagiarism is tempting because it promises a falsely convenient way to avoid doing the necessary work (especially when time is limited because of other responsibilities) and because commercial online suppliers of term papers tempt us with the ease with which we can just buy a paper. In addition, as the deadline for an assigned research paper looms and our level of stress increases, it's sometimes hard to worry about documenting sources adequately at the last moment. Also, it's so easy to fall into the trap of cutting and pasting into our writing what we find on the Internet and not documenting what we lift off our computer screen. Inadequate note taking can cause last-minute confusion about which source was used or whether the notes in a computer file are our own or someone else's. So it's important at the start of the research process—before searching for information that will be used in the research paper—to think about how to avoid plagiarism and how to take careful notes (see Chapter 63 for strategies to use for note taking, and see the following checklist for tips to avoiding plagiarism as you write).

Checklist

AVOIDING PLAGIARISM

- Start your paper early, as soon as you get your assignment. Cases of plagiarism sometimes arise because students procrastinate (wait until the last minute) to start their papers and then panic because they feel as though they can't get them done in time. The best way to prevent these feelings is to start your paper early.

- Begin your research process early so you have enough time to read and understand your source material.

- Take notes as your read your source material. This will make it easier for you to remember passages to quote, paraphrase, or summarize and include in your paper.

- Indicate in your notes which passages are quoted, paraphrased, or summarized. You can do this by labeling them with a *Q, P,* or *S.*

- Record all URLs (Web addresses) of Web pages you use for research. This will make it easier for you to cite your sources and find information again if you need it later.

- Add information to your bibliography page every time you use a new source. This will help you make sure that you cite all of your sources properly in your paper.

- Ask your instructor or a writing center tutor for help if you are unsure about how to approach your assignment or how to cite your sources.

Exercise 64.1 Proofreading Practice

While doing research for a paper on unnecessary uses of fossil fuels, the writer recorded several lines from an outside source that might be useful. The writer then wrote the paragraph presented here. Highlight or underline the sentences or phrases in the writer's paragraph that should have been documented to avoid plagiarism.

Source
This is an excerpt from an article that the writer of the research paper read and recorded.

> Engines designed for regular fuel don't improve on premium and sometimes run worse. And today's engines designed for premium run fine on regular, too, their makers say, though power declines slightly.
>
> But premium lovers are passionate. "I would rather simply curtail driving rather than switch grades," says Bill Teater of Mount Vernon, Ohio, who put high-test in both his Cadillacs, though only one recommends it. He's sure both the DeVille and the Escalade run rough and lack pep on regular.
>
> Prejudice and preference aside, engineers, scientists and the federal government say there's little need for premium.

> Work Cited
>
> Healy, James. "Why Use Premium Gas When Regular Will Do?" USA Today 30 July 2003. 11 Apr. 2004 <http://www.usatoday.com/money/autos/2003-07-30-premiumgas_x.htm>.

Writer's Paragraph
This is a paragraph from the final research paper.

> Many drivers prefer to put premium gas in their tank because they think they will get better mileage or more power from their car engines. They may also be following instructions in their owner's manual. Also, they want to avoid engine knock. So when they go to the gas station, they often choose premium gas without realizing they don't require that extra octane. Too many drivers today are paying unnecessarily high prices for premium gas when their cars don't need it. In fact, engineers, scientists, and the federal government say there's little need for premium. Engines designed for regular fuel don't improve on premium and sometimes run worse. In addition, today's engines designed for premium run fine on

regular, too, their makers say, though power declines slightly. When drivers want to save money, it's wise to ignore the ads and get regular octane gas instead.

Exercise 64.2 Revision Practice

Revise the writer's paragraph in Exercise 64.1 so that it contains the documentation that should have been included. Use either MLA or APA format (see Chapters 66 and 67).

Exercise 64.3 Learning About Plagiarism Policies

To help you think about how plagiarism is described, read a few statements on plagiarism, beginning with your school's statement, the statement developed by the Writing Program Administrators organization (http://wpacouncil.org/files/WPAplagiarism.pdf), and similar ones available on the Web written for other colleges. (See the Web site for this book for some URLs.) Consider the similarities and differences among these statements, and describe them in a paragraph or two. What do you think might account for differences?

64b RECOGNIZING PLAGIARISM AND DOCUMENTING SOURCES RESPONSIBLY

The implications of plagiarism are explained in 64a; this section will help you recognize and avoid it as you write. This is especially important if you come from another country or culture where copying the words of others is a school exercise or where there is a strong sense of all property being communal. In some cultures, educated writers are expected to know and incorporate the thinking of great scholars, and it may be considered an insult to the reader to mention the names of those scholars, implying that the reader is not acquainted with these scholarly works. However, in the United States, this is not the case, and writers are always expected to acknowledge their sources and give public credit to the appropriate person or group. Moreover, publishing copyrighted material without authorization is a violation of U.S. copyright law.

Material on the Internet is so easily downloaded that it's not always apparent when working with your notes that the information you have collected comes from a source that needs to be cited. Despite this, you need to learn when to acknowledge your sources as you summarize, paraphrase, or quote the words of others.

Hint

UNDERSTANDING THE THREE TYPES OF PLAGIARISM

Plagiarism occurs in three ways, and it is helpful to keep these in mind as you check your work to be sure you haven't plagiarized.

■ Using someone's exact words without putting quotation marks around the words and without citing the source.

■ Changing another person's words into your own words by paraphrasing or summarizing without citing the source. (Putting information you find into your own words without citing the source is perhaps the most common pitfall that results in plagiarism.)

■ Stating ideas or research specifically attributed to another person or persons without citing the source. However, information and ideas that are widely known and agreed on are considered common knowledge and do not need to have a documented source (see 64b1).

1. Common Knowledge: Information That Does Not Require Documentation

Common knowledge, that body of general ideas we share with our readers, does not have to be documented. Common knowledge consists of standard information on a subject that many people know, information that is widely shared and can be found in numerous sources without reference to any source. This applies to common historical information. For example, it is common knowledge that the Declaration of Independence was adopted in 1776 and that George Washington was the first U.S. president. This also applies to common physical or scientific facts, such as the fact that the earth is the third planet from the sun and the fact that water is composed of hydrogen and oxygen molecules. Specific details or statistics about these topics might not be considered common knowledge, however, and you should provide proper documentation to show where the ideas or study results came from.

Common knowledge may also include more specific ideas or concepts, depending on the expertise of the audience with whom you are sharing information. For example, if your audience is composed of educators, it's common knowledge among this group that U.S. schoolchildren aren't well acquainted with geography. However, if you cite test results documenting the extent of the problem or use the words and ideas of a knowledgeable person about the causes of the problem, that is not common knowledge and needs documentation. Similarly, it is common knowledge among most Americans that solar power is one answer to future energy needs. However, forecasts about how widely solar power may be used twenty years from now would be the work of some person or group studying the subject, and documentation would be needed. As one more example, a popular topic on television is that obesity is a widespread health problem in the United States. A statement to that effect does not need to be documented, but if you're writing about the occurrence of obesity and find statistics for various segments of the population, the source must be cited. Common knowledge also consists of facts widely available in a variety of standard reference books.

Field research you conduct also does not need to be documented, though you should indicate that you are reporting your own findings. If you quote someone you interviewed, you do need to document how you conducted the interview (personal interview, e-mail message, phone), the person's name, and the date of the interview or exchange. If you're reporting the results of your own study or survey, you should explain when and how the study or survey took place.

2. Information That Requires Documentation

When we use the ideas, findings, data, conclusions, arguments, and words of others, we need to acknowledge that we are borrowing their work and inserting it in our own by documenting it. If you are arguing for a particular viewpoint and find someone who expresses that viewpoint, you may want to include it. That, of course, will require that you document who that person is and where you found that source.

Avoiding Plagiarism: An Example

Original Source
One of the most obvious—and most important—approaches to saving rainforests is to protect them in national parks, the same way that industrialized nations such as the United States and Canada safeguard their tropical wonders. Yet so far fewer than 5 percent of the world's tropical forests are included in parks or other kinds of protected areas. Most of the developing countries that house these forests simply do not have enough money to buy land and set up park systems. And many of the nations that do establish parks are then unable to pay park rangers to protect the land. These unprotected parks routinely are invaded by poor, local people who desperately need the forest's wood, food, land, or products to sell. The areas are often called "paper parks" because they exist on paper but not in reality.

(Tangley, Laura. *The Rainforest: Earth at Risk.* New York: Chelsea, 1992. 105–06.)

Accidental (and Unacceptable) Plagiarism
The problem of saving the world's rainforests has become a matter of great public concern. There are a number of solutions being offered, but the most obvious and most important approach is to protect them in national parks. This is the same way that industrialized nations such as the United States and Canada safeguard their natural wonders. In poorer nations, this does not work because they do not have enough money to buy land and set up park systems. What happens is that when they don't have money, they are unable to pay park rangers to protect the land. Without any protection of the land

Checklist

CHECKING YOUR WORK FOR PLAGIARISM

▪ Read your paper and ask yourself whether your readers can properly identify which ideas and words are yours and which are from the sources you cite. Make sure that you cite all of the ideas that aren't your own and aren't considered common knowledge.

▪ Check to make sure your paper isn't a string of quotations from your sources. Even though you're using research and ideas from other sources, you should still show your authority in the paper. Try paraphrasing some ideas, but use parenthetical citations to show where your ideas came from.

▪ Consider whether your paper predominantly reflects your words, phrases, and integration of ideas. Check to see whether your thesis provides unity to the ideas expressed in the full paper. Also check your topic sentences to make sure they provide unity to the ideas presented in your paragraphs.

▪ Make sure that all of the sources on your Works Cited or References page are referenced in the body of the paper and vice versa. To do this, read your paper. Every time you come across a parenthetical reference, check off that source on your Works Cited or References page. At the end of your paper, all of the sources on your Works Cited page should be checked off. If you have some that aren't checked, see whether you need to insert corresponding parenthetical references or whether the sources need to be removed from the Works Cited page. If you find that you parenthetically refer to sources that aren't on your Works Cited page, add them to your list.

by rangers, poor people come in and invade because they <u>desperately need the forest's wood, food, land, or products to sell</u>. These parks then don't really exist as parks.

[In this paragraph the words, phrases, and ideas from the original source are underlined. Note how much of this paraphrase comes from the original source and how the author has neglected to signal to the reader that this material comes from another source.]

Acceptable Paraphrase
The problem of saving the world's rainforests has become a matter of great public concern. Of the approaches being considered, Laura Tangley, in *The Rainforest,* considers one of the most important solutions to be turning rainforests into national parks. Tangley points out, however, that this is a solution only for industrialized nations such as the United States and

Canada because they have the funding to keep national parks protected from poachers. In developing nations that cannot afford park rangers, the local populations are not prevented from taking wood, food, land, or forest products that they can sell. Tangley states that such forests, because they are not protected from human destruction, "exist on paper but not in reality" (106).

Exercise 64.4 Proofreading for Plagiarism

In the following paragraph, the writer has included some material that should have been documented. Highlight or underline the sentence or sentences you suspect need to have documentation.

Many students today wonder if a college education is really worth the effort and expense. Tuition has gone up over the last few years, and many students need to work or take out loans if their parents cannot help fund their college years. However, a college education is definitely worth its cost in terms of both learning more about the world and earning a higher income later. College offers students the opportunity to learn about many different subjects such as history, philosophy, biology, and business management, and having a college education can result in being better off financially later on. While the average student leaves college roughly $17,000 in debt, he or she will make roughly $1 million more over a lifetime than someone who has not gone to college. So while no one wants to graduate and face a large debt that has to be paid off, that college degree will help the person earn much more and also pay off that debt.

Exercise 64.5 Practice Citing Sources

Add citations in MLA format to the following paragraph, which incorporates material from the two sources listed here, and attach a Works Cited list. For information on parenthetical citations and references in MLA format, see Chapter 66.

■ Quotations from the essay titled "Rethinking Urban Transport" in the book *State of the World, 2001* by Marcia D. Lowe, published in New York City in 2002 by W. W. Norton

"Cities with streets designed for cars instead of people are increasingly unlivable" (56).

"Traffic congestion, now a fact of life in major cities, has stretched rush hours to 12 hours or longer in Seoul and 14 in Rio de Janeiro. In 1989, London traffic broke a record with a 53-kilometer backup of cars at a near standstill" (57).

"Roaring engines and blaring horns cause distress and hypertension, as in downtown Cairo, where noise levels are 10 times the limit set by health and safety standards" (57).

- Quotations from the book *Planning for a Livable Tomorrow* by Irwin Lipperman, published in New York City in 1992 by Nathanson Press

    "City space is rapidly being eaten up by automobiles. Parking in a city center can use up to 20% or 30% of the available space, and suburban malls often have parking lots bigger than the malls themselves" (99).

    "Automobile pollutants in the air inhaled by urbanites increase the likelihood of lung disorders and make bronchial problems more severe, especially among the elderly" (108).

- Student paragraph from a research paper on the topic of city planning

    Another important concern in city planning is to formulate proposals to eliminate or reduce problems caused by automobiles. Cities with streets designed for cars instead of people are increasingly unlivable, for cars cause congestion, pollution, and noise. Providing more public transportation can reduce these problems, but it is not likely that city dwellers will give up owning cars. Therefore, solutions are needed for parking, which already uses up as much as 20 to 30 percent of the space available in downtown areas, and for rush hour traffic, which now extends to more than twelve hours in Seoul and to fourteen hours in Rio de Janeiro. Pollution, another urban problem caused partly by cars, needs to be controlled. Automobile emissions cause lung disorders and aggravate bronchial problems. In addition, noise from automobiles must be curbed. Noise has already become a health problem in cities such as Cairo, where noise levels are already ten times the acceptable standard for human health.

64c SUMMARIZING WITHOUT PLAGIARIZING

A **summary** is a brief restatement of the main ideas in a source, using your own words.

As you write, you will want to include summaries of other people's writing when you refer to their ideas but do not wish to use a direct quote. Good reasons for using summaries are that the source has unnecessary detail, the writer's phrasing is not particularly memorable, and you want to keep your writing concise. When you include a summary, you need to cite the source to give credit to the writer. (See Chapters 66, 67, and 68 for information on how to cite your sources and 64a and 64b on what plagiarism is and how to avoid it.) Unlike paraphrases (see 64d), summaries are shorter than the original source because they include only the main points of the source.

Checklist

IDENTIFYING CHARACTERISTICS OF SUMMARIES

- Summaries are written in your own words, not copied from your source.
- Summaries include only the main points, omitting details, facts, examples, illustrations, direct quotations, and other specifics.
- Summaries use fewer words than the source being summarized.
- Summaries are objective and do not include your own interpretation or reflect your slant on the material.

To write a summary, follow these steps:

1. Read the original source carefully and thoughtfully.
2. After the first reading, ask yourself what the author's major point is.
3. Go back and reread the source, making a few notes in the margin.
4. Look away from your source, and then, like a newscaster, panelist, or speaker reporting to a group, finish the sentence: "This person is saying that . . ."
5. Write down what you've just said.
6. Go back and reread both the source and your notes in the margins to check that you've correctly remembered and included the main points.
7. Revise your summary as needed.

Summary: An Example

Original Source

As human beings have populated the lands of the earth, we have pushed out other forms of life. It seemed to some that our impact must stop at the ocean's edge, but that has not proved to be so. By overharvesting the living bounty of the sea and by flushing the wastes and by-products of our societies from the land into the ocean, we have managed to impoverish, if not destroy, living ecosystems there as well.

(Thorne-Miller, Boyce, and John G. Catena. *The Living Ocean: Understanding and Protecting Marine Biodiversity*. Washington: Island, 1991. 3–4.)

Unacceptable Summary

Humans have populated the lands of the earth, but by overharvesting the bounty of the sea and flushing the wastes of our societies into the ocean, they are destroying sea life.

[Long stretches of text in this example are taken directly from the original source and could be considered plagiarized. This example is also lacking a parenthetical reference.]

Acceptable Summary

People have destroyed numerous forms of life on land and are now doing the same with oceans. Overfishing and dumping waste products into the waters have caused the destruction of various forms of ocean life (Thorne-Miller and Catena 3-4).

64d PARAPHRASING WITHOUT PLAGIARIZING

A **paraphrase** restates information from a source, using your own words.

Checklist

IDENTIFYING CHARACTERISTICS OF PARAPHRASES

- A paraphrase has approximately the same number of words as the source. (A summary, by contrast, is much shorter.)
- Paraphrases use your own words, not those of the source.
- Paraphrases are more detailed than summaries.
- Paraphrases are objective and do not include your own interpretation or slant on the material.

Unlike a summary (see 64c), a paraphrase is approximately the same length as the source and contains more detail than a summary would. To write a paraphrase, follow these steps:

1. Read the original passage as many times as is needed to understand its full meaning.
2. As you read, take notes, using your own words, if that helps.
3. Put the original source aside and write a draft of your paraphrase, using your notes if needed.
4. Check your version against the original source by rereading the original to be sure you've included all the ideas from the source.
5. If you find a phrase worth quoting in your own writing, use quotation marks in the paraphrase to identify your borrowing, and note the page number.

Paraphrase: An Example

Original Source

Nationally, women's enrollment began to overtake men's in the early 1980's. In the last couple of years, the gap has widened enough to alarm state education boards, researchers, and higher-education policy wonks, who worry that men are falling behind even as women are succeeding.

Colleges are responding by trying to entice more young men to enroll—adding engineering programs and football teams, changing the color palette of their admissions brochures from pastel to primary, and quietly tweaking their standards to give male applicants a leg up. The gender gap is already changing classroom dynamics, rerouting social relationships, and paving a dangerous path toward a lopsided future, say some policy analysts.

(Wilson, Robin. "The New Gender Divide." *The Chronicle of Higher Education* 26 Jan. 2007: A36–A39.)

Unacceptable Paraphrase

There is an increasing gap between the number of men and women attending college. This gap has widened enough to worry state education boards, researchers, and higher-education policy wonks. Colleges are trying to entice more young men to enroll. To grab men's attention, they are adding engineering programs and football teams. They are also tweaking their admissions standards. This gap is affecting classroom dynamics and social relationships, making a dangerous path toward a lopsided future.

[This example contains many long stretches of text that are taken directly from the original source. The language and sentence structure of this example are too close to the original text and could be considered plagiarized. This example is also missing a parenthetical reference.]

Unacceptable Paraphrase

Across the nation, female enrollment began to take over men's in the early 1980s. Recently, the divide has broadened enough to distress state education boards, researchers, and higher-education policymakers, who are concerned that males are dropping behind even as females are succeeding. Colleges are answering by working to attract more men—adding engineering programs and football teams, changing the colors of admissions brochures, and quietly changing standards to give male applicants a leg up. The gender gap is already altering classrooms, changing social relationships, and creating a negative path for the future (Wilson A36).

[The language and sentence structure of this example are too close to the original text and could be considered plagiarized.]

Acceptable Paraphrase

Policymakers and educational specialists are increasingly concerned about the decrease in the number of males enrolling in college, noting that the disparity in the percentages of men and women in college is beginning to reshape academic environments and may have adverse consequences in coming years. To reverse this trend, several colleges have adjusted their admissions standards, adopted male-oriented marketing strategies, and started new athletic programs in efforts to increase the number of men attending their institutions (Wilson A36).

[The main ideas of the original are communicated here in the writer's own language and sentence structures. A parenthetical citation indicates where the ideas originally came from.]

Exercise 64.6 Paraphrasing and Summarizing Practice

Rewrite each of the following paragraphs, first as a summary of the content and then as a paraphrase. Cite your sources appropriately.

Original Source

This winter, a sparkling diamond landed in front of a technician at the Gemological Institute of America in New York City. He ran tests, noted the stone was man-made, and graded it as he would any diamond. It was the gem industry's strongest acknowledgment yet that lab-grown diamonds are just as real as natural ones.

For years, De Beers, the world's largest purveyor of natural diamonds, argued against the acceptance and GIA grading of lab-grown stones. But since 2003, synthetic diamond production has taken off, driven by consumer demand for merchandise that's environmentally friendly (no open-pit mines), sociopolitically neutral (no blood diamonds), and monopoly-free (not controlled by De Beers). As a result, Gemesis, the leading manufacturer of gem-quality diamonds, has expanded operations rapidly. Three years ago, the company had 24 diamond-producing machines; now it has hundreds—matching the cash-value output of a small mine—and is turning on a new one every other day. "At this point, we operate like any other mine," says Clark McEwen, COO of Gemesis. "We produce rough diamonds in our machines and sell to distributors who do the cutting and polishing."

(Davis, Joshua. "Lab-Grown Diamonds Make the Cut." *Wired* February 2007: 40.)

64e USING QUOTATION MARKS TO AVOID PLAGIARIZING

A **quotation** is the record of the exact words of a written or spoken source, indicated by surrounding the words with quotation marks.

Every quotation should be accompanied by a citation acknowledging its source.

1. When to Quote

Follow these guidelines for using quotations effectively.

- Use quotations as evidence, as support, or as further explanation of what you have written. Quotations are not substitutes for stating your point in your own words.

- Use quotations sparingly. Too many quotations strung together with very little of your own writing makes a paper look like a scrapbook of pasted-together sources, not a thoughtful integration of what is known about a subject. (See 64f on integrating sources into your writing.)

- Use quotations that illustrate the author's own viewpoint or style, or quote excerpts that would not be as effective if rewritten in different words. Effective quotations are succinct or particularly well phrased.
- Introduce quotations with words that signal the relationship of the quotation to the rest of your discussion (see 64f).

Checklist

DETERMINING WHEN TO USE QUOTATIONS

- Quote when the writer's words are especially vivid, memorable, or expressive.
- Quote when an expert explains so clearly and concisely that a paraphrase would be less clear or would contain more words. Quoting can also help you emphasize the expertise or authority of your source.
- Quote when the words the source uses are important to the discussion.

Original Source Worth Quoting
When asked to comment on the recent investigations of government fraud, Senator Smith said to a *New York Times* reporter, "Their ability to undermine our economy is exceeded only by their stupidity in thinking that they wouldn't get caught."

("Fraud Hearings." *New York Times* 18 Nov. 2003, late ed.: A4.)

[This statement is worth quoting because restating it in different words would probably take more words and have less punch.]

Original Source Worth Paraphrasing
When asked in a television interview to comment on the recent investigations of government fraud, Senator Smith said, "These huge payments for materials that should have cost less will now cost the government money because they will increase our budget deficit more than we anticipated."

(Smith, Saul. Interview with Nina Totenberg. *Nightline*. ABC. WILI, Chicago. 23 Nov. 2003.)

[This statement is a good candidate for paraphrasing, with a reference to Senator Smith, because the statement is not particularly concise, well phrased, or characteristic of a particular person's way of saying something.]

Acceptable Paraphrase
During a televised interview, Senator Smith responded to a question about investigations of government fraud by noting that overpayments on materials will cause an unexpected increase in the budget deficit.

2. How to Quote

When you quote, use the exact words of the original source. Place the entire quotation within quotation marks, and use a parenthetical reference to give credit to your source.

Original Source
Markets work best when people make independent decisions about how much a commodity—in this case, a C.E.O.—is worth. They stop working well when people simply imitate what others are doing, or when non-market factors (like how well you get along with the boss) intrude. In the end, the very things that make people likely to join a board—connections, business experience, sociability—are also the things that make them less effective once they do.

(Surowiecki, James. "The Sky-High Club." *The New Yorker* 22 Jan. 2007: 32.)

[This article looks at the culture of corporate executive boards and the very high salaries given to some chief executive officers of major companies.]

Unacceptable Quotation
Some people criticize the high salaries some corporate executives receive, stating the very things that make people likely to join a board—connections, business experience, sociability—are also the things that make them less effective once they do.

[The quoted material is not placed inside quotation marks, and no parenthetical citation is used to indicate the original source. This is a plagiarized passage.]

Unacceptable Quotation
New Yorker writer James Surowiecki criticizes the high salaries some corporate executives receive, stating, "In the end, the things that make people likely to join a board make them less effective once they do."

[The material inside the quotation marks is not taken word for word from the original source. Ellipses should be inserted to indicate omitted words (see 64e5). Also, a parenthetical citation should be added to indicate the page number.]

Acceptable Quotation
New Yorker writer James Surowiecki criticizes the astronomical salaries some corporate executives earn despite their lackluster work performance, stating, "In the end, the very things that make people likely to join a board—connections, business experience, sociability—are also the things that make them less effective once they do" (32).

[The quotation is introduced effectively, and the material inside the quotation marks is taken word for word from the original source. A parenthetical citation indicates the page on which this quotation can be found in Surowiecki's article.]

3. Types of Quotations

Quoting Prose

Short quotations   If your quotation runs to no more than four typed lines, make it part of your paragraph and use quotation marks around it (see 42a).

> During the summer of 1974, at a crucial stage of development in the Apollo program, national interest in NASA was sharply diverted by the Watergate affair. As Joseph Trento, an investigative reporter, explains in his book on the Apollo program, "The nation was sitting on the edge of its collective seat wondering if Richard Nixon would leave us in peace or pull the whole system down with him" (142).

(Trento, Joseph. *Prescription for Disaster.* New York: Crown, 1987.)

Long quotations (block quotations)   If the quotation is more than four typed lines, set it off by indenting one inch or ten spaces from the left margin in MLA style (one-half inch or five spaces in APA style). Double-space the quotation, and do not use quotation marks.

> In his book on the Apollo and space shuttle programs, Joseph Trento reports on the final mission in the Apollo program:
>
> > The last mission involving the Apollo hardware nearly ended in tragedy for the American crew. After reentry the crew opened a pressure release valve to equalize the command module atmosphere with the earth's atmosphere. But the reaction control rockets failed to shut down, and deadly nitrogen tetroxide oxydizer gas entered the cabin's breathing air. The crew survived the incident, but some at Houston and in Washington wondered if the layoff from manned flight hadn't put the crew at risk. (144)

(Trento, Joseph. *Prescription for Disaster.* New York: Crown, 1987.)

Quoting Poetry

If you are quoting from a poem, follow the guidelines in 42a2.

Quoting Dialogue

If you are quoting the speech of two or more people who are talking, start a new paragraph for each change of speaker (see 42a3).

4. Capitalization of Quotations

Capitalize the first word of directly quoted speech in the following situations:

- When the first quoted word begins a sentence

  She said, "He likes to talk about football, especially when the Super Bowl is coming up."

■ When the words in the dialogue are a fragment

"He likes to talk about football," she said. "Especially when the Super Bowl is coming up."

Don't capitalize quoted speech in the following situations:

■ When the first quoted word is not the beginning of a sentence

She said that he likes talking about football, "especially when the Super Bowl is coming up."

■ When the quotation is interrupted and then continues in the same sentence

"He likes to talk about football," she said, "especially when the Super Bowl is coming up."

5. Punctuation of Quotations

Comma

When you introduce a quotation, use a comma after expressions such as *he said, she asked,* or *Brady wrote.*

As R. F. Notel explains, "The gestures people use to greet each other differ greatly from one culture to another."

When the quotation follows *that,* do not use a comma and do not capitalize the first letter of the first word in the quotation.

The public relations director noted that "newsletters to alumni are the best source of good publicity—and donations."

Colon

Use the colon to introduce a quotation that follows a complete sentence or is displayed as a block quotation (see 64e3).

The selection of juries has become a very complex and closely researched process. Henry Wang, a leading market research analyst, shares an interesting insight: "In addition to employing social scientists, some lawyers now practice beforehand with 'shadow juries,' groups of twelve people demographically similar to an actual jury" (94).

(Wang, Henry. "Marketing's Invasion of Our Legal System." *Today's Marketing* 15 Mar. 2004: 90–115.)

End Punctuation

Put periods before the closing quotation marks. If the quotation contains an exclamation point or a question mark, include that before the closing quotation marks. However, if an exclamation point or question mark is needed as part of the sentence but is not part of the quotation, put the mark after the closing quotation marks.

Matt explained, "I didn't mean to upset her."

The stage director issued his usual command to the actor: "Work with me!"

Did she really say, "I quit"?

Brackets

Occasionally, you may need to add some information within a quotation, insert words to make the quotation fit your sentence, or indicate with *sic* that you are quoting your source exactly even though you recognize an error there. When you insert any words within the quotation, set off your words with brackets (see 45d).

> "During President Carter's administration, Press [Frank Press, Carter's science adviser] indicated his strong bias against funding applied research" (Milltek 220).

> (Milltek, Steffen. "Science Suffers from Political Disinterest." *Research Quarterly* 36.2 [2002]: 218–27.)

Ellipsis (for Omitted Words)

When you omit words from a quotation, use an ellipsis (three spaced periods) to indicate that material has been left out (see 45e).

Original Source
Contributing editors are people whose names are listed on the masthead of a magazine but who are usually not on the staff. Basically, they're freelance writers with a good track record of producing ideas and articles prolifically.

(Truf, Leon. *Journalism Today.* Boston: Nottingham, 2001. 72.)

Use of Quotation
Not all the names listed on the masthead of a magazine are regular staff members. Some, as Truf explains, are freelancers who have "a good track record of producing . . . articles prolifically" (72).

Single Quotation Marks for Words Originally Quoted in Another Source

When you are enclosing a quotation within a quotation, use a single quotation mark (the apostrophe on a keyboard) before and after the embedded quotation. In MLA citation style, add the words *qtd. in* to your parenthetical reference to show that the words were originally quoted in another source.

> When describing a new antibiotic-resistant strain of bacteria infecting injured American troops in Iraq, Arjun Srinivasan, an epidemiologist with the Centers for Disease Control, stated, "'These bacteria are developing very,

very quickly. . . . The bad news is that we're many years away from having new drugs to treat them. It should be a call to arms'" (qtd. in Silberman 136).

(Silberman, Steve. "The Invisible Enemy." *Wired* Feb. 2007: 132+.)

For more information on the use of punctuation with quotation marks, see 42d.

64f USING SIGNAL WORDS AND PHRASES TO INTEGRATE SOURCES

When you summarize, paraphrase, or quote from outside sources in your writing, you need to identify each source and explain its connection to what you are writing about. You can do this by using signal words. Because signal words tell the reader what to expect or how to interpret the material in advance, they help you integrate the material smoothly and seamlessly into your writing. If you don't do this, readers will feel a bump when the writing moves from your words to those of the source material. It's also possible that the reader will not fully understand or appreciate what the source is adding to your writing. Moreover, without signal words, you as the writer lose control of the paper if the sources seem to dominate your own voice.

To create smooth transitions and use sources effectively, consider the following suggestions.

■ *Explain how the source material is connected to the rest of the paragraph.* Always show your readers the connection between the reference and the point you are making. Introduce the material by showing a logical link, or add a follow-up comment that integrates a quotation into your paragraph.

Although most experts predict that high-definition television will not replace the current system in the near future, one spokesperson for the electronics industry says that global competition will force this sooner than most people anticipate: "American consumers aren't going to settle for the old technology when they travel abroad and see the brilliant clarity of high-definition television now available in other countries" (Marklen 7).

■ *Use the name of the source and, if appropriate, that person's credentials as an authority.*

The treatment of osteoporosis usually includes medications to improve bone density, but Dr. Matthew Benjamin, head of the Department of Osteoporosis Research at the University of Ottawa, warns that the most commonly prescribed medications also have potentially dangerous side effects that have not been adequately studied.

■ *Use a verb to indicate the source's stance or attitude toward what is quoted.* Does the source think the statement is very important

("Professor Mehta *stressed* . . .")? take a position on an issue ("The senator *argued* . . .)? remain neutral about what is stated ("The researcher *reported* . . .")? When writing about literature and most other humanities subjects, use the present tense. Science writers generally use present tense verbs, except when writing about research that has been completed ("When studying the effects of constant illumination on corn seedlings, Jenner *found* that . . .").

Although many automobile owner's manuals state that only premium gas should be used, Martin Messing, a consulting engineer for the Mobil Oil Company, points out that he personally uses regular gas in his car, despite what his owner's manual says (90). Messing maintains that he sees no difference in the performance of his car, despite the recomendation that he should use premium. Auto engineer Luis Montenegro, who works for the federal government, explains that "the main advantage of premium-grade gas is that automobile manufacturers can advertise that the new model of their automobile has a few more horsepower than older models" ("Auto Performance" 136).

■ *Limit the use of quotations.* When a paragraph has a string of quotations and references to source material connected by a few words from the writer, the writer has lost control of the paper and abandoned it to the voices and opinions of other writers. The result can seem like a cut-and-paste scrapbook of materials from other people. A few good quotations, used sparingly and integrated smoothly, will be much more effective.

■ *Use signal words and phrases with quotations.* When you are quoting from sources, use words and phrases that prepare your reader for the quotation that will follow and that add smooth transitions from your words to the quotation.

■ *Be sure each source is included in your list of works cited.* (See Chapters 66, 67, and 68.)

Signal Phrases

It is often effective to use the author's name in the phrase that introduces the quotation. The phrase helps the quotation fit neatly into the discussion.

As the film critic Leon Baberman has noted, ". . ." (43).

Maya Moon answers her critics by saying, ". . ." (9).

Dr. Rahmo Milwoicz clarifies this point succinctly when he writes, ". . ." (108).

". . . ," as Luanne Yah explains, ". . ." (36).

According to J. S. Locanno, an expert in restoring prairie land, ". . ." (27).

In his personal journals, Churchill often deplored . . . (49).

Despite strong opposition, Millard has steadfastly maintained that . . . (72).

The Consumer Safety Bureau has recently revealed the results of . . . (144).

The animal rights activists repeatedly condemn the use of . . . (90).

After studying the noise in the engine, the mechanic concluded that . . . (63).

When lawyers for the defense questioned Emilie Maynard on the witness stand, she conceded that . . . (18).

Try This

TO INTRODUCE QUOTED, PARAPHRASED, OR SUMMARIZED WORDS

To add variety to the verbs you use, try using the following signal words:

acknowledges	condemns	points out
adds	considers	predicts
admits	contends	proposes
advises	denies	rejects
agrees	describes	reports
argues	disagrees	responds
asks	emphasizes	reveals
asserts	explains	says
believes	finds	shows
claims	holds	speculates
comments	insists	suggests
complains	maintains	thinks
concedes	notes	warns
concludes	observes	writes

Although it is hard to predict the future of the toy industry, Robert Lillo, a senior analyst at the American Economics Institute, warns that "the bottom may fall out of the electronic game industry as CD-ROMs gobble up that market with cheaper, more elaborate products with better graphics" (21).

(Lillo, Robert. "The Electronic Industry Braces for Hard Times." *Business Weekly* 14 Feb. 1996: 18–23.)

In 1990, when the United Nations International Human Rights Commission predicted that "there will be an outburst of major violations of human rights in Yugoslavia within the next few years" (14), few people in Europe or the United States paid attention to the warning.

(United Nations. International Human Rights Commission. *The Future of Human Rights in Eastern Europe.* New York: United Nations, 1990.)

Your writing will be smoother if you use signal worlds to introduce other people's ideas or words into your paragraphs. In the following two examples, notice the difference in the way the quotes are integrated into the text.

Quotation Not Integrated into the Paragraph

Modern farming techniques are different from those used twenty years ago. John Hessian, an Iowa soybean grower, says, "Without a computer program to plan my crop allotments or to record my expenses, I'd be back in the dark ages of guessing what to do." New computer software programs are being developed commercially and are selling well.

(Hessian, John. Personal interview. 27 July 1998.)

[The quotation here is abruptly dropped into the paragraph, without an introduction and without a clear indication from the writer as to how Hessian's statement relates to the ideas being discussed.]

Revised Paragraph

Modern farming techniques differ from those of twenty years ago. John Hessian, an Iowa soybean grower who relies heavily on computers, explains, "Without a computer program to plan my crop allotments or to record my expenses, I'd be back in the dark ages of guessing what to do." Commercial software programs, such as those used by Hessian for crop allotments and budgeting, are being developed and are selling well.

[This revision explains how Hessian's statement confirms the point being made.]

Exercise 64.7 Pattern Practice

Using the patterns of the samples presented here, write your own brief paragraphs using the same or similar signal words or phrases. An example, with signal words and phrases underlined, is provided.

Pattern: Unlike many in the music industry who believe that the music album will continue to sell well, Nedra Cummins, a leading expert in the music industry's forecasting of trends, claims that the album is disappearing.

Sentence in the Same Pattern: Although sales of music albums continue to dwindle, Roland Lefker, a spokesperson for Midtown Recordings, defends the future of the album by saying that recording stars will continue to cut albums rather than single songs to be downloaded.

1. Annual CD sales have been declining; one leading market researcher notes, "There has been a 30 percent decline in CD purchases over the past five years."

2. Fee-based downloading of single songs may be the way music is purchased in the future. A recent study by one recording company reported that on the most frequently used Web sites offering downloads, the top ten in popularity were all individual songs.

3. When long-playing records came into existence, they allowed artists to record several songs on the same LP and to experiment with creating longer works. "We suddenly had a new freedom to let songs expand into ten- to fifteen-minute lengths," observes a recording star of the 1960s.

Exercise 64.8 Writing Practice

Assume that you are writing a paper on the topics listed here. Using the information in 64e and 64f, write a paragraph that quotes the source directly.

1. *Possible topics:* Causes of school violence, effects of school violence, safety in schools

Not all school violence is caused by students. Outsiders (students from other schools, students who have been expelled, or adults) go into schools to rob, attack, kidnap, rape, or murder students or staff members. This can occur when an outsider wants to harm a specific individual. For example, a gang member may seek revenge on someone who happens to be a student and attack him or her at school. Or violence can occur when one person attacks another at random on school grounds. For example, a drug addict may enter a school to rob or steal and may assault a teacher or student.

It is important to remember that school crime affects more than just the victim and the perpetrator. It affects the whole school. Students may become fearful, angry, and frustrated. They may feel guilty that they were not able to prevent the incident, and they may even suffer long-term psychological problems. Like an adult whose home has been burglarized, students may feel violated. Their sense of security may be damaged, possibly never to be fully repaired.

(Day, Nancy. *Violence in Schools: Learning in Fear*. Springfield: Enslow, 1996. 12.)

2. *Possible topics:* Prenatal care, substance abuse during pregnancy, the effects of drugs on a fetus or newborn

Heavy exposure before birth to alcohol, tobacco, or narcotic drugs can cause a great variety of problems. In particular, exposure to these substances can lead not only to a decrease in the number of brain cells due to interference with cellular replication in critical periods of growth but also to damage to the connections between parts of the brain. A smaller brain can result. Cocaine and crack raise the blood pressure, close off small capillaries, and damage brain substance in developing areas of the brain. In addition, an addicted mother tends to eat poorly, and malnutrition in the developing fetus adds to its vulnerability. If an addicted person continues to ingest these toxins toward the latter part of the pregnancy, the baby is likely to have mild or major interference in the transmission of messages from one part of the brain to another.

At birth, the baby's behavior will reflect these disorders in neurotransmission through slowness to respond to stimuli, unreachableness, and apparent attempts to maintain a sleep state. They can be so volatile that they appear to have no state in which they can take in information from the environment, digest it, and respond appropriately. These babies can be at high risk for abuse or neglect. They are not only unrewarding to their already depressed, addicted mothers, but they give back only negative or disorganized responses. They are extremely difficult to feed and to organize for sleep. Their potential for failing to thrive is enormous.

(Brazelton, T. Berry. *Touchpoints: Your Child's Emotional and Behavioral Development.* New York: Longman, 1992. 14.)

3. *Possible topics:* Coping at college, verbal self-defense

Sometimes, in spite of all your best intentions, you find yourself in a situation where you have really fouled it up. You are 100 percent in the wrong, you have no excuse for what you've done, and disaster approaches. Let us say, for example, that you enrolled in a class, went to it three or four times, did none of the work, forgot to drop it before the deadline, and are going to flunk. Or let's say that you challenged an instructor on some information and got nowhere trying to convince him or her that you were right; then you talked to a counselor, who got nowhere trying to convince you that you were wrong; next you spent quite a lot of time doing your duty to the other students in the class by telling them individually that the instructor is completely confused; and now, much too late, you have discovered that it is you who are in error. Either of these will do as a standard example of impending academic doom.

In such a case, there's only one thing you can do, and you're not going to like it. Go to the instructor's office hour, sit down, and level. Say that you are there because you've done whatever ridiculous thing you have done, that you already know you have no excuse for it, and that you have come in to clear it up as best you can. Do not rationalize; do not talk about how this would never have happened if it hadn't been for some other instructor's behavior; do not mention something the instructor you are talking to should have done to ward this off; do not, in other words, try to spread your guilt around. Level and be done with it.

(Elgin, Suzette Haden. *The Gentle Art of Verbal Self-Defense.* New York: Dorset, 1988. 260.)

65

WRITING THE RESEARCH PAPER

65a GETTING STARTED

Chapters 1 through 6 discuss how to write a paper; reviewing those chapters will help you get started writing your research paper. However, although those earlier chapters help with shorter papers, you now have a more complex task at hand—integrating material, making decisions about how to organize all of the information you've collected, working your sources smoothly into your writing, and producing a draft. If you are anxious about confronting this stage of the research paper, try breaking the task into several steps (see the "Try This" box below). If you are a writer who writes more efficiently by first starting to write and then going back to plan or by planning mentally and then writing, you may want to start in that way.

Once you have an overview of how you are going to proceed, assemble all of the information you have collected as you conducted your research, and review it while asking yourself the appropriate questions for each:

- What is the assignment? How long should the paper be?

- What is the goal of the paper? to argue in order to persuade others to accept your conclusion? to report what you found and not draw any conclusions? to survey what is known about a subject? to review? to analyze? to evaluate? to inform?

- What is your working thesis? (That may change as you write, but if someone asks what your paper is about, can you restate your thesis in a sentence that summarizes your paper?)

- Who is the audience for this paper? How much background will your readers have? What new information will you be offering that needs explanation?

- What will the subtopics of the thesis be? (Again, this is a working list and may be revised as you plan further and as you write the paper.)

- What graphics, subheads, and other visuals will you include? (See 6a, 6b, and 6c.)

Try This

TO DIVIDE WRITING TASKS INTO SMALLER STEPS

Help yourself by constructing a plan for what you are going to do and in what order you'll proceed. Here are some steps you might take:

▶

1. Review the assignment, your goal, and your thesis.
2. Assemble your sources.
3. Decide on subtopics.
4. Sort your information under each subtopic.
5. Check to see if you need more information or want to eliminate a section that no longer seems relevant.
6. Write a draft.
7. Get some feedback on your draft.
8. Revise.
9. Proofread.

Go back and repeat steps as necessary. Set deadlines for each step if that helps (and think of a reward you'll enjoy when that part is finished).

After constructing a schedule for yourself, start earlier than you planned, to allow for any problems or unanticipated extra time that is needed for some part.

65b PLANNING AND ORGANIZING

If you work effectively and comfortably with outlines, try writing an outline (see 2a and 6c). You could also group your material into major sections in some visual way and then draw connections or a road map of how you plan to organize the paper.

Sort your material in the order you've decided on, and then check to see whether you have gathered enough information for each subtopic. This step helps you see whether you need to eliminate some weak subtopics or find additional material for some subtopic that should remain in the paper but doesn't yet have adequate support for your point.

Try This

TO REVIEW YOUR PLAN OF ORGANIZATION

After you've decided on a tentative order or outline, check to see if it works by trying these strategies:

■ Talk yourself through the outline or road map to see whether it works well.

■ Develop some subheads (if you plan to use them) to help you see the sections of the paper.

▶

- Explain to a fellow student or writing center tutor how you'll proceed, and ask for feedback.

- Decide on a working title, and see whether all of the sections fit appropriately under that title.

- Assume the role of a reader, and see whether the information proceeds in a way that allows you to follow along without getting lost or needing more connections.

- Ask yourself what point you will make in each section. Does the information in that section support your point? (You want to use sources to *support* your point, not to make the point.)

65c WRITING A DRAFT

Some writers prefer to write their introduction first, but others like to write sections of the paper and then come back to the introduction. As you write, consider the purpose of an introduction:

- *To interest the reader.* You can do this by asking a question that the research paper will answer, or you can offer an interesting or unexpected fact that draws readers into the paper because they want to know more. You can also explain to readers why they should know about this subject.

- *To help the reader move into the world of your topic.* Introduce your topic in a way that helps the reader anticipate what the context of your subject is, perhaps by explaining it, providing needed background, or giving examples.

- *To offer a summary of what will be discussed in the paper.* You can help the reader anticipate what the paper will be about by previewing what will be discussed.

As you draft the paper, keep the outline or road map nearby so that you can refer to it as you proceed. Some material may get rearranged as you write, but that's common. To help you keep to your plan or outline, you may want to revise the outline to reflect the changes in the organization.

Review the material on using signal words, summaries, paraphrases, and quotations (see 64c through 64f) so that you integrate your sources effectively. Decide which information is common knowledge and doesn't need to have a source listed and which information needs documentation (see 64b). You'll also want to review Chapter 5 on presenting your material with visual effectiveness and Chapter 6 on document design, especially if you are including subheads, graphs, tables, or other visuals.

As you start writing the conclusion of your paper, look back at your working thesis to see if you have adequately covered the topic and supported your thesis. Does the thesis need to be revised? If so, does the introduction need to be revised? Does the title fit the paper? A conclusion can look backward by summarizing what was covered or forward to future action. Consider possible purposes of a conclusion:

■ *To remind your readers of what they've learned.* If your paper discusses a complex topic, you can summarize what you have written. Does this summary adequately support the thesis of the paper?

■ *To help the reader see the significance of the topic.* Remind the reader of the significance of the topic by restating its importance to them.

■ *To look forward.* You can forecast what might happen next, what future research might be needed, or what action step readers might take based on what you have presented.

List your sources at the end of the paper as a Works Cited list if you are using MLA format (see Chapter 66) or as References if you are following APA style (see Chapter 67).

65d REVIEWING THE DRAFT

After you have written a working draft, put it away for a day or two to get some distance from it. If you try rereading the whole paper immediately after finishing the first draft, you won't be able to review it as effectively. For example, after a day or two, you may notice that information that was in your mind is not completely written in the paper and has to be added. You might also see a rough jump between ideas where a transition is needed. When you do go back to the paper, try reading it aloud and listen as you read. You are likely to hear sentences you want to rewrite and sections you decide need revising. Review the list of higher-order concerns listed in 2e to check on your purpose, thesis, audience, organization, and development. Also review your outline to see if it reflects the plan of the paper that you wrote.

Then seek feedback from other readers, such as a peer review group, if your instructor includes this in your class, or a writing center tutor. Feedback from others is very useful, so don't omit this helpful stage in developing your paper. Some writers are reluctant to let anyone other than their instructor read the paper, but once they do make an appointment to talk with a writing tutor, they realize how important and helpful this can be.

65e REVISING, EDITING, AND CHECKING THE FORMAT

After you have reread the paper yourself and received feedback from others, you are ready to revise. You may want to repeat the reviewing stage after you revise the first time and get more feedback. Some writers go through three or four drafts or revise sections over and over until they are satisfied. This will take time, but it is often necessary to be sure the paper is as effective and well written as you want it to be. After all the researching you've done, you want the paper to reflect your skill by presenting your best effort.

Then check the later-order concerns (see 2f) of grammar and mechanics. Remember that the spell-checker on your computer is not likely to catch all typos and misspellings, so read over the paper carefully. Look back at previous papers that instructors have graded to remind yourself of any grammatical errors you are prone to making so that you can correct them now. Finally, look over the formatting of the paper to be sure your documentation is correct. Also, do a final check to see that all the sources cited in the paper are in the list at the end of the paper and that you've deleted all the sources in the list that you didn't use. A final review of 6c will help you make sure that the formatting of the entire paper is appropriate.

66

DOCUMENTING IN MLA STYLE

As you research your topic, you will be building on the work of others. Your work can in turn contribute to the pool of knowledge about the topic for others who will read and depend on your research. The process of documentation requires that you acknowledge everyone whose work you have summarized, paraphrased, and quoted in your research paper so that readers of your work can find the sources you have used.

Documentation formats can vary, depending on the field of study and instructor preference, so it's wise to check with your instructor to see which documentation style to use. Unless you are asked to use another documentation format, use the format recommended by the **Modern Language Association (MLA)** for research papers in the arts and the humanities. The latest style manuals published by the MLA are the following, but check to see whether more current guidelines have succeeded them (www.mla.org/style):

> Gibaldi, Joseph. *MLA Handbook for Writers of Research Papers.* 6th ed. New York: MLA, 2003.

> Gibaldi, Joseph. *MLA Style Manual and Guide to Scholarly Publishing.* 2nd ed. New York: MLA, 1998.

MLA style is explained here, American Psychological Association (APA) format is explained in Chapter 67, and your library will have manuals for other fields as well. For information on some other styles, including the *Chicago Manual* style, Council of Science Editors (CSE) style, and others, see Chapter 68. Newspapers and other publishing companies, businesses, and large organizations often have their own preferred formats, which are explained in their own style manuals.

Why Styles Are Different

Some writers wonder why there are different styles to choose from for citing references. The differences between the styles are important because they reflect the major concerns of each field of study and the people who will use that style. MLA style is the preferred style in English; in this field, authors are important, and the whole names of authors are included. In APA format, there are often multiple authors, which are indicated only by initials for first and middle names. In MLA style, the title is placed after the authors' names, and the publication date is placed later in the citation, indicating that older texts may be just as valuable as newer ones. In APA style, however, the currency of research is very important, so the date appears after the authors' names. Because MLA is widely used in composition courses, the MLA publishes a handbook for student use and attempts to keep up with students' needs to document sources. For a comparison to APA, which is another frequently used style for citing sources with a different audience, see Chapter 67.

Major Features of MLA Style

- In in-text citations, give the author's last name and the page number of the source within the sentence. For in-text citations that occur after long quoted material that is indented, the citation comes after the sentence and after the period.

- Use full first and last names and middle initials of authors.

- Capitalize all major words in book and periodical titles, and underline titles or put them in italics. Enclose article and chapter titles in quotation marks.

- In a Works Cited list at the end of the paper, give full publication information, alphabetized by author.

The Three Parts of MLA Citation Format

1. *In-text citations.* In your paper, you need parenthetical references to acknowledge words, ideas, and facts you've taken from outside sources.

2. *Endnotes.* If you need to add material that would disrupt your paper if it were included in the text, include such notes at the end of the paper.

3. *Works Cited list.* At the end of your paper, include a list of the sources from which you have quoted, summarized, or paraphrased.

(For proofreading and pattern practice in MLA Works Cited format, see Exercises 66.1 and 66.2 on pp. 446–447).

66a IN-TEXT CITATIONS

The purpose of in-text citations is to help your reader find the appropriate reference in the Works Cited list at the end of the paper. You may have previously used footnotes to indicate each source as you used it, but MLA format recommends parenthetical citations, depending on how much information you include in your sentence or in your introduction to a quotation. Try to be brief, but not at the expense of clarity, and remember to use signal words and phrases (see 64f).

1. Author's Name Not Given in the Text If the author's name is not in your sentence, put the last name in parentheses, leave a space with no punctuation, and then indicate the page number.

> Recent research on sleep and dreaming indicates that dreams move backward in time as the night progresses (Dement 72).

2. Author's Name Given in the Text If you include the author's name in the sentence, only the page number is needed in parentheses.

> Freud states that "a dream is the fulfillment of a wish" (154).

3. Two or More Works by the Same Author If you used two or more different sources by the same author, when you cite one of them, put a comma after the author's last name and include a shortened version of the title and the page reference. If the author's name is in the text, include only the title and page reference.

> One current theory emphasizes the principle that dreams express "profound aspects of personality" (Foulkes, Sleep 144).
>
> (or)
>
> Foulkes's investigation shows that young children's dreams are "rather simple and unemotional" (Children's Dreams 90).

4. Two or Three Authors If your source has two or three authors, either name them in your sentence or include the names in parentheses.

> Jeffrey and Milanovitch argue that the recently reported statistics for teen pregnancies are inaccurate (112).
>
> (or)
>
> The recently reported statistics for teen pregnancies are said to be inaccurate (Jeffrey and Milanovitch 112).

5. More Than Three Authors If your source has more than three authors, either use the first author's last name followed by *et al.* (which means "and others") or list all the last names.

> The conclusion drawn from a survey on the growth of the Internet, conducted by Martin et al., is that global usage will double within two years (36).
>
> (or)
>
> Recent figures on the growth of the Internet indicate that global usage will double within two years (Martin, Ober, Mancuso, and Blum 36).

6. Unknown Author If the author is unknown, use a shortened form of the title in your citation.

> More detailed nutritional information in food labels is proving to be a great advantage to diabetics ("New Labeling Laws" 3).

7. Corporate Author or Government Document Use the name of the corporation or government agency, shortened or in full. If the name is long, try to include it in your sentence to avoid extending the parenthetical reference.

> The United Nations Regional Flood Containment Commission has been studying weather patterns that contribute to flooding in Africa (4).

8. Entire Work If you cite an entire work, it is preferable to include the author's name in the text.

> Lafmun was the first to argue that small infants respond to music.

9. Literary Work If you refer to classic prose works, such as novels or plays, that are available in several editions, it is helpful to provide more information than just a page reference in the edition you used. A chapter number, for example, might help readers locate the reference in any copy they find. In such a reference, give the page number first, add a semicolon, and then give other identifying information.

> In The Prince, Machiavelli reminds us that although some people manage to jump from humble origins to great power, such people find their greatest challenge to be staying in power: "Those who rise from private citizens to be princes merely by fortune have little trouble in rising but very much trouble in maintaining their position" (23; ch. 7).

For verse plays and poems, omit page numbers and use act, scene, canto, and line numbers separated by periods. For lines, use the word *line* or *lines* in the first reference, and then afterward give only the numbers.

> Eliot again reminds us of society's superficiality in "The Love Song of J. Alfred Prufrock": "There will be time, there will be time / To prepare a face to meet the faces that you meet" (lines 26-27).

10. Biblical and Other Sacred Texts Because sacred texts are available in several editions from various publishers, it is helpful to provide more information than just a page reference. For the first reference in your document, give the shortened title of the work (underlined), followed by a comma. Then add the abbreviated title of the chapter. Add the verse number, followed by a period, and the line numbers. For additional references, give only the abbreviated chapter title, verse, and line numbers.

> The Old Testament emphasizes the seriousness of the passage to adulthood: "Banish anxiety from your mind, and put away pain from your body; for youth and the dawn of life are vanity" (New Oxford Annotated Bible, Eccles. 11.10). In his first letter, Paul echoes this sobering view of adulthood (1 Cor. 13.11–12).

11. Multivolume Work When you cite a volume number as well as a page reference for a multivolume work, separate the two by a colon and a space. Do not use the word *volume* or *page*.

> In his History of the Civil War, Jimmersen traces the economic influences that contributed to the decisions of several states to stay in the Union (3: 798-823).

12. Indirect Source It is preferable to cite the original source. If you have to rely on a secondhand source—words from one source quoted in a work by someone else—start the citation with the abbreviation *qtd. in.*

> Although Newman has established a high degree of accuracy for such tests, he reminds us that "no test like this is ever completely and totally accurate" (qtd. in Mazor 33).

13. Two or More Sources If you refer to more than one work in the same parenthetical citation, separate the references by a semicolon.

Recent attempts to control the rapid destruction of the rainforests in Central

America have met with little success (Costanza 22; Kinderman 94).

14. Work Listed by Title For sources listed by title in your list of works cited, use the title in your sentence or in the parenthetical citation. If you shorten the title because it is long, use a shortened form that begins with the word by which it is alphabetized in your Works Cited list.

The video excerpts revealed sophisticated techniques unknown in the early

science-fiction movies ("Making Today's Sci-Fi Flicks" 27).

15. Work from a Library Database For works from library databases, start with the word by which the source is alphabetized in your Works Cited list. If you are able to view a PDF version of the original print file (meaning that it looks exactly the same as the original print publication), use the exact page numbers. If you are viewing the work in Web page format, do not use page numbers.

Mountain biking has yet to be considered a full-fledged mainstream sport, due

in part to the challenges faced by the advertising industry in marketing the

mountain-biking lifestyle (Smith 66).

Advertisers are now using custom-designed bottles, superheroes, and new

flavors to market bottled water to children (Hein).

16. Work from an Online or Electronic Source For works from on-line or electronic sources, start with the word by which the source is alphabetized in your Works Cited list (see 66c). Because Web pages may vary in length when printed out on paper (due to printer settings, font settings, and computer preferences), page numbers for online sources in HTML format are not considered stable references for citation purposes. Therefore, don't use page numbers to cite your source. If the source contains numbered paragraphs, however, you may include paragraph numbers. To indicate paragraph numbers, follow the words with which you begin your citation with a comma. Then add *par* or *pars* (followed by a period) to indicate paragraphs, and then add the paragraph number or numbers used. Also, if your source is in PDF format, you may include page numbers.

The World Wide Web is a helpful source for community groups seeking

information on how to protest projects that damage the local environment

("Environmental Activism").

A number of popular romantic comedies from the late 1990s suggest that women

can only succeed at maintaining their femininity by paying less attention to their

careers (Negra, par. 6).

17. Long Quotation If a quotation runs more than four typed lines, set it off by indenting one inch or ten spaces from the left margin. Double-space the quotation, and do not use quotation marks. At the end of the quote, place the parenthetical citation after the period. Do not place another period after the final parenthesis.

Thomas Friedman argues that Americans need to prepare today's students for tomorrow's challenges in the global marketplace:

> Our fate can be different, but only if we start doing things differently. It takes fifteen years to train a scientist or advanced engineer, starting from when that young man or woman first gets hooked on science or math in elementary school. Therefore, we should be embarking immediately on an all-hands-on-deck, no-holds-barred, no-budget-too-large crash program for science and engineering education. They have to be educated through a long process, because, ladies and gentlemen, this really *is* rocket science. (359)

(Friedman, Thomas L. The World Is Flat: A Brief History of the Twenty-First Century, Updated and Expanded. New York: Farrar, 2006.)

66b ENDNOTES

When you have additional comments or information that would disrupt the paper, cite the information in endnotes numbered consecutively through the paper. Put the number at the end of the phrase, clause, or sentence containing the material you are referring to, after the punctuation. Raise the number above the line, with no punctuation. Leave no extra space before the number.

The treasure hunt for sixteenth-century pirate loot buried in Nova Scotia began in 1927,[3] but hunting was discontinued when the treasure seekers found the site flooded at high tide.[4]

At the end of your paper, begin a new sheet with the heading "Notes," but do not underline the heading or put it in quotation marks. Leave a one-inch margin at the top, center the heading, double-space, and then begin listing your notes. For each note, indent five spaces, raise the number above the line, leave one space, and begin the note. Double-space, and if the note continues on the next line, begin that line at the left-hand margin. The format is different from that used in the Works Cited section. For a book reference, the author's name appears in normal order, followed by a comma and the underlined title; the city, publisher, and date in parentheses; and a page reference. For a journal article, the author's name and article title are followed by the volume (and issue number, if necessary), the date (in parentheses), and a page reference.

³Some historians argue that this widely accepted date is inaccurate.

See Jerome Flynn, <u>Buried Treasures</u> (New York: Newport, 1978) 29-43.

⁴Greater detail can be found in Avery Jones and Jessica Lund, "The

Nova Scotia Mystery Treasure," <u>Contemporary History</u> 9 (1985): 81-83.

If you are asked to use footnotes instead of endnotes, place them at the bottoms of the pages on which the text is cited, beginning four lines (two double spaces) below the text. Single-space footnotes, but double-space between them. Number them consecutively through the paper.

66c   WORKS CITED LIST

The list of works cited includes all sources you cite in your paper. Do not include other materials you read but didn't specifically refer to in your paper. Arrange the list alphabetically by the last name of the author; if there is no author, alphabetize by the first word of the title (ignore the articles *A, An,* and *The*).

For the Works Cited section, begin a new sheet of paper, leave a one-inch margin at the top, center the heading "Works Cited" (with no underlining or quotation marks), and then double-space before the first entry. For each entry, begin at the left-hand margin for the first line, and indent five spaces (or one-half inch) for additional lines in the entry. Double-space throughout. Place the Works Cited list at the end of your paper after the notes, if you have any. See the Works Cited page in the sample MLA-formatted paper on pages 448–463.

Books

Each reference has three parts: (1) author, (2) title, and (3) publication information. Each part is followed by a period and one space.

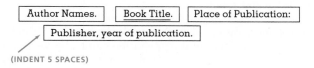

(INDENT 5 SPACES)

Author   Use the author's full name: last name first, followed by a comma, and then the first name and any middle initial or name. End the name with a period and one space.

Title   Give the full title, including the subtitle, if any. Put a colon and then a space between the title and subtitle. Underline the title or put it in italics (check to see if your instructor has a preference) (see Chapter 46), and end with a period and a space. Capitalize all words except articles, prepositions, and coordinating conjunctions, unless they are the first or last words.

Publication information Include the following:

1. The **city** where the work was published (if it's not on the title page, look on the back of that page), followed by a colon and a space. Do not include the state for cities in the United States. If several cities are listed, cite only the first. For cities outside the United States that are not well known, add the abbreviation for the country or, in Canada, the province.

2. The **name of the publisher,** followed by a comma. Shorten the names of publishers by omitting articles at the beginning of the name (*A, An, The*) and business names or descriptive words (*Books, Co., Press,* etc.). For university presses, use UP (Ohio State UP, U of Utah P). If more than one person's name is part of the company name, cite only the first name (Prentice, Simon, etc.), and if the company name is commonly known to your readers by an acronym, use the acronym (GPO, NCTE, IBM, etc.).

   Publishers sometimes put books under imprints. An imprint is a name of a subdivision or specialized line of books printed by a publisher. The imprint name usually appears with the publisher's name on the title page. If the work is published as an imprint, list the name of the imprint, immediately followed by a hyphen and the name of the publisher (Talese-Doubleday, Viking-Penguin, Belknap-Harvard UP, etc.).

3. The **date of publication.** If there are several dates, use the most recent. If there is no year of publication, use the most recent copyright date.

Example

> Boehmke, Frederick J. The Indirect Effect of Direct Legislation: How Institutions Shape Interest Group Systems. Columbus: Ohio State UP, 2005.

Articles in Periodicals

Periodicals are published regularly on a fixed schedule. Some, particularly newspapers and magazines, usually appear daily, weekly, or monthly; scholarly journals are typically published less often. Some publications, such as *Time* and *Wired,* are easily recognized as magazines, and others, such as *Scientific American,* are cited as magazines but are closer to scholarly journals in their content.

Scholarly Journals

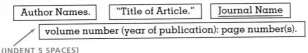

| Author Names. | "Title of Article." | Journal Name |

volume number (year of publication): page number(s).

(INDENT 5 SPACES)

Magazines

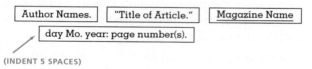

(INDENT 5 SPACES)

Newspapers

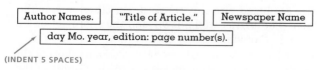

(INDENT 5 SPACES)

References for periodicals, like those for books, have three major parts: (1) author, (2) title, and (3) publication information, each followed by a period.

Author Follow the guidelines for authors of books.

Title Follow the guidelines for articles, putting the title in quotation marks, without underlining or italics. Place the period before the closing quotation mark.

Publication information Give the journal title (underlined), the volume number, the year of publication (in parentheses), a colon, and then the pages for the complete article, followed by a period. Articles that appear within the same 100 pages can be listed with inclusive page numbers. For example, if you use an article on pages 745 to 796, the pages can be listed as 745–96. For articles that have interrupted pagination, a plus sign can be added after the first page number of the publication. For example, if an article runs from pages 24–26 and then jumps to page 152, the page numbers can simply be listed as 24+.

Example

Sen, Sudipta. "Imperial Subjects on Trial: On the Legal Identity of Britons in Late-Eighteenth-Century India." Journal of British Studies 45 (2006): 532-55.

Sources from Online Library Databases or Subscription Services

For works located in library databases or subscription services, follow the guidelines for the print source, and then list additional information about the database and library from which the information was accessed. Not all libraries carry the same resources in their online databases or subscription services, so a reader might need information about the library in order to retrieve the work. The reference will have up to seven main parts:

(1) author, (2) title, (3) print publication information, (4) name of database, (5) name of database provider, (6) name of library system, library, city, and state, and (7) access details, each followed by a period.

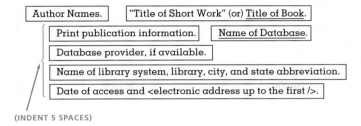

(INDENT 5 SPACES)

Author   Follow the guidelines for authors of books.

Title   For an article, put the title in quotation marks, without underlining or italics. Place the period before the closing quotation mark. For an entire book, follow the guidelines for books and underline the title.

Publication information   Follow the guidelines for books, magazines, journals, or newspapers, depending on your source.

Database details   Give the name of the database you used, underlined, followed by a period. If there is a database provider named, list that, followed by a period.

Library details   Then add the name of your university, school, or library system, followed by a comma, and then give the name of the library, with "library" abbreviated as *Lib.*, not underlined or italicized. Add the city in which the library is located, followed by a comma, and the abbreviated name of the state. End with a period.

Access details   Give the date on which you accessed the site. Then add the URL information for the home page of the Web site from which you accessed the source, which includes the Web address up to the first slash (/), enclosed in angle brackets (<>). End with a period.

Example

Loomis, Carol J. "Warren Buffett Gives It Away." Fortune 10 July 2006: 56.

   Expanded Academic ASAP. Thomson Gale. Francis Marion U, Rogers

   Lib., Florence, SC. 29 Dec. 2006 <http://web5.infotrac.galegroup.com/>.

Basic Web Site Sources

The reference for an online source will have up to six main parts: (1) author, (2) title of Web page, (3) title of Web site, (4) date of publication, revision, or update, (5) name of institutional or corporate site provider, and

(6) access details, each followed by a period. Web sites, however, do not always provide all of this information, especially authors, dates of publication, and names of institutional or corporate providers. In such cases, none of that information can be included.

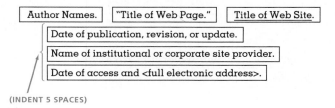

(INDENT 5 SPACES)

Try This

TO LOCATE THE HOME PAGE OF A WEB SITE OR ONLINE RESOURCE

When you locate resources on the Internet, especially when you access them through a search engine, you often see long, confusing Web addresses that look something like this:

> http://ses.library.usyd.edu.au/bitstream/2123/518/1/
> adt-NU20030602.10342102whole.pdf

When you are looking for the author, publication date, editor, or site provider of a Web site, it can be helpful to access the site's home page. Try looking for a link to the home page on the very top of the Web page. Also look for menus on the left side of the screen that indicate a link to a home page.

You can also locate the home page by clicking on the electronic address/URL of the site, deleting all of the information after the first slash (/), and hitting the *Enter* button on your keyboard. You should see something like this:

> http://ses.library.usyd.edu.au/

Then hit *Enter*. You should be able to see the home page or site provider of the Web site.

Author   Follow the guidelines for authors of books.

Title of Web page   Think of a Web page on a Web site like an article in a magazine—a part of a larger work. Follow the guidelines for articles, putting the title in quotation marks. Insert a period before the closing quotation mark. If no author is indicated, begin with the title of the Web page.

Title of Web site   Follow the guidelines for books, underlining the title. If you aren't sure about the title of the Web site, you can often find it by going to the site's home page. If an editor is listed, add the name here, following the abbreviation *Ed.* (not italicized or underlined). The name of the editor can sometimes be located on a "credits" page on the Web site.

Date of publication, revision, or update   Look for this information on the bottom of the Web page you are viewing. If there is a copyright date or year, cite that. Place a period after the date.

Institutional or corporate site provider   If there is a sponsoring organization, such as an educational institution, company, or nonprofit organization, cite it, followed by a period. This information, if available, can usually be found at the bottom of the home page or on a credits page.

Access details   Give the date you accessed the site, and add the entire URL (the network address), enclosed in angle brackets. If the URL is long and needs to extend to a second line, break it only after a slash and don't insert a space or hyphen. If the URL is extremely long and unwieldy, you can include the URL for just the home page, and then add "Keywords:" and the keywords you used to find the information on the site (see Works Cited entry 92 for an example). You can also type "Path:" and list the names of the buttons or links you clicked to get from the home page to the page you used for your research. End the entry with a period.

Example

Emery, Gene. "Study Tracks Big Growth in Drug Ads." ABCNews. 15 Aug.

2007. 19 Aug. 2007 <http://abcnews.go.com/Health/Drugs/

wireStory?id=3483903>.

Print Sources Posted Online

For a print source posted online, the reference will have up to eight main parts: (1) author, (2) title of Web page, article, or short work, or the title of a book or long work, (3) original print publication information, (4) title of Web site, (5) editor names, (6) date of publication, revision, or update, (7) name of institutional or corporate site provider, and (8) access details, each followed by a period. Web sites, however, do not always list all of this information, especially dates of publication, editors, and names of institutional or corporate providers. In such cases, none of that information can be included.

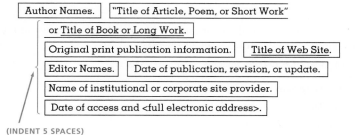

(INDENT 5 SPACES)

Author Follow the guidelines for authors of books.

Title of article, poem, or short work, or title of a book or long work
For titles of articles, poems, or other short works, put the title in quotation marks. Insert a period before the closing quotation mark. For titles of books or long works, underline them, and add a period at the end.

Original print publication information Include all of the publication information for the original print source.

Title of Web site Follow guidelines for books, underlining titles. If you are not sure about the title of the Web site, you can often find it by going to its home page.

Editor names Identify the editor or editors, if available, following the abbreviation *Ed.* (not italicized or underlined). The name of the editor can sometimes be located on a "credits" page on the Web site.

Date of publication, revision, or update Look for this information on the bottom of the Web page you are viewing. If there is a copyright date or year, cite that. Place a period after the date.

Institutional or corporate site provider If there is a sponsoring organization, such as an educational institution, company, or nonprofit organization, cite it, followed by a period. This information, if available, can usually be found at the bottom of the home page or on a credits page.

Access details Give the date you accessed the site as well as the entire URL, enclosed in angle brackets. If the URL is long, break only after a slash and don't insert a space or hyphen. End with a period.

Example

Corelli, Marie. The Passing of a Great Queen. London, Methuen, 1901.

Victorian Women Writers Project. Ed. Perry Willett. 19 Jan. 2001.

U of Indiana. 29 Dec. 2006 <http://www.indiana.edu/~letrs/vwwp/
corelli/passing.html>.

Examples of MLA Works Cited

Books

1. One Author To cite books from online library databases, see entry 39. To cite books accessed online, see entry 50.

Smith, Zadie. On Beauty. New York: Penguin, 2005.

2. Two or Three Authors Reverse name of first author only.

Roizen, Michael F., and Mehmet C. Oz. You: The Owner's Manual.
New York: Harper, 2005.

> Israel, Susan E., Dorothy A. Sisk, and Cathy Collins Block.
>> Collaborative Literacy: Using Gifted Strategies to Enhance
>> Learning for Every Student. Thousand Oaks: Corwin, 2007.

3. More Than Three Authors For more than three authors, you may list only the first author's name and add *et al.* (for "and others"), or you may give all names in full in the order in which they appear on the title page.

> Orlik, Peter B., et al. Exploring Electronic Media: Chronicles and
>> Challenges. Malden: Blackwell, 2007.

(or)

> Orlik, Peter B., Steven D. Anderson, Louis A. Day, and W. Lawrence
>> Patrick. Exploring Electronic Media: Chronicles and
>> Challenges. Malden: Blackwell, 2007.

4. More Than One Work by the Same Author Use the author's name in the first entry only. From then on, type three hyphens and a period, and then begin the next title. Alphabetize by title. If the person edited or translated another work in your list, use a comma and *ed.* or *trans.* after the three hyphens.

> Amis, Martin. The Information. New York: Harmony, 1995.
>
> ---. Yellow Dog. New York: Miramax, 2003.

5. Work with a Publisher's Imprint Publishers sometimes put books under imprints or special names that usually appear with the publisher's name on the title page. Include the imprint name, a hyphen, and the name of the publisher (e.g., Belknap-Harvard UP, Vintage-Random, or Grove-Atlantic).

> McEwan, Ian. Saturday. New York: Talese-Doubleday, 2005.

6. Republished Work State the original publication date after the title of the book. In the publication information that follows, put the date of publication for the current version.

> Greene, Graham. The Comedians. 1965. New York: Penguin, 2005.

7. Anthology/Collected Works An *anthology* is a book that contains several smaller works. If the anthology contains works from several authors, list the editor or editors first. Use the abbreviation *ed.* for one editor and *eds.* for more than one editor. If the anthology contains works by a single author, list the author first and include the editor or editors (if present) after the title. When adding the name of an editor or editors after the title of the work, use the abbreviation *Ed.* (which means "Edited by"). To cite one or more works in an anthology, see entries 8 and 9.

> Tuma, Keith, ed. <u>Anthology of Twentieth-Century British and Irish</u>
> <u>Poetry</u>. New York: Oxford UP, 2001.
>
> James, Henry. <u>The Complete Notebooks of Henry James</u>. Ed. Leon
> Edel and Lyall H. Powers. New York: Oxford UP, 1987.

8. Work in an Anthology/Collected Works State the author and title of the work first, and then give the title and other information about the anthology, including the page on which the selection appears. Include the original publication date after the title of the work if it is different from the publication date of the anthology/collected works.

> Alexie, Sherman. "Ghost Dance." <u>McSweeney's Mammoth Treasury</u>
> <u>of Thrilling Tales</u>. Ed. Michael Chabon. New York:
> Vintage-Random, 2003. 341-53.
>
> Fitzgerald, F. Scott. "Bernice Bobs Her Hair." 1920. <u>The Short Stories</u>
> <u>of F. Scott Fitzgerald</u>. Ed. Matthew J. Bruccoli. New York:
> Scribner's, 1989. 25-47.
>
> Shelley, Percy Bysshe. "Ozymandias." 1818. <u>Literature: An</u>
> <u>Introduction to Fiction, Poetry, and Drama</u>. 8th ed. Ed. X. J.
> Kennedy and Dana Gioia. New York: Longman, 2002. 1096-97.

9. Two or More Works in the Same Anthology/Collected Works If you cite two or more works from the same collection and wish to avoid unnecessary repetition, you may include a complete entry for the collection and then cross-reference the works to that collection. In the cross-reference, include the author and title of the work, the last name of the editor of the collection, and the page numbers. For previously published material, you may include the original date of publication after the title of the work.

> Grand, Sarah. "A New Sensation." 1899. Richardson 231-43.
>
> Richardson, Angelique, ed. <u>Women Who Did: Stories by Men and</u>
> <u>Women, 1890-1914</u>. New York: Penguin, 2005.
>
> Wharton, Edith. "The Reckoning." 1904. Richardson 296-317.

10. Scholarly Collection/Work That Names an Editor Use the abbreviation *ed.* for one editor and *eds.* for more than one editor.

> Kunka, Andrew J., and Michele Troy, eds. <u>May Sinclair: Moving</u>
> <u>towards the Modern</u>. Burlington: Ashgate, 2006.

11. Article in a Scholarly Collection/Work That Names an Editor
Include the author's name, and add the article title (in quotation marks).

Then name the scholarly collection and the editor or editors. If a selection has been published before, give that information and then use *Rpt. in* (for "Reprinted in") with the anthology information.

> Brantlinger, Patrick. "What Is 'Sensational' about the 'Sensation Novel'?" Nineteenth-Century Fiction 37 (1982): 1-28. Rpt. in Wilkie Collins. Ed. Lyn Pickett. New York: St. Martin's, 1998. 30-57.

> Kail, Harvey. "Separation, Initiation, and Return: Tutor Training Manuals and Writing Center Lore." The Center Will Hold: Critical Perspectives of Writing Center Scholarship. Ed. Michael A. Pemberton and Joyce Kincaid. Logan: Utah State UP, 2003. 74-95.

12. Work with an Author and an Editor If there is an editor in addition to an author, but it is not an anthology (see entry 7), give the editor's name after the title. Before the editor's name, put the abbreviation *Ed.* (for "Edited by").

> Kolakowski, Leszek. My Correct Views on Everything. Ed. Zbigniew Janowski. South Bend: St. Augustine's, 2005.

13. Second or Later Edition

> Wolfram, Walt, and Natalie Schilling-Estes. American English. 2nd ed. Malden: Blackwell, 2006.

14. Work That Names a Translator Use the abbreviation *Trans.* (for "Translated by").

> Changeux, Jean-Pierre. The Physiology of Truth: Neuroscience and Human Knowledge. Trans. M. B. De Bevoise. Cambridge: Belknap-Harvard UP, 2004.

15. Work by a Corporate Author

> Microsoft Corporation. Inside Out: Microsoft—In Our Own Words. New York: Warner, 2000.

16. Work by an Unknown Author

> Terrorist Hunter: The Extraordinary Story of a Woman Who Went Undercover to Infiltrate the Radical Islamic Groups Operating in America. New York: Ecco-Harper, 2003.

17. Work That Has More Than One Volume If you are citing two or more volumes of a work in your paper, put references to volume and page numbers in the parenthetical citations. If you are citing only one of the volumes in your paper, state the number of that volume in the Works Cited list, and give publication information for that volume alone.

> Spodek, Howard. The World's History. 3rd ed. 2 vols. Upper Saddle
>
>   River: Prentice, 2006.
>
> Lewis, C. S. The Collected Letters of C. S. Lewis. Ed. Walter Hooper.
>
>   Vol. 3. San Francisco: Harper, 2007.

18. Article in a Dictionary, Encyclopedia, or Reference Book Treat an encyclopedia article or a dictionary entry from a well-known reference book like a piece in an anthology, but do not cite the editor of the reference work. If the article is signed, give the author first. If it is unsigned, give the title first. If articles are arranged alphabetically, omit volume and page numbers. When citing familiar reference books, list only the edition and year of publication. For less familiar reference books, especially those that have been published only once, give all publication information, but omit page numbers if arranged alphabetically.

> "Bioluminescence." The Columbia Encyclopedia. 6th ed. 2001.
>
> Miller, Catherine. "Informed Consent." Encyclopedia of
>
>   Psychotherapy. Ed. Michel Hersen and William H. Sledge.
>
>   2 vols. San Diego: Academic, 2002.
>
> "Semaphore." Merriam-Webster's Collegiate Dictionary. 11th ed.
>
>   2003.

To cite an article from an online dictionary, encyclopedia, or reference database, see entry 58.

19. Introduction, Foreword, Preface, or Afterword Start the entry with the author of the part you are citing. Then add the information about the book, followed by the page numbers where that part appears. If the author of the part is not the author of the book, use the word *By* and give the book author's full name. If the author of the part and the book are the same, use *By* and the author's last name only.

> Annan, Kofi A. Foreword. In His Own Words. By Nelson Mandela.
>
>   New York: Little, 2003. xiii-xiv.
>
> Langland, Elizabeth. Introduction. Telling Tales: Gender and
>
>   Narrative Form in Victorian Literature and Culture. By
>
>   Langland. Columbus: Ohio State UP, 2002. xiii-xxiii.

20. Work with a Title Within a Title If a title that is normally underlined appears within another title, do not underline it or put it inside quotation marks.

Welsh, Alexander. Dickens Redressed: The Art of Bleak House and

Hard Times. New Haven: Yale UP, 2000.

21. Work in a Series If the title page or a preceding page of the book you are citing indicates that it is part of a series, include the series name, without underlining or quotation marks, and the series number, followed by a period, before the publication information. Use common abbreviations for words in the series name.

Haimo, Ethan. Schoenberg's Transformation of Musical Language.

Music in the Twentieth Century 22. Cambridge: Cambridge UP,

2006.

22. Government Publication Use the abbreviation *GPO* for publications from the Government Printing Office. If a specific author is not named, list the government agency issuing the work as the author.

United States. Office of the President. Budget of the United States

Government, Fiscal Year 2007. Washington: GPO, 2006.

United States. Dept. of Education. Tutor-Trainer's Resource

Handbook. Washington: GPO, 1973.

To cite a government publication consulted online, see entry 59.

23. Proceedings of a Conference If the proceedings of a conference are published, treat the entry like a book and add the name, date, and location of the conference if such information isn't included in the title.

Raven, Peter H., ed. Nature and Human Society: The Quest

for a Sustainable World. Proc. of the 1997 Forum on

Biodiversity, Washington, DC. Washington: Natl.

Acad., 2000.

Grant, Carl, ed. Proceedings of the National Association for

Multicultural Education: Seventh Annual NAME Conference,

October 29-November 2, 1997, Albuquerque, NM. Mahwah:

Erlbaum, 1999.

24. Biblical and Other Sacred Texts

The Bible: Authorized King James Version with Apocrypha. Ed.

Robert Carroll and Stephen Prickett. Oxford: Oxford UP, 1998.

The Jewish Study Bible: Tanakh Translation, Torah, Nevi'im,

Kethuvim. Trans. Jewish Publication Society. Ed. Adele Berlin,

Marc Zvi Brettle, and Michael Fishbane. Oxford: Oxford UP, 2003.

To cite an online text of a sacred text, see entry 60.

25. Graphic Novel MLA does not offer a specific example for this in its handbook; however, this format follows the general conventions of MLA style. List the names of the writer and the artist together as co-creators of the work, followed by the title of the book (underlined). If the graphic novel is a collection of previously published comics, include the number of included issues, followed by the city, publisher, and years of original publication. Then use *Rpt. in* (for "Reprinted in") and add the title of the graphic novel (underlined), followed by *book* (in square brackets) and the original publication dates.

> Loeb, Jeph, and Tim Sale. Batman: Dark Victory. 14 issues.
>> New York: DC, 1999-2000. Rpt. in Batman: Dark Victory [book].
>> New York: DC, 2001.
> Vaughan, Brian K., and Niko Henrichon. Pride of Baghdad. New
>> York: Vertigo-DC, 2006.

Articles in Periodicals

26. Scholarly Journal with Continuous Paging Most scholarly journals have continuous pagination throughout the entire volume for all of the issues published in a single year. At the end of the year, all issues in that volume are bound together and stored on shelves by the year of the volume. To find a particular issue on the shelf, you need only the volume number and the page, not the issue number.

> Goode, Mike. "Blakespotting." PMLA 121 (2006): 769-86.

To cite a journal article from an online library database, see entry 36. To cite an article from an online journal, see entry 52.

27. Scholarly Journal That Pages Each Issue Separately If each issue of the journal starts with page 1, include the volume and issue number.

> Gardner, Phillip, and William Ramsey. "The Polyvalent Mission of
>> Writing Centers." Writing Center Journal 25.1 (2005): 25-42.

To cite a journal article from an online library database, see entry 36. To cite an article from an online journal, see entry 52.

28. Monthly or Bimonthly Magazine Article For a magazine published every month or every two months, give the month or months (abbreviated except for May, June, and July) and year, plus the page numbers. Don't add the volume and issue numbers. If the article does not appear on consecutive pages, give the first page followed by a plus sign.

> Bardach, Ann Louise. "Twilight of the Assassins." Atlantic
>> Nov. 2006: 88+.
> Nelson, Michael J. "Snob Classics." Cracked Nov.-Dec. 2006: 60-61.

To cite a magazine article from an online library database, see entry 37. To cite an online magazine article, see entry 53.

29. Weekly or Biweekly Magazine Article For a magazine published every week or every two weeks, give the complete date, beginning with the day and abbreviating the month (except for May, June, or July). If the article does not appear on consecutive pages, give the first page followed by a plus sign.

> Drumming, Neil. "High Wire Act." Entertainment Weekly 22 Sept.
>
> 2006: 54-57.

To cite a magazine article from an online library database, see entry 37. To cite an online magazine article, see entry 53.

30. Newspaper Article Provide the author's name and the title of the article. Then add the name of the newspaper as it appears on the masthead, omitting any introductory article such as *The.* If the city of publication isn't included in the name, add the city in square brackets after the name: *Journal-Courier* [Trenton]. If the paper is nationally circulated, such as the *Wall Street Journal,* don't add the city of publication. Abbreviate all months except for May, June, and July. Give any information about the edition, and follow it with a colon and page numbers. If the article is not printed on consecutive pages, give only the first page number followed by a plus sign.

> Steel, Emily. "Novel Program Blends Charity and Marketing." Wall
>
> Street Journal 20 Dec. 2006: B1+.
>
> Stech, Katy. "Congress Gives $36.8M for Hospital." Post and Courier
>
> [Charleston] 17 Dec. 2006: B1.

To cite a newspaper article from an online library database, see entry 38. To cite an online newspaper article, see entry 54.

31. Unsigned Article

> "The System of Down." Esquire Jan. 2007: 48.

32. Editorial or Letter to the Editor If you are citing an editorial, add the word *Editorial* after its title. Use the word *Letter* after the author of a letter to the editor.

> "The Story of the Numbers." Editorial. New York Times 16 Dec. 2006,
>
> late ed.: A16.
>
> Salisbury, Alan B. Letter. Washington Post 15 Dec. 2006: A34.

To cite an editorial or letter to the editor published in an online publication, see entry 56.

33. Review of a Work Include the reviewer's name and title of the review, if any, followed by the words *Rev. of* (for "Review of"), the title of the work being reviewed, a comma, the word *by,* and then the author's name. If the work has no title and isn't signed, begin the entry with *Rev. of,* and in your list of works cited, alphabetize under the title of the work being reviewed.

> Gleiberman, Owen. "Of Human Bondage." Rev. of Casino Royale,
>
> dir. Martin Campbell. Entertainment Weekly 24 Nov. 2006:
>
> 79-80.
>
> Rev. of The Beak of the Finch, by Jonathan Weiner. Science Weekly
>
> 12 Dec. 1995: 36.
>
> Sheffield, Rob. Rev. of Kingdom Come, by Jay-Z. Rolling Stone
>
> 14 Dec. 2006: 119-20.

To cite a review in an online publication, see entry 55.

34. Published Interview For interviews published, recorded, or broadcast on television or radio, begin with the name of the person interviewed, the title of the interview in quotation marks (if there is no title, use the word *Interview*), the interviewer's name if known, and any relevant publication information.

> Brown, Peter. "Just Say No to Direct to Video." Interview with Lucas
>
> Graves. Wired Apr. 2006: 44.

To cite an interview published online, see entry 57. To cite a personal, telephone, or e-mail interview, see entry 88. To cite a radio or television interview, see entry 89. To cite an online radio or television interview, see entry 90.

35. Article in a Microform Collection of Articles

> Gilman, Elias. "New Programs for School Reform." Charleston
>
> Herald 18 Jan. 1991: 14. Newsbank: School Reform 14 (1991):
>
> fiche 1, grids A7-12.

Electronic Sources

Library databases or subscription services Many libraries subscribe to online services that allow users to access digitized versions of articles that have originally appeared in print magazines, journals, and newspapers (see Chapter 60b for more information). When citing sources located through online subscription services such as InfoTrac, LexisNexis, EBSCOhost, Science Direct, and NewsBank, you need to include additional information in your Works Cited entries to show where the sources were located and how they could be retrieved. After providing the standard reference for the print form of the work, add the name of the database (underlined). If you are viewing a specialized database, also provide the name of the service provider, which is the name of the company or organization that hosts the database or subscription service. Then add the name of your library system and the city and state in which the library is located (this information will vary depending on the library you use). Complete the entry with the date of access and the Web address (or URL) of the database's home page (the URL information up to the first /).

36. Journal Article Located in a Library Database or Subscription Service

> Miller, Christopher R. "Jane Austen's Aesthetics and Ethics of Surprise." Narrative 13 (2005): 238-60. MLA International Bibliography. EBSCOhost. U of South Carolina Lib., Columbia, SC. 27 Dec. 2006 <http://web.ebscohost.com.pallas2.tcl.sc.edu/>.

37. Magazine Article Located in a Library Database or Subscription Service

> Boo, Katherine. "The Best Job in Town." New Yorker 5 July 2004: 56+. Expanded Academic ASAP Plus. Thomson Gale. Francis Marion U, Rogers Lib., Florence, SC. 7 June 2005 <http://web7.infotrac.galegroup.com/>.

38. Newspaper Article Located in a Library Database or Subscription Service

> Davis, Mark. "Baby Giant Panda Takes the Next Step." Journal-Constitution [Atlanta] 22 Dec. 2006: F2. Custom Newspapers. Thomson Gale. U of South Carolina Sumter, Anderson Lib., Sumter, SC. 29 Dec. 2006 <http://find.galegroup.com/>.

39. Book Located in a Library Database or Subscription Service

> Day, Gary. Class. New York: Routledge-Taylor, 2001. NetLibrary. Francis Marion U, Rogers Lib., Florence, SC. 29 Dec. 2006 <http://libcatalog.fmarion.edu/>.

Internet and Online Databases MLA has formats documenting many types of Internet sources. However, if you can't find one that fits your source, follow the guidelines the MLA offers for all in-text citations (see 66a):

- References to sources in your paper should be clear and should allow your reader to find each source in your Works Cited section. Usually, this means indicating the author or the first item for that entry in your Works Cited list.

- If possible, indicate where the specific information being cited is located in the source. For many Web sites, however, this is not possible.

For citing sources from the World Wide Web, see the MLA's guidelines on its Web site (www.mla.org). The MLA guidelines, recognizing that online sources may lack some of the standard information included in citations, recommend that you include as many items from the following list as you can.

- *Name.* Include the name of the author, editor, compiler, or translator, with last name listed before first name, followed by an abbreviation such as *ed.* or *trans.*, if needed.

- *Title.* List in quotation marks the title of the short work (poem, short story, article, and so on) within a scholarly project, database, or periodical or the title of a posting (found in the subject line) to a discussion list or forum, followed by the description *Online posting.*

- *Title of book* (underlined).

- *Name of editor, compiler, or translator.* If it isn't already cited as the first item in the entry, include the name of the editor, compiler, or translator of the text, preceded by an abbreviation such as *Ed.* or *Trans.*

- *Publication information for any print version of the source.*

- *Title of project or site.* List the title of the scholarly project, database, periodical, or professional or personal site (underlined) or, for a professional or personal site with no title, include a description such as *Home page* (neither underlined nor in quotation marks).

- *Name of editor.* List the name of the editor of the scholarly project or database, if available.

- *Version number of the source.* If it isn't listed as part of the title, include the version number of the source or, for a journal, give the volume number, issue number, or other identifying number.

- *Date.* List the date of electronic publication, the latest update, or the posting.

- *Name of subscription service.* If the source is located through a library subscription service, list the name of the subscription service, as well as the name and location of the subscribing institution.

- *List or forum name.* For a posting to a discussion list or forum, include the name of the list or forum.

- *Numbers.* Give the total number of pages, paragraphs, or other sections, if numbered.

- *Organization or institution name.* Identify the sponsoring organization or institution.

- *Date of access.* Give the date you accessed the source.

■ *Electronic address.* Place the electronic address, or URL, between angle brackets: < >. If you have to divide the address so that it starts on one line and continues on to the next, break the address only after a slash. Never add hyphens or permit your word processing software to add hyphens.

40. Entire Web Site List the name of the author or editor, if available. Then list the name of the site (underlined). Next list the date of publication or revision (if available), the institutional provider (if available), and the date of access. Then provide the exact URL of the home page in brackets.

> Attack of the Show. 29 Dec. 2006. G4TV. 29 Dec. 2006
>
> > <http://www.g4tv.com/attackoftheshow/index.html>.
>
> Bonobo Conservation Initiative. 2002. 17 Dec. 2006
>
> > <http://www.bonobo.org/>.
>
> Hunt, Ben. Web Design from Scratch. 27 Dec. 2006
>
> > <http://www.webdesignfromscratch.com/>.
>
> International Spy Museum. 15 Oct. 2006. 15 Oct. 2006
>
> > <http://www.spymuseum.org/index.asp>.
>
> Nee, Brendan. BrendanNee.com. Nov. 2002. 23 Dec. 2006
>
> > <http://www.bnee.com/>.

41. Page on a Web Site A Web page is a single page on a Web site. Think of a Web page on a Web site like a chapter in a book—it is a small part of the entire work. After the author's name (if available), place the name of the Web page in quotation marks. Provide the exact URL for the Web page in angle brackets at the end of the citation.

> Hunt, Ben. "Graphic Design." Web Design from Scratch. 2 Mar. 2006.
>
> > 27 Dec. 2006 <http://www.webdesignfromscratch.com/
> >
> > graphic-design.cfm>.
>
> Johnson, Stephen. "AOTS Hosts Kevin Pereira and Olivia Munn."
>
> > Attack of the Show. 15 Apr. 2006. G4TV. 29 Dec. 2006
> >
> > <http://www.g4tv.com/attackoftheshow/features/53663/
> >
> > AOTS_hosts_Kevin_Pereira_and_Olivia_Munn.html>.
>
> "Language of Espionage." International Spy Museum. 15 Oct. 2006.
>
> > 15 Oct. 2006 <http://www.spymuseum.org/educate/loe.asp>.
>
> Nee, Brendan. "Urban Sprawl: A Case Study of La Crosse, WI."
>
> > BrendanNee.com. Nov. 2002. 23 Dec. 2006 <http://www.bnee.com/
> >
> > research/urban-sprawl-a-case-study-of-la-crosse-wi/>.
>
> "Where Do Bonobos Live?" Bonobo Conservation Initiative. 2002.
>
> > 17 Dec. 2006 <http://www.bonobo.org/wheredobonobolive.html>.

42. Home Page for an Academic Course The title of the course should not be underlined or placed in quotation marks.

> Frick, Ted. Website Design, Management, and Evaluation
>
> in Education. Course home page. Aug.-Dec. 2006.
>
> Dept. of Education, Indiana U. 21 Dec. 2006.
>
> <http://www.indiana.edu/~istf500/frick06fall/>.

43. Home Page for Academic Department

> English. Dept. home page. U of Minnesota. 13 Dec. 2006
>
> <http://english.cla.umn.edu/>.

44. Scholarly Project Accessed Online

> Sapir, J. David. "Ethnographic Photography." Fixing Shadows: Still
>
> Photography. U of Virginia, Dept. of Anthropology. Sept. 2006.
>
> 21 Dec. 2006 <http://people.virginia.edu/~ds8s/>.

45. Personal Home Page

> Kaplan, Hannah. Home page. 31 Jan. 2004. 8 Feb. 2004
>
> <http://www.mcs.com/~dkaplan/hannah.html>.
>
> Timberlake, Justin. Home page. 2006. 23 Dec. 2006
>
> <http://www.justintimberlake.com/>.

46. Personal Page on a Social Networking Web Site

> Panettiere, Hayden. MySpace: Hayden Panettiere. 29 Dec. 2006
>
> <http://www.myspace.com/haydenpanettiere>.

47. Section of a Personal Page on a Social Networking Web Site If the URL is very long, add *Path:* after the URL and list the names of links that will take readers to the cited page.

> Kutcher, Ashton. "Berlin." MySpace: Ashton Kutcher. 2 Oct. 2006.
>
> 29 Dec. 2006 <http://www.myspace.com/ashtonkutcher>.
>
> Path: View All Blog Entries.
>
> Moosie. Comment. MySpace: Kaysar. 29 Dec. 2006. 29 Dec 2006
>
> <http://profile.myspace.com/
>
> index.cfm?fuseaction=user.viewprofile&friendid=24258997>.

48. Entire Blog List the blog owner as the author. If the blog owner uses a pseudonym or handle, use that name.

> Dean Dad. Confessions of a Community College Dean. 26 Dec. 2006
>
> <http://suburbdad.blogspot.com/>.
>
> Little Professor. The Little Professor. 23 Dec. 2006
>
> <http://littleprofessor.typepad.com/the_little_professor/>.

Sims, Chris. Chris's Invincible Super-Blog. 2007. 22 Aug. 2007

<http://the-isb.com/>.

Zúniga, Markos Moulitsas. Daily Kos: State of the Nation. 27 Dec.

2006 <http://www.dailykos.com/>.

49. Posting on a Blog Include the title of the posting in quotation marks after the name of the blog owner. If the posting is from a writer other than the blog owner, list the author of the posting, the title of the posting (in quotation marks), the blog title (underlined), and then *By* and the blog owner.

Dean Dad. "Intrusive Advisement." Confessions of a Community

College Dean. 21 Dec. 2006. 26 Dec. 2006 <http://

suburbdad.blogspot.com/>.

Devilstower. "You Have the Power." Daily Kos: State of the Nation.

By Markos Moulitsas Zúniga. 24 Dec. 2006. 27 Dec. 2006

<http://www.dailykos.com/main/3>.

Little Professor. "Rules for Writing Neo-Victorian Novels." The Little

Professor. 15 Mar. 2006. 27 Dec. 2006 <http://

littleprofessor.typepad.com/the_little_professor/2006/03/

rules_for_writi.html>.

Sims, Chris. "After-Action Report: HeroesCon 2007." Chris's

Invincible Super-Blog. 18 June 2007. 27 Aug. 2007 <http://

the-isb .com/?p=55>.

50. Entire Book Accessed Online Provide the name of the author and text. Include the original date of the text, if available. Add the editor's name, publication information, and the date of the edition of the text, if available. Then list the name of the site provider (underlined) and the date the work was posted online. Follow that with the date of access and an exact URL.

Braddon, Mary Elizabeth. Lady Audley's Secret. 1861-62. Ed. David

Skilton. New York: Oxford UP, 1998. Questia. 23 Dec. 2006

<http://www.questia.com/PM.qst?a=o&d=57366610>.

Christie, Agatha. The Mysterious Affair at Styles. 1920. Project

Gutenberg. Mar. 1997. 21 Dec. 2006 <http://www.gutenberg.org/

catalog/world/readfile?fk_files=37415>.

Fitzgerald, F. Scott. This Side of Paradise. New York: Scribner, 1920.

Bartleby.com. July 1999. 21 Dec. 2006 <http://www.bartleby.com/

115/>.

51. Poem Accessed Online Provide the name of the author and text. Include the original date of the text, if available. Add the editor's name, publication information, and the date of the edition of the text, if available. Then list the name of the site provider (underlined) and the date the work was posted online. Follow that with the date of access and an exact URL.

> Angelou, Maya. "Still I Rise." New York: Random, 1978. Poets.org.
>
> 23 Nov. 2006 <http://www.poets.org/viewmedia.php/prmMID/15623>.
>
> Arnold, Matthew. "Dover Beach." 1867. A Victorian Anthology,
>
> 1837-1895. Ed. Edmund Clarence Stedman. Cambridge:
>
> Riverside, 1895. Bartleby.com. Apr. 2003. 18 Nov. 2006
>
> <http://bartleby.com/246/420.html>.

52. Article in an Online Journal If page numbers are visible, include them in the citation. If a total number of page numbers or paragraphs is presented, include them after the publication date. If no page numbers are present, omit them. Include the date of access and the exact URL. Treat sources located through Google Scholar or other full-text online databases like sources from library databases (see entry 36).

> Bandfield, Joshua L. "Global Mineral Distributions on Mars."
>
> Journal of Geophysical Research 107 (2002): 21 pp. Google
>
> Scholar. 27 Dec. 2006 <http://ivis.eps.pitt.edu/courses/mars/
>
> papers/bandfield_jgr_2002.pdf>.
>
> Blumner, Jacob S. "A Writing Center-Education Department
>
> Collaboration: Training Teachers to Work One-on-One."
>
> Praxis: A Writing Center Journal 3.2 (2006). 27 Jan. 2007
>
> <http://projects.uwc.utexas.edu/praxis/?q=node/79>.
>
> Roth, Elaine. "Black and White Masculinity in Three Steven
>
> Soderbergh Films." Genders 43 (2006): 45 pars. 21 Dec. 2006
>
> <http://www.genders.org/g43/g43_roth.html>.

53. Article in an Online Magazine

> Ellison, Katherine. "Shopping for Carbon Credits." Salon 2 July
>
> 2007. 20 July 2007 <http://www.salon.com/news/feature/
>
> 2007/07/02/carbon_credits/index.html>.
>
> Singel, Ryan. "Spammer Slammer Targets Politics." Wired News
>
> 14 Dec. 2006. 27 Dec. 2006 <http://www.wired.com/news/
>
> technology/0,72291-0.html?tw=wn_politics_2>.

54. Article in an Online Newspaper or Newswire

> Rust, Suzanne. "Threatened Frogs Get Reprieve in Milwaukee."
>
> Milwaukee Journal Sentinel Online 17 Dec. 2006. 24 Dec. 2006
>
> <http://www.jsonline.com/story/index.aspx?id=542931>.

"Study Shows Jet Lag May Be Harmful." United Press International
26 Dec. 2006. 26 Dec. 2006 <http://www.upi.com/NewsTrack/
view.php?StoryID=20061226-035150-7797r>.

55. Online Review of a Work

Lumenick, Lou. "Crowning Achievement Proves Actress Is Queen of
Queens." Rev. of The Queen, dir. Stephen Frears. New York
Post Online Edition 28 Sept. 2006. 23 Dec. 2006
<http://www.nypost.com/seven/09282006/entertainment/
movies/crowning_achievement_movies_lou_lumenick.htm>.

Michel, Sia. Rev. of The Sweet Escape, by Gwen Stefani.
Entertainment Weekly.com 1 Dec. 2006. 23 Dec. 2006
<http://www.ew.com/ew/article/review/music/
0,6115,1564580_4_0_,00.html>.

56. Editorial or Letter to the Editor Published Online

Austin, Leonard B. "Lawsuits Aren't Fun and Games."
Letter. Newsday.com 28 Dec. 2006. 28 Dec. 2006
<http://www.newsday.com/news/opinion/letters/>.

Flono, Fannie. "State Tests Hinder Students When Standards Low."
Editorial. Charlotte Observer 27 Oct. 2006. 23 Dec. 2006
<http://www.charlotte.com/mld/charlotte/news/columnists/
fannie_flono/15860266.htm>.

57. Interview Published Online

Ishiguro, Kazuo. "Myths and Metaphors." Interview with Jennie
Rothenberg. Atlantic Unbound 7 Apr. 2005. 23 Oct. 2006
<http://www.theatlantic.com/doc/200504u/int2005-04-07>.

58. Article in an Online Dictionary, Encyclopedia, or Reference Database

"Onomatopoeia." Merriam-Webster Online. 2006. 11 Dec. 2006
<http://www.m-w.com/dictionary/onomatopoeia>.

"Peru." HighBeam Encyclopedia. 2006. 12 Nov. 2006 <http://
www.encyclopedia.com/doc/1E1-Peru.html>.

59. Government Publication Online If the URL is very long and complicated, you can list the URL for the Web site's search page, as shown here with the Government Printing Office example.

Canada. Department of National Defence. "Operation StealthComm:
Semaphore Flags." Canadian Navy. 31 Aug. 2006. 27 Dec. 2006
<http://www.navy.forces.ca/cms_youth/youth_ sc_sema2_e.asp>.

United States. Senate. Committee on Foreign Relations. Hearings on
the Policy Options for Iraq. 109th Congress., 1st sess. Washington:
GPO, 2006. 18 Dec. 2006 <http://www.gpoaccess.gov>.

60. Online Version of a Biblical or Other Sacred Texts

The Bible: King James Version. Blue Letter Bible. 28 Nov. 2006
<http://www.blueletterbible.org/kjv/Gen/Gen001.html#top>.

61. Posting to an E-Mail List

Wood, Eileen. "Re: Basic Citation Tags." Online posting. 5 Oct. 2000.
LegalXML Citations Workgroup Listserv Archive. 2 June 2004
<http://camlaw.rutgers.edu/~jjoerg/citations/l.id>.

62. E-Mail Communication

Hampton, Hayes. "Recent Film Criticism." E-mail to the author.
5 July 2006.

63. Real-Time Communication/Instant Messaging (IM) This format applies to an online forum (such as a MUD or a MOO) and instant messaging programs. Cite the name of the sender, the topic of discussion, and the date of communication. Then include the communication forum and the date of access. Include a URL, if available.

Garlenum, Karl. Online discussion of peer tutoring. 27 Nov. 1998.
WRITE-C/MOO. 2 Dec. 1998 <telnet://write-c.udel.edu:2341>.

Kehrwald, Kevin. Online discussion of Oscar nominations.
20 Feb. 2006. Windows Live Messenger. 20 Feb. 2006.

64. Podcast After the title, include the word *Podcast*, followed by a period. Provide a URL if one is available.

Marshall, Peter. "BBC Radio News." Podcast. BBC. 26 Dec. 2006. MP3.
iTunes. 29 Dec. 2006.

Sims, Andrew, et al. "The Beginning of the End: Show #69."
Podcast. MuggleCast. 22 Dec. 2006. 24 Aug. 2007
<http://media.mugglenet.com/mugglecast/mc2006_12_22LB.mp3>.

Tracy, Elizabeth, and Rick Lang. "Week of December 29, 2006."
Podcast. Johns Hopkins Medicine. 29 Dec. 2006. <http://
www.hopkinsmedicine.org/mediaII/Podcasts/pod62.mp3>.

CD-ROMs and other portable databases Some databases are sources in electronic form that are stored on CD-ROMs or DVDs and have to be read on computers (that is, they can be carried around, unlike online databases, which are explained on page 430). When citing these sources, state the medium of publication (such as CD-ROM), the vendor's name, and the date of electronic publication.

65. Material Accessed from a Periodically Published Database on CD-ROM If no printed source is indicated, include author, title of material (in quotation marks), date of material (if given), title of database (underlined), publication medium, name of vendor, and electronic publication date.

> Anstor, Marylee. "Nutrition for Pregnant Women." New York Times
>
> > 12 Apr. 1994, late ed.: C1. New York Times Ondisc. CD-ROM.
> >
> > UMI-ProQuest. Oct. 1994.
>
> Institute for Virus Research. "Coenzyme-Cell Wall Interaction."
>
> > 14 Feb. 1995. Institutes for Health Research. CD-ROM. Health
> >
> > Studies Source Search. June 1995.

66. Publication on CD-ROM or DVD Many CD-ROM and DVD works are published, like books, without updates or regular revisions. Cite these like books, but add a description of the medium of publication.

> Flanagan, Caitlin. "Bringing Up Baby." New Yorker 15 Nov. 2004:
>
> > 46+. The Complete New Yorker. DVD. New York: Random, 2005.
>
> Mattmer, Tobias. "Discovering Jane Austen." Discovering Authors.
>
> > Vers. 1.0. CD-ROM. Detroit: Gale, 1992.

67. Computer Software/Video Game References to computer software are similar to references to CD-ROM or DVD materials (see entries 66 and 77).

> McProof. Vers. 3.2.1. DVD-ROM. Salt Lake City: Lexpertise, 2002.
>
> Sid Meier's Civilization IV. CD-ROM. New York: 2K-Firaxis, 2005.

68. Map on CD-ROM

> "California." Map. Rand McNally Street Finder Deluxe. CD-ROM.
>
> > Rand, 2000.

Additional Sources in Print, Audio, Video, Online, or Other Formats

69. Television Program Include the title of the episode (in quotation marks), the title of the program (underlined), the title of the series (if available, with no underlining or quotation marks), the name of the network, the call letters and city of the local station (if relevant), and the broadcast date. If pertinent, add information such as the names of the performers, director, narrator, or host.

> "Final Grades." The Wire. HBO. 10 Dec. 2006.
>
> When Parents Are Deployed. Host Cuba Gooding, Jr. PBS. SCETV,
>
> > Columbia, SC. 27 Dec. 2006.

70. Online Television Program If viewed online, include the name of the Web site, date of access, and URL.

> "Every Man for Himself." Lost. Dir. Stephen Williams. Perf. Matthew
>
> > Fox, Josh Holloway, and Evangeline Lilly. ABC.com. 25 Oct. 2006.
> >
> > 28 Dec. 2006 <http://dynamic.abc.go.com/streaming/
> >
> > player?mk=20152749&cid=7>.

71. Radio Program

> "Judging James Bond." On Point. Host Tom Ashbrook. Natl. Public
>
> > Radio. WBUR Radio, Boston. 20 Nov. 2006.

72. Online Radio Program If accessed online, include the name of the Web site, date of access, and URL.

> "The Women of Rwanda." The Connection. Host Dick Gordon.
>
> > The Connection.org. 22 Apr. 2004. 28 Dec. 2006 <http://
> >
> > www.theconnection.org/shows/2004/04/20040422_b_main.asp>.

73. Sound Recording/CD Depending on which you want to emphasize, cite the composer, conductor, or performer first. Then list the title (underlined); artist; manufacturer; and year of issue (if unknown, write *n.d.* for "no date"). Place a comma between manufacturer and date, with periods following all other items.

> Perlman, Itzhak. Mozart Violin Concertos nos. 3 and 5. Wiener
>
> > Philharmoniker Orch. Cond. James Levine. Deutsche
> >
> > Grammophon, 1983.
>
> U2. "Vertigo." How to Dismantle an Atomic Bomb. Interscope, 2005.

74. Sound Recording/MP3/Music Download For MP3s and other music downloads, indicate file type before the name of the manufacturer.

> Killers. "When You Were Young." Sam's Town. MP3. Island, 2006.

75. Film Viewed in a Theater Begin a reference to a film with the title (underlined), and include the director, distributor, and year. You may also include the names of the screenwriter, performers, and producer. Include other data that seem relevant, and give the original release date (if relevant) and the medium before the name of the distributor. (See also entries 76–78.)

The Departed. Dir. Martin Scorsese. Perf. Leonardo DiCaprio, Matt
 Damon, and Jack Nicholson. Warner, 2006.

Pride and Prejudice. By Jane Austen. Dir. Joe Wright. Perf. Keira
 Knightly and Matthew Macfadyen. Focus, 2005.

76. Film, Emphasis on the Director

Gaghan, Stephen, dir. Syriana. Perf. George Clooney, Matt Damon,
 and Jeffrey Wright. Warner, 2005.

77. Video Recording on Videocassette or DVD Include the original release date for films rereleased on video or DVD, when relevant.

King Kong. Dir. Peter Jackson. Perf. Naomi Watts, Jack Black, and
 Adrien Brody. DVD. Universal, 2006.

Spellbound. Dir. Alfred Hitchcock. Perf. Gregory Peck and Ingrid
 Bergman. 1945. DVD. Criterion, 2002.

78. Video Recording Posted Online List the name or pseudonym of the person who posted the video recording, if available.

Judsonlaipply. "Evolution of Dance." Perf. Judson Laipply. YouTube.
 6 Apr. 2006. 17 Nov. 2006 <http://www.youtube.com/
 watch?v=dMH0bHeiRNg>.

Transfinitejoy. "The Protagonist and the Pterodactyl." YouTube.
 8 Dec. 2006. 15 Dec. 2006. <http://www.youtube.com/
 watch?v=KyGX7gldDXs>.

79. Live Performance of a Play Like a reference to a film (see entry 75), references to performances usually begin with the title and include similar information. Include the theater and city where the performance was given, separated by a comma and followed by a period, and the date of the performance.

The Beaux' Strategem. By George Farquhar. Dir. Michael Kahn. Perf.
 Christopher Innvar, Veanne Cox, Christian Conn, and Julia
 Coffey. Shakespeare Theatre, Washington, DC. 11 Nov. 2006.

80. Musical Composition Begin with the composer's name. Underline the title of an opera, a ballet, or a piece of music with a name, but put quotation marks around the name of an individual song. If the composition is known only by number, form, or key, do not underline or use quotation marks. If the score is published, cite it like a book, but do not capitalize abbreviations such as *no.* and *op.* You may include the date after the title.

Bach, Johann Sebastian. Brandenburg Concertos.

Bach, Johann Sebastian. Orchestral Suite no. 1 in C major.

81. Work of Art Begin with the artist's name; underline the title of the work; and include the date of the work and the institution that houses the work or the person who owns it, followed by a comma and the city.

> Dalí, Salvador. Forgotten Horizon. 1936. Tate Mod., London.

82. Work of Art in a Print Source Follow the information in entry 81, but add the appropriate publication information for your print source, citing the page, slide, figure, or plate number.

> Lichtenstein, Roy. Drowning Girl. 1963. Museum of Mod. Art, New
>
> York. Roy Lichtenstein. By Janis Hendrickson. Berlin: Taschen,
>
> 1988. 31.

83. Online Work of Art Follow the information in entry 81, but add the appropriate publication information for the Web site on which an image of the work of art is posted.

> Monet, Claude. Waterloo Bridge, London, at Sunset. 1904. National
>
> Gallery of Art, Washington, DC. National Gallery of Art.
>
> 28 Dec. 2006 <http://www.nga.gov/cgi-bin/
>
> pinfo?Object=61112+0+none>.

84. Photograph Cite a photograph in a museum as a work of art. Cite a published photograph by indicating the name of the photographer and the publication information needed to locate the source (see entry 82).

> Gursky, Andreas. Times Square, New York. 1997. Museum of Mod.
>
> Art, New York.

85. Online Photograph Follow the guidelines in entry 84, but add the appropriate publication information for the Web site on which the image is posted.

> Carson, Niall. Chilled Primates. 30 Dec. 2005. MSNBC.com.
>
> 21 Dec. 2006 <http://www.msnbc.msn.com/id/16094272/>.

86. Personal Photograph For a personal photograph, name the subject and location of your photo. Then include *Personal photograph by author* and the date of the photo.

> Lincoln Memorial, Washington, DC. Personal photograph by author.
>
> 16 Nov. 2006.

87. Letter or Memo For a letter sent to you, name the letter writer, followed by *Letter to the author* and the date. For a letter in an archival collection, include the name of the archive, followed by a period. Add the institution name and city. Cite a published letter like a work in an anthology (see entry 8), but include the date of the letter.

> Blumen, Lado. Letter to Lui Han. 14 Oct. 1998. Lado Blumen Papers.
>
>> Minneapolis Museum of Art Lib., Minneapolis.
>
> Johnson, Jeffrey. Letter to the author. 7 May 2007.
>
> Nafman, Theresa. Memo to Narragansett School Board.
>
>> Narragansett High School, Boston. 3 May 2004.
>
> West, Rebecca. "To Bertrand Russell." Sept. 1929. Selected Letters of
>
>> Rebecca West. Ed. Bonnie Kime Scott. New Haven: Yale UP,
>>
>> 2000. 114-17.

88. Personal, Telephone, or E-Mail Interview If you conducted the interview, start with the name of the person interviewed, the type of interview (*Personal interview, Telephone interview, E-mail interview*), and the date.

> Epes, Heather. Personal interview. 15 Dec. 2006.
>
> Flannagan, Rebecca. Telephone interview. 3 Apr. 2006.
>
> Krier, April. E-mail interview. 9 June 2006.

89. Radio or Television Interview

> Owen, Clive. Interview with Charlie Rose. The Charlie Rose Show.
>
>> PBS. SCETV, Columbia, SC. 23 Dec. 2006.

90. Online Radio or Television Interview If accessed online, include the name of the Web site, date of access, and URL.

> Carter, Jimmy. Interview with Terry Gross. Fresh Air with Terry
>
>> Gross. NPR.com. 27 Nov. 2006. 28 Dec. 2006 <http://www.npr.org/
>>
>> templates/story/story.php?storyId=6543594>.

91. Map or Chart Treat a map or chart like a book without an author (see entry 16), but add the descriptive label *Map* or *Chart*.

> New York. Map. Chicago: Rand, 1995.

To cite a map on CD-ROM, see entry 68.

92. Online Map or Chart Follow the guidelines in entry 91. Then include the name of the Web site, date of access, and URL.

> "Los Angeles." Map. Mapquest. 15 Dec. 2006 <http://
>
>> www.mapquest.com>. Keywords: Los Angeles.

93. Cartoon or Comic Strip Begin with the cartoonist's name, followed by the title of the cartoon or strip (if any) in quotation marks and a descriptive label (*Cartoon* or *Comic strip*), and conclude with the usual publication information. For a cartoon or comic strip found online, add the relevant Internet information.

> Amend, Bill. "Foxtrot." Comic strip. <u>Morning News</u> [Florence] 21 Dec.
> 2006: D3.

94. Online Cartoon or Comic Strip Follow the guidelines in entry 93. Then include the name of the Web site, date of access, and URL.

> Lang, Bob. "Looking Out for Number One." Cartoon. <u>CNN.com</u>. 11
> May 2007. 24 Aug. 2007 <http://www.cnn.com/POLITICS/
> analysis/toons/2007/05/11/lang/index.html>.

95. Advertisement Begin with the name of the product, company, or institution that is the subject of the advertisement, followed by the descriptive label *Advertisement,* and conclude with the usual publication information.

> Sony BDP-S1 Blu-ray Disc Player. Advertisement. <u>Entertainment</u>
> <u>Weekly</u> 5 Jan. 2007: 38-39.

96. Commercial Follow the format for citing a television show in entry 69, identifying the network and date viewed.

> Mercedes-Benz. Advertisement. CNN. 28 Dec. 2006.

97. Online Advertisement Follow the format in entry 41 for citing a Web page on a Web site.

> Apple Computer. Advertisement. <u>Apple.com</u>. 28 Dec. 2006
> <http://www.apple.com/>.

98. Lecture, Speech, or Address Begin with the speaker's name, followed by the title of the presentation in quotation marks. Add the meeting and sponsoring organization, location, and date. Use a descriptive label such as *Address* or *Speech* if there is no title.

> Villanueva, Victor. "Blind: Talking of the New Racism."
> International Writing Center Association Convention.
> Minneapolis Hyatt Regency, Minneapolis. 21 Oct. 2005.
> Wiesel, Elie. Address. Koger Center, U of South Carolina, Columbia.
> 12 Sept. 2006.

99. Online Lecture, Speech, or Address Follow the guidelines in entry 98. Then include the name of the Web site, date of access, and URL.

> Eisenhower, Dwight D. "D-Day Invasion Order." Speech. 5 June 1944.
> <u>History.com</u>. 27 Dec. 2006 <http://www.history.com/
> media.do?action=clip&id=1106>.

Friedman, Thomas. "The World Is Flat." Lecture. MIT. 16 May

2005. MITWorld. 20 Sept. 2006 <http://mitworld.mit.edu/video/

266/>.

100. Pamphlet Cite a pamphlet like a book. If from a government agency, cite with the appropriate attribution.

How to Fit a Bicycle Helmet. Arlington: Bicycle Helmet Safety Inst.,

2006.

United States. Dept. of the Interior. Natl. Park Service. The White

House. Washington: GPO, 2006.

101. Online Pamphlet Follow the example in entry 100. Then include the name of the Web site, date of access, and URL.

Using Graphic Novels in the Classroom. New York: Graphix-

Scholastic, 2005. Scholastic. 28 Dec. 2006 <http://

www.scholastic.com/graphix/Scholastic_BoneDiscussion.pdf>.

102. Comic Book List the names of the writer and the artist together as co-creators of the work, followed by the title of the book (underlined). List the issue number and add the year of publication in parentheses. Follow this with the city and name of the publisher (also see entry 25).

Heinberg, Allan, and Terry Dodson. Wonder Woman 3 (2006). New York: DC.

103. Online Comic Book Follow the example in entry 102. Then include the name of the Web site, date of access, and URL.

Ellis, Warren, and Stuart Immonen. Nextwave 1 (2006). Marvel

Comics. 29 Dec. 2006 <http://www.marvel.com/digitalcomics/

view.htm?iid=1094&title=NEXTWAVE1>.

104. Published Dissertation Treat a published dissertation like a book, but include dissertation information before the publication information. You may add the University Microfilms International (UMI) order number after the date if UMI published the work.

Heafner, Christopher Allen. Transcendental Teaching: A

Reinvention of American Education. Diss. U of South Carolina,

2005. Ann Arbor: UMI, 2005. AAT 3181954.

105. Online Published Dissertation Follow the example for a published dissertation in entry 104. Then include the name of the Web site, date of access, and URL. If accessed through a library subscription service, provide the online information, following the example in entries 36–39.

Maloney, Kathleen A. Mirrored Images—English and India:

Women's Educational Opportunities in Literature, 1844-1898.

Diss. Purdue U, 2002. Ann Arbor: UMI, 2002. AAT 3099182.

ProQuest. U of South Carolina Lib., Columbia, SC. 28 Dec. 2006

<http://proquest.umi.com.pallas2.tcl.sc.edu/>.

106. Abstract of a Dissertation Begin with the publication information for the original work, and then add the information for the journal in which the abstract appears. If accessed online, then include the name of the Web site, date of access, and URL. If accessed through a library subscription service, provide the online information, following the example in entries 36–39.

McGuy, Timothy. "Campaign Rhetoric of Conservatives in the 1994

Congressional Elections." Diss. Johns Hopkins U, 1995. DAI 56

(1996): 1402A.

107. Unpublished Dissertation Put the title of an unpublished dissertation in quotation marks and include the descriptive label *Diss.*, followed by the name of the university granting the degree, a comma, and the year.

Tibbur, Matthew. "Computer-Mediated Intervention in Early

Childhood Stuttering." Diss. Stanford U, 1991.

Exercise 66.1 Proofreading Practice

The following examples contain errors in MLA Works Cited citation format. Correct each of them by consulting the examples on the preceding pages.

1. Book with One Author

Ali, Monica. "Brick Lane." New York, Scribner, 2003.

2. Work in an Anthology

Brooks, Gwendolyn. "Kitchenette Building." 1945. Ed. Valerie Lee.

The Prentice Hall Anthology of African American Women's

Literature. Upper Saddle River, NJ: Prentice Hall. 193. 2006.

3. Article in a Magazine

Paul Theroux, "Living with Geese." Smithsonian: December 2006, 38-44.

4. Web Page on a Web Site

Norris, Molly Frances. "Harry Potter the Healer." ABC News,

21 July 2007. 23 July 2007. Retrieved from <http://

abcnews.go.com/Health/story?id=3401421&page=1>.

Exercise 66.2 Pattern Practice

Prepare a Works Cited page containing an entry for each of the following sources using the guidelines and examples on the preceding pages.

1. Book with One Author

Author: Diane Setterfield
Title: *The Thirteenth Tale*
Publisher: Atria Books
Place of publication: New York
Date of publication: 2006

2. Work in an Anthology

Author: Andre Dubus
Title of anthology: *Masculinities: Interdisciplinary Readings*
Title of work: "A Father's Story"
Page numbers of selection: 181–194
Editor of anthology: Mark Hussey
Publisher: Prentice Hall
Place of publication: Upper Saddle River, New Jersey
Date of publication: 2003

3. Article in a Weekly Magazine

Author: Jeffrey Toobin
Title of magazine: *The New Yorker*
Title of article: "Killing Habeas Corpus"
Date of publication: December 4, 2006
Page numbers of selection: 46+

4. Article from an Online Magazine

Author: Mark Benjamin
Site name: *Salon*
Article title: "Post-Traumatic Futility Disorder"
Date of publication: 12/21/06
Access date: 1/18/07
URL: http://www.salon.com/news/feature/2006/12/21/ptsd/index.html

66d SAMPLE MLA-STYLE RESEARCH PAPER

A sample MLA-style research paper, beginning on page 448, illustrates how to insert in-text citations and create a Works Cited page. The sample paper doesn't include a title page. Title pages are not required in MLA style; however, you should ask your instructor if he or she would like you to include one with your paper.

1/2 INCH

Bryant 1

1 INCH

Liza Bryant

Dr. Jennifer Kunka

English 200

April 24, 2007

Crumbling Buildings and Broken Dreams:

South Carolina's Rural Students Deserve Better

Imagine you are walking into your new school, and as you start up the steps to go to the front door, the steps begin to creak and give way underneath your feet. Once inside, you walk down the hallway of a school built in the nineteenth century, and the sights do not get any better. You can focus only on the peeling paint chips and the rotting molding. The hallway smells like sewage, the water fountains do not work, and plywood patches cover the floor. Along with all of this, you are freezing because it is thirty degrees outside and the heating in the building does not work. You walk into your classroom, and students are bundled up in their jackets and gloves; they can barely pay attention to the teachers because they are trying to stay warm. Continuing to look around the classroom, you find that the desks are about to fall apart. Looking up, you see spots in the ceiling where there is water damage from the leaking roof. You begin to wonder how students learn in this type of environment. You thought that you had experienced the worst, but you walk into the restroom and spot a snake lying underneath the sink (Ferillo). You ask yourself how you could possibly concentrate on learning in a school like this.

Unfortunately, such educational environments are not uncommon for many rural South Carolina students, according to Bud Ferillo's documentary Corridor of Shame: The Neglect of South Carolina's Rural Schools. Because of the way schools are funded, students in several rural areas of South Carolina are not getting the quality education they deserve. Many rural students must cope with unsafe building conditions and insufficient educational resources, and, with everything else they endure in their lives, they

1 INCH

Comments

1. Page numbers should be included in the upper-right corner of the page, ½" below the top edge of the page. Include your last name, then one space and the page number.

2. Notice the order of information here (the writer's name, the instructor's name, the course title, and the date), all double-spaced and justified to the left margin.

3. The title is centered. Titles of papers should not be in quotation marks or underlined.

4. In the first paragraph, the writer tries to grab the readers' attention with a vivid description, including details about the conditions in several South Carolina schools mentioned in Bud Ferillo's *Corridor of Shame* documentary. By drawing readers into this description, the writer builds her emotional appeal.

Bryant 2

often make the decision to drop out. This educational problem, however, can be alleviated with additional funding from the state. The state of South Carolina expects to receive a budget surplus of $1 billion for 2007 (Adcox). The state legislature should use a significant portion of this money to make an investment in South Carolina's future by improving physical conditions in these rural schools and giving these students a true opportunity to succeed.

South Carolina had the lowest high school graduation rate in the nation in 2003 (Drake, "Publication"). According to "South Carolina: Quality Counts 2007," an annual education report released by Education Week, the 2003 graduation rate in South Carolina was only 52.5%, which was 17.1% lower than the national average of 69.6% ("South Carolina: Quality" 5). Furthermore, South Carolina Kids Count, an organization that monitors the health and education of South Carolina's children, notes that several of the rural school districts along the Interstate 95 corridor had 2005 graduation rates well below the state average. For example, the Allendale County graduation rate was reported at 30.4%, Dillon County District 2 noted a 39.7% graduation rate, and Marion County District 7 counted a 45.7% graduation rate (South Carolina Kids 4). Graduation rates in South Carolina's rural counties are particularly low, and the state must take action to address this problem.

According to Corridor of Shame, some rural schools in these counties are literally falling apart. Some rural schools in operation today date back to 1896. They are worn down, cold in the winter, hot in the summer, hazardous, and infested not only with bugs but also with larger animals, such as poisonous snakes. Many buildings have leaky roofs, rotting doors and walls, and buckling floors. One school is using a locker room for its reading center; the room is so run down that it cannot be used as a locker room anymore. At another school, the ceiling in a first-grade classroom collapsed on top of students' heads. At yet another school, a recent fire drill failed because the alarm system did not work. Numerous schools

Comments

5. When this writer cites material from Web sites in the body of her paper, she does not include page numbers in the parenthetical citation, according to MLA style.

6. In her thesis statement, the writer clearly states who (the South Carolina state legislature) should do what (pay for improvements to school buildings) to address the problems described in the first paragraph.

7. The writer uses two articles by the same author, John Drake, in this paper. To differentiate between two sources, include the author's last name, a comma, and the first word or two of the source title. "Publication" is in quotation marks because it is the name of an article from a news service.

8. Offering a brief description of this organization adds credibility to the writer's use of this source.

9. Because this document was accessed online in a PDF format, page numbers can be listed in the parenthetical citation. For HTML-formatted online materials, page numbers are not listed (see 66a16 for in-text citations for online sources).

10. Descriptions of the physical conditions of some rural South Carolina schools help the writer show the seriousness of this problem.

featured in this documentary had sewage problems in classrooms and in hallways (Ferillo). When it rains, students should not have to   11 worry about horrible smells, water in the hallways, or bugs coming up through the drains. These buildings need help, but some are too far gone to be helped. The ones in this condition just need to be replaced with better, safer facilities for the children of South Carolina.

Citizens in these rural districts lack the funding to improve these schools on their own. South Carolina schools are funded by   12 local property taxes. Many of these dilapidated schools are located in counties with traditionally low property values. Furthermore, these economic problems have been exacerbated by the high unemployment rates in these counties. The South Carolina Statistical Abstract notes that Marion, Allendale, Dillon, and Orangeburg Counties have all experienced double-digit unemployment rates during the last six years ("Annual"). The   13 conditions of these rural schools contrast sharply with those in wealthier school districts near Columbia and Charleston, creating vast disparities in the educational experiences students receive across South Carolina.

Several rural school districts along the I-95 corridor have sued the state of South Carolina on grounds that it was not providing   14 students with a "minimally adequate education," as mandated by the state constitution (Kropf A1). In the case of Abbeville County   15 School District v. State of South Carolina, Judge Thomas W. Cooper, Jr., ruled that early childhood education was not being funded adequately; however, he did not mandate repairs to existing school buildings or increases in teachers' salaries, which many felt also needed to be addressed (Drake, "Judge"). Many educators are   16 particularly disappointed that Judge Cooper did not address the physical conditions of school buildings. Tom Truitt, former executive director of the Pee Dee Education Center, stated, "I really do not understand how he could have failed to have done

Comments

11. The documentary is cited by the director's name.

12. The writer provides additional background information in this paragraph to explain why local school districts can't address these problems on their own.

13. These statistical data show the severity of the economic problems in these rural counties.

14. This paragraph provides additional background about the rural school problems, showing that several school districts have already tried to rectify the problem by suing the state.

15. Newspaper articles are cited with section letters and page numbers.

16. Page numbers aren't used for HTML-formatted material accessed from library databases.

Bryant 4

something on facilities" (qtd. in Drake, "Judge"). Every aspect of   17

a child's education matters, and just fixing early childhood   18

education is not going to make a sufficient change in our

graduation rates.

    The state of South Carolina should use its budget surplus

to give students the resources they need to excel in a safe

environment that is conducive to learning. How can children   19

be expected to learn in cold, damp, smelly, rotting buildings,

sometimes infested with bugs and snakes? Any child would be

distracted in such unsafe and uncomfortable surroundings, yet

many rural students are forced to endure such conditions every

day. A school should be a warm and inviting place because it is   20

where children spend most of their time. These learning

opportunities should be provided in safe, comfortable buildings.

    Furthermore, the state of South Carolina sends its students the

wrong message by requiring that they attend schools that are

unsafe and do not promote learning. In The Tipping Point: How

Little Things Can Make a Big Difference, author Malcolm Gladwell

defines "the Power of Context," arguing that "children are

powerfully shaped by their external environment, that the features

of our immediate social and physical world . . . play a huge role in   21

shaping who we are and how we act" (168). Consequently, every   22

day that a school remains in disrepair is another day that a

student is reminded that education is not important and may be

encouraged to drop out. By investing the budget surplus in these

rural schools, South Carolina can foster environments that promote

education and discourage students from leaving school.

    In addition, investing the state budget surplus in these rural   23

schools will be an investment in the future of the entire state

of South Carolina. Considering the devastating percentage of

dropouts, the state of South Carolina should want to help to make a

change. Funding South Carolina schools would help to bring that

change by upgrading old school buildings or building new ones,

Comments

17. The writer uses this quote from Truitt, a respected source, to illustrate the frustration that educators felt regarding the judge's decision.

18. Truitt's statement appeared in Drake's article, which is considered a secondary source of information. Here, the writer includes the quote from Truitt and cites it as an indirect source. This indirect source is indicated in the parenthetical reference by using "qtd. in" (for "quoted in") before the citation information.

19. With this paragraph, the writer shifts to providing reasons for readers to accept her argument.

20. The writer makes an emotional appeal here, asking readers to think about how children would feel about learning in such conditions.

21. The ellipsis (. . .) indicates that some words were removed from the original quotation.

22. The author's name is included earlier in this sentence, so the page number in this parenthetical citation is sufficient.

23. Note the transitional phrases the writer uses to move from reason to reason in this section of the paper.

Bryant 5

giving teachers the resources they truly need to provide students a quality education. The National Dropout Prevention Center/ Network reports that dropouts have damaging effects on state economies. In areas with a high percentage of dropouts, personal incomes and employment rates drop enormously, crime rates increase, and literacy levels decrease (National). A dropout's personal income is about $9,245 less than a high school graduate's per year, and only about 40% of dropouts become employed (National). High school dropouts account for about 75% of prison inmates, also putting a damper on state economies (National). These local school problems have negative effects on the entire state. An editorial in Columbia's State newspaper emphasizes the economic benefits tied to educating children:

> [I]f we want to compete in a global economy . . . and start building an economy that can support a prosperous lifestyle, then we have to start working together to make sure that the kids in rural Clarendon County not only show up in first grade as prepared to learn as those in Richland 2, but also have books and teachers and classroom environments that are just as conducive to learning. ("Stop")

The legislature needs to address the educational needs of all South Carolina children for the state to advance economically.

In fairness, all South Carolina students—not just those in wealthy school districts—should receive a high-quality education. While wealthier school districts, like those near Columbia and Charleston, have the resources, materials, and teachers needed to be successful, many rural school districts do not and are unable to give students the education they need to become leaders in the world. Because of the vast disparities in property values and tax collection rates, wealthier school districts are better equipped to educate their students, leaving the rural areas of South Carolina to fend for themselves because they have smaller tax bases from

24

25

26

27

Comments

24. The National Dropout Prevention Center/Network is listed on the Works Cited page as a corporate/organizational author.

25. Note the brackets [ ] indicate a word was altered from the original text. Also, the ellipsis (. . .) was added to show words were removed from the original text. When using brackets and ellipsis in quotations, it is important to maintain the core meaning and integrity of the original quotation.

26. For quotations that are more than four typed lines, use the long quote format. Note this long quote is indented 1" on the left. Also, the period is located before the citation rather than after.

27. Here, the writer appeals to a sense of equality, noting that all children in South Carolina deserve a good education.

which to fund their schools (Ferillo). It is the state's responsibility to give all South Carolina students a quality education in safe, comfortable learning environments.

While many people recognize that the conditions in these rural schools are unacceptable, some citizens believe that state tax money should not be used to address the problems of these local school districts. However, South Carolina citizens need to recognize that these local school problems have an impact on the entire state, eventually costing all state taxpayers. Students who drop out and have trouble securing employment put financial pressure on our public assistance and prison systems. Furthermore, new businesses will not invest in South Carolina if we do not produce skilled, educated workers. We have to put money into our schools so students are prepared for the world and the workforce. Our economy loses money from unskilled workers every day, and it is time to stop the trend and give rural school districts what they need to educate our young people.

Others argue that the state budget surplus should go toward other problems, not public schools. Some legislators have argued the surplus should be used for the elimination of the grocery tax, improved health care, and road improvement projects. Others believe that the surplus should be returned to state taxpayers in the form of income tax relief (Adcox). Indeed there are many problems in South Carolina that could be alleviated or eliminated by increased funding. However, the educational problems that come from the underfunding of rural school districts negatively compound many other problems in our state, such as high unemployment and crime rates. The most important investment our state can make is in the safety and education of South Carolina's children.

Children in South Carolina need our state government to step in and save the day. Students should not have to go to school in unsafe conditions that distract them from learning. Increased

28

29

30

31

Comments

28. In this paragraph, the writer shifts to addressing some concerns she anticipates readers will have regarding her proposal.

29. The writer uses a logical appeal here. She shows that state taxpayers should contribute money to alleviate problems within these local school districts because these local problems have an impact on the entire state.

30. Here the writer offers a concession to readers' concerns—that the budget surplus could be used to address other worthy issues. By conceding, she shows the common ground she shares with her readers. However, the writer moves on to show that the school funding issue contributes to many of the other problems that taxpayers may wish to address with these funds.

31. In the concluding paragraph, the writer summarizes her argument and emphasizes the importance of solving this problem. She then ends by looking forward to a positive outcome that could result from her thesis.

funding for rural school improvements would do wonders in some students' lives. It would give them hope and show them that the state cares about their future, as well as show them that dropping out of school is not the answer. All South Carolina citizens need to understand that we must give schools adequate funding to reach all our students. Once students can concentrate on graduating, success will be commonplace instead of for a select few.   32

Comment

32. The writer ends the paper with a strong statement, again appealing to readers' beliefs in equality and fair treatment.

Works Cited

Adcox, Seanna. "S.C. Senate Begins Work on State's $7.3 Billion Budget." State [Columbia] 9 Apr. 2007. 15 Apr. 2007 <http://www.thestate.com/312/story/31098.html>.

"Annual Average Unemployment Rates by County (2001-2005)." South Carolina Statistical Abstract. 2007. 12 Apr. 2007 <http://www.ors2.state.sc.us/abstract/chapter8/employment21.asp>.

Drake, John. "Judge Rules in School Funding Case." Associated Press State and Local Wire 29 Dec. 2005. LexisNexis. Francis Marion U, Rogers Lib., Florence, SC. 17 Apr. 2007 <http://web.lexis-nexis.com>.

---. "Publication Ranks SC's Graduation Rate Worst in Nation." Associated Press State and Local Wire 20 June 2006. LexisNexis. Francis Marion U, Rogers Lib., Florence. 17 Apr. 2007 <http://web.lexis-nexis.com>.

Ferillo, Bud, dir. Corridor of Shame: The Neglect of South Carolina's Rural Schools. DVD. Ferillo & Assoc., 2005.

Gladwell, Malcolm. The Tipping Point: How Little Things Can Make a Big Difference. New York: Little, 2000.

Kropf, Schuyler. "Court Gives S.C. Schools Partial Win." Post and Courier [Charleston] 30 Dec. 2005: A1.

National Dropout Prevention Center/Network. "Quick Facts." National Dropout Prevention Center/Network. 24 Mar. 2004. 16 Apr. 2007 <http://www.dropoutprevention.org/stats/quick_facts/econ_impact.htm>.

South Carolina Kids Count. "Kids Count Reflects on Judge Cooper's Ruling." South Carolina Kids Count. 12 Apr. 2007 <http://www.sckidscount.org/cooper.pdf>.

"South Carolina: Quality Counts 2007." Education Week Jan. 2007. 12 Apr. 2007 <http://www.edweek.org/media/ew/qc/2007/17shr.sc.h26.pdf>.

"Stop Delaying, Start Educating All Our Kids." Editorial. State [Columbia] 21 Nov. 2006. LexisNexis. Francis Marion U, Rogers Lib., Florence, SC. 15 Apr. 2007 <http://web.lexis-nexis.com>.

1 INCH

1/2 INCH

1 INCH

1 INCH

1 INCH

33

34

35

36

37

38

39

40

41

42

43

Comments

33. The Works Cited list begins on a separate page, with the title centered on the page.

34. The entire page is double-spaced. It is formatted in the "hanging indent" style, with all lines following the first line of each entry indented one-half inch. All entries are alphabetized.

35. This source is a Web page from a newspaper's Web site. When the city in which the newspaper is published is not indicated in the newspaper title, add the city name in square [ ] brackets.

36. Both of the sources by John Drake are newswire articles located in a library database. Note that the entry includes the name of the database, the name of the school and library system, and the library's city and state. It also includes the date the writer accessed this material and the home page of the database's Web site.

37. The three hyphens and a period (---.) at the beginning of this entry indicate this article was written by the same author (John Drake) as the previous entry.

38. This source is a documentary film on DVD. It is cited with emphasis on the director's name.

39. This source is a book with a single author.

40. This source is a newspaper article.

41. This source is a Web page on a Web site. The site is listed as a corporate/organizational author.

42. This source is a report on the *Education Week* Web site.

43. As indicated after the article title, this source is an editorial. It was located in a library database.

67
DOCUMENTING IN APA STYLE

The format prescribed by the **American Psychological Association (APA)** is used to document papers in fields such as psychology, sociology, business, economics, nursing, social work, and criminology. Ask for your instructor's preference. For APA format, follow the guidelines offered here and consult the *Publication Manual of the American Psychological Association* (5th ed., Washington, D.C.: American Psychological Association, 2001). Also follow the most current guidelines for citing electronic and online sources in the *APA Style Guide to Electronic References* (Washington, D.C.: American Psychological Association, 2007), which are included in this guide. Check for further updates on the APA Web site (apastyle.apa.org).

In Chapter 66, you'll find an explanation of why documentation styles are different, according to the priorities of the fields in which they are used. Researchers in social sciences use APA because their writing mainly reports research. Dates are important because newer research progresses from previous research, so the date of publication comes after the names of the authors. Authors' first names are given in initials only because the focus is on the research, not the authors.

Similarities and Differences Between APA and MLA

- APA and MLA use parenthetical citations in the text to refer readers to sources at the end of the paper.

- APA and MLA both use numbered notes to add information that would interrupt the flow of the writing.

- APA lists of works mentioned in the paper are called "References"; MLA lists are "Works Cited."

- Unlike MLA, APA includes the publication date in parenthetical citations, and the date appears after the author's name in the References.

- APA lists of authors include only the initials for the first and middle names.

- APA and MLA use of capitalization and italics in titles differs.

Features of APA Style

- The paper begins with a brief abstract or summary.

- For in-text citations, give the author's last name and the source's year of publication.

- In quotations, put signal words (see 64f) in past tense ("Smith reported") or present perfect tense ("as Smith has reported").

■ In the References list at the end of the paper, give full publication information, alphabetized by author.

■ Use full last names but only initials of first and middle names of authors.

■ Capitalize only the first word and proper names in book and article titles, but capitalize all major words in journal titles. Use italics for book and journal titles; do not put article titles in quotation marks.

■ Use the ampersand (&) instead of the word *and* with authors' names in parenthetical citations, tables, captions, and the References.

67a IN-TEXT CITATIONS

When you use APA format and refer to sources in your text, include the author's name and date of publication. For direct quotations, include the page number also.

1. Direct Quotations When you quote a source, end with quotation marks and give the author, year, and page number in parentheses.

> In coastal areas, natural catastrophe insurance "is either impossible to come by or has skyrocketed past affordable" (Richter, 2006, p. 28).

2. Author's Name Given in the Text Cite only the year of publication in parentheses.

> When Patel (2006) reproduced the study, she noted an increase in levels of carbon dioxide.

If the year appears in the sentence, don't add parenthetical information. If you refer to the same study again in the paragraph with the source's name, you don't have to cite the year again if it is clear that the same study is being referred to.

> Patel also noted a corresponding decrease in oxygen levels.

3. Author's Name Not Given in the Text Cite the name and year, separated by a comma.

> In a recent study of response times (Chung, 2005), no change was noticed.

4. Work by Multiple Authors For two authors, cite both names every time you refer to the source. Use *and* in the text, but use an ampersand (&) in parenthetical material, tables, captions, and the References list.

> Best and Wickham (2006) noted their data refuted the results of a similar study on oxygen molecules (Singh & Wong, 2003).

For three, four, or five authors, include all authors (and date) the first time you cite the source. For additional references to the same work, use

only the first author's name and *et al.* (for "and others"), with no underlining or italics.

Ellison, Mayer, Brunerd, and Keif (1987) studied supervisors who were given no

training.

Later, when Ellison et al. (1987) continued their study of these same

supervisors, they added a one-week training program.

For six or more authors, cite only the first author and *et al.* and the year
for all references.

Mokach et al. (1989) noted no improvement in norms for participant scores.

5. Group as Author The name of the group that serves as the author
(for example, a government agency or a corporation) is usually spelled out
every time it appears in a citation. If the name is long but easily identified by its abbreviation and you want to switch to the abbreviation, give
the abbreviation in parentheses when the entire name first appears.

In 1992, when the National Institutes of Mental Health (NIMH) prepared its report,

no field data on this epidemic were available. However, NIMH agreed that future

reports would correct this deficiency.

6. Unknown Author When a work has no author indicated, cite the
first few words of the title and the year.

One magazine article ("Fueling the Rise," 2006) noted the rapid growth in spending.

7. Authors with the Same Last Name When two or more authors in
the References have the same last name, include their initials in text
citations.

Until T. A. Wilman (1994) studied the initial survey (M. R. Wilman, 1993), no

reports were issued.

8. Two or More Works in the Same Citation When two or more works
are cited within the same parentheses, arrange them in the order in which
they appear in the References list, and separate them with semicolons.

Several studies (Canin, 1989; Duniere, 1987; Pferman & Chu, 1991) reported

similar behavior patterns in such cases.

9. Biblical and Classical Works Reference entries are not necessary
for major classical works such as the Bible and ancient Greek and Roman
works, but identify the version you used in the first citation in your text.
If appropriate, in each citation, include the part (book, chapter, lines).

When Abraham saw three men passing his tent, he asked them to stop and not

pass by him (Gen. 18:3, Revised Standard Version).

This was known (Aristotle, trans. 1931) to be prevalent among young men with these symptoms.

10. Specific Parts of a Source To cite a specific part of a source, include the page, chapter, figure, or table, and use the abbreviations *p.* (for "page") and *chap.* (for "chapter").

No work was done on interaction of long-term memory and computer programming (Sitwa & Shiu, 1993, p. 224), but recently Takamuru (1996, chap. 6) reported studies that have considered this interaction.

For an electronic source that contains no page number, cite the paragraph number with the paragraph symbol (¶) or abbreviation for paragraph (*para.*). When no paragraph number is given, cite the heading and the number of the paragraph following it.

The two methods showed a significant difference (Smith, 2000, ¶ 2) when repeated with a different age group.

No further study indicated any change in the results (Thomasus, 2001, Conclusion section, para. 3).

11. Personal Communications Personal communications include letters, memos, telephone conversations, and electronic communications such as e-mail, discussion groups, and messages on electronic bulletin boards that are not archived. Because the data can't be recovered, these are included only in the text, not in the References list. Include the initials and last name of the communicator and as exact a date as possible. (For electronic sources that can be documented, see 67c.)

According to P. P. Roy (personal communication, December 21, 2006), the possibility of change is small.

12. World Wide Web To cite a Web site in the text (but not a specific document), include the Web address. See 67c for more information.

Consult the Web site for the American Psychological Association (http://apastyle.apa.org) for updates on how to cite Internet sources.

67b FOOTNOTES

In your paper, you may need footnotes to expand on content and to acknowledge copyrighted material. Content footnotes add important information that can't be integrated into the text, but they are distracting and should be used only if they strengthen the discussion. Copyright permission footnotes acknowledge the source of quotations and other materials that are copyrighted. Number the footnotes consecutively with superscript arabic numerals, and include the footnotes on a separate page after the References.

67c REFERENCES LIST

Arrange all entries in alphabetical order by the author's last name; for several works by one author, arrange by year of publication with the earliest one first. For each entry in the list, the first line begins at the left margin and all following lines are indented five spaces.

Parts of the References Entry for a Book

Information appears in the order given here.

> | Author, F. M. |

List the last name of the author or editor (followed by a comma) and the initials of the first and middle name (followed by periods). Use commas to separate a list of two or more names, and use an ampersand (&) before the last name in the list.

> Taleb, N. N.

> | (Year). |

Provide the year of publication in parentheses, followed by a period.

> (2007).

> | Book title: Subtitle. |

Give the full title, including the subtitle, in italics. Capitalize only the first word of the title and subtitle, the first word after a colon, and any proper nouns. For a second or later edition, add the edition number in parentheses after the title. If there are editors, compilers, or translators, list these in a separate set of parentheses immediately after the title or after the edition number. End with a period.

> *The black swan: The impact of the highly improbable.*

> | City: Publisher. |

Include the city, a colon, and the publisher's name. End with a period.

> New York: Random House.

Complete citation

> Taleb, N. N. (2007). *The black swan: The impact of the highly improbable.* New York: Random House.

Parts of the References Entry for a Journal Article

Information appears in the order given here.

> | Author, F. M. |

List the last name of the author (followed by a comma) and the initials of the first and middle names (followed by periods). Use commas to separate a list of two or more names, and use an ampersand (&) before the last name in the list.

> Gaiber-Maitlin, S.

(Year).

Provide the year of publication in parentheses, followed by a period.

> (2007).

Article title: Subtitle.

Include the full title and subtitle. Capitalize the first word of the title, first word after a colon, and proper nouns. End with a period.

> The psychological needs of military personnel and families.

Journal Title: Subtitle,

Give the full title, including the subtitle, in italics. Capitalize the first word in the title and subtitle and all other words except articles, conjunctions, and short prepositions. End with a comma.

> *Monitor in Psychology,*

Volume number(issue number), page numbers.

Give the volume number in italics. If the journal is paginated separately by issue, add the issue number in parentheses directly after the volume number. Don't put a space between the volume number and the parenthesis before the issue number, and don't italicize the issue number. Add a comma, the page numbers of the article, and a period.

> *38*(1), 56–57.

Complete citation

> Gaiber-Maitlin, S. (2007). The psychological needs of military
>
> personnel and families. *Monitor in Psychology, 38*(1), 56–57.

Start the References list on a new page, with the word *References* centered at the top of the page, and double-space all entries.

Examples of APA References

Books

1. One Author

> Anderson, C. (2006). *The long tail: Why the future of business is*
>
> *selling less of more.* New York: Hyperion.

2. Two to Six Authors

> Levitt, S. D., & Dubner, S. J. (2005). *Freakonomics: A rogue economist explores the hidden side of everything.* New York: Morrow.
>
> Nevid, J. S., Rathus, S. A., & Greene, B. (2006). *Abnormal psychology in a changing world* (6th ed.). Upper Saddle River, NJ: Prentice Hall.

3. Seven or More Authors List the first six authors' names, and add *et al.* (which means "and others") to indicate additional authors.

> Wolfe, S. M., Sasich, L. D., Lurie, P., Hope, R. E., Barbehenn, E., Knapp, D. E., et al. (2005). *Worst pills, best pills: A consumer's guide to avoiding drug-induced death or illness.* New York: Pocket Books.

4. More Than One Work by the Same Author Include the author's name in all references and arrange by year of publication, the earliest first.

> Kilmonto, R. J. (1983). *Culture and ethnicity.* Washington, DC: American Psychiatric Press.
>
> Kilmonto, R. J. (1989). *Cultural adaptations.* New York: HarperCollins.

5. Republished Work

> Darwin, C. (1985). *The origin of species by means of natural selection* (J. W. Burrow, Ed.). New York: Penguin. (Original work published 1859)

6. Anthology, Scholarly Collection, or Work That Names an Editor

> Brettell, C. B., & Sargent, C. F. (Eds.). (2005). *Gender in cross-cultural perspective* (4th ed.). Upper Saddle River, NJ: Prentice Hall.

7. Article or Chapter in an Anthology, Scholarly Collection, or Work That Names an Editor

> Ball, J. D., & Peake, T. H. (2006). Brief psychotherapy in the U.S. military: Principles and applications. In C. H. Kennedy & E. A. Zillmer (Eds.), *Military psychology: Clinical and operational applications* (pp. 61–73). New York: Guilford Press.

8. Second or Later Edition Place the number of the edition in parentheses after the book title. If the book is a revised edition, instead of a number, place *Rev. ed.* in parentheses after the book title.

> Drafke, M. (2006). *The human side of organizations* (9th ed.). Upper Saddle River, NJ: Prentice Hall.

9. Work with an Author and an Editor

Kolakowski, L. (1984). *My correct views on everything* (Z. Janowski, Ed.). South Bend, IN: St. Augustine's Press.

10. Work That Names a Translator

Bourdieu, P. (1984). *Distinction: A social critique on the judgement of taste* (R. Nice, Trans.). Cambridge, MA: Harvard University Press. (Original work published 1979)

11. Work by a Group or Corporate Author

American Heart Association. (2005). *No-fad diet: A personal plan for healthy weight loss.* New York: Clarkson Potter.

12. Work by an Unknown Author

Professional guide to assessment. (2006). Philadelphia: Lippincott Williams & Wilkins.

13. Work That Has More Than One Volume

Donovan, W. (Ed.). (1979–1986). *Social sciences: A history* (Vols. 1–5). New York: Hollins.

14. Signed Article in a Dictionary, Encyclopedia, or Reference Book

Miller, C. (2002). Informed consent. In M. Herzen & W. Sledge (Eds.), *Encyclopedia of psychotherapy* (Vol. 2, pp. 17–24). San Diego, CA: Elsevier Science.

15. Unsigned Article in a Dictionary, Encyclopedia, or Reference Book If using a multivolume work, add volume number after book title (see entry 13).

Psychodrama. (2002). In *Merriam-Webster's collegiate dictionary* (11th ed., p. 1004). Springfield, MA: Merriam-Webster.

16. Introduction, Foreword, Preface, or Afterword List the author of the section first. Include the page numbers after the title of the book.

Annan, K. (2003). Foreword. In N. Mandela, *In his own words* (pp. xiii–xiv). New York: Little, Brown.

17. Government Publication

Office of the President. (2006). *Budget of the United States government, fiscal year 2007.* Washington, DC: U.S. Government Printing Office.

18. Proceedings of a Conference Cite as an article in a scholarly collection. If article is published in a journal, follow the guidelines for entries 22 or 23.

> Salvucci, D. D., & Macuga, K. L. (2001). Predicting the effects of cell-
> phone dialing on driving performance. In E. M. Altmann, A.
> Cleeremans, C. D. Schunn, & W. D. Gray (Eds.), *Proceedings of*
> *the 2001 fourth annual international conference on cognitive*
> *modeling* (pp. 25–30). Mahwah, NJ: Erlbaum.

19. Technical or Research Report If there is a report number, include it in parentheses after the title.

> Birney, A. F., & Hall, M. M. (1981). *Early identification of children*
> *with written language disabilities* (Rep. No. 81-502).
> Washington, DC: National Education Association.

20. Report from a University If a report number is provided, place it in parentheses after the title, as in entry 19.

> Stukel, J. (2004). *More good works: A state of the university report.*
> Urbana-Champaign: University of Illinois, Office for
> University Relations.

21. Biblical and Classical Works Major classical works, such as the Bible and ancient Greek and Roman works, are not listed in the References. Instead, they are cited in the paper when referred to. See 67a for in-text citation format and examples.

Articles in Periodicals

22. Article in a Journal Paginated Continuously

> Pasnak, R., Cooke, W. D., & Hendricks, C. (2006). Enhancing
> academic performance by strengthening class-inclusion
> reasoning. *Journal of Psychology, 140,* 603–613.

23. Article in a Journal Paginated Separately by Issue

> Cubitt, S. (2006). Grayscale video and the shift to color. *Art Journal,*
> *65*(3), 40–53.

24. Article in a Monthly or Bimonthly Magazine Include the volume number in italics after the magazine title.

> Roberts, D. (2006, June). Below the rim. *Smithsonian, 37,* 54–65.

25. Article in a Weekly or Biweekly Magazine Include the volume number in italics after the magazine title.

> Gannon, F. (2006, December 11). Beyond bird flu: Other potential
>
> epidemics. *The New Yorker, 82,* 61.

26. Article in a Newspaper For newspaper articles, use *p.* (for a single page) or *pp.* (for multiple pages) before the page numbers.

> Banerjee, N. (2004, September 1). Many feeling pinch after newest
>
> surge in U.S. fuel prices. *The New York Times,* p. A1.

27. Unsigned Article

> U.S. assigns terror score to international travelers. (2006, December
>
> 1). *The New York Times,* p. A28.

28. Letter to the Editor

> Tippmann, J. R. (2006, October). Design's next diva [Letter to the
>
> editor]. *Fast Company, 109,* 18.

29. Review of a Work If the review is untitled, use the material in brackets as the title and indicate whether the review is of a book, film, or video; the brackets indicate the material is a description of form and content, not a title.

> Epstein, P. R. (2006). [Review of the motion picture *An Inconvenient*
>
> *Truth*]. *British Medical Journal, 332,* 1397.
>
> Mookherjee, N. (2006). Archeology and history [Review of the book
>
> *Social memory and history: Anthropological perspectives*].
>
> *Journal of the Royal Anthropological Institute, 12,* 957–958.

30. Published Interview Cite published interviews like articles in journals, newspapers, and magazines, and list the interviewer as the author.

> Worth, J. (2006, November). Punk rock capitalism? *New*
>
> *Internationalist, 395,* 16–17.

Electronic Sources

The APA has published the *APA Style Guide to Electronic References* (Washington, D.C.: American Psychological Association, 2007) to provide current guidelines for citing electronic and online sources. This guide updates information presented in the *Publication Manual of the American Psychological Association* (5th ed.). Check periodically for updates to the *APA Style Guide to Electronic References* on the APA Web site (apastyle.apa.org). The goal of each reference is to credit the author and to help your reader find the material. Follow these guidelines for creating your References list:

Author names Include the name(s) of the author(s) in the same format used for books and journals.

Date of publication Include the date in parentheses following the name(s) of the author(s), followed by a period. If no date is available, write (n.d.) for "no date."

Titles Do not use italics when listing names of articles and pages within Web sites. Use italics for titles of books, periodicals, and most whole Web sites.

Publication information For journal articles retrieved online, always list the volume and issue number.

Retrieval information A retrieval line generally begins with "Retrieved from" and the URL. In some cases, a retrieval line is not necessary, but in other cases, more information may be needed:

■ *Databases* Include the names of databases in the retrieval line only if the source is rare, a print version is difficult to locate, or the material is available only on a small number of databases. Otherwise, for materials located on widely available databases, including library subscription services, do not include a retrieval line (see entries 33 and 34).

■ *Date of retrieval* Include the date you accessed the material only if the item retrieved does not have a publication date, is very likely to be updated or changed, or is from a reference book (see entry 41).

■ *DOI* Some journal articles are now identified by DOI (Digital Object Identifier) numbers. A DOI is a unique electronic code assigned to an online journal article. Even if a journal article is moved to a new Web site, the DOI for that article will remain the same. The DOI can often be located on the first page on an online article. For journal articles indicated by a DOI, include the DOI number after the publication information (see entry 31). For online journal articles without DOIs, include the URL.

■ *URL* Include the full URL for most works accessed online. Include the home page URL (up to the first /) when accessing materials available only by search or subscription, online encyclopedias or dictionaries, or material in frames format. If you have to divide the URL onto two or more lines, break the address before slashes and punctuation marks (except within "http://"), and never add a hyphen. Write the URL like the rest of your text; do not use underlining, italics, angle brackets, or an end period.

31. **Journal Article with a DOI** Include the volume and issue number. List the DOI at the end of the entry. If accessed through a database

or subscription service, include page numbers (if available), but do not name the database. If accessed on a Web site, do not list a URL.

Floen, S. K., & Elklit, A. (2007). Psychiatric diagnoses, trauma, and

suicidiality. *Annals of General Psychiatry, 6*(12).

doi:10.1186/1744-859X-6-12

32. Online Journal Article with No DOI Include volume and issue numbers for online journal articles. Add a retrieval line with the URL.

Prell, C. (2006). Social capital as network capital: Looking at the role

of social networks among not-for-profits. *Sociological*

Research Online, 11(4). Retrieved from

http://www.socresonline.org.uk/11/4/prell.html

33. Journal Article with No DOI from an Online Database, Library Database, or Subscription Service Always include volume and issue numbers for journals accessed online. If the article does not have a DOI (see p. 476) but is widely available through library databases and subscription services, cite it like a print journal article and do not name the database. Name the database *only* if the source is rare or is only available on a small number of databases.

Richter, A. (2006). Insurance catastrophe. *Journal of Property*

Management, 71(6), 28–32.

Wright, W. K. (1916). Psychology and the war. *Psychological*

Bulletin, 13(12), 462–466. Retrieved from PsycINFO database.

34. Magazine or Newspaper Article from an Online Database, Library Database, or Subscription Service Follow the same citation format you would use for a print magazine or newspaper article. For print articles widely available through library databases and subscription services, no retrieval line is necessary. Add a retrieval line that names the database only if the source is rare or available only on a small number of databases.

Colvin, G. (2007, May 14). Business is back. *Fortune, 155,* 40.

Smith, C. S. (1898, July 3). Wartime prosperity. *The New York Times,*

p. 18. Retrieved from The Historical New York Times database.

35. Article in an Online Newspaper Include the URL for the newspaper's home page.

Schmeltzer, J. (2007, January 2). Starbucks plans to cut trans

fats. *Chicago Tribune.* Retrieved from

http://www.chicagotribune.com

36. Article in an Online Magazine If a volume number is available, include it after the magazine title, in italics, followed by a period (see entry 37).

> Reitz, V. (2006, October 1). Engineering for fun and profit. *Medical*
>
> *Design Magazine Online.* Retrieved from
>
> http://www.medicaldesign.com/articles/ID/13233

37. Exclusive Online Magazine Content Use this format for online content not available in the print version of a magazine.

> Wilson, D. (2007, June 26). Everything I need to know about (real)
>
> robots I learned from Transformers [Online exclusive]. *Wired,*
>
> *15.* Retrieved from http://www.wired.com/entertainment
>
> /Hollywood/magazine/15-07/trans_know

38. Online Review of a Work

> Scott, A. O. (2006, December 29). In gloom of war, a child's paradise
>
> [Review of the motion picture *Pan's labyrinth*]. *The New York*
>
> *Times.* Retrieved from http://www.nytimes.com

39. Entire Book Accessed Online

> James, W. (1907). *Pragmatism.* Retrieved from
>
> http://www.gutenberg.org/etext/5116

40. Book Chapter Accessed Online

> Klein, L. R. (1986). Macroeconomic modeling and forecasting. In N. J.
>
> Smelser & D. R. Gerstein (Eds.), *Behavioral and social science:*
>
> *50 years of discovery* (pp. 95–110). Retrieved from http://
>
> books.nap.edu/openbook.php?record_id=611&page=95

41. Online Dictionary, Encyclopedia, or Reference Book Article In the retrieval line, include the date you accessed the site and the URL for the home or search page.

> Pashmina. (n.d.). In *Merriam-Webster's online dictionary.* Retrieved
>
> August 30, 2007, from http://www.m-w.com/dictionary/
>
> Vermeil. (2007). In *Encyclopedia Britannica online.* Retrieved
>
> September 1, 2007, from http://www.britannica.com

42. Page on a Web Site Add the date of access to the retrieval line only if the URL or content is likely to change.

Clayton, V. (2007, August 10). Think like a marketer to get kids to eat
   healthy. *MSNBC*. Retrieved from http://www.msnbc.msn.com
   /id/20204504

43. Stand-Alone Internet Document with No Author or Date When the date of publication is not available, include the retrieval date.

Curriculum overview 2. (n.d.). Retrieved January 2, 2007, from
   http://www.marlborough.k12.ct.us/Brochure/Grade%202.htm

44. Chapter or Section of an Internet Document

Commission on the Intelligence Capabilities of the United States
   Regarding Weapons of Mass Destruction. (2005, March 31).
   Case study: Iraq. In *Report to the President* (chap. 1). Retrieved
   from http://www.wmd.gov/report/report.html

45. Posting on a Blog

Finchsimgate, P. (2007, January 3). More fishie science. Message
   posted to http://www.thechemblog.com

46. Wiki Article Wikis are Web sites that are written and edited by many people. Assess the credibility of such sources before including them in your work. Wikis are likely to be updated, so include the retrieval date in your entry.

Monopoly. (2006, July 14). Retrieved August 31, 2007, from The
   Economics Wiki: http://economics.wikia.com/wiki/Monopoly

47. Message Posted to an Electronic Mailing List or Newsgroup Add information about accessing the message if it is archived online.

Roberts, M. (2007, May 31). Re: Authorizing users [Msg 343]. Message
   posted to ILLIAD-L electronic mailing list, archived at
   http://listserv.vt.edu/cgi-bin/wa?A2=ind0705&L
   =illiad-l&T=0&P=39229

Woodgate, J. (2001, July 16). Calif. to change their voltage? [Msg 1].
   Message posted to news://sci.electronics.design

48. Abstract Accessed Online

Madachy, R., Boehm, B., & Lane, J. A. (2006). Assessing hybrid
   incremental processes for SISOS development [Abstract].
   Retrieved from http://sunset.usc.edu/csse/TECHRPTS/2006
   /2006_main.html

49. Published Dissertation Accessed from a Database Add the dissertation file number at the end of the entry.

> Negre, F. (2005). *Biosynthesis and regulation of floral scent in snapdragon and petunia flowers.* Retrieved from ProQuest Digital Dissertations. (AAT 3210759).

50. U.S. Government Report Available from the GPO (Government Printing Office) Access Database

> U.S. General Accounting Office. (2003, May 15). *Rebuilding Iraq* (Publication No. GAO-03-792R). Retrieved from General Accounting Office Reports Online via GPO Access database.

51. Audio Podcast

> Inskeep, S. (Host). (2007, June 8). Bono presses G-8 leaders on Africa aid. *Morning Edition.* Podcast retrieved from http://www.npr.org /templates/story /story.php?storyId=10830589
>
> Ryssdal, K. (Host). (2007, January 2). Marketplace. Podcast retrieved from iTunes.

52. Computer Program or Software Reference entries are unnecessary for most popular software programs. This citation format applies only to specialized software programs. If software is downloaded, omit city and publisher, and then add *Available from* and the URL.

> Gangnopahdhav, A. (1994). Data analyzer for e-mail usage [Software]. Princeton, NJ: MasterMinders.

53. E-Mail and Instant Messaging (IM) Personal e-mail, instant messaging, and other electronic communications that are not archived are identified as personal communications in the paper and are not listed in the References.

Additional Sources in Print, Audio, Video, Online, or Other Formats

54. Personal, Telephone, and E-Mail Interview Personal, telephone, and e-mail interviews are not included in the References. Instead, use a parenthetical citation in the text. See entry 30 for citing a published interview.

55. Television Series Start with the name, and then in parentheses the person's function (for example, *Producer*). After the title, insert *Television series* enclosed in brackets, followed by a period. Add the place the broadcast originated from, a colon, and the broadcasting network.

Abams, J. J., Burk, B., Cuse, C., & Lindelof, D. (Executive Producers).
(2004–2007). *Lost* [Television series]. New York: ABC.

56. Episode from a Television Series

Armus, A., Foster, N. K. (Writers), & Dawson, R. (Director). (2007,
February 12). Run! [Television series episode]. In A. Arkush &
T. Kring (Producers), *Heroes*. New York: NBC.

57. Television Series Episode Podcast

Young, R. (Writer/Director/Producer), & Smith, H. (Writer). (2004,
November 16). Is Wal-Mart good for America? [Television
series episode]. In D. Fanning & M. Sullivan (Executive
Producers), *Frontline*. Podcast retrieved from
http://www.pbs.org/wgbh/pages/frontline/shows
/walmart/view

58. Radio Broadcast Also see audio podcast (entry 51).

Amari, C., & Wolski, R. (Producers). (2004, May 29). *Twilight time*
[Radio program]. Chicago: WGN Radio.

59. Audio Recording on CD Also see audio podcast (entry 51).

Sedaris, D. (Speaker). (2003, October 9). *David Sedaris live at
Carnegie Hall* [CD]. New York: Little, Brown.

60. Music Recording on CD or MP3

Mayer, J. (2006). Waiting on the world to change. On *Continuum*
[CD]. New York: Aware/Columbia.
West, K. (2007). Stronger [MP3]. Retrieved from iTunes.

61. Motion Picture Released Theatrically

Reitman, J. (Writer/Director), & Sacks, D. O. (Producer). (2006). *Thank
you for smoking* [Motion picture]. United States: Fox
Searchlight.

62. DVD

Allen, W. (Writer/Director), Jaffe, C. H., & Rollins, J. (Producers).
(2006). *Match point* [DVD]. United States: Dreamworks.
(Original release date 2005).

63. Online Video Recording

Voltz, S., & Grobe, F. (2006). The Diet Coke and Mentos experiments [Video file]. Video posted to http://www.eepybird.com /dcm1.html

64. Live Performance of a Play

Farquhar, G. (Author), & Kahn, M. (Director). (2006, November 11). *The beaux' strategem* [Theatrical performance]. Shakespeare Theatre, Washington, DC.

65. Print or Online Map

Georgia. (2004). [Map]. Skokie, IL: Rand McNally.

San Diego. (2007). [Map]. Retrieved from http://www.mapquest.com

66. Lecture Notes or Multimedia Slides

Hughes, S. W. (2001). *Scannable resumes* [PowerPoint slides]. Retrieved from Purdue University Online Writing Lab Web site: http://owl.english.purdue.edu/workshops/pp /scannable.ppt

67. Online or In-Person Lecture, Speech, or Address

Chomsky, N. (2004, February 15). *The militarization of science and space.* Lecture at MIT. Cambridge, MA. Retrieved from http://mitworld.mit.edu/video/182

Villanueva, V. (2005, October 21). *Blind: Talking of the new racism.* Address to the International Writing Center Association Convention. Minneapolis, MN.

68. Broadcast, Online, or Print Advertisement

American Express. (2007, January 3). [Advertisement]. Atlanta: CNN.

Apple. (2007). iPod Shuffle [Advertisement]. Retrieved from http://www.apple.com/ipodshuffle/ads

MasterCard (2006, June). [Advertisement]. *Smithsonian, 37,* 25.

69. Print or Online Brochure If the publisher is also the author, list *Author* as the publisher.

Starbucks Coffee Company. (2005). *You, Starbucks, and nutrition* [Brochure]. Seattle, WA: Author.

World Health Organization. (2005). *Global action against cancer* [Brochure]. Retrieved from http://www.who.int/cancer/media /GlobalActionCancerEnglfull.pdf

67d   SAMPLE APA-STYLE RESEARCH PAPER

A sample student research paper using APA format and documentation begins on page 484. For all pages, leave a margin of at least one inch on all sides. For more on paper preparation, see 6c.

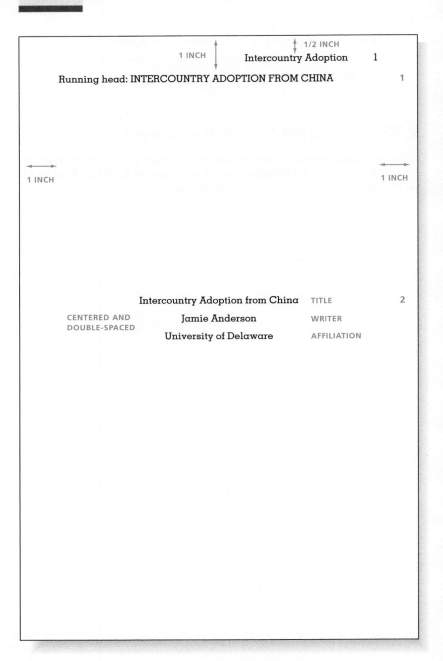

1 INCH

1/2 INCH

Intercountry Adoption   1

Running head: INTERCOUNTRY ADOPTION FROM CHINA   1

1 INCH

1 INCH

Intercountry Adoption from China   TITLE   2

CENTERED AND
DOUBLE-SPACED   Jamie Anderson   WRITER

University of Delaware   AFFILIATION

(Proportions shown in the margins of the APA paper are not actual but have
been adjusted to fit space limitations of this book. Follow actual dimensions
indicated and your instructor's directions.)

Comments

1. The title page has a running head typed in capital letters at top left (specifically to be used for publication purposes). Note that for all research papers, the entire essay has an abbreviated running head (in this case, "Intercountry Adoption") in a header with the page number, justified to the right margin.

2. The title, byline (writer's name), and affiliation (writer's college) are double-spaced and centered on the page. According to the APA manual, this information is all that is required for a professional publication. Many instructors prefer that you include the title, your name, instructor's name, course, and date instead (see 6c), so check with your instructor.

1 INCH

1/2 INCH
Intercountry Adoption   2

Abstract   3

Adoption of children from other countries by American families has
increased dramatically since World War II, and in the past decade,
adoptions of Chinese children have risen from a few hundred to over
5,000. Studies on the effects of intercountry adoption from China reveal
both positive and negative results. Negatives include identity confusion,
1 INCH racism, and developmental delays. With understanding and support,   1 INCH
however, adoptive parents can overcome these obstacles. In addition to
published research, personal experiences of real adoptive families are
cited. Intercountry adoption is found to be a generally positive
experience for both parents and children.   4

Comments

3. The second page of the essay begins with an abstract. Note the title (Abstract), centered at the top of the page.

4. The abstract should summarize an essay briefly (in about one hundred words) and accurately. Major assertions and research findings should be stated.

Intercountry Adoption from China

Intercountry adoption, the process of adopting children from across international borders, has been taking place in the United States since the years immediately following World War II. According to Rojewski and Rojewski (2001), there were 7,948 intercountry adoptions in the United States in 1989; in 1998, that number rose to 15,774, accounting for 12% to 13% of all adoptions (p. 3). Even more impressive has been the extreme growth in number of adoptions from China. In 1992, only 201 children were brought into the United States from China. By 2000, that number had increased to 5,053 children (p. 3). Studies on the process and effects of intercountry adoption from China have revealed both positive and negative results. While the effects of intercountry adoption from China are far-reaching for both the adoptee and the adoptive parents, there is no reason why intercountry adoption from China should be opposed.

Intercountry adoption was first generally done for humanitarian reasons. The first children to be adopted internationally were European orphans. This also occurred after both the Korean War in the 1950s and the Vietnam War in the 1970s (Rojewski & Rojewski, 2001, p. 2). Triseliotis (1993) suggests that the motive for intercountry adoption at these times was mostly to rescue children who were negatively affected by war. Today, however, the most common reason for intercountry adoption is for childless couples to become parents.

There are specific reasons why China has become such a popular place from which to adopt. In 1979, the Chinese government implemented a one-child-per-couple policy. The law, intended to help control the growing Chinese population, enforced a strict one-child policy in urban areas and a "one-son/two-child" rule in rural parts of the country (Rojewski & Rojewski, 2001, p. 5). Since the law's passage, hundreds of thousands of baby girls have been abandoned each year, for the most part because of the social

Comments

5. The title of the essay is repeated on the third page, centered.

6. APA style favors signal phrases (see 64f) using authors' names, always followed by the date of publication of the source being cited.

7. Parenthetical page references in APA style require the abbreviation *p.* before the page number. Note also that if a signal phrase is used, the name is omitted from the parenthetical reference.

8. Within the same paragraph, if the source being cited is the same as the previous source, only the page number need be given.

9. It is clear from this thesis that while the essay will address both positives and negatives of adoption of Chinese children into the United States, it will conclude that the practice should continue.

10. Here begins a section that sketches the history of intercountry adoption and accounts for its growing popularity.

11. If no signal phrase is used, authors' names, publication dates, and page numbers go in parentheses, separated by commas. Note that an ampersand (&) replaces the word *and* between authors' names in a parenthetical citation.

preference for sons, who are able to carry on the family name, perform heavier work, and support their parents when they reach old age. Tessler, Gamache, and Liu (1999) report that in 1992, partly in response to this situation, the People's Republic of China passed a law formalizing the process of intercountry adoption from China. Gravois (2004) notes that "95 percent of children available for adoption in China are girls" (para. 5). Tessler et al. (1999) also note that "eligibility, health status of prospective children, and cultural and personal interests may all be involved . . . in leading one to adopt from China" (pp. 79–80).

Because intercountry adoption from China is relatively new, studies are still under way on its effects on the adopted children and the adoptive families. Enough research has been done already, however, for most experts to take a position on the practice.

The majority of those who are opposed cite racial and cultural differences as their biggest concern. Intercountry adoptees can feel caught between identities. Are they American, Chinese, or both? Integrating the two cultures can be a very difficult process, one that some fear adoptive parents fail to recognize. Tessler et al. (1999) agree that "the most negative potential outcome of bicultural socialization is that children develop no strong attachment to either culture, thus feeling isolated and alone, without a strong reference group" (p. 25). Another reason cited in opposition to intercountry adoption is that the adopted child will be more exposed to racism. This is another area that many adoptive parents are not equipped to handle. Finally, developmental delays are likely in internationally adopted children. In such areas as speech, mental capabilities, and height and weight, "as many as three-fourths of all Chinese adoptees experience some type of developmental delay for a period of time after adoption" (Rojewski & Rojewski, 2001, p. 61).

Those who support intercountry adoption from China cite other studies that reinforce their beliefs. One study cited by

Comments

12. If a work has three or more authors, all authors (up to five) are named in the first citation of the work, but only the first author's name, followed by *et al.,* is used thereafter. (If a work has six or more authors, the form using *et al.* is used for all citations, including the first.)

13. Note in this paragraph the skillful use of three different sources to offer a coherent reason for the growth in adoption of Chinese children.

14. This transitional paragraph signals the end of the section on the history of intercountry adoption and the beginning of a new section that addresses more directly the thesis stated at the end of the paper's first paragraph about the advisability of intercountry adoption.

15. This paragraph summarizes three strong objections to intercountry adoption. If we remember the general thesis (at the end of paragraph one), we shouldn't be surprised when these objections are addressed later in the essay.

Vonk (2001) concluded that 75% to 80% of adopted children have positive relationships with their adoptive parents and experience no higher rates of educational or behavioral problems than children living with their birth parents (p. 248). Researchers have not been able to find substantial evidence that children adopted internationally are more likely to suffer long-term educational, social, or emotional conflicts. Others who support intercountry adoption believe that by allowing these underprivileged children into the country, more attention will be given to the fact that there are still thousands of other children suffering. Still others believe that it would be immoral not to allow children to be removed from orphanages and institutions when there are good homes available for them in other countries (Triseliotis, 1993). Rojewski and Rojewski (2001) flatly state, "There is no factual basis for the arguments used to oppose intercountry adoption. They are without merit" (p. 21).   16

The issue of adjustment is the most discussed variable   17
concerning intercountry adoption from China. It affects not only the adopted child but the parents and the rest of the family as well. Before considering adopting a child from another country, families need to realize that the status of their entire family will change to multicultural. According to a source from the National Adoption Information Clearinghouse, "When you adopt a child of another   18
race or culture, it is not only the child who is different. Your family becomes a 'different' family" ("Transracial," 2002, para. 8).   19
Prospective adoptive parents have to think about whether or not extended family members or friends will have any problems accepting their decision to adopt internationally. So even though the biggest adjustment awaits the adoptee, the adoptive parents will have adjustments to deal with as well.

The way parents choose to deal with the integration of the Chinese and American cultures can have a startling influence on the child's overall adjustment. Some who oppose intercountry adoption from China believe that the task is too hard for many

Comments

16. This paragraph counters the preceding one with reasons in favor of intercountry adoption.

17. The essay returns here to the objections raised in the fifth paragraph. This will occupy the essay for the next eight paragraphs.

18. An introductory phrase that identifies an expert source in this way can strengthen the effect of the information presented.

19. Because this source is unsigned, the parenthetical reference includes the first word of the Web page title in quotation marks. Because it is a Web source, it is also indicated by a paragraph number instead of a page number.

parents: "Parents must find a difficult balance that neither sets the child apart as being different nor denies the child's origins" (Rojewski & Rojewski, 2001, p. 96). Vonk (2001) concluded that parents need to be educated in the following categories in order to help their adopted child adjust properly: "racial awareness," "survival skills," and "multicultural [family] planning" (pp. 249–251). *Racial awareness* refers to the degree to which the parents recognize how race affects their own lives and how it will affect the life of their adopted child. *Survival skills* refer to the skills that parents teach their child about dealing with racism. It is imperative that adoptees receive the necessary "help to develop strong self-images despite racism" (p. 251). Some techniques include talking openly about racial issues, practicing answers to potentially harmful comments, and showing no personal tolerance for racist remarks. *Multicultural family planning* advocates a hands-on approach to helping the child learn more about his or her culture (p. 251).

Parents can help their child achieve balance between cultures in many ways. Open communication regarding cultural differences seems to be the most important factor. Children have to be encouraged to discuss how they feel because they are the ones who most acutely deal with the effects of bicultural socialization. Another important factor in achieving balance is the incorporation of Chinese culture and heritage into all aspects of the child's life. Suggested ways to do so include acknowledging different facets of Chinese culture, interacting with other Chinese people, and celebrating adoption-related events. According to Dickinson (2002), many families also choose to celebrate the child's native holidays and rituals, such as the Chinese New Year (para. 10). Parents can help their child interact with other members of their race by joining playgroups with other adoptees, living in culturally diverse neighborhoods, and finding positive role models of Chinese ethnicity. Ways to celebrate adoption-related events consist of

20

21

Comments

20. Note how the abstract generalization about the need for open communication is followed by a concrete example (see 32c).

21. Here the author uses the transitional device of repetition in the sentence to repeat the phrase "important factor" introduced earlier in the paragraph (see 19a).

including the child's birth name in her newly given American name. Parents can also acknowledge the day that the parents first met the child. This practice, "referred to by many as 'Gotcha Day,' was the most frequently celebrated of all adoption-related events" (Rojewski & Rojewski, 2001, p. 97). By acknowledging cultural differences in these ways, adoptees are likely to develop a sense of trust for their parents, positive attitudes toward family members, self-esteem, and better resilience against racism.

With the increasing numbers of Chinese children being adopted by U.S. families, the number of support groups for adoptive families is also growing. The largest of these groups is Families with Children from China (FCC). All chapters of this organization have three shared goals: "to support families who've adopted in China," "to encourage adoption from China," and "to advocate for and support children remaining in orphanages in China" (cited in Tessler et al., 1999, p. 61). The FCC hosts family picnics, Chinese festivals, and playgroups, among other events, to help adoptees and their new families adjust.

Even with help from the adoptive parents, adoptees still "must struggle to integrate an identity that includes acceptance of their own physical appearance, their birth heritage, and the heritage of their upbringing" (Vonk, 2001, p. 249). Although adoptees must deal with these struggles throughout their lives, some important steps normally occur during specific life stages. During infancy, the biggest adjustments for the adoptee are learning to trust and making the transition to a new home and family. Parents are responsible for building parent-child relationships at this point, along with deciding how to acknowledge cultural heritage. During the toddler and preschool years, parents need to begin preparing their children for awareness of their adoption and how to handle it. The middle years of childhood, between the ages of 6 and 12, are when most adjustment issues surface. Abandonment issues are generally discovered for the first time, and "the loss of one's

Comment

22. Although Anderson is quoting the goals of Families with Children from China, she found the quotations in another source: Tessler, Gamache, and Liu (1999). Note her way of letting the reader know this.

roots and identity may cause the child difficulty in establishing a sense of self and birth heritage" (Rojewski & Rojewski, 2001, p. 45). Also, the first exposure to racism and prejudice usually occurs during this time. Adolescence can be a very difficult time for intercountry adoptees, because "these young people have to contend with all of the usual challenges of adolescence plus being adopted, and most often being placed in a family that has a different ethnic and racial background than their own" (p. 48). Although all of these stages can be difficult, the more accepting that adoptees become of their culture and heritage, the easier the time of adjustment will be for them.

Other developmental adjustments sometimes need to be addressed. Many adoptees suffer from some kind of mental or physical delay. Most "problems, if and when they arise, most likely are related to preadoptive experiences such as neglect, malnutrition, or separation trauma," not postadoptive factors (Vonk, 2001, p. 248). These children have been found to catch up very quickly once adjusted (p. 248). Tan, Marfo, and Dedrick (2007) also note that special needs children adopted from China experience no greater developmental delays than other adopted Chinese children.   23

With all of the attention that has been paid to the adjustment process, it is no wonder that intercountry adoption from China is generally regarded in such a positive light. Personal experiences of adoptive parents reflect these positive findings as well. Christine   24
Bondonese, a physical therapist from Allentown, Pennsylvania, adopted Maia, a baby girl from China, three years ago. Overall, the family's experience has been very positive. They have dealt with many adjustment issues. Developmental delays were an original concern. Bondonese said, "Maia was 8 months old when we brought her home. However, the doctor told us she was more like 6 months old—she had mild delays—but caught up quickly with no special help" (personal communication, November 11, 2002). Now 4 years   25
old, Maia has started attending preschool and has adapted very

Comments

23. The last of the objections raised in the fifth paragraph has now been addressed.

24. These transition sentences introduce a short section of original research in the form of interviews with two families who have adopted Chinese children.

25. Because conversations and interviews do not contain what the APA considers "recoverable data," they are cited in the text but are not listed on the reference page.

well. Bondonese said that both "socially and academically, she is at the top of her class." To help integrate both cultures, the family belongs to a local chapter of the FCC and keeps many Chinese things in their home, including books and music. Maia has had to adjust to many new things since she was brought to the United States, but Bondonese said that the most important thing the family has been able to give her to help in the adjustment process is "lots of love!"

The Lauffer family has also had a positive adoption experience. John and Johanna Lauffer adopted Janie from China when she was 9 months old. Janie also experienced some developmental delays, but Johanna Lauffer said that "now at the age of 3 [she] is doing great. Her doctor said she is right in line with where she should be" (personal communication, November 15, 2002). To help integrate the two cultures, the Lauffers brought many things back from China to keep in their home, and they frequently talk about the fact that Janie is adopted and from China. Johanna Lauffer said, "I am not too sure how much she is absorbing now, but we hope it will help." Most adoptive families face similar issues, but with appropriate parenting and plenty of love, adopted babies from China are usually able to adapt relatively easily.

While there still are opposing views regarding the subject of intercountry adoption from China, the consensus seems to be that the benefits of this type of adoption far outweigh the negatives. With all of the suffering children in the world today, there is no reason why the availability of good homes should be ignored, whether or not they require the children to be adopted into a different country. Many children do suffer some type of developmental delay at their time of arrival, but the vast majority overcome these early delays with few problems. Adoptees also need to make many psychological adjustments, but with proper care and attention, they can overcome these problems. Overall, intercountry adoption from China benefits everyone involved in the process.

26

27

Comments

26. Place square brackets around words that you insert into a quotation. This should only be done to clarify information or build a grammatical sentence structure. It is very important, however, to maintain the original author's intended meaning.

27. This return to the basic thesis of the essay (in spite of negatives, intercountry adoption is recommended) signals the beginning of the conclusion. Anderson restates the major points in favor of intercountry adoption.

References

Dickinson, A. (2002, August 26). Bicultural kids: Parents who adopt children of a different ethnicity are enjoying the best of both worlds. *Time, 160,* B1+.

Gravois, J. (2004, January 16). Bringing up babes. *Slate.* Retrieved from http://www.slate.com/id/2093899

Rojewski, J. W., & Rojewski, J. L. (2001). *Intercountry adoption from China.* Westport, CT: Bergin & Garvey.

Tan, X. T., Marfo, K., & Dedrick, R. F. (2007). Special needs adoption from China: Exploring child-level indicators, adoptive family characteristics, and correlates of behavioral adjustment. *Children and Youth Services Review, 29*(10), 1269–1285. doi:10.1016/j.childyouth.2007.05.001

Tessler, R., Gamache, G., & Liu, L. (1999). *West meets East: Americans adopt Chinese children.* Westport, CT: Bergin & Garvey.

Transracial and transcultural adoption. (2002, March 3). *National adoption information clearinghouse.* Retrieved from http://www.calib.com/naic/pubs/f_trans.html

Triseliotis, J. (1993). Intercountry adoption: In whose best interest? In M. Humphrey & H. Humphrey (Eds.), *Intercountry adoption: Practical experiences* (pp. 119–137). New York: Tavistock/Routledge.

Vonk, M. E. (2001, July). Cultural competence for transracial adoptive parents. *Social Work, 46,* 246–255.

1 INCH

1 INCH

28

29

30

31

32

33

34

35

36

37

1 INCH

Comments

28. The title of the bibliography page is "References" and is centered.

29. In titles (of articles and books, for example), capitalize only the first word, the first word after a colon, and proper nouns. Italicize the titles of books, periodicals, motion pictures, and CDs.

30. This source is an online version of a print magazine article located on a library database (see entry 34 in 67c). For articles widely available on databases, no retrieval line naming the database is necessary.

31. Use the last name but only the initial(s) (not the whole first name) of the author, and follow this with the publication date in parentheses and then a period. An Internet address (URL) is not placed in brackets, and the final period is omitted.

32. The Tan, Marfo, and Dedrick article was accessed on the ScienceDirect database. This article has been assigned a DOI (Digital Object Identifier). When referencing a DOI-assigned journal article that has been accessed online or in a database, include the DOI number at the end of the citation (see entry 31 in 67c).

33. If there is more than one author, all the names and first initials are reversed: last name first, then first name initial or initials.

34. If no author's name appears on the original source, which is often the case with Internet documents, the first item in the entry is the title, followed (like a name) by the date of publication.

35. The article cited here is from an edited volume of essays. Editors' names appear with initial first, then last name.

36. Include all digits in page ranges.

37. This source was accessed in PDF format from a library database. For materials widely available on databases, do not add a retrieval line naming the database in your entry (see entry 33 in 67c).

68
DOCUMENTING IN OTHER STYLES

68a *CHICAGO MANUAL OF STYLE* (CM)

In disciplines such as history and other humanities, the preferred style is that of *The Chicago Manual of Style* (15th ed., 2003), which is also explained in a shorter volume intended for student writers, *A Manual for Writers of Term Papers, Theses, and Dissertations* (7th ed., 2007), by Kate L. Turabian et al.

When you use CM style, you may use notes or endnotes to acknowledge sources in the text, or you may use in-text citations that refer the reader to a bibliography at the end of the paper.

1. Numbered Notes

■ *Numbering in the text.* Numbered notes are used to indicate publication information. They also add explanations and other material that would otherwise interrupt the main text. Citations should be numbered consecutively with superscript numbers ([1]). Put the note number at the end of the sentence or end of a clause immediately following the punctuation mark. Don't insert a space between the punctuation mark and the superscript number.

> The violence in the Raj at that time was more pronounced than it had been in the previous conflict.[4] As Peter Holman has noted, "The military police were at a loss to stem the tide of bloodshed."[5]

■ *Placing notes.* List notes at the bottom of the page as footnotes or at the end of the essay as endnotes.

■ *Spacing notes.* Single-space within each note, and insert one blank line between each note. Indent the first line of each note the same space that you indent paragraphs.

■ *Ordering the parts of notes.* Begin with the author's first and last names, add the title, and then include the publishing information and page numbers.

■ *Punctuating, capitalizing, and abbreviating.* Use commas between elements, and put publishing information within parentheses. Include the page number, but omit the abbreviation *p.* or *pp.* Italicize titles of books and periodicals. Capitalize titles of articles, books, and journals. Use quotation marks around titles of periodical articles and sections of books.

■ *Using a bibliography page.* The use of a bibliography page is optional with the use of notes.

Ordering Notes in a Paper

The first time a source is cited, all relevant information is included. Later citations for that source are shortened. In most cases, note the author's last name, a shortened version of the title, and the page or pages being cited, omitting *p.* or *pp.* Use a comma after the author name and after the title and a period at the end.

If you wish, you may use *Ibid.* to refer to the work in the directly preceding note or, if the page is different, use *Ibid.* followed by a comma and the page number.

> 6. Peter Holman, *The History of the Raj: Nineteenth and Twentieth Centuries* (New York: Dorset Press, 1996), 18.
>
> 7. Martin Joos, *The Five Clocks* (New York: Harcourt, Brace, 1962), 5.
>
> 8. Holman, *History of the Raj*, 34–36.
>
> 9. Ibid., 72.

2. Author-Date Citation Format

The author-date citation format requires both in-text citations and a bibliography page. In-text citations in *Chicago Manual* style are similar, but not identical, to those in APA style (see 67a).

■ Up to three authors are cited by last name. If there are four or more authors, list only the first author's last name, followed by *et al.*

■ The date of publication is given next, with no intervening punctuation.

■ If a page number is required, it is given following a comma.

Here are some typical author-date citations in CM style:

> (Patel 2004, 18)
>
> (Newhouse and Zuzu 1889)
>
> (Baez et al. 2004, 244)
>
> As explained by Patel (2004, 18), . . .

For online or electronic works without page numbers, indicate the section title (if available) under which the specific reference can be located:

> (Quinn 2006, under "Espionage")

Every work cited in the body of your paper must have an entry in the Bibliography at the end of the paper, and every work appearing in the Bibliography must be cited at least once in the body of the paper.

Note that the *Chicago Manual* also permits bibliography entries to follow the order and capitalization scheme of APA style (see 67c), with one major difference: the date is *not* enclosed in parentheses.

3. Bibliography in CM Style

There are some stylistic differences between footnotes or endnotes and Bibliography entries. Whereas the names in notes appear in natural order (first name, then last name), the bibliography inverts the first author's name, with last name first. Elements in the bibliography are separated by periods, not commas and parentheses.

> Gladwell, Malcolm. *Blink: The Power of Thinking Without Thinking*. New
>
> York: Little, Brown, 2005.

Title your list "Bibliography," "Works Cited," or "References."

Start the first line of each entry at the left margin, and indent all other lines in the entry. Single-space within each entry, and insert one blank line between each entry. Indent each line after the first with the same space that you indent paragraphs. Include all of the same elements as in a note for that source, but do not put parentheses around the publishing information.

Italicize titles of books and periodicals. Use quotation marks around titles of periodicals and sections of books.

Parts of the Bibliography Entry for a Book

Information appears in the order given here.

Author. Give the full names of all authors (or editors or translators).

Title: Subtitle. Give the full title, including subtitle, in italics. If adding an editor, end with a comma instead of a period.

Editor, compiler, or translator. List these, if any, if in addition to the author.

Volume number. For a multivolume work, give the total number of volumes if the work is being referred to as a whole. If a single volume is being cited, identify only that one by number.

Title of individual volume. List the volume title, if applicable. If adding page numbers for a specific work, end with a comma instead of a period.

Page numbers. Give page numbers when a chapter or other section of a book is being cited. Use an inclusive number format (write 211–40, not 211–240).

City: Publisher, Year. Include the city, the publisher's name, and the date of publication. For an online book, add the electronic address, and place the access date in parentheses.

Books

In the examples, *N* stands for note format and *B* stands for bibliography format. See the note in 68a2 regarding an alternative bibliography format. Notes and bibliography entries should be single-spaced, with a blank line between each entry. For ease of reading, however, the examples below are double spaced.

1. One Author

N: 1. Seymour M. Hersh, *Chain of Command: The Road from 9/11 to Abu Ghraib* (New York: HarperCollins, 2004), 97.

B: Hersh, Seymour M. *Chain of Command: The Road from 9/11 to Abu Ghraib.* New York: HarperCollins, 2004.

2. Two Authors

N: 2. Shoshana Felman and Dori Laub, *Testimony: Crises of Witnessing in Literature, Psychoanalysis, and History* (New York: Routledge, 1992), 57.

B: Felman, Shoshana, and Dori Laub. *Testimony: Crises of Witnessing in Literature, Psychoanalysis, and History.* New York: Routledge, 1992.

3. Three Authors

N: 3. Glen Stout, Charles Vitchers, and Robert Gray, *Nine Months at Ground Zero: The Story of the Brotherhood of Workers Who Took on a Job like No Other* (New York: Scribner, 2006), 90–91.

B: Stout, Glen, Charles Vitchers, and Robert Gray. *Nine Months at Ground Zero: The Story of the Brotherhood of Workers Who Took on a Job like No Other.* New York: Scribner, 2006.

4. Four or More Authors

In the notes format, list the first author and add *et al.* or *and others* with no intervening punctuation.

N: 4. James A. Baker III et al., *The Iraq Study Group Report: The Way Forward—a New Approach* (New York: Vintage, 2006), 27.

In the bibliography format, list all authors for a work between four and ten authors. If the work has eleven or more authors, list the first seven authors and add *et al.* with no intervening punctuation.

B: Baker, James A., III, Lee H. Hamilton, Lawrence S. Eagleburger, Vernon E. Jordan Jr., Edwin Meese III, Sandra Day O'Connor, Leon E. Panetta, William J. Perry, Charles S. Robb, and Alan K. Simpson. *The Iraq Study Group Report: The Way Forward—a New Approach.* New York: Vintage, 2006.

5. Book with an Unknown Author

N: 5. *The Second World War: A World in Flames* (Oxford: Osprey, 2004), 30–31.

B: *The Second World War: A World in Flames.* Oxford: Osprey, 2004.

6. Book with an Editor

N: 6. Nancy P. McKee and Linda Stone, eds., *Readings on Gender and Culture in America* (Upper Saddle River, NJ: Prentice Hall, 2002), 1–2.

B: McKee, Nancy P., and Linda Stone, eds. *Readings on Gender and Culture in America.* Upper Saddle River, NJ: Prentice Hall, 2002.

7. Second or Later Edition

N: 7. Nancy Bonvillain, *Women and Men: Cultural Constructs of Gender,* 3rd ed. (Upper Saddle River, NJ: Prentice Hall, 2001), 39–41.

B: Bonvillain, Nancy. *Women and Men: Cultural Constructs of Gender.* 3rd ed. Upper Saddle River, NJ: Prentice Hall, 2001.

8. Reprinted Book

N: 8. Edith Wharton, *House of Mirth* (1905; repr., New York: Penguin, 1986), 64–65.

B: Wharton, Edith. *House of Mirth.* 1905. Reprint, New York: Penguin, 1986.

9. Selection or Book Chapter in an Anthology/Scholarly Collection

N: 9. Stuart Moulthrop, "No War Machine," in *Reading Matters: Narratives in the New Media Ecology,* ed. Joseph Tabbi and Michael Wutz (Ithaca, NY: Cornell University Press, 1997), 280.

B: Moulthrop, Stuart. "No War Machine." In *Reading Matters: Narratives in the New Media Ecology,* edited by Joseph Tabbi and Michael Wutz, 269–92. Ithaca, NY: Cornell University Press, 1997.

10. Multivolume Book When following the notes format and using a book that doesn't have an individual volume title, omit the volume reference immediately after the book title. Then, after the facts of publication, insert the volume number (followed by a colon) and page numbers (i.e., 2:45–96).

N: 10. Roy T. Matthews and F. Dewitt Platt, *The Western Humanities,* vol. 2, *The Renaissance to the Present,* 5th ed. (New York: McGraw-Hill, 2004), 297–98.

B: Matthews, Roy T., and F. Dewitt Platt. *The Western Humanities.*
        Vol. 2, *The Renaissance to the Present.* 5th ed. New York:
        McGraw-Hill, 2004.

11. Book with a Title Within the Title

N: 11. Rebello, Stephen, *Alfred Hitchcock and the Making of
        "Psycho"* (New York: St. Martin's Griffin, 1998), 60.

B: Rebello, Stephen. *Alfred Hitchcock and the Making of "Psycho."*
        New York: St. Martin's Griffin, 1998.

12. Government Publication

N: 12. Office of the President, *Budget of the United States
        Government, Fiscal Year 2007* (Washington, DC: Government
        Printing Office, 2006), 11.

B: Office of the President. *Budget of the United States Government,
        Fiscal Year 2007.* Washington, DC: Government Printing
        Office, 2006.

13. Article in a Reference Book Don't include the volume or page number. Instead, cite the term in the reference book under which the information is contained. Use the abbreviation *s.v.* for *sub verbo,* meaning "under the word," and place the term in quotation marks. Well-known reference books are not listed in the bibliography as long as the title is cited in the text.

N: 13. *Encyclopaedia Britannica,* 15th ed., s.v. "Parks, Rosa."

14. Biblical or Other Scriptural Reference Include the book (abbreviated with no underlining or italics), chapter, and verse, but no page number. Scriptural references are usually cited in the notes or in the parenthetical citation.

N: 14. Gen. 21:14–18.

Periodicals

15. Article in a Journal If no issue number is available, it can't be included.

N: 15. Fredrik Logevall, "Lyndon Johnson and Vietnam,"
        Presidential Studies Quarterly 34, no. 1 (2004): 102.

B: Logevall, Fredrik. "Lyndon Johnson and Vietnam." *Presidential
        Studies Quarterly* 34, no. 1 (2004): 100–12.

16. Article in a Magazine While referenced page numbers should be included in the notes entry, page numbers for the full article are optional for the bibliographic entry.

N: 16. George Packer, "Knowing the Enemy," *New Yorker*,

December 18, 2006, 62.

B: Packer, George. "Knowing the Enemy." *New Yorker*, December 18,

2006, 60–69.

17. Article in a Newspaper No page numbers are listed. If you are citing a specific edition of the paper, you may add a comma after the year and list the edition (e.g., late edition, Southeast edition), followed by a period.

N: 17. Somini Sengupta, "Interests Drive U.S. to Back a Nuclear

India." *New York Times*, December 10, 2006.

B: Sengupta, Somini. "Interests Drive U.S. to Back a Nuclear India."

New York Times, December 10, 2006.

18. Book Review

N: 18. Kevin Warwick, review of *Beyond the Image Machine:*

A History of Visual Technologies, by David Tomas,

Modernism/Modernity 13 (January 2006): 213.

B: Warwick, Kevin. Review of *Beyond the Image Machine: A History*

of Visual Technologies, by David Tomas.

Modernism/Modernity 13 (January 2006): 212–14.

Online and Electronic Sources

19. Article from a Print Journal, Magazine, or Newspaper Located in a Library Database or Subscription Service Follow the citation format for the print version of the text, and then provide the electronic address to the entry page of the database or subscription service, usually the URL up to the first slash (/).

N: 19. Bill Powell, "When Outlaws Get the Bomb," *Time*,

October 23, 2006, 32, http://find.galegroup.com/ (accessed January 2,

2007).

B: Powell, Bill. "When Outlaws Get the Bomb." *Time*, October 23,

2006, 32. http://find.galegroup.com/ (accessed

January 2, 2007).

20. Entire Web Site Unless the name of the Web site is the name of an online journal, magazine, newspaper, or book, don't italicize it.

N: 20. San Diego Zoo, http://www.sandiegozoo.org/

(accessed January 2, 2007).

B: San Diego Zoo. http://www.sandiegozoo.org/ (accessed
            January 2, 2007).

21. Page on a Web Site Unless the name of the Web site is the name of an online journal, magazine, newspaper, or book, don't italicize it.

N: 21. Andrew Hollinger, "Muslims Make Holocaust Museum
            Appearance," United States Holocaust Memorial Museum
            (December 20, 2006), http://www.ushmm.org/museum/press/
            archives/detail.php?category=07-general&content=2006-12-20
            (accessed January 2, 2007).

B: Hollinger, Andrew. "Muslims Make Holocaust Museum
            Appearance." United States Holocaust Memorial Museum.
            December 20, 2006. http://www.ushmm.org/museum/press/
            archives/detail.php?category=07-general&content=2006-12-20
            (accessed January 2, 2007).

22. Article from an Online Journal, Magazine, or Newspaper Follow the guidelines for the print version of the source. Then add the full electronic address and the access date.

N: 22. Dinesh Joseph Wadiwel, "Sovereignty, Torture, and
            Blood: Tracing Genealogies and Rethinking Politics," *Borderlands*
            5, no. 1 (May 2006), http://www.borderlandsejournal.adelaide.edu.au/
            vol5no1_2006/wadiwel_blood.htm (accessed December 23, 2006).

B: Wadiwel, Dinesh Joseph. "Sovereignty, Torture, and Blood:
            Tracing Genealogies and Rethinking Politics." *Borderlands*
            5, no. 1 (May 2006). http://www.borderlandsejournal.adelaide.edu.au/
            vol5no1_2006/wadiwel_blood.htm (accessed December 23,
            2006).

23. Entire Blog Don't italicize the title of the blog.

N: 23. Political Cortex: Brain Food for the Body Politic,
            http://www.politicalcortex.com/ (accessed November 20, 2006).

B: Political Cortex: Brain Food for the Body Politic. http://
            www.politicalcortex.com/ (accessed November 20, 2006).

24. Posting on a Blog If the author's real name is unknown, add *pseud.* in square brackets. Don't italicize the title of the blog.

N: 24. Arnold [pseud.], comment on "Close," The Little Professor,
            comment posted December 28, 2006, http://
            littleprofessor.typepad.com/the_little_professor/2006/12/
            close.html#comments (accessed January 2, 2007).

B: Arnold [pseud.]. Comment on "Close." The Little Professor.
December 28, 2006. http://littleprofessor.typepad.com/
the_little_professor/2006/12/close.html#comments
(accessed January 2, 2007).

25. Online Government Document

N: 25. National Council on Disability, *Creating Livable
Communities* (Washington, DC: National Council on Disability,
October 31, 2006), 10, http://www.ncd.gov/newsroom/publications/
2006/pdf/livable_communities.pdf (accessed January 3, 2007).

B: National Council on Disability. *Creating Livable Communities*.
Washington, DC: National Council on Disability, October 31,
2006. http://www.ncd.gov/newsroom/publications/2006/pdf/
livable_communities.pdf (accessed January 3, 2007).

26. E-Mail Message or Posting to a Mailing List E-mail messages
and postings to mailing lists usually appear only in the notes or parenthetical citation, not in the bibliography. Add an electronic address and access date at the end of the entry if the posting is archived on a Web site.

N: 26. Dora Dodger-Gilbert, e-mail message to Veterinary
Questions and Viewpoints mailing list, January 3, 2007.

27. Daniel Kaplan, e-mail message to the author,
September 23, 2004.

27. CD-ROM or DVD-ROM

N: 28. *All-Movie Guide*, CD-ROM (Corel, 1996).

B: *All-Movie Guide*. CD-ROM. Corel, 1996.

28. Podcast, MP3, or Other Downloaded Material Add the provider
and file format at the end of the entry.

N: 29. Melvyn Bragg, Roger Crowley, Judith Herrin, and Colin
Imber, "The Siege of Constantinople," *BBC Radio 4: In Our Time*
(December 28, 2006), iTunes MP3.

30. Kanye West, *Late Registration* (New York: Roc-a-Fella
Records, 2005), iTunes MP3.

B: Bragg, Melvyn, Roger Crowley, Judith Herrin, and Colin Imber.
"The Siege of Constantinople." *BBC Radio 4: In Our Time*. December
28, 2006. iTunes MP3.

West, Kanye. *Late Registration*. New York: Roc-a-Fella Records, 2005.
iTunes MP3.

Other Sources

29. Unpublished Dissertation

N: 31. Arnold Mayniew, "Historical Perceptions of Royal
Prerogative" (PhD diss., University of Illinois, 1991), 32–37.

B: Mayniew, Arnold. "Historical Perceptions of Royal Prerogative."
PhD diss., University of Illinois, 1991.

30. Television Interview

N: 32. Barack Obama, interview by Tim Russert, *Meet the Press*,
NBC, October 22, 2006.

B: Obama, Barack. Interview by Tim Russert. *Meet the Press*. NBC.
October 22, 2006.

31. Personal or Telephone Interview In the author-date format, personal communications are acknowledged in the text but not in the bibliography.

N: 33. Kenneth Autrey, interview by the author, October 24, 2006,
Florence, South Carolina.

34. John Sutton, telephone interview by the author, December 1,
2006.

32. Film on Videotape or DVD

N: 35. *Good Night, and Good Luck*, DVD, directed by George
Clooney (2005; Burbank, CA: Warner Home Video, 2006).

B: *Good Night, and Good Luck*. DVD. Directed by George Clooney.
2005. Burbank, CA: Warner Home Video, 2006.

33. Sound Recording Include the product number (often located on the spine of a CD) at the end of the entry.

N: 36. Johann Sebastian Bach, *Four Concerti for Various
Instruments*, Orchestra of St. Luke's, dir. Michael Feldman,
Musical Heritage Society, CD 512268T.

B: Bach, Johann Sebastian. *Four Concerti for Various Instruments*.
Orchestra of St. Luke's, dir. Michael Feldman. Musical
Heritage Society, CD 512268T.

34. Source Quoted from Another Source Quotations from secondary sources should ordinarily be avoided. If, however, the original source is unavailable, list both sources in the entry.

N: 37. H. H. Dubs, "An Ancient Chinese Mystery Cult," *Harvard Theological Review* 35 (1942): 223, quoted in Susan Naquin, *Millenarian Rebellion in China: The Eight Trigrams Uprising of 1813* (New Haven, CT: Yale University Press, 1976), 288.

B: Dubs, H. H. "An Ancient Chinese Mystery Cult." *Harvard Theological Review* 35 (1942): 223. Quoted in Susan Naquin, *Millenarian Rebellion in China: The Eight Trigrams Uprising of 1813*. New Haven, CT: Yale University Press, 1976, 288.

68b COUNCIL OF SCIENCE EDITORS (CSE)

Writers in the physical and life sciences follow the documentation style developed by the Council of Science Editors (CSE), found in *Scientific Style and Format: The CSE Manual for Authors, Editors, and Publishers* (7th ed., 2006). Mathematicians and those in other scientific fields also use this style. (See 68c for a list of style manuals for other scientific fields.) Check to see whether your instructor has a preference for a documentation format to use.

The *CSE Manual* offers three documentation styles. Again, ask your instructor which one is preferred for your papers, or you can check a current journal in the field. The three styles are *name-year*, *citation-sequence*, and *citation-name*.

1. Name-Year Format

Authors' names and publication dates are included in parenthetical citations in the text, closely resembling *Chicago Manual* name-date style (see 68a).

In-Text Citation

The earlier studies done on this virus (Fong and Townes 1992; Mindlin 1994) reported similar results. However, one of these studies (Mindlin 1994) noted a mutated strain.

In the list of references at the end of the paper, the names are listed alphabetically with the date after the name. Journal titles are abbreviated, without periods.

Reference List Entry

Fong L, Townes HC. 1992. Viral longevity. Biol Rep. 27(2):129-45.

2. Citation-Sequence Style

References may instead be cited by means of in-text superscript numbers (numbers set above the line, such as [1] and [2]) that refer to a list of numbered references at the end of the paper. The references are numbered sequentially in the order in which they are cited in the text, and later references to the same work use the original number. When you have two or more sources cited at once, put the numbers in sequence, separated with commas but no spaces.

In-Text Citation

Earlier studies on this virus [1,4,9] reported similar results. However, one of these studies [4] noted a mutated strain.

In the list of references, the entries are listed in the order in which they are cited in the paper, not alphabetically.

Reference List Entry

1. Fong L, Townes HC. Viral longevity. Biol Rep. 1992;27(2):129-45.

3. Citation-Name Style

In this style, all sources are first listed on the References page in alphabetical order by authors' names and then assigned a number in sequence. These numbers are then used to correspond to in-text superscript numbers. Other than the change in numbering, the in-text and the reference list citation formats are the same as that used for the citation-sequence style.

4. CSE References List

At the end of the paper, include a list titled "References" or "Cited References." As you can tell from the examples in 68b1 and 68b2, the placement of the date depends on which style you use.

- *Name-date style.* Put the date after the author's name. Arrange the list alphabetically by last names. Do not indent any lines in the entries.
- *Citation-sequence and citation-name styles.* For books, put the date after the publisher's name. For periodicals, put the date after the periodical name. Arrange the list by number. Put the number at the left margin, followed by a period and a space and then the authors' names.

5. References in CSE Style

Use periods between major divisions of the entry.

Author. | Start with the last name first, no comma, and initials without periods for first and middle names. Separate authors' names with commas. End the list of authors' names with a period.

Title. | For books and article titles, capitalize only the first word and proper nouns. Do not underline, italicize, or use quotation marks. For journals, abbreviate titles and capitalize all major words.

City of publication (state abbreviation): publisher; publication date. | Include a semicolon and a space between the name of the publisher and the date. Use a semicolon with no space between the date and volume number of the journal. Abbreviate months. End with a period.

Pages. | For books, you may include the total number of pages, with p. after the number. End the entry with a period. For journal articles, show the page numbers and end with a period.

All numbered references shown are in the citation-sequence format. References should be single-spaced, with a blank line between each entry. For ease of reading, however, the examples below are double spaced.

1. Book with One Author

1. Woit P. Not even wrong: the failure of string theory and the search for unity in physical law. New York: Basic Books; 2006. 291 p.

2. Book with More Than One Author If there are more than ten authors, list the first ten and add *et al.* or *and others*.

2. French S, Krause D. Identityin physics: a historical, philosophical, and format analysis. New York: Oxford University Press; 2006. 422 p.

3. Anthology, Scholarly Collection, or Work That Names an Editor

3. Fraser LH, Keddy PA, editors. The world's largest wetlands: ecology and conservation. New York: Cambridge University Press; 2005. 488 p.

4. Article or Chapter in an Anthology, Scholarly Collection, or Work That Names an Editor

4. Terborgh J. The green world hypothesis revisited. In: Ray JC, Redford KH, Steneck RS, Berger J, editors. Large carnivores and the conservation of biodiversity. Washington (DC): Island Press; 2005. p 82-99.

5. Work by a Group or Corporate Author

> 5. Council of Science Editors, Style Manual Committee. Scientific style and format: the CSE manual for authors, editors, and publishers. 7th ed. Reston (VA): The Council; 2006. 658 p.

6. Article in a Journal or Magazine

> 6. Wang Y, Wang R. Imaging using parallel integrals in optical projection tomography. Phys Med Biol. 2006;51(12):6023-32.

7. Article in a Newspaper Provide the page number and column number of the beginning of the article.

> 7. Edwards H. Aquarium shows off new views. Seattle Times (Metro Ed.). 2007 Jun 15;Sect. A:1 (col.1).

8. Article with No Author Begin the entry with the article title.

9. Editorial After the title, add [editorial].

10. Journal Article in a Library Database or Subscription Service

> 8. Hulme M, Turnpenny J. Understanding and managing climate change: the UK experience [Internet]. Geog J 2004 [cited 2007 Jun 15];170(2):105-15. Available from: http://www.fmarion.edu/academics/ journalarticlesanddatabases after clicking InfoTrac and then clicking Expanded Academic ASAP and searching by article title.

11. Article in an Online Journal

> 9. Pribram KH. What makes humanity humane. J Biomed Discov Collab [Internet]. 2006 Nov 29 [cited 2007 Jan 3];1(14):1-7. Available from: http://www.j-biomed-discovery.com/content/pdf/ 1747-5333-1-14.pdf.

12. Entire Web Site

> 10. Gray W. Tropical meteorology project [Internet]. c1994-2003. Fort Collins: Colorado State University; [updated 2007 May 30; cited 2007 Jun 15]. Available from: http://hurricane.atmos.colostate.edu/.

13. E-Mail and Instant Messaging (IM) Personal e-mail, instant messaging, and other personal communications are identified in the body of the paper and are not listed in the References.

68c RESOURCES FOR OTHER STYLES

Anthropology

The Chicago Manual of Style, 15th ed. Chicago: U of Chicago P, 2003. (See 68a.)

Chemistry

Coghill, Anne M., and Lorrin R. Garson, eds. *The ACS Style Guide: A Manual for Authors and Editors*. 3rd ed. New York: Oxford UP, 2006.

Education

American Psychological Association. *Publication Manual of the American Psychological Association*. 5th ed. Washington: APA, 2001. (See Chapter 67.)

American Psychological Association. *APA Style Guide to Electronic References*. Washington: APA, 2007.

Gibaldi, Joseph. *MLA Handbook for Writers of Research Papers*. 6th ed. New York: Mod. Lang. Assn. of Amer., 2003. (See Chapter 66.)

English

Gibaldi, Joseph. *MLA Handbook for Writers of Research Papers*. 6th ed. New York: Mod. Lang. Assn. of Amer., 2003. (See Chapter 66.)

History

The Chicago Manual of Style, 15th ed. Chicago: U of Chicago P, 2003. (See 68a.)

Journalism

Connolly, William, and Allan Siegal. *New York Times Manual of Style and Usage*. Rev. ed. New York: Crown-Three Rivers, 2002.

Goldstein, Norm, et al. *Associated Press Style Book and Briefing on Media Law*. Rev. and updated ed. Portland: Perseus, 2007.

Mathematics

American Mathematical Society. *The AMS Author Handbook: General Instructions for Preparing Manuscripts*. Rev. ed. Providence:

AMS, 1996. *American Mathematical Society*. 2 Jan. 2007 <ftp://ftp.ams.org/pub/author-info/documentation/handbk.pdf>.

Medicine

Iverson, Cheryl, et al., ed. *American Medical Association Manual of Style: A Guide for Authors and Editors*. 9th ed. Baltimore: Williams, 1997.

Music

The Chicago Manual of Style, 15th ed. Chicago: U of Chicago P, 2003. (See 68a.)

Philosophy

The Chicago Manual of Style, 15th ed. Chicago: U of Chicago P, 2003. (See 68a.)

Physics and Astronomy

American Institute of Physics. *AIP Style Manual*. 4th ed. New York: AIP, 1997. *American Institute of Physics*. 2 Jan. 2007 <http://www.aip.org/pubservs/style/4thed/toc.html>.

Political Science

Lane, Michael K. *Style Manual for Political Science*. Rev. ed. Washington: Amer. Political Science Assn., 2002.

Psychology

American Psychological Association. *Publication Manual of the American Psychological Association*. 5th ed. Washington: APA, 2001. (See Chapter 67.)

American Psychological Association. *APA Style Guide to Electronic References*. Washington: APA, 2007.

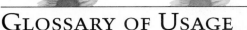

GLOSSARY OF USAGE

This list includes words and phrases you may be uncertain about when writing. If you have questions about a word not included here, try the index to this book to see whether the word is discussed elsewhere.

A, an: Use *a* before words that begin with a consonant (for example, *a* cat, *a* house) and before words beginning with a vowel that sounds like a consonant (*a* one-way street, *a* union). Use *an* before words that begin with a vowel (*an* egg, *an* ice cube) and before words with a silent *h* (*an* hour). (See 20b.)

Accept, except: *Accept,* a verb, means "to agree to," "to believe," or "to receive."

> The detective **accepted** his account of the event and did not hold him as a suspect in the case.

Except, a verb, means "to exclude" or "to leave out," and *except,* a preposition, means "leaving out."

> Because he didn't know any of the answers, he was **excepted** from the list of contestants and asked to leave.

> **Except** for brussel sprouts, which I hate, I eat most vegetables.

Advice, advise: *Advice* is a noun, and *advise* is a verb.

> She always offers too much **advice.**

> Would you **advise** me about choosing the right course?

Affect, effect: Most frequently, *affect,* which means "to influence," is used as a verb, and *effect,* which means "a result," is used as a noun.

> The weather **affects** my ability to study.

> What **effect** does too much coffee have on your concentration?

However, *effect,* meaning "to cause" or "to bring about," is also used as a verb.

> The new traffic enforcement laws **effected** a change in people's driving habits.

Common phrases with *effect* include *in effect* and *to that effect.*

Ain't: This is a nonstandard way of saying *am not, is not, has not, have not,* etc.

All ready, already: *All ready* means "prepared"; *already* means "beforehand" or "by this time."

> The courses for the meal are **all ready** to be served.

> When I got home, she was **already** there.

All right, alright: *All right* is two words, not one. *Alright* is an incorrect form.

All together, altogether: *All together* means "in a group," and *altogether* means "entirely," "totally."

> We were **all together** again after our separate vacations.

> He was not **altogether** happy about the outcome of the test.

Alot, a lot: *Alot* is an incorrect form of *a lot.*

a.m., p.m. (*or*) A.M., P.M.: Use these with numbers, not as substitutes for the words *morning* or *evening.*

> We meet every ~~A.M.~~ for an exercise class.
> ^ morning at 9 A.M.

Among, between: Use *among* when referring to three or more things and *between* when referring to two things.

> The decision was discussed **among** all members of the committee.

> I had to decide **between** the chocolate mousse pie and the almond ice cream.

Amount, number: Use *amount* for things or ideas that can't be counted. For example, furniture is a general term for items that can't be counted. That is, we can't say "one furniture" or "two furnitures." Use *number* for things that can be counted, as, for example, four chairs or three tables.

> He had a huge **amount** of work to finish before the deadline.

> A **number** of people saw the accident.

An: See the entry for *a, an.*

Anybody, any body: See the entry for *anyone, any one.*

Anyone, any one: *Anyone* means "any person at all." *Any one* refers to a specific person or thing in a group. There are similar distinctions for other words ending in *-one* and *-body* (for example, *everybody, every body; anybody, any body;* and *someone, some one*).

> The teacher asked if **anyone** knew the answer.

> **Any one** of those children could have taken the ball.

Anyways, anywheres: These are nonstandard forms for *anyway* and *anywhere.*

Any more, anymore: *Any more* is a phrase referring to one or more items.

> Are there **any more** potato chips?

Anymore is an adverb meaning "now," "henceforth".

> I don't want to see her **anymore**.

As, as if, as though, like: Use *as* in a comparison (not *like*) when there is an equality intended or when the meaning is "in the function of."

> Celia acted **as** (not *like*) the leader when the group was getting organized. [Celia = leader]

Use *as if* or *as though* for the subjunctive.

> He spent his money **as if** [or **as though**] he were rich.

Use *like* in a comparison (not *as*) when the meaning is "in the manner of" or "to the same degree as."

> The boy swam **like** a fish.

Don't use *like* as the opening word in a clause in formal writing.

> **Informal: Like** I thought, he was unable to predict the weather.

> **Formal: As** I thought, he was unable to predict the weather.

Assure, ensure, insure: *Assure* means "to declare" or "to promise"; *ensure* means "to make safe or certain," and *insure* means "to protect with a contract of insurance."

> I **assure** you that I am trying to find your lost package.

> Some people claim that eating properly **ensures** good health.

> This policy also **insures** my car against theft.

Awful, awfully: *Awful* is an adjective meaning "inspiring awe" or "extremely unpleasant."

> He was involved in an **awful** accident.

Awfully is an adverb used in informal writing to mean "very." It should be avoided in formal writing.

> **Informal: The dog was awfully dirty.**

Awhile, a while: *Awhile* is an adverb meaning "for a short time" and modifies a verb:

> He talked **awhile** and then left.

A while is an article with the noun *while* and means "a period of time." As the object of a preposition, the spelling is always *a while*.

> We talked on the phone for **a while**.

Bad, badly: *Bad* is an adjective and is used after linking verbs. *Badly* is an adverb.

> The wheat crop looked **bad** [not *badly*] because of lack of rain.

There was a **bad** flood last summer.

The building was **badly** constructed and unable to withstand the strong winds.

Because of, due to: *Because of* means "on account of" or "for the reason that."

> **Because of** having had a minor automobile accident, she was nervous about driving again.

Due to is used after a linking verb.

> His success was **due to** hard work.

Beside, besides: *Beside* is a preposition meaning "at the side of," "compared with," or "having nothing to do with." *Besides* is a preposition meaning "in addition to" or "other than." *Besides* as an adverb means "also" or "moreover." Don't confuse *beside* with *besides*.

> That is **beside** the point.

> **Besides** the radio, they had no other means of contact with the outside world.

> **Besides,** I enjoyed the concert.

Between, among: See the entry for *among, between*.

Breath, breathe: *Breath* is a noun, and *breathe* is a verb.

> She held her **breath** when she dived into the water.

> Learn to **breathe** deeply when you swim.

Can, may: *Can* is a verb that expresses ability, knowledge, or capacity.

> He **can** play both the violin and the cello.

May is a verb that expresses possibility or permission. Careful writers avoid using *can* to mean permission.

> **May** [not *Can*] I sit here?

Can't hardly: This is incorrect because it is a double negative.

> can
> She ~~can't~~ hardly hear normal voice levels.

Choose, chose: *Choose* is the present tense of the verb, and *chose* is the past tense.

> Jennie always **chooses** strawberry ice cream.

> Yesterday, she even **chose** strawberry-flavored popcorn.

Cloth, clothe: *Cloth* is a noun, and *clothe* is a verb.

> Here is some **cloth** for a new scarf.

> His paycheck helps feed and **clothe** many people in his family.

Compared to, compared with: Use *compared to* when showing that two things are alike. Use *compared with* when showing similarities and differences.

> The speaker **compared** the economy **to** a roller coaster because both have sudden ups and downs.

> The detective **compared** the fingerprints **with** other sets from a previous crime.

Could of: This is incorrect. Instead use *could have.*

Data: This is the plural form of *datum.* In informal usage, *data* is used as a singular noun, with a singular verb. However, you should treat *data* as a plural in academic writing.

> **Informal:** The **data** is inconclusive.

> **Formal:** The **data** are inconclusive.

Desert, dessert: *Desert* is a noun meaning "arid place" and a verb meaning "to abandon."

> While exploring the Mojave **Desert,** they **deserted** their friends when danger appeared.

Dessert is a noun meaning "sweet course at the end of a meal."

> They ordered cherry pie for **dessert.**

Different from, different than: *Different from* is always correct, but some writers use *different than* if there is a clause following this phrase.

> This program is **different from** the others.

> That is a **different** result **than** they predicted.

Done: The past tense forms of the verb *do* are *did* and *done. Did* is the simple form that needs no additional verb as a helper. *Done* is the past form that requires the helper *have.* Some writers make the mistake of interchanging *did* and *done.*

> They ~~done~~ it again.   (*or*)   They ^ done it again.
>   did   have

Due to, because of: See the entry for *because of, due to.*

Effect, affect: See the entry for *affect, effect.*

Ensure: See the entry for *assure, ensure, insure.*

Etc.: This is an abbreviation of the Latin *et cetera,* meaning "and the rest." It should be used sparingly, if at all, in formal academic writing. Substitute other phrases such as *and so forth* or *and so on.*

Everybody, every body: See the entry for *anyone, any one.*

Everyday, every day: *Everyday* means "occurring every day, common, usual, suitable for ordinary days."

Having ice cream for dessert became an **everyday** occurrence.

Every day is a phrase in which the noun *day* is modified by the adjective *every* and means "each day."

Every day she was at camp, she overslept and missed breakfast.

Everyone, every one: See the entry for *anyone, any one.*

Except, accept: See the entry for *accept, except.*

Farther, further: Although some writers use these words interchangeably, dictionary definitions differentiate them. *Farther* is used when actual distance is involved, and *further* is used to mean "to a greater extent," "more."

The house is **farther** from the road than I realized.

That was **furthest** from my thoughts at the time.

Fewer, less: *Fewer* is used for things that can be counted (*fewer* trees, *fewer* people). *Less* is used for ideas; abstractions; things that are thought of collectively, not separately (*less* trouble, *less* furniture); and things that are measured by amount, not number (*less* milk, *less* fuel).

Goes, says: *Goes* is a nonstandard replacement for *says.*

When I give him a book to read, he ~~goes~~ *says,* "What's it about?"

Gone, went: These are past tense forms of the verb *go. Went* is the simple form that needs no additional verb as a helper. *Gone* is the past form that requires the helper *have.* Some writers make the mistake of interchanging *went* and *gone.*

They already ~~gone~~ *went (or) had gone* away before I woke up.

Good, well: *Good* is an adjective and therefore describes only nouns. *Well* is an adverb and therefore describes adjectives, other adverbs, and verbs. The word *well* is used as an adjective only in the sense of "in good health."

She is a **good** driver.

The stereo works ~~good~~ *well.*

I feel ~~good~~ *well.*

Got, have: *Got* is the past tense of *get* and should not be used in place of *have.* Similarly, *got to* should not be used as a substitute for *must. Have got to* is an informal substitute for *must.*

have
Do you ~~got~~ any pennies for the meter?

must
I ~~got to~~ go now.

Informal: You **have got to** see that movie.

Great: This adjective is overworked in its formal meaning of "very enjoy-able," "good," or "wonderful" and should be reserved for its more exact meanings, such as "of remarkable ability," "intense," or "high degree of."

Informal: That was a **great** movie.

More Exact: The vaccine was a **great** discovery.
The map went into **great** detail.

Have, got: See the entry for _got, have._

Have, of: _Have,_ not _of,_ should follow verbs such as _could, might, must,_ and _should._

have
They should ~~of~~ called by now.

Hear, here: _Hear_ is a verb.

Did you **hear** that?

Here indicates a place.

Come over **here.**

Hisself: This is a nonstandard substitute for _himself._

Hopefully: This adverb means "in a hopeful way." Many people consider the meaning "it is to be hoped" unacceptable.

Acceptable: He listened **hopefully** for the knock at the door.

Often Considered Unacceptable: Hopefully, it will not rain tonight.

I: Although some people discourage the use of _I_ in formal essays, it is acceptable. If you wish to eliminate the use of _I,_ see 21d on passive verbs.

Imply, infer: Some writers use these verbs interchangeably, but careful writers maintain the distinction between the two. _Imply_ means "to suggest without stating directly," "to hint." _Infer_ means "to form an opinion based on facts or reasoning."

The tone of her voice **implied** that he was stupid.

The anthropologist **inferred** that this was a burial site for prehistoric people.

Insure: See the entry for _assure, ensure, insure._

Irregardless: This is an incorrect form of the word *regardless.*

Is when, is why, is where, is because: These are incorrect forms for definitions. See Chapter 16 on faulty predication.

> **Faulty Predication:** Nervousness is when my palms sweat.

> **Revised:** When I am nervous, my palms sweat.

> **Revised:** Nervousness is a state of being very uneasy or agitated.

Its, it's: *Its* is a personal pronoun in the possessive case. *It's* is a contraction for *it is.*

> The kitten licked **its** paw.

> **It's** a good time for a vacation.

Kind, sort: These two forms are singular and should be used with *this* or *that.* Use *kinds* or *sorts* with *these* or *those.*

> This **kind** of cloud often indicates that there will be heavy rain.

> These **sorts** of plants are regarded as weeds.

Lay, lie: *Lay* is a verb that needs an object and should not be used in place of *lie,* a verb that takes no direct object. *Lay* is also the past tense form of *lie.*

> He should l̶a̶y̶ ^{*lie*} down and rest awhile. Yesterday he *lay* down for a short nap.

> You can l̶i̶e̶ ^{*lay*} that package on the front table.

Leave, let: *Leave* means "to go away," and *let* means "to permit." It is incorrect to use *leave* when you mean *let.*

> L̶e̶a̶v̶e̶ ^{*Let*} me get that for you.

Less, fewer: See the entry for *fewer, less.*

Let, leave: See the entry for *leave, let.*

Like, as: See the entry for *as, as if, as though, like.*

Like for: The phrase "I'd like for you to do that" is incorrect. Omit *for.*

May, can: See the entry for *can, may.*

Most: It is incorrect to use *most* as a substitute for *almost.*

Nowheres: This is an incorrect form of *nowhere.*

Number, amount: See the entry for *amount, number.*

Of, have: See the entry for *have, of.*

Off of: It is incorrect to write *off of* for *off* in a phrase such as *off the table.*

OK, O.K., okay: These can be used informally but should not be used in formal or academic writing.

Quiet, quit, quite: *Quiet* is an adjective meaning "without sound or noise."

Mornings are a **quiet** time.

Quit is a verb meaning "to give up," "to abandon."

He **quit** working on it.

Quite is an adverb meaning "very," "entirely."

That painting is **quite** nice.

Reason . . . because: This is redundant. Instead of *because,* use *that.*

that

The reason she dropped the course is ~~because~~ she couldn't keep up with the homework.

Less Wordy Revision: She dropped the course because she couldn't keep up with the homework.

Reason why: Using *why* is redundant. Drop the word *why.*

The reason ~~why~~ I called is to remind you of your promise.

Saw, seen: These are past tense forms of the verb *see. Saw* is the simple form that needs no additional verb as a helper. *Seen* is the past form that requires the helper *have.* Some writers make the mistake of interchanging *saw* and *seen.*

saw   *have*

They ~~seen~~ it happen.   (*or*)   They seen it happen.

Set, sit: *Set* means "to place" and is followed by a direct object. *Sit* means "to be seated." It is incorrect to substitute *set* for *sit.*

sit

Come in and ~~set~~ down.

Set

~~Sit~~ the flowers on the table.

Should of: This is incorrect. Instead, use *should have.*

Sit, set: See the entry for *set, sit.*

Somebody, some body: See the entry for *anyone, any one.*

Someone, some one: See the entry for *anyone, any one.*

Sort, kind: See the entry for *kind, sort.*

Such: This is an overworked word when used in place of *very* or *extremely.*

Sure: The use of *sure* as an adverb is informal. Careful writers use *surely* instead.

> **Informal:** I **sure** hope you can join us.

> **Revised:** I **surely** hope you can join us.

Than, then: *Than* is a conjunction that introduces the second element in a comparison. *Then* is an adverb that means "at that time," "next," "after that," "also," or "in that case."

> She is taller **than** I am.

> He picked up the ticket and **then** left the house.

That there, this here, these here, those there: These are incorrect forms for *that, this, these, those* (omit *there* and *here*).

That, which: Use *that* for essential clauses and *which* for nonessential clauses. Some writers also use *which* for essential clauses. (See 23b and Chapter 29.)

Their, there, they're: *Their* is a possessive pronoun; *there* means "in, at, or to that place"; and *they're* is a contraction for "they are."

> **Their** house has been sold.

> **There** is the parking lot.

> **They're** both good swimmers.

Theirself, theirselves, themself: These are all incorrect forms for *themselves.*

Them: It is incorrect to use *them* in place of the pronoun *these* or *those.*

> Look at ~~them~~ *those* apples.

Then, than: See the entry for *than, then.*

To, too, two: *To* is a preposition; *too* is an adverb meaning "very" or "also"; and *two* is a number.

He brought his bass guitar **to** the party.

He brought his drums **too.**

He had **two** music stands.

Toward, towards: Both are accepted forms with the same meaning, but *toward* is preferred.

Use to: This is incorrect for the modal meaning *formerly.* Instead, use *used to.*

Want for: Omit the incorrect *for* in phrases such as "I want for you to come here."

Well, good: See the entry for *good, well.*

Went, gone: See the entry for *gone, went.*

Were, we're, where: *Were* is a verb.

They **were** singing.

We're is a contraction meaning "we are."

We're about to leave here.

Where indicates a place.

Where is he?

Where: It is incorrect to use *where* to mean *when* or *that.*

The Fourth of July is a holiday ~~where~~ *when* the town council shoots off fireworks.

I see ~~where~~ *that* there is now a ban on capturing panthers.

Where . . . at: This is a redundant form. Omit *at.*

This is where the picnic is ~~at~~.

Which, that: See the entry for *that, which.*

While, awhile: See the entry for *awhile, a while.*

Who, whom: Use *who* for the subject case; use *whom* for the object case.

He is the person **who** signs that form.

He is the person **whom** I asked for help.

Who's, whose: *Who's* is a contraction for *who is; whose* is a possessive pronoun.

Who's included on that list?

Whose wristwatch is this?

Your, you're: *Your* is a possessive pronoun; *you're* is a contraction for *you are.*

Your hands are cold.

You're a great success.

Glossary of Grammatical Terms

Absolutes: Words or phrases that modify whole sentences rather than parts of sentences or individual words. An absolute phrase, which consists of a noun and participle, can be placed anywhere in the sentence but needs to be set off from the sentence by commas.

The snow having finally stopped, the football game began.
(ABSOLUTE PHRASE)

Abstract nouns: Nouns that refer to ideas, qualities, generalized concepts, and conditions and that do not have plural forms. (See Chapter 55.)

happiness, pride, furniture, trouble, sincerity

Active voice: See *voice*.

Adjectives: Words that modify nouns and pronouns. (See Chapter 24.) Descriptive adjectives have three forms:

Positive: red, clean, beautiful, offensive

Comparative (for comparing two things): redder, cleaner, more beautiful, less offensive

Superlative (for comparing more than two things): reddest, cleanest, most beautiful, least offensive

Adjective clauses: See *dependent clauses.*

Adverbs: Words that modify verbs, verb forms, adjectives, and other adverbs. (See Chapter 24.) Descriptive adverbs have three forms:

Positive: fast, graceful, awkward

Comparative (for comparing two things): faster, more graceful, less awkward

Superlative (for comparing more than two things): fastest, most graceful, least awkward

Adverb clauses: See *dependent clauses.*

Agreement: The use of the corresponding form for related words in order to have them agree in number, person, or gender. (See 15a and 23b.)

John runs.

[Both subject and verb are singular.]

533

It is necessary to flush the **pipes** regularly so that **they** don't freeze.

[Both subjects, *it* and *they,* are in third person; *they* agrees in number with the antecedent, *pipes.*]

Antecedents: Words or groups of words to which pronouns refer.

When the **bell** rang, **it** was loud.

[*Bell* is the antecedent of *it.*]

Antonyms: Words with opposite meanings.

Word	Antonym
hot	cold
fast	slow
noisy	quiet

Appositives: Nonessential phrases and clauses that follow nouns and identify or explain them. (See Chapter 29.)

My uncle, **who lives in Wyoming,** is taking surfing lessons in Florida.
    (APPOSITIVE)

Articles: See *noun determiners.*

Auxiliary verbs: Helping verbs used with main verbs in verb phrases.

should be going
(AUXILIARY VERB)

has taken
(AUXILIARY VERB)

Cardinal numbers: See *noun determiners.*

Case: The form or position of a noun or pronoun that shows its use or relationship to other words in a sentence. The three cases in English are (1) *subject* (*subjective* or *nominative case*), (2) *object* (*objective case*), and (3) *possessive* (*genitive case*). (See 23a.)

Clauses: Groups of related words that contain both subjects and predicates and function as sentences or as parts of sentences. Clauses are either *independent* (*main*) or *dependent* (*subordinate*). (See Chapter 28.)

Clichés: Overused or tired expressions that no longer communicate effectively. (See 35a.)

Collective nouns: Nouns that refer to groups of people or things, such as a *committee, team,* or *jury.* When the group includes a number of members acting as a unit and is the subject of the sentence, the verb is also singular. (See 11g and 22a.)

> The **jury** has made a decision.

Colloquialisms: Words or phrases used in casual conversation and writing. (See 36e.)

Comma splice: A punctuation error in which two or more independent clauses in a compound sentence are separated only by a comma and lacks a coordinating conjunction. (See 10a.)

> , but (*or*);
> Jesse said he couldn't loan out his computer/ that was typical of his responses to requests.

Common nouns: Nouns that refer to general rather than specific categories of people, places, and things and are not capitalized. (See 22a and Chapter 55.)

> basket   person   history   tractor

Comparative: The form of adjectives and adverbs used when two things are being compared. (See *adjectives, adverbs,* and 24c.)

Complements: The adjectives or nouns to which linking verbs link their subjects.

> Phyllis was **tired.**
>   (COMPLEMENT)

> She became a **musician.**
>   (COMPLEMENT)

Complex sentences: Sentences with at least one independent clause and at least one dependent clause, arranged in any order. (See 30b3.)

Compound-complex sentences: Sentences with at least two independent clauses and at least one dependent clause, arranged in any order. (See 30b4.)

Compound nouns: Nouns such as *swimming pool, dropout, roommate,* and *stepmother,* made up of more than one word.

Compound sentences: Sentences with two or more independent clauses and no dependent clauses. (See 30b2.)

Concrete words: Words that refer to people and things that can be perceived by the senses. (See 32c.)

Conjugations: See *verbs.*

Conjunctions: Words that connect other words, phrases, and clauses in sentences. Coordinating conjunctions connect independent clauses; subordinating conjunctions connect dependent or subordinating clauses with independent or main clauses.

Coordinating Conjunctions: and, but, for, nor, or, so, yet

Some Subordinating Conjunctions: after, although, because, if, since, until, while

Conjunctive adverbs: Words that begin or join independent clauses. (See 28a.)

consequently   however   therefore   thus   moreover

Connotation: The attitudes and emotional overtones beyond the direct definition of a word. (See 36d.) For example, the words *plump* and *fat* both mean fleshy, but *plump* has a more positive connotation than *fat*.

Consistency: Agreement, especially maintaining the same voice with pronouns, the same tense with verbs, and the same tone, voice, or mode of discourse. (See Chapter 15.)

Coordinate: Of equal importance. Two independent clauses in the same sentence are coordinate because they have equal importance and the same emphasis. (See 17a and 28a.)

Coordinating conjunctions: See *conjunctions*.

Correlative conjunctions: Words that work in pairs and give emphasis.

both . . . and   neither . . . nor   either . . . or   not only . . . but also

Count nouns: Nouns that name things that can be counted because they can be divided into separate and distinct units. (See Chapter 55.)

Dangling modifiers: Phrases or clauses in which the doer of the action is not clearly indicated. (See 13a.)

Tim thought
Having missed an opportunity to study, the exam seemed especially difficult.
                                ^

Declarative mood: See *mood*.

Demonstrative pronouns: Pronouns that refer to things. (See *noun determiners* and 22b.)

this   that   these   those

Denotation: The dictionary definition of a word. (See 36d.)

Dependent clauses (subordinate clauses): Clauses that cannot stand alone as complete sentences. (See 28b.) There are two kinds of dependent clauses: adverb clauses and adjective clauses. *Adverb clauses* begin with subordinating conjunctions such as *after, if, because, while,* and *when. Adjective* *clauses* tell more about nouns or pronouns in sentences and begin with words such as *who, which, that, whose,* and *whom.*

Determiners: See *noun determiners.*

Diagramming: See *sentence diagrams.*

Direct and indirect quotations: *Direct quotations* are the exact words said by someone or the exact words in print that are being copied. *Indirect quotations* aren't the exact words but a rephrasing or summarizing of someone else's words. (See 42a.)

Direct discourse: See *mode of discourse.*

Direct objects: Nouns or pronouns that follow a transitive verb and complete the meaning or receive the action of the verb. The direct object answers the question *what?* or *whom?*

Ellipsis: A series of three periods indicating that words have been omitted from material being quoted. (See 45e.)

Essential and nonessential clauses and phrases: *Essential* (also called *restrictive*) clauses and phrases appear after nouns and are necessary or essential to complete the meaning of the sentence. *Nonessential* (also called *nonrestrictive*) clauses and phrases appear after nouns and add extra information, but that information can be removed from the sentence without altering the meaning. (See Chapter 29.)

> Apples **that are green** are not sweet.
>> (ESSENTIAL CLAUSE)

> Golden Delicious apples, **which are yellow,** are sweet.
>> (NONESSENTIAL CLAUSE)

Excessive coordination: Stringing too many equal clauses together with coordinators into one sentence. (See 17a.)

Excessive subordination: Stringing too many subordinate clauses together in a complex sentence. (See 17b.)

Faulty coordination: Combining in one sentence two independent clauses that either are unequal in importance or have little or no connection to each other. (See 17a.)

Faulty parallelism: See *nonparallel structure.*

Faulty predication: An improper or illogical fit between a predicate and its subject. This happens most often after forms of the verb *be.* (See Chapter 16.)

> He
> ~~The reason he~~ was late ~~was~~ because he had to study.

Fragments: Groups of words punctuated as sentences that either do not have both a subject and a complete verb or are dependent clauses. (See Chapter 12.)

Whenever we wanted to pick fresh fruit while we were staying on my
, we would head for the apple orchard with buckets
grandmother's farm .

Fused sentences: Punctuation errors (also called *run-ons*) in which there is no punctuation between independent clauses in the sentence. (See 10b.)

;
Jennifer never learned how to ask politely she just took what she wanted.

General words: Words that refer to whole categories or large classes of items. (See 32b.) See also *specific words.*

Gerunds: Verbal forms ending in *-ing* that function as nouns. (See *phrases* and 21b.)

Aaron enjoys **cooking. Jogging** is another of his favorite pastimes.
(GERUND) (GERUND)

Helping verbs: See *auxiliary verbs.*

Homonyms: Words that sound alike but are spelled differently and have different meanings. (See 50e.)

hear/here   passed/past   buy/by

Idioms: Expressions meaning something beyond the simple definition or literal sense of the words. For example, idioms such as "short and sweet" or "wearing his heart on his sleeve" are not intended to be taken literally. (See Chapter 58.)

Imperative mood: See *mood.*

Indefinite pronouns: Pronouns that take the place of generic, unidentified, or unnamed nouns. (See 22b5 and 23b5.)

anyone   everyone   nobody   something

Independent clauses: Clauses that can stand alone as complete sentences. They do not depend on other clauses to complete their meaning. (See 28a.)

Indicative mood: See *mood.*

Indirect discourse: See *mode of discourse.*

Indirect objects: Words that follow transitive verbs and come before direct objects. They indicate the one to whom or for whom something is given, said, or done and answer the question *to what?* or *to whom?* Indirect objects can always be replaced by a prepositional phrase beginning with *to* or *for.* (See 23a2.)

Alice gave **me** some money.
(INDIRECT OBJECT)

Alice gave some money **to me.**
(OBJECT OF PREPOSITION)

Infinitives: Phrases made up of the present form of the verb preceded by *to.* Infinitives can have subjects, objects, complements, or modifiers. (See *phrases* and 21b.)

Everyone wanted **to swim** in the new pool.
(INFINITIVE)

Intensifiers: Modifying words used for emphasis.

She **most** certainly did fix that car!

Interjections: Words used as exclamations.

Oh, I don't think I want to know about that.

Interrogative pronouns: Pronouns used in questions. (See 22b.)

who   whose   whom   which   that

Intransitive verbs: See *verbs.*

Irregular verbs: Verbs in which the past tense forms or the past participles are not formed by adding *-ed* or *-d.* (See 21c4.)

do, did, done   begin, began, begun

Jargon: Words and phrases that are either the specialized language of various fields or, in a negative sense, unnecessarily technical or inflated terms. (See 36f.)

Linking verbs: Verbs linking the subject to the subject complement. The most common linking verbs are *appear, seem, become, feel, look, taste, sound,* and forms of *be.*

I **feel** sleepy.
(LINKING VERB)

He **became** president of the club.
(LINKING VERB)

Misplaced modifiers: Modifiers not placed next to or close to the words being modified. (See 13b.)

We saw an advertisement for an excellent new home theater system on television.

Modal verbs: Helping verbs such as *shall, should, will, would, can, could, may, might, must, ought to,* and *used to* that express an attitude such as interest, possibility, or obligation. (See 21f and 52a.)

Mode of discourse: *Direct discourse* repeats the exact words that someone says, and *indirect discourse* reports the words but changes some of them. (See 15e.)

Everett said, **"I want to become a physicist."**
(DIRECT DISCOURSE)

Everett said **that he wanted to become a physicist.**
(INDIRECT DISCOURSE)

Modifiers: Words or groups of words that describe or limit other words, phrases, and clauses. The most common modifiers are adjectives and adverbs. (See Chapter 24.)

Mood: The verb's indication that a sentence expresses a fact (the declarative or indicative mood), expresses some doubt or something contrary to fact or states a recommendation (the subjunctive mood), or issues a command (the imperative mood). (See 21e.)

Noncount nouns: Nouns that name things that can't be counted because they are abstractions or things that cannot be cut into parts. (See Chapter 55.)

Nonessential clauses and phrases: See *essential and nonessential clauses and phrases.*

Nonparallel structure: Lack of parallelism that occurs when similar items are not in the same grammatical form. (See 14b.)

Nonrestrictive clauses and phrases: See *essential and nonessential clauses and phrases.*

Nouns: Words that name people, places, things, and ideas and can have plural or possessive endings. Nouns function as *subjects, direct objects, predicate nominatives, objects of prepositions,* and *indirect objects.* (See 22a.)

Noun clauses: Subordinate clauses used as nouns.

What I see here is adequate.
(NOUN CLAUSE)

Noun determiners: Words that signal that a noun is about to follow. They stand next to their nouns or can be separated from them by adjectives. Some noun determiners can also function as nouns. There are five types of noun determiners.

1. Articles (see 56c): *the* (definite); *a, an* (indefinite)
2. Demonstratives: *this, that, these, those*
3. Possessives: *my, our, your, his, her, its, their*
4. Cardinal numbers: *one, two, three,* and so on
5. Miscellaneous: *all, another, each, every, much,* and others

Noun phrases: See *phrases.*

Number: The quantity expressed by a noun or pronoun, either singular (one) or plural (more than one).

Object case of pronouns: The case needed when the pronoun is the direct or indirect object of the verb or the object of a preposition. (See 23a.)

Singular	Plural
First person: *me*	First person: *us*
Second person: *you*	Second person: *you*
Third person: *him, her, it*	Third person: *them*

Object complements: The adjectives in predicates modifying the object of the verb (not the subject).

The enlargement makes the picture **clear**.
(OBJECT COMPLEMENT)

Object of the preposition: A noun or pronoun following the preposition. The preposition, its object, and any modifiers make up a *prepositional phrase.* (See 23a2.)

This present is for **Daniel**.
(OBJECT OF THE PREPOSITION *FOR*)

She knocked twice **on the big wooden door.**
(PREPOSITIONAL PHRASE)

Objects: See *direct objects* and *object complements.*

Parallel construction: Two or more items listed or compared and written in the same grammatical form, indicating that they are equal elements. When items are not in the same grammatical form, they lack parallel structure (this error is often called *faulty parallelism*). (See Chapter 14.)

She was sure that **being an apprentice in a photographer's studio** would be more useful than **being a student in photography classes**.

[The phrases in bold type are parallel because they have the same grammatical form.]

Paraphrase: Restatement of information from a source, using your own words. (See 64d.)

Parenthetical elements: Nonessential words, phrases, and clauses set off by commas, dashes, or parentheses.

Participles: Verb forms that may be part of the complete verb or function as adjectives or adverbs. The present participle ends in *-ing,* and the past participle usually ends in *-ed, -d, -n,* or *-t.* (See *phrases* and 21b.)

> **Present participles:** *running, sleeping, digging*
> She is **running** for mayor in this campaign.

> **Past participles:** *elected, deleted, chosen, sent*
> The **elected** candidate will take office in January.

Parts of speech: The eight classes into which words are grouped according to their function, place, meaning, and use in a sentence: *nouns, pronouns, verbs, adjectives, adverbs, prepositions, conjunctions,* and *interjections.*

Passive voice: See *voice.*

Past participles: See *participles.*

Perfect progressive tense: See *verb tenses.*

Perfect tenses: See *verb tenses.*

Person: There are three persons in English. (See 23a.)

> **First person:** Who is speaking (*I* or *we*)

> **Second person:** Who is spoken to (*you*)

> **Third person:** Who is spoken about (*he, she, it, they, anyone,* etc.)

Personal pronouns: Pronouns that refer to people or things. (See 23a.)

PERSONAL PRONOUNS			
	Subject	**Object**	**Possessive**
Singular			
First person	*I*	*me*	*my, mine*
Second person	*you*	*you*	*your, yours*
Third person	*he, she, it*	*him, her, it*	*his, her, hers, its*
Plural			
First person	*we*	*us*	*our, ours*
Second person	*you*	*you*	*your, yours*
Third person	*they*	*them*	*their, theirs*

Phrasal verbs: Verbs that consist of two or more words that help express the meaning. (See 52b.)

Phrases: Groups of related words without subjects and predicates. (See Chapter 27.)

Verb phrases function as verbs.

She **has been eating** too much sugar.
    (VERB PHRASE)

Noun phrases function as nouns.

A **major winter storm** hit **the eastern coast of Maine.**
    (NOUN PHRASE)   (NOUN PHRASE)

Prepositional phrases usually function as modifiers.

That book **of hers** is overdue at the library.
    (PREPOSITIONAL PHRASE)

Participial phrases, gerund phrases, infinitive phrases, appositive phrases, and absolute phrases function as adjectives, adverbs, or nouns.

Participial Phrase: I saw people **staring at my peculiar-looking haircut.**

Gerund Phrase: **Downloading music from the Internet** can be illegal.

Infinitive Phrase: He likes **to give expensive presents.**

Appositive Phrase: You ought to see Dr. Elman, **a dermatologist.**

Absolute Phrase: **The test done,** he sighed with relief.

Plagiarism: Situation that results when a writer fails to document a source, presenting someone else's words and ideas as the writer's own work. (See Chapter 64.)

Positive: The form of an adjective or adverb when no comparison is made. (See *adjectives, adverbs,* and 24c.)

Possessive pronouns: See *personal pronouns, noun determiners,* and 23a.

Predicates: Words or groups of words that express action or state of being in a sentence and consist of one or more verbs, plus any complements or modifiers.

Predicate adjectives: See *subject complements.*

Predicate nominatives: See *subject complements.*

Prefixes: Word parts added to the beginning of words. (See 50c3.)

Prefix	Word
bio- (life)	biography
mis- (wrong, bad)	misspell

Prepositional phrases: See *phrases.*

Prepositions: Words that link and relate their objects (usually nouns or pronouns) to some other word or words in a sentence. Prepositions usually precede their objects but may follow the objects and appear at the end of the sentence. (See Chapters 25 and 57.)

The waiter gave the check **to my date** by mistake.
                                   (PREPOSITIONAL PHRASE)

I wonder **what** she is asking **for.**
(OBJECT OF THE PREPOSITION)   (PREPOSITION)

Progressive tenses: See *verb tenses.*

Pronoun case: The form of a pronoun that is needed in a particular sentence. (See *subjects, direct objects, indirect objects, case,* and 23a.)

Pronoun reference: The relationship between the pronoun and the noun (antecedent) for which it is substituting. (See 23b.)

Pronouns: Words that substitute for nouns. (See 22b.) Pronouns should refer to previously stated nouns, called *antecedents.*

When **Josh** came in, **he** brought some firewood.
      (ANTECEDENT)   (PRONOUN)

Pronouns have eight forms: *personal, demonstrative, relative, interrogative, indefinite, possessive, reflexive,* and *reciprocal.*

Proper nouns: Words that name specific people, places, and things. Proper nouns are always capitalized. (See Chapter 55.)

Copenhagen   Honda   U.S. House of Representatives   Spanish

Quotations: Record of the exact words of a written or spoken source, set off by quotation marks. Block (or long) quotations are indented. (See Chapter 42 and 64e.)

Reciprocal pronouns: Pronouns that refer to individual parts of plural terms. (See 22b8.)

Reflexive pronouns: Pronouns that show someone or something in the sentence is acting for itself or on itself. Because a reflexive pronoun must refer to a word in a sentence, it isn't the subject or direct object. If used to show emphasis, reflexive pronouns are called *intensive pronouns.* (See 22b7.)

Singular	**Plural**
First person: *myself*	First person: *ourselves*
Second person: *yourself*	Second person: *yourselves*
Third person: *himself, herself, itself*	Third person: *themselves*

She returned the book **herself** rather than giving it to her roommate to
                        (REFLEXIVE PRONOUN)
bring back.

Relative pronouns: Pronouns that show the relationship of a dependent clause to a noun in the sentence. Relative pronouns (*that, which, who, whom, whose*) substitute for nouns already mentioned in sentences and introduce adjective or noun clauses. (See 22b3.)

This was the movie **that** won the Academy Award.

Restrictive clauses and phrases: See *essential and nonessential clauses and phrases.*

Run-on sentences: See *fused sentences* and 10b.

Sentences: Groups of words that have at least one independent clause (a complete unit of thought with a subject and predicate). (See Chapter 30.) Sentences can be classified by their structure as *simple, compound, complex,* and *compound-complex.*

Simple: One independent clause

Compound: Two or more independent clauses

Complex: One or more independent clauses and one or more dependent clauses

Compound-Complex: Two or more independent clauses and one or more dependent clauses

Sentences can also be classified by their function as *declarative, interrogative, imperative,* and *exclamatory.*

Declarative: Makes a statement.

Interrogative: Asks a question.

Imperative: Issues a command.

Exclamatory: Makes an exclamation.

Sentence diagrams: Structured sketches that show the relationships within sentences.

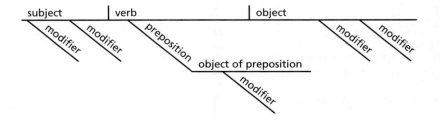

Marnie's cousin, who has no taste in food, ordered a hamburger with coleslaw at the Chinese restaurant.

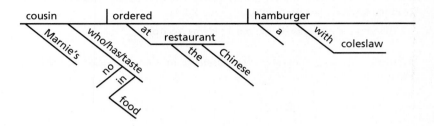

Sentence fragments: See *fragments.*

Simple sentences: See *sentences* and 30b1.

Simple tenses: See *verb tenses.*

Slang: Terms that either are invented or are given new definitions in order to be novel or unconventional. They are generally considered inappropriate in formal writing. (See 36e.)

Specific words: Words that identify items in a group. (See 32b.) See also *general words.*

Split infinitives: Phrases in which modifiers are inserted between *to* and the verb. Some people object to split infinitives, but others consider them grammatically acceptable.

   to quickly turn   to easily reach   to forcefully enter

Standard English: Generally accepted language that conforms to established rules of grammar, sentence structure, punctuation, and spelling. (See 36a.)

Subject: The word or words in a sentence that act or are acted on by the verb or are linked by the verb to one or more other words in the sentence. The *simple subject* consists of only the noun or other main word or words, and the *complete subject* includes all modifiers with the simple subject. (See Chapter 26.)

   Harvey objected to his roommate's alarm clock going off at 7 A.M.

   [*Harvey* is the subject.]

   Every single one of the people in the room heard her giggle.

   [The simple subject is *one;* the complete subject is the whole phrase.]

Subject case of pronouns: See *personal pronouns* and 23a1.

Subject complement: The noun or adjective in the predicate (*predicate nominative* or *adjective*) that refers to the same entity as the subject in sentences with linking verbs, such as *feel, look, smell, sound, taste, seem,* and forms of *be*.

> She feels **happy.**
>   (SUBJECT COMPLEMENT)
>
> He is a **pharmacist.**
>   (SUBJECT COMPLEMENT)

Subject-verb agreement: Agreement in number and person between subjects and verb endings in sentences. (See Chapter 11.)

Subjunctive mood: See *mood*.

Subordinating conjunctions: Words such as *although, if, until,* and *when* that join two clauses and make one subordinate to the other.

> She is late. She overslept.
>
> She is late **because** she overslept.

Subordination: Placing one clause in a subordinate or dependent relationship to another in a sentence because it is less important and depends for its meaning on the other clause. (See 17b.)

Suffixes: Word parts added to the ends of words. (See 50c3.)

Suffix	Word
-ful	careful
-less	nameless

Summaries: Brief restatements of the main idea in a source, using your own words. (See 64c.)

Superlative: See *adjectives, adverbs,* and 24c.

Synonyms: Words with similar meanings.

Word	Synonym
damp	moist
pretty	attractive

Tense: See *verb tenses*.

Tone: The attitude or level of formality reflected in the word choices in a piece of writing. (See 15c and 36b.)

Transitions: Words in sentences that show relationships between sentences and paragraphs. (See Chapter 19.)

Transitive verbs: See *verbs*.

Two-word verbs: See *phrasal verbs*.

Verbals: Words that are derived from verbs but do not act as verbs in sentences. Three types of verbals are *infinitives, participles,* and *gerunds*. (See *gerunds, infinitives, participles,* and 21b.)

> **Infinitives:** to + verb
>
> > to wind   to say

> **Participles:** Words used as modifiers or with helping verbs. The present participle ends in -*ing*, and many past participles end in -*d* or -*ed*.
>
> > The dog is **panting.**
> > (PRESENT PARTICIPLE)
> >
> > He bought only **used** clothing.
> > (PAST PARTICIPLE)

> **Gerunds:** Present participles used as nouns.
>
> > **Smiling** was not a natural act for her.
> > (GERUND)

Verbs: Words or groups of words (verb phrases) in predicates that express action, show a state of being, or act as a link between the subject and the rest of the predicate. Verbs change form to show time (tense), mood, and voice and are classified as *transitive, intransitive,* and *linking verbs*. (See Chapter 21.)

> Transitive verbs require objects to complete the predicate.
>
> > He **cut** the cardboard **box** with his knife.
> > (TRANSITIVE VERB)   (OBJECT)

> Intransitive verbs don't require objects.
>
> > My ancient cat often **lies** on the porch.
> > (INTRANSITIVE VERB)

> Linking verbs link the subject to the following noun or adjective.
>
> > The trees **are** bare.
> > (LINKING VERB)

Verb phrases: See *verbs*.

Verb tenses: The time indicated by the verb form in the past, present, or future. (See 21c.)

Present Tense

Simple Present: Describes actions or situations that exist now and are habitually or generally true.

I **walk** to class every afternoon.

Present Progressive: Indicates activity in progress, not finished, or continuing.

He **is studying** Swedish.

Present Perfect: Describes single or repeated actions that were completed in the past or began in the past and lead up to and include the present.

She **has lived** in Alaska for two years.

Present Perfect Progressive: Indicates action that began in the past, continues to the present, and may continue into the future.

They **have been building** that parking garage for six months.

Past Tense

Simple Past: Describes completed actions or conditions in the past.

They **ate** breakfast in the cafeteria.

Past Progressive: Indicates that past action took place over a period of time.

He **was swimming** when the storm began.

Past Perfect: Indicates that an action or event was completed before another event in the past.

No one **had heard** about the crisis when the newscast began.

Past Perfect Progressive: Indicates an ongoing condition in the past that has ended.

I **had been planning** my trip to Mexico when I heard about the earthquake.

Future Tense

Simple Future: Indicates actions or events in the future.

The store **will open** at 9 A.M.

Future Progressive: Indicates future action that will continue for some time.

I **will be working** on that project next week.

Future Perfect: Indicates action that will be completed by or before a specified time in the future.

Next summer, they **will have been** here for twenty years.

Future Perfect Progressive: Indicates ongoing actions or conditions until a specific time in the future.

By tomorrow, I **will have been waiting** for the delivery for one month.

VERB CONJUGATIONS

Verbs change form to express time (tense). (See 17c.) Regular verbs change in predictable ways, as shown here. Irregular verb forms differ and should be memorized; the table uses the verb *go* as an example.

Regular Verbs

Present Tense

Simple present:

I walk	we walk
you walk	you walk
he, she, it walks	they walk

Present progressive:

I am walking	we are walking
you are walking	you are walking
he, she, it is walking	they are walking

Present perfect:

I have walked	we have walked
you have walked	you have walked
he, she, it has walked	they have walked

Present perfect progressive:

I have been walking	we have been walking
you have been walking	you have been walking
he, she, it has been walking	they have been walking

Past Tense

Simple past:

I walked	we walked
you walked	you walked
he, she, it walked	they walked

Past progressive:

I was walking	we were walking
you were walking	you were walking
he, she, it was walking	they were walking

Past perfect:

I had walked	we had walked
you had walked	you had walked
he, she, it had walked	they had walked

Past perfect progressive:

I had been walking	we had been walking
you had been walking	you had been walking
he, she, it had been walking	they had been walking

Future Tense

Simple future:

I will walk	we will walk
you will walk	you will walk
he, she, it will walk	they will walk

Future progressive:

I will be walking	we will be walking
you will be walking	you will be walking
he, she, it will be walking	they will be walking

Future perfect:

I will have walked	we will have walked
you will have walked	you will have walked
he, she, it will have walked	they will have walked

Future perfect progressive:

I will have been walking	we will have been walking
you will have been walking	you will have been walking
he, she, it will have been walking	they will have been walking

Irregular Verbs

Present Tense

Simple present:

I go	we go
you go	you go
he, she, it goes	they go

Present progressive:

I am going	we are going
you are going	you are going
he, she, it is going	they are going

Present perfect:

I have gone	we have gone
you have gone	you have gone
he, she, it has gone	they have gone

Present perfect progressive:

I have been going	we have been going
you have been going	you have been going
he, she, it has been going	they have been going

Past Tense

Simple past:

I went	we went
you went	you went
he, she, it went	they went

▶

Past progressive:

I was going	we were going
you were going	you were going
he, she, it was going	they were going

Past perfect:

I had gone	we had gone
you had gone	you had gone
he, she, it had gone	they had gone

Past perfect progressive:

I had been going	we had been going
you had been going	you had been going
he, she, it had been going	they had been going

Future Tense

Simple future:

I will go	we will go
you will go	you will go
he, she, it will go	they will go

Future progressive:

I will be going	we will be going
you will be going	you will be going
he, she, it will be going	they will be going

Future perfect:

I will have gone	we will have gone
you will have gone	you will have gone
he, she, it will have gone	they will have gone

Future perfect progressive:

I will have been going	we will have been going
you will have been going	you will have been going
he, she, it will have been going	they will have been going

Voice: Verbs are either in the *active* or *passive* voice. In the active voice, the subject performs the action of the verb. In the passive, the subject receives the action. (See 15d and 21d.)

The dog **bit** the boy.
(ACTIVE VERB)

The boy **was bitten** by the dog.
(PASSIVE VERB)

INDEX

Contents